Lunch Wore a
SPEEDO

Other Books by Jim Toomey

Sherman's Lagoon: Ate That, What's Next?

Poodle: The Other White Meat

An Illustrated Guide to Shark Etiquette

Another Day in Paradise

Greetings from Sherman's Lagoon

Surf's Up!

The Shark Diaries

Catch of the Day

A Day at the Beach

Surfer Safari

Planet of the Hairless Beach Apes

Yarns & Shanties (and Other Nautical Baloney)

Sharks Just Wanna Have Fun

Confessions of a Swinging Single Sea Turtle

Discover Your Inner Hermit Crab

Never Bite Anything That Bites Back

Think Like a Shark

Here We Go Again

Treasuries

Sherman's Lagoon 1991 to 2001: Greatest Hits and Near Misses

In Shark Years I'm Dead: Sherman's Lagoon Turns Fifteen

Lunch Wore a SPEEDO

The Nineteenth Sherman's Lagoon Collection

by Jim Toomey

SURF BOARDS
DIVE GEAR
SWIM WEAR
YARD SALE

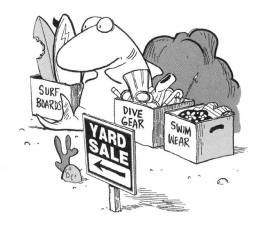

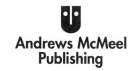

Andrews McMeel Publishing

Kansas City • Sydney • London

To my parents, Mary and John Toomey,
for keeping their sense of humor through it all.

jt

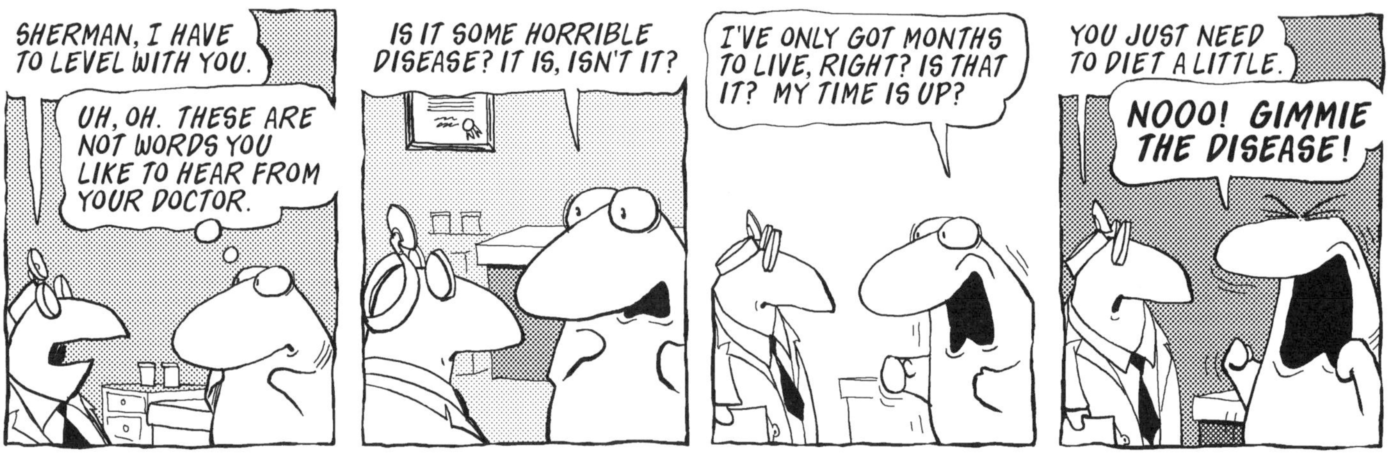
SHERMAN, I HAVE TO LEVEL WITH YOU.
UH, OH. THESE ARE NOT WORDS YOU LIKE TO HEAR FROM YOUR DOCTOR.
IS IT SOME HORRIBLE DISEASE? IT IS, ISN'T IT?
I'VE ONLY GOT MONTHS TO LIVE, RIGHT? IS THAT IT? MY TIME IS UP?
YOU JUST NEED TO DIET A LITTLE.
NOOO! GIMMIE THE DISEASE!

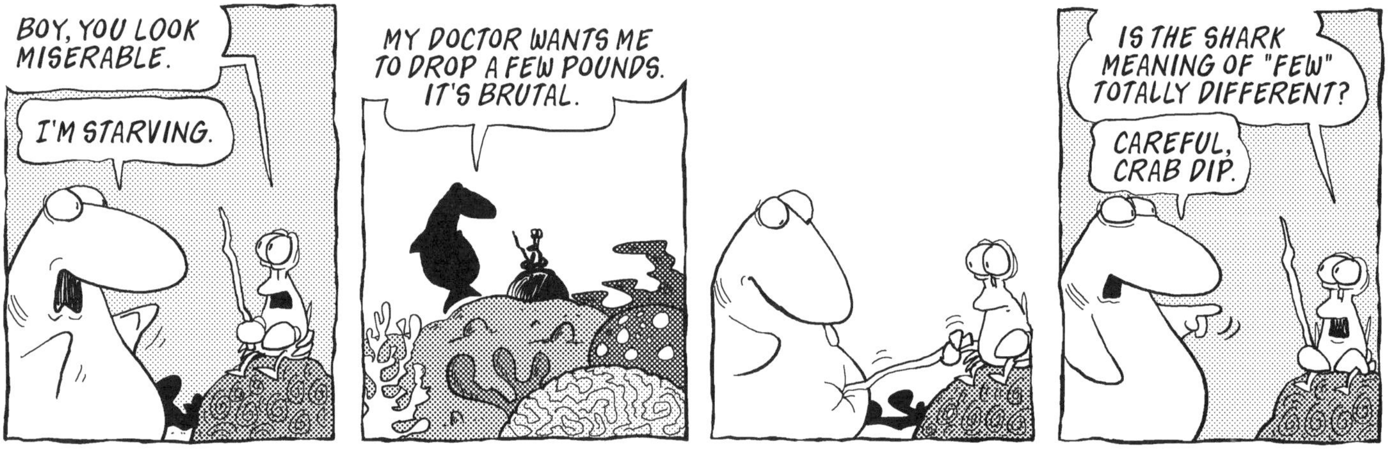
BOY, YOU LOOK MISERABLE.
I'M STARVING.
MY DOCTOR WANTS ME TO DROP A FEW POUNDS. IT'S BRUTAL.
IS THE SHARK MEANING OF "FEW" TOTALLY DIFFERENT?
CAREFUL, CRAB DIP.

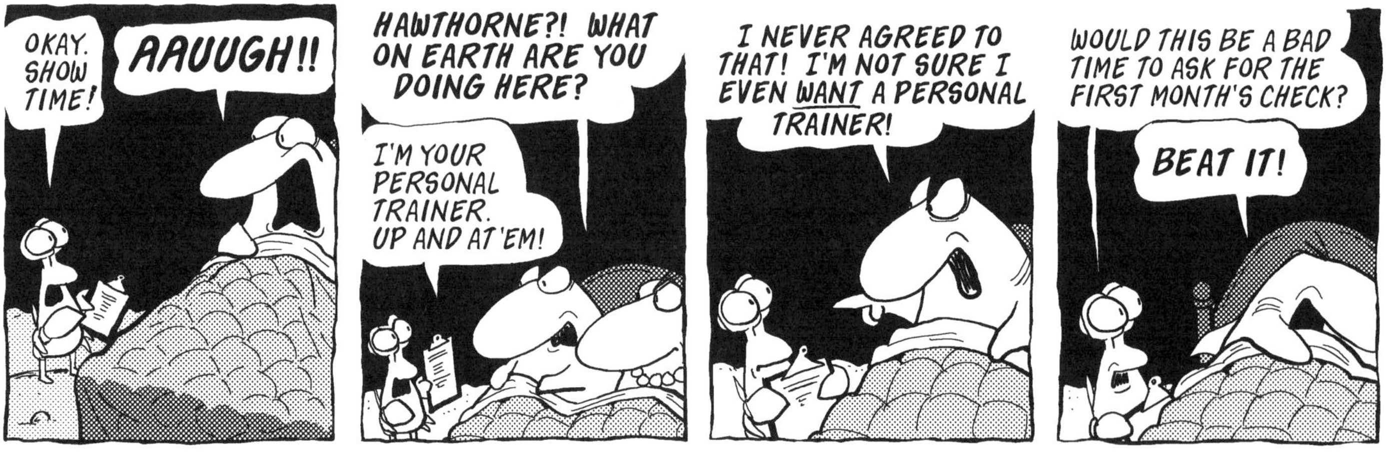
OKAY. SHOW TIME!
AAUUGH!!
HAWTHORNE?! WHAT ON EARTH ARE YOU DOING HERE?
I'M YOUR PERSONAL TRAINER. UP AND AT 'EM!
I NEVER AGREED TO THAT! I'M NOT SURE I EVEN WANT A PERSONAL TRAINER!
WOULD THIS BE A BAD TIME TO ASK FOR THE FIRST MONTH'S CHECK?
BEAT IT!

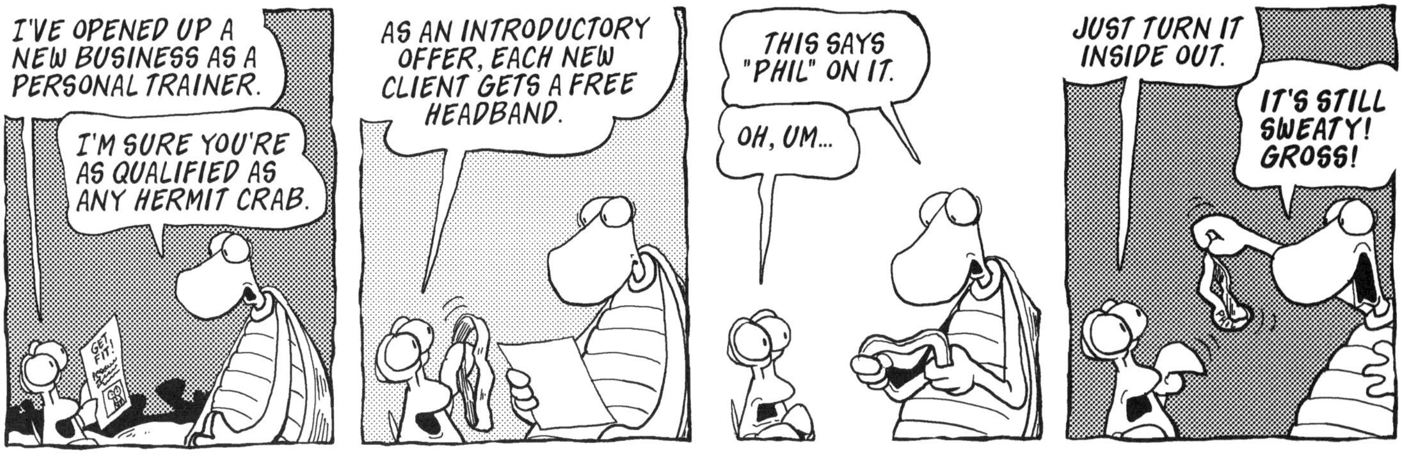
I'VE OPENED UP A NEW BUSINESS AS A PERSONAL TRAINER.
I'M SURE YOU'RE AS QUALIFIED AS ANY HERMIT CRAB.
GET FIT!
AS AN INTRODUCTORY OFFER, EACH NEW CLIENT GETS A FREE HEADBAND.
THIS SAYS "PHIL" ON IT.
OH, UM...
JUST TURN IT INSIDE OUT.
IT'S STILL SWEATY! GROSS!

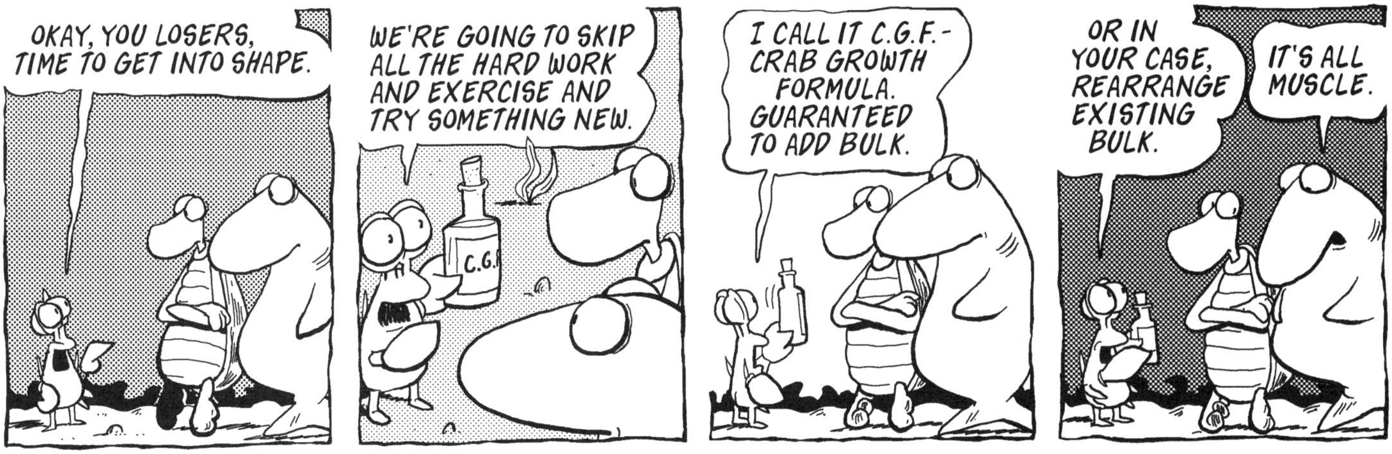
OKAY, YOU LOSERS, TIME TO GET INTO SHAPE.
WE'RE GOING TO SKIP ALL THE HARD WORK AND EXERCISE AND TRY SOMETHING NEW.
I CALL IT C.G.F.- CRAB GROWTH FORMULA. GUARANTEED TO ADD BULK.
OR IN YOUR CASE, REARRANGE EXISTING BULK.
IT'S ALL MUSCLE.

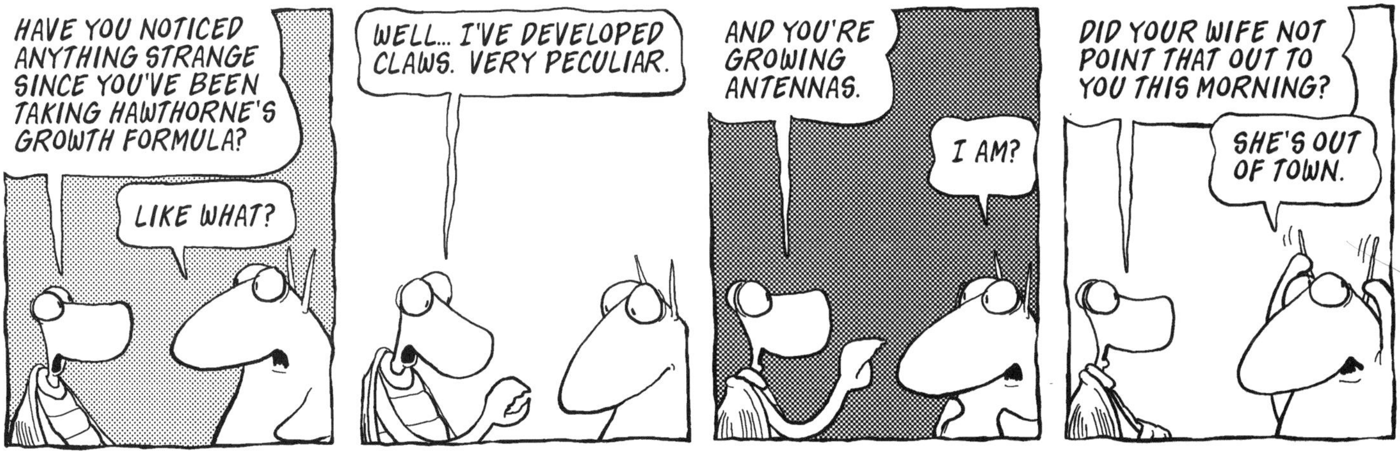
HAVE YOU NOTICED ANYTHING STRANGE SINCE YOU'VE BEEN TAKING HAWTHORNE'S GROWTH FORMULA?
LIKE WHAT?
WELL... I'VE DEVELOPED CLAWS. VERY PECULIAR.
AND YOU'RE GROWING ANTENNAS.
I AM?
DID YOUR WIFE NOT POINT THAT OUT TO YOU THIS MORNING?
SHE'S OUT OF TOWN.

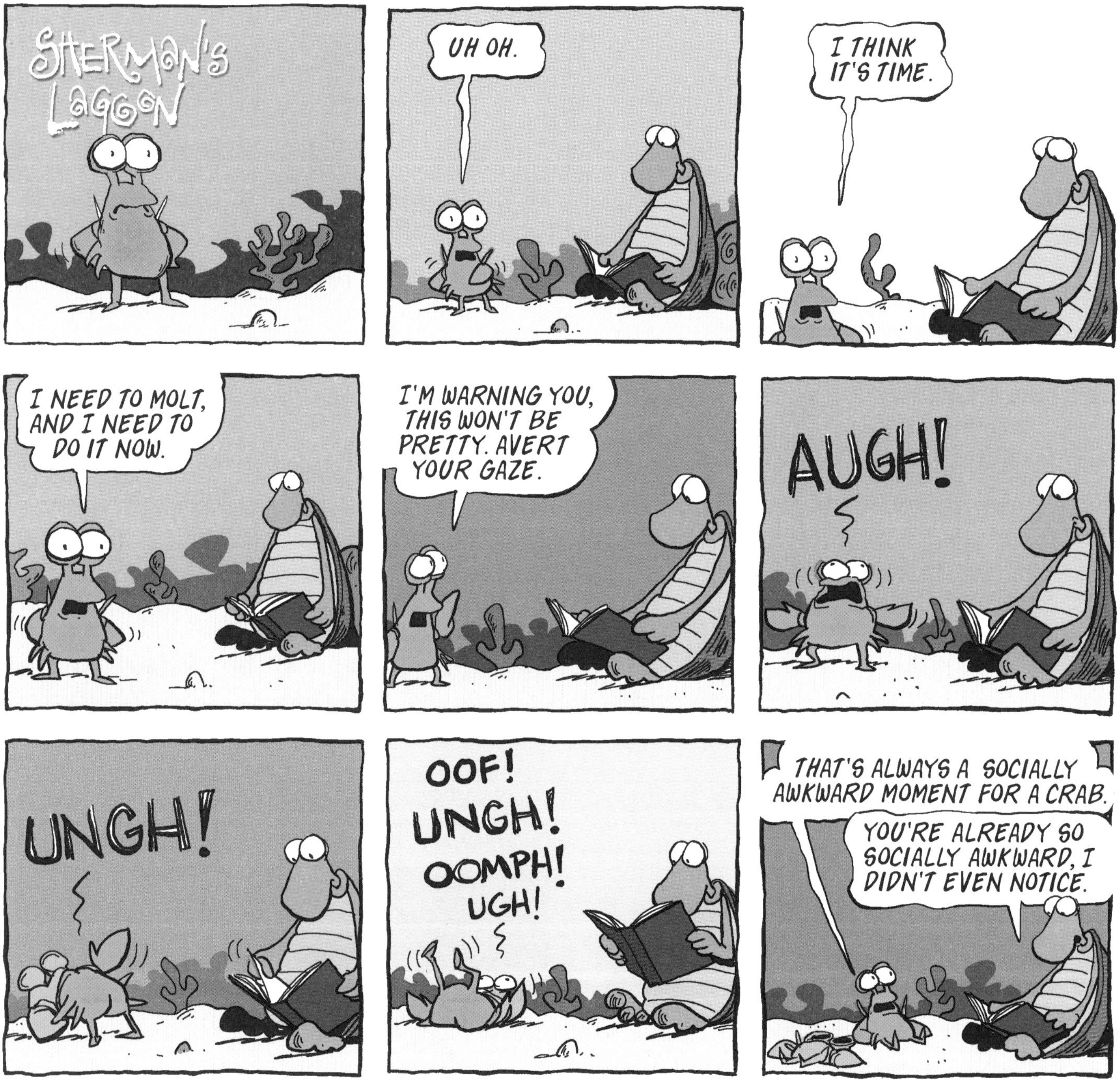
SHERMAN'S LAGOON
UH OH.
I THINK IT'S TIME.
I NEED TO MOLT, AND I NEED TO DO IT NOW.
I'M WARNING YOU, THIS WON'T BE PRETTY. AVERT YOUR GAZE.
AUGH!
UNGH!
OOF! UNGH! OOMPH! UGH!
THAT'S ALWAYS A SOCIALLY AWKWARD MOMENT FOR A CRAB.
YOU'RE ALREADY SO SOCIALLY AWKWARD, I DIDN'T EVEN NOTICE.

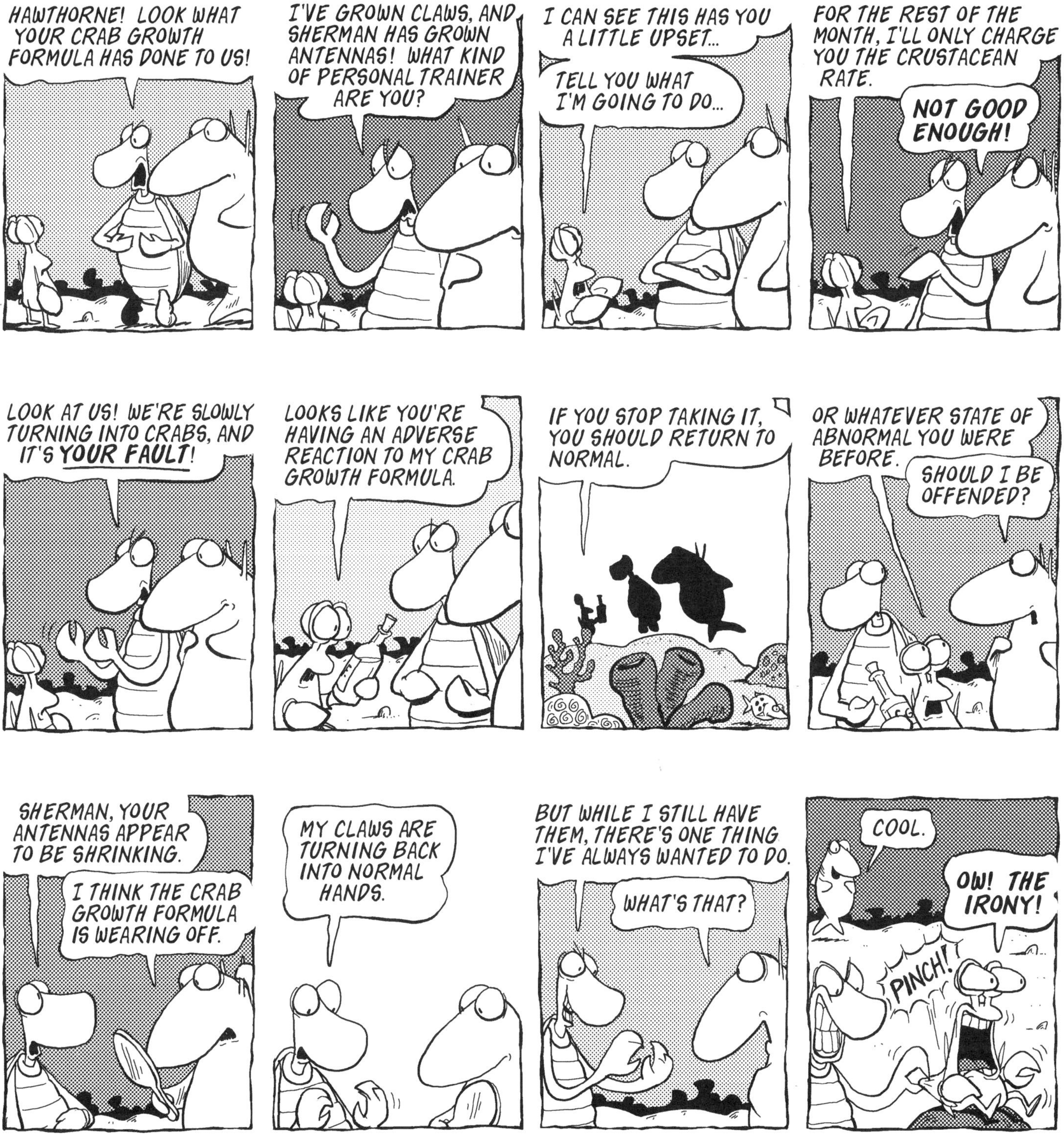
HAWTHORNE! LOOK WHAT YOUR CRAB GROWTH FORMULA HAS DONE TO US!
I'VE GROWN CLAWS, AND SHERMAN HAS GROWN ANTENNAS! WHAT KIND OF PERSONAL TRAINER ARE YOU?
I CAN SEE THIS HAS YOU A LITTLE UPSET...
TELL YOU WHAT I'M GOING TO DO...
FOR THE REST OF THE MONTH, I'LL ONLY CHARGE YOU THE CRUSTACEAN RATE.
NOT GOOD ENOUGH!
LOOK AT US! WE'RE SLOWLY TURNING INTO CRABS, AND IT'S YOUR FAULT!
LOOKS LIKE YOU'RE HAVING AN ADVERSE REACTION TO MY CRAB GROWTH FORMULA.
IF YOU STOP TAKING IT, YOU SHOULD RETURN TO NORMAL.
OR WHATEVER STATE OF ABNORMAL YOU WERE BEFORE.
SHOULD I BE OFFENDED?
SHERMAN, YOUR ANTENNAS APPEAR TO BE SHRINKING.
I THINK THE CRAB GROWTH FORMULA IS WEARING OFF.
MY CLAWS ARE TURNING BACK INTO NORMAL HANDS.
BUT WHILE I STILL HAVE THEM, THERE'S ONE THING I'VE ALWAYS WANTED TO DO.
WHAT'S THAT?
COOL.
OW! THE IRONY!
PINCH!

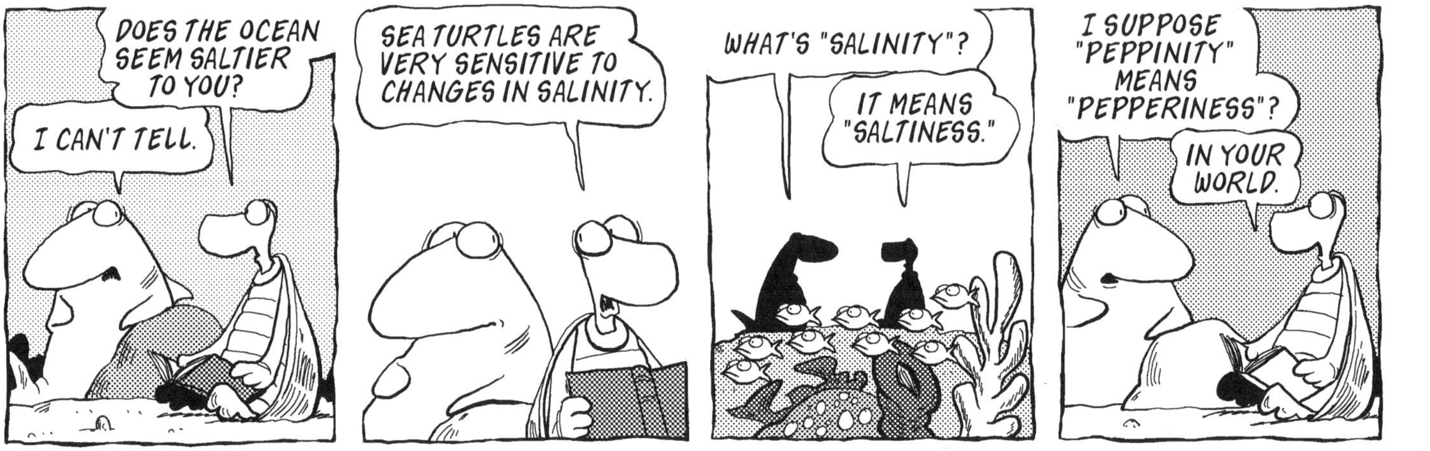
DOES THE OCEAN SEEM SALTIER TO YOU?
I CAN'T TELL.
SEA TURTLES ARE VERY SENSITIVE TO CHANGES IN SALINITY.
WHAT'S "SALINITY"?
IT MEANS "SALTINESS."
I SUPPOSE "PEPPINITY" MEANS "PEPPERINESS"?
IN YOUR WORLD.

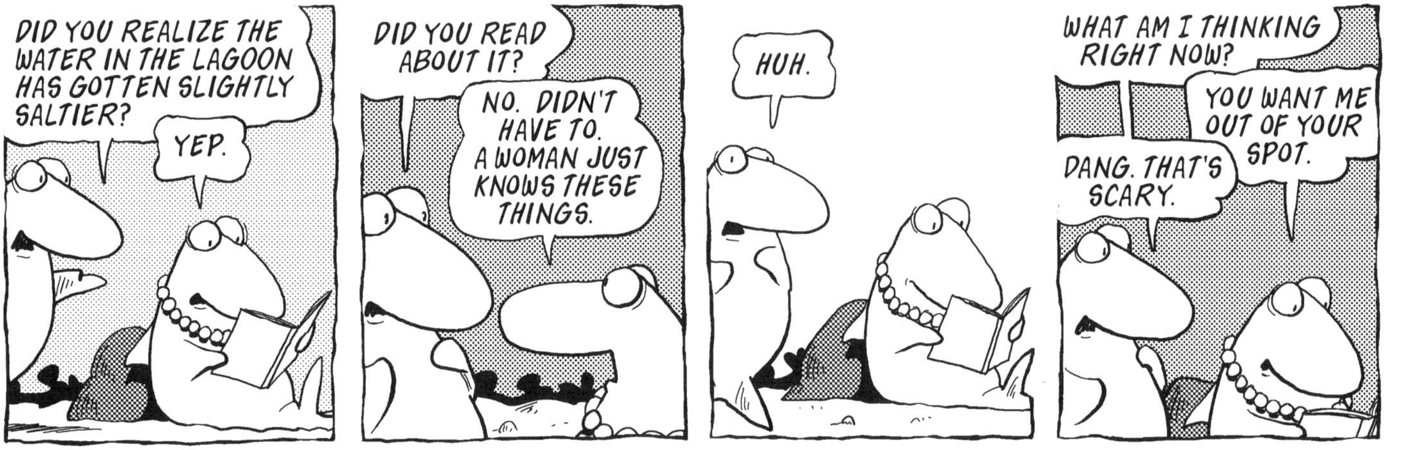
DID YOU REALIZE THE WATER IN THE LAGOON HAS GOTTEN SLIGHTLY SALTIER?
YEP.
DID YOU READ ABOUT IT?
NO. DIDN'T HAVE TO. A WOMAN JUST KNOWS THESE THINGS.
HUH.
WHAT AM I THINKING RIGHT NOW?
YOU WANT ME OUT OF YOUR SPOT.
DANG. THAT'S SCARY.

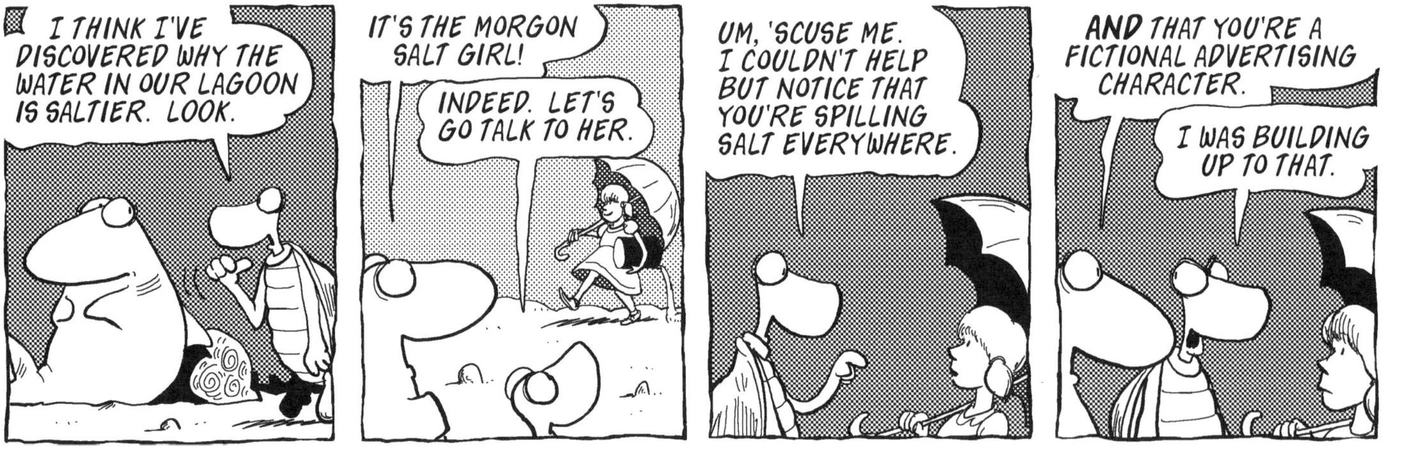
I THINK I'VE DISCOVERED WHY THE WATER IN OUR LAGOON IS SALTIER. LOOK.
IT'S THE MORGON SALT GIRL!
INDEED. LET'S GO TALK TO HER.
UM, 'SCUSE ME. I COULDN'T HELP BUT NOTICE THAT YOU'RE SPILLING SALT EVERYWHERE.
AND THAT YOU'RE A FICTIONAL ADVERTISING CHARACTER.
I WAS BUILDING UP TO THAT.

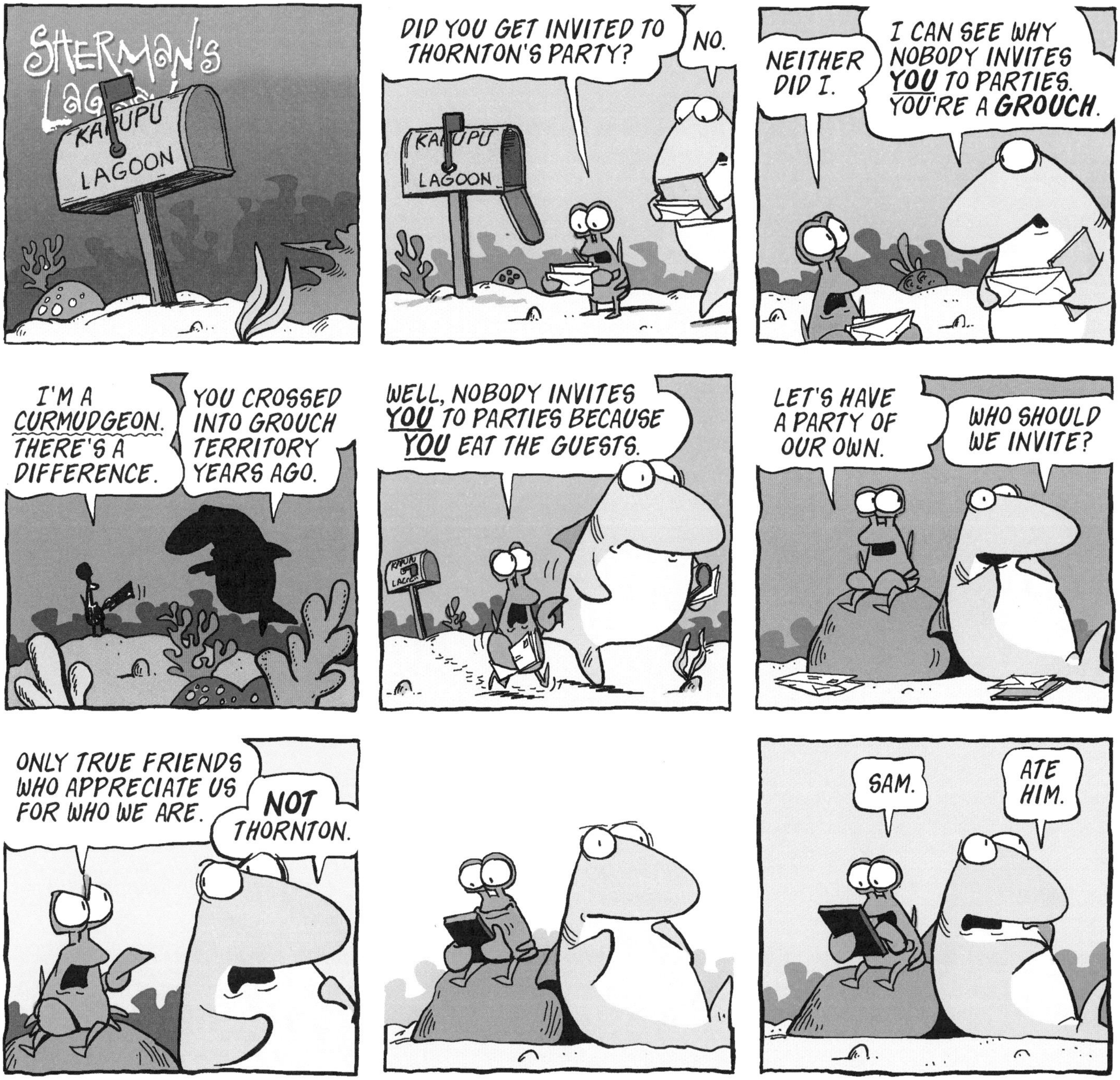
SHERMAN'S LAGOON
KAHUPU LAGOON
DID YOU GET INVITED TO THORNTON'S PARTY?
NO.
NEITHER DID I.
I CAN SEE WHY NOBODY INVITES YOU TO PARTIES. YOU'RE A GROUCH.
I'M A CURMUDGEON. THERE'S A DIFFERENCE.
YOU CROSSED INTO GROUCH TERRITORY YEARS AGO.
WELL, NOBODY INVITES YOU TO PARTIES BECAUSE YOU EAT THE GUESTS.
LET'S HAVE A PARTY OF OUR OWN.
WHO SHOULD WE INVITE?
ONLY TRUE FRIENDS WHO APPRECIATE US FOR WHO WE ARE.
NOT THORNTON.
SAM.
ATE HIM.

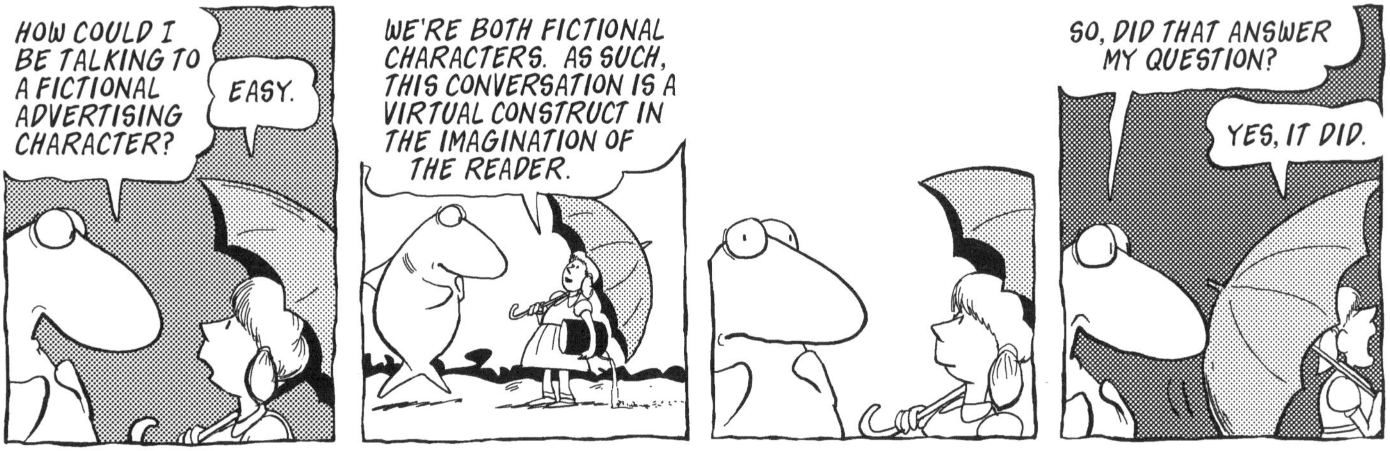
HOW COULD I BE TALKING TO A FICTIONAL ADVERTISING CHARACTER?
EASY.
WE'RE BOTH FICTIONAL CHARACTERS. AS SUCH, THIS CONVERSATION IS A VIRTUAL CONSTRUCT IN THE IMAGINATION OF THE READER.
SO, DID THAT ANSWER MY QUESTION?
YES, IT DID.

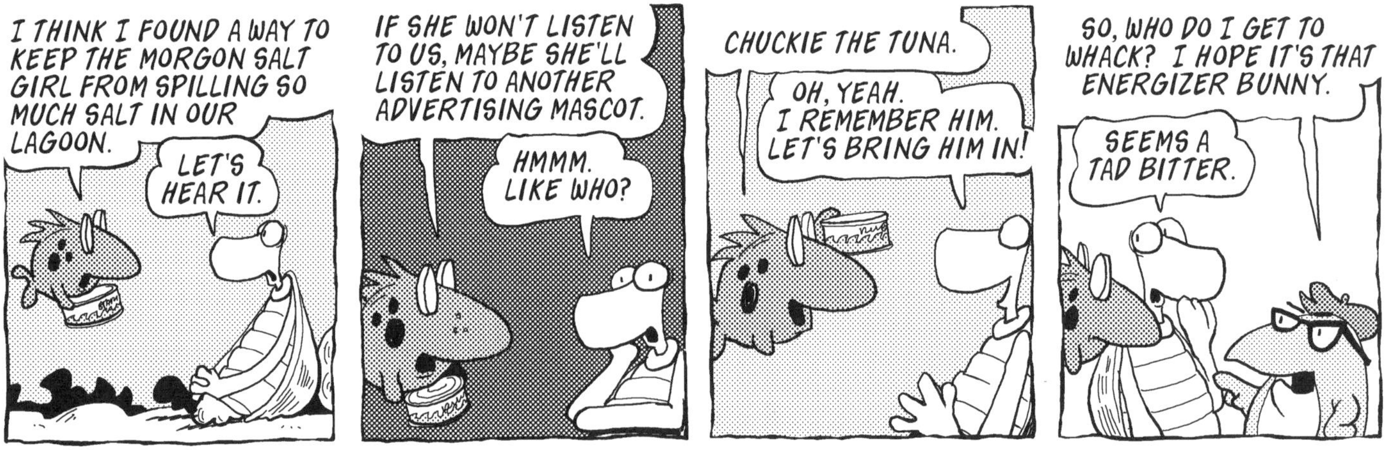
I THINK I FOUND A WAY TO KEEP THE MORGON SALT GIRL FROM SPILLING SO MUCH SALT IN OUR LAGOON.
LET'S HEAR IT.
IF SHE WON'T LISTEN TO US, MAYBE SHE'LL LISTEN TO ANOTHER ADVERTISING MASCOT.
HMMM. LIKE WHO?
CHUCKIE THE TUNA.
OH, YEAH. I REMEMBER HIM. LET'S BRING HIM IN!
SO, WHO DO I GET TO WHACK? I HOPE IT'S THAT ENERGIZER BUNNY.
SEEMS A TAD BITTER.

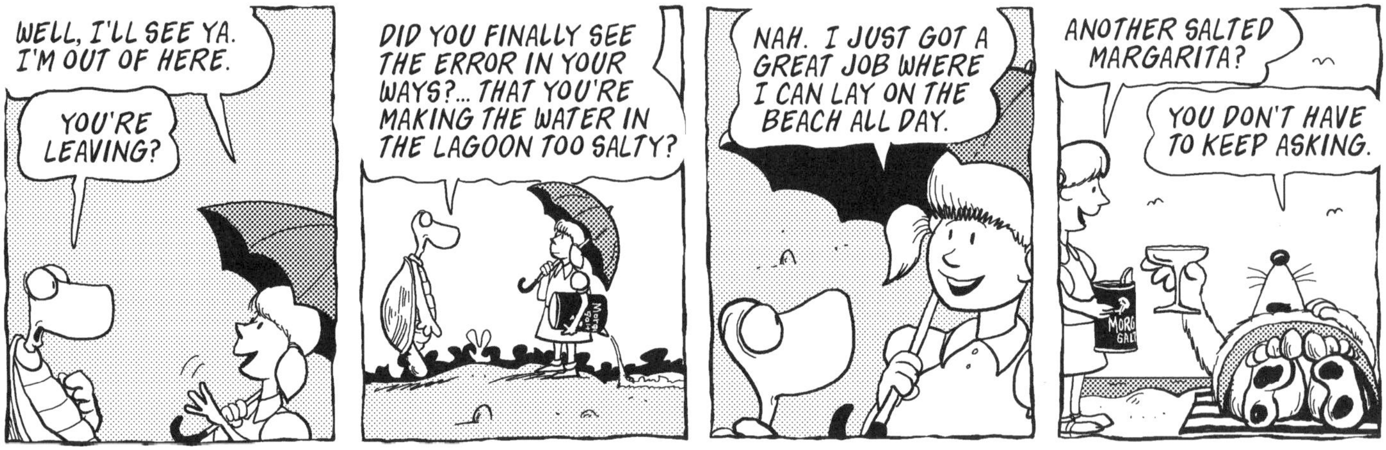
WELL, I'LL SEE YA. I'M OUT OF HERE.
YOU'RE LEAVING?
DID YOU FINALLY SEE THE ERROR IN YOUR WAYS?... THAT YOU'RE MAKING THE WATER IN THE LAGOON TOO SALTY?
NAH. I JUST GOT A GREAT JOB WHERE I CAN LAY ON THE BEACH ALL DAY.
ANOTHER SALTED MARGARITA?
YOU DON'T HAVE TO KEEP ASKING.

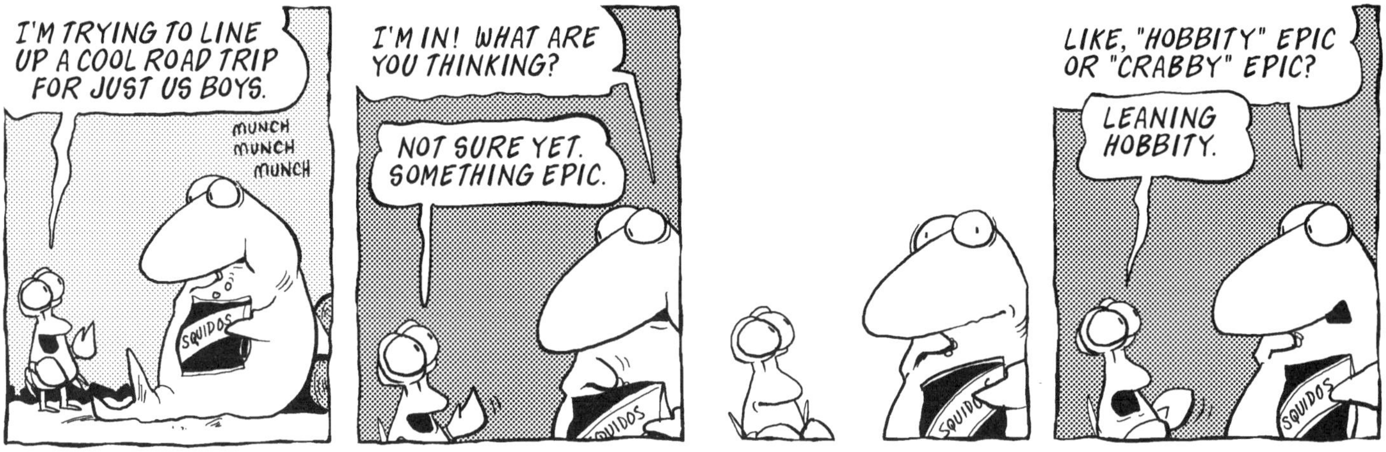
I'M TRYING TO LINE UP A COOL ROAD TRIP FOR JUST US BOYS.
MUNCH MUNCH MUNCH
SQUIDOS
I'M IN! WHAT ARE YOU THINKING?
NOT SURE YET. SOMETHING EPIC.
SQUIDOS
SQUIDOS
LIKE, "HOBBITY" EPIC OR "CRABBY" EPIC?
LEANING HOBBITY.
SQUIDOS

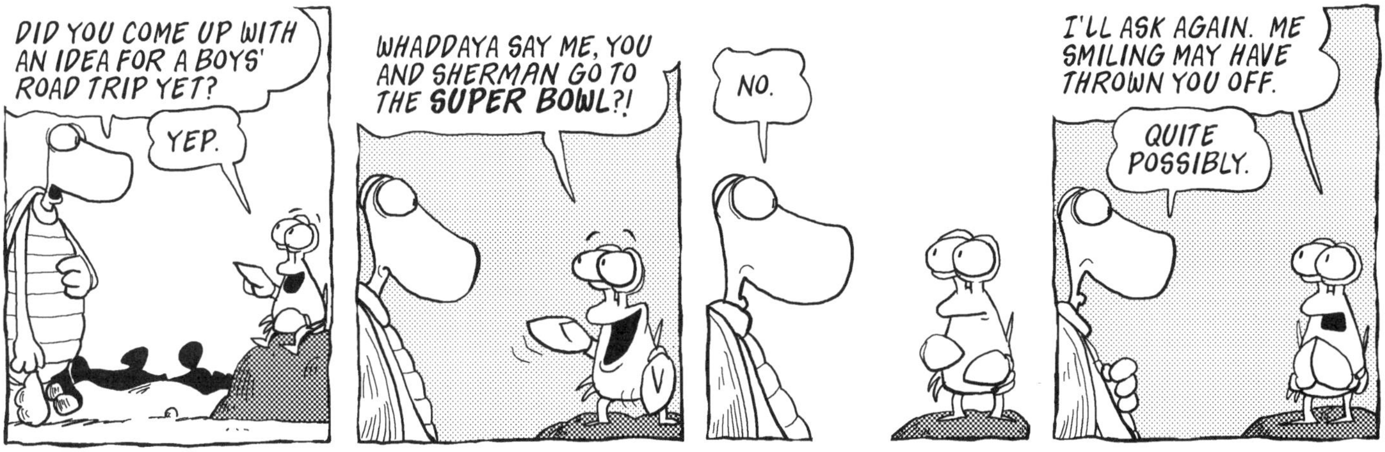
DID YOU COME UP WITH AN IDEA FOR A BOYS' ROAD TRIP YET?
YEP.
WHADDAYA SAY ME, YOU AND SHERMAN GO TO THE SUPER BOWL?!
NO.
I'LL ASK AGAIN. ME SMILING MAY HAVE THROWN YOU OFF.
QUITE POSSIBLY.

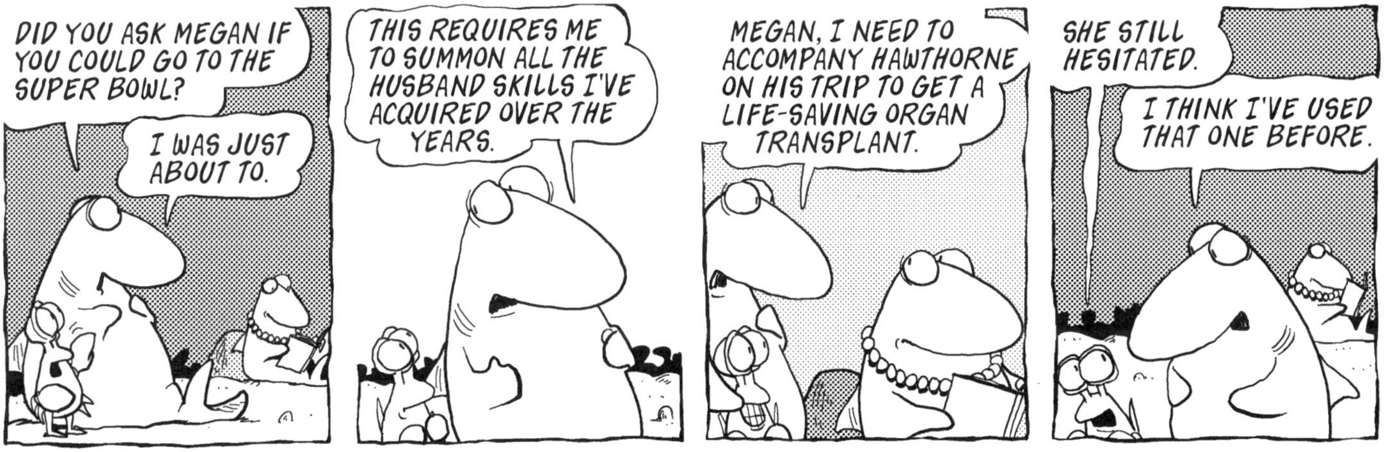
DID YOU ASK MEGAN IF YOU COULD GO TO THE SUPER BOWL?
I WAS JUST ABOUT TO.
THIS REQUIRES ME TO SUMMON ALL THE HUSBAND SKILLS I'VE ACQUIRED OVER THE YEARS.
MEGAN, I NEED TO ACCOMPANY HAWTHORNE ON HIS TRIP TO GET A LIFE-SAVING ORGAN TRANSPLANT.
SHE STILL HESITATED.
I THINK I'VE USED THAT ONE BEFORE.

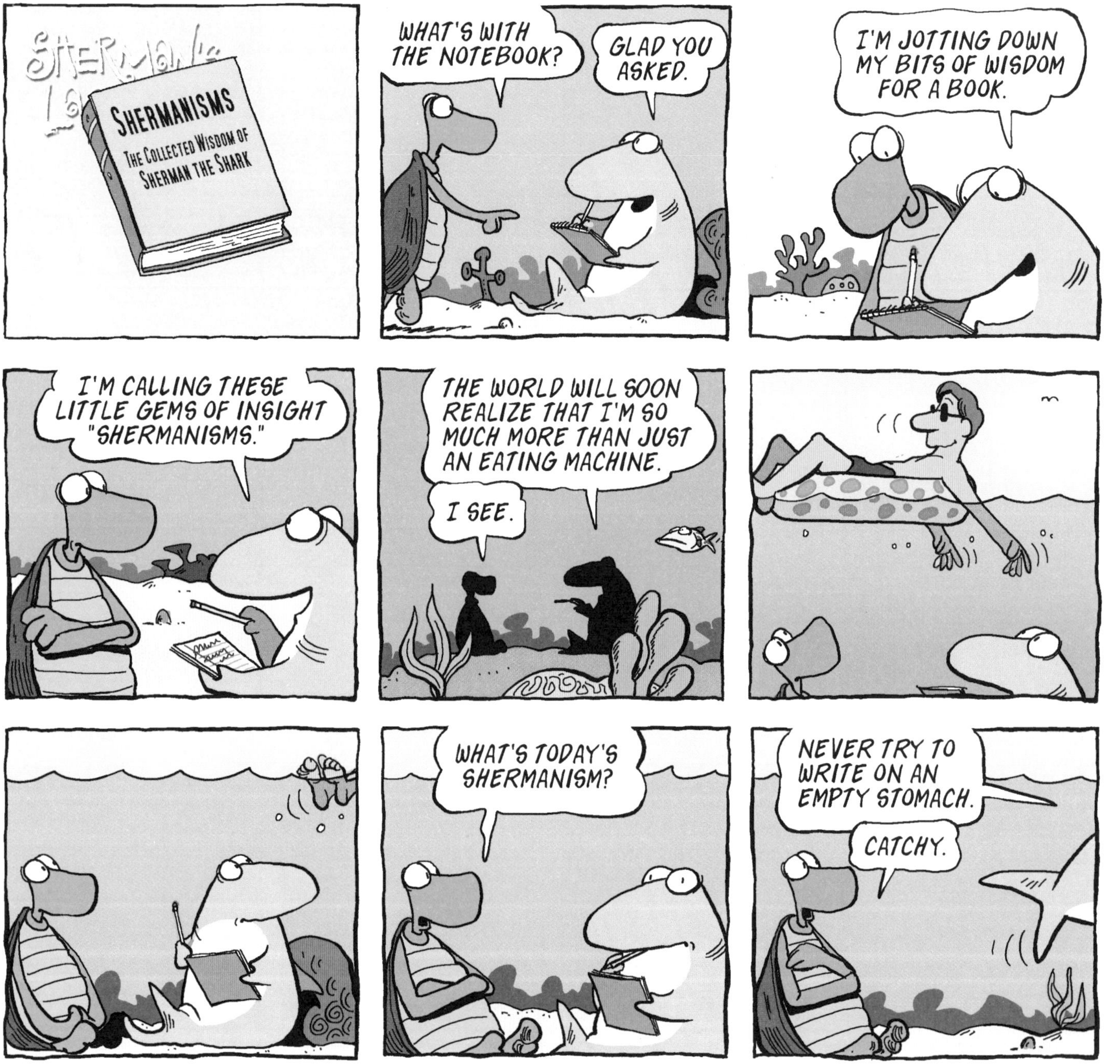
SHERMAN'S LAGOON
SHERMANISMS
THE COLLECTED WISDOM OF SHERMAN THE SHARK
WHAT'S WITH THE NOTEBOOK?
GLAD YOU ASKED.
I'M JOTTING DOWN MY BITS OF WISDOM FOR A BOOK.
I'M CALLING THESE LITTLE GEMS OF INSIGHT "SHERMANISMS."
THE WORLD WILL SOON REALIZE THAT I'M SO MUCH MORE THAN JUST AN EATING MACHINE.
I SEE.
WHAT'S TODAY'S SHERMANISM?
NEVER TRY TO WRITE ON AN EMPTY STOMACH.
CATCHY.

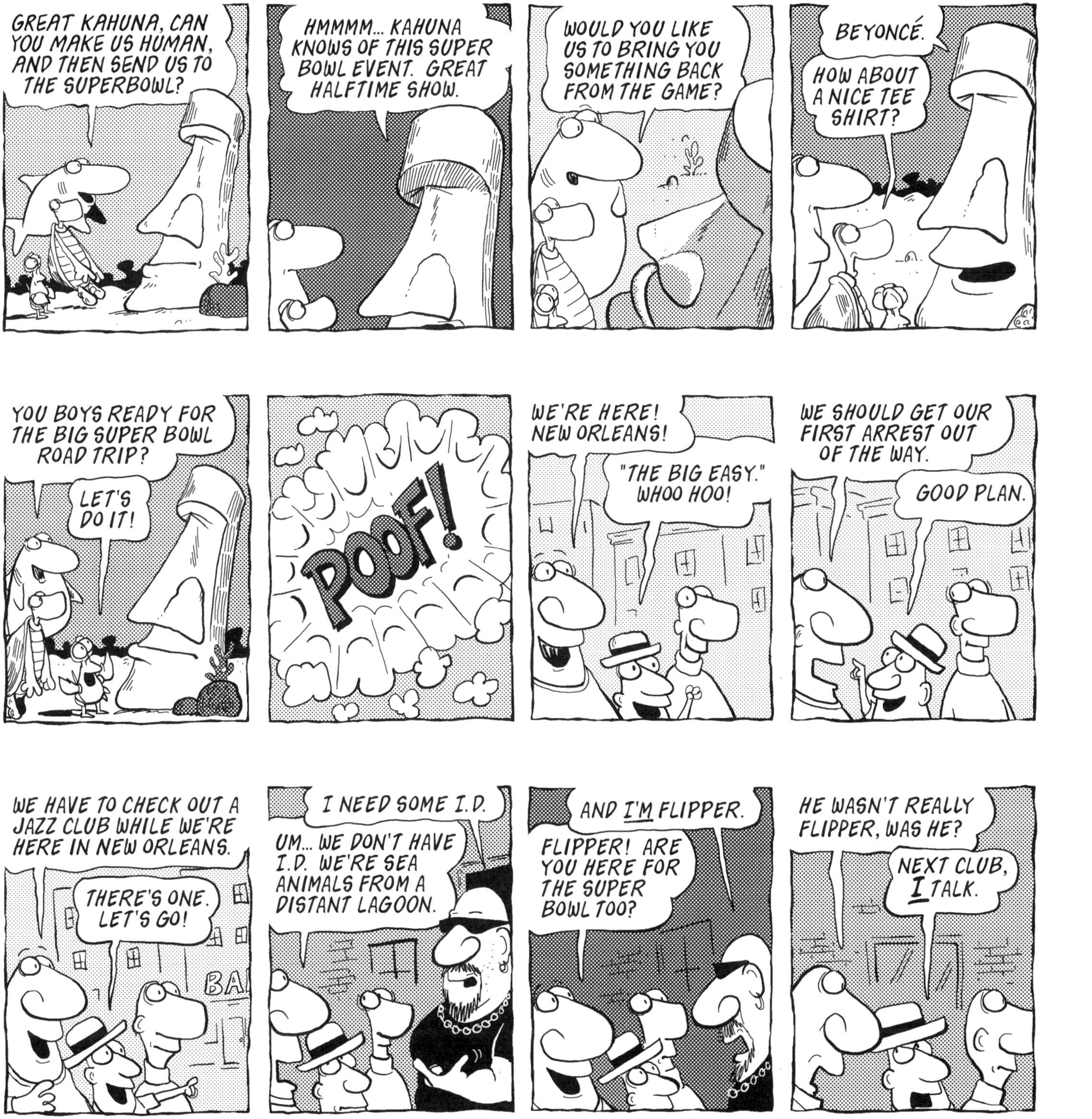
GREAT KAHUNA, CAN YOU MAKE US HUMAN, AND THEN SEND US TO THE SUPERBOWL?
HMMMM... KAHUNA KNOWS OF THIS SUPER BOWL EVENT. GREAT HALFTIME SHOW.
WOULD YOU LIKE US TO BRING YOU SOMETHING BACK FROM THE GAME?
BEYONCÉ.
HOW ABOUT A NICE TEE SHIRT?
YOU BOYS READY FOR THE BIG SUPER BOWL ROAD TRIP?
LET'S DO IT!
POOF!
WE'RE HERE! NEW ORLEANS!
"THE BIG EASY." WHOO HOO!
WE SHOULD GET OUR FIRST ARREST OUT OF THE WAY.
GOOD PLAN.
WE HAVE TO CHECK OUT A JAZZ CLUB WHILE WE'RE HERE IN NEW ORLEANS.
THERE'S ONE. LET'S GO!
BA
I NEED SOME I.D.
UM... WE DON'T HAVE I.D. WE'RE SEA ANIMALS FROM A DISTANT LAGOON.
AND I'M FLIPPER.
FLIPPER! ARE YOU HERE FOR THE SUPER BOWL TOO?
HE WASN'T REALLY FLIPPER, WAS HE?
NEXT CLUB, I TALK.

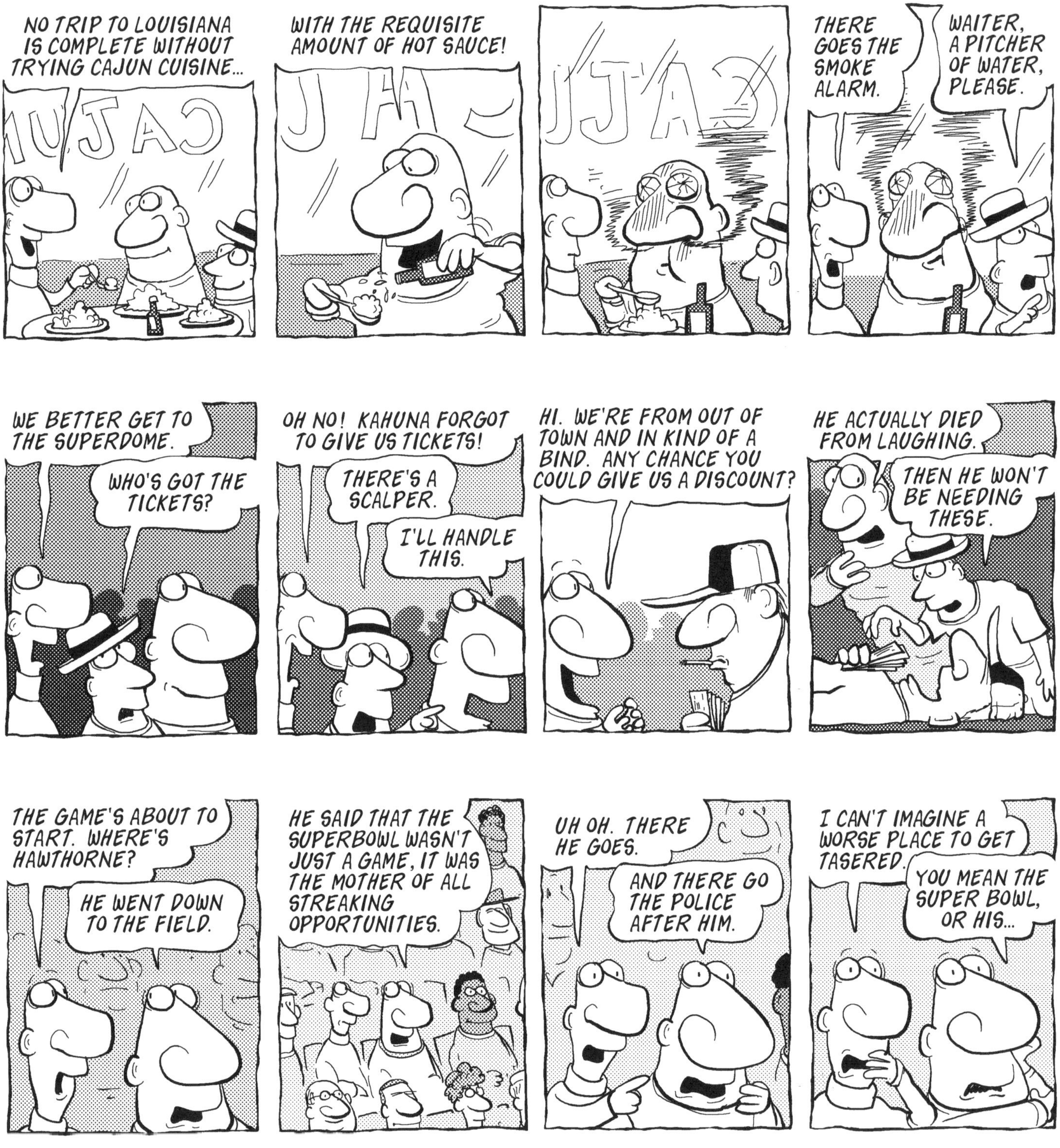
NO TRIP TO LOUISIANA IS COMPLETE WITHOUT TRYING CAJUN CUISINE...
WITH THE REQUISITE AMOUNT OF HOT SAUCE!
THERE GOES THE SMOKE ALARM.
WAITER, A PITCHER OF WATER, PLEASE.
WE BETTER GET TO THE SUPERDOME.
WHO'S GOT THE TICKETS?
OH NO! KAHUNA FORGOT TO GIVE US TICKETS!
THERE'S A SCALPER.
I'LL HANDLE THIS.
HI. WE'RE FROM OUT OF TOWN AND IN KIND OF A BIND. ANY CHANCE YOU COULD GIVE US A DISCOUNT?
HE ACTUALLY DIED FROM LAUGHING.
THEN HE WON'T BE NEEDING THESE.
THE GAME'S ABOUT TO START. WHERE'S HAWTHORNE?
HE WENT DOWN TO THE FIELD.
HE SAID THAT THE SUPERBOWL WASN'T JUST A GAME, IT WAS THE MOTHER OF ALL STREAKING OPPORTUNITIES.
UH OH. THERE HE GOES.
AND THERE GO THE POLICE AFTER HIM.
I CAN'T IMAGINE A WORSE PLACE TO GET TASERED.
YOU MEAN THE SUPER BOWL, OR HIS...

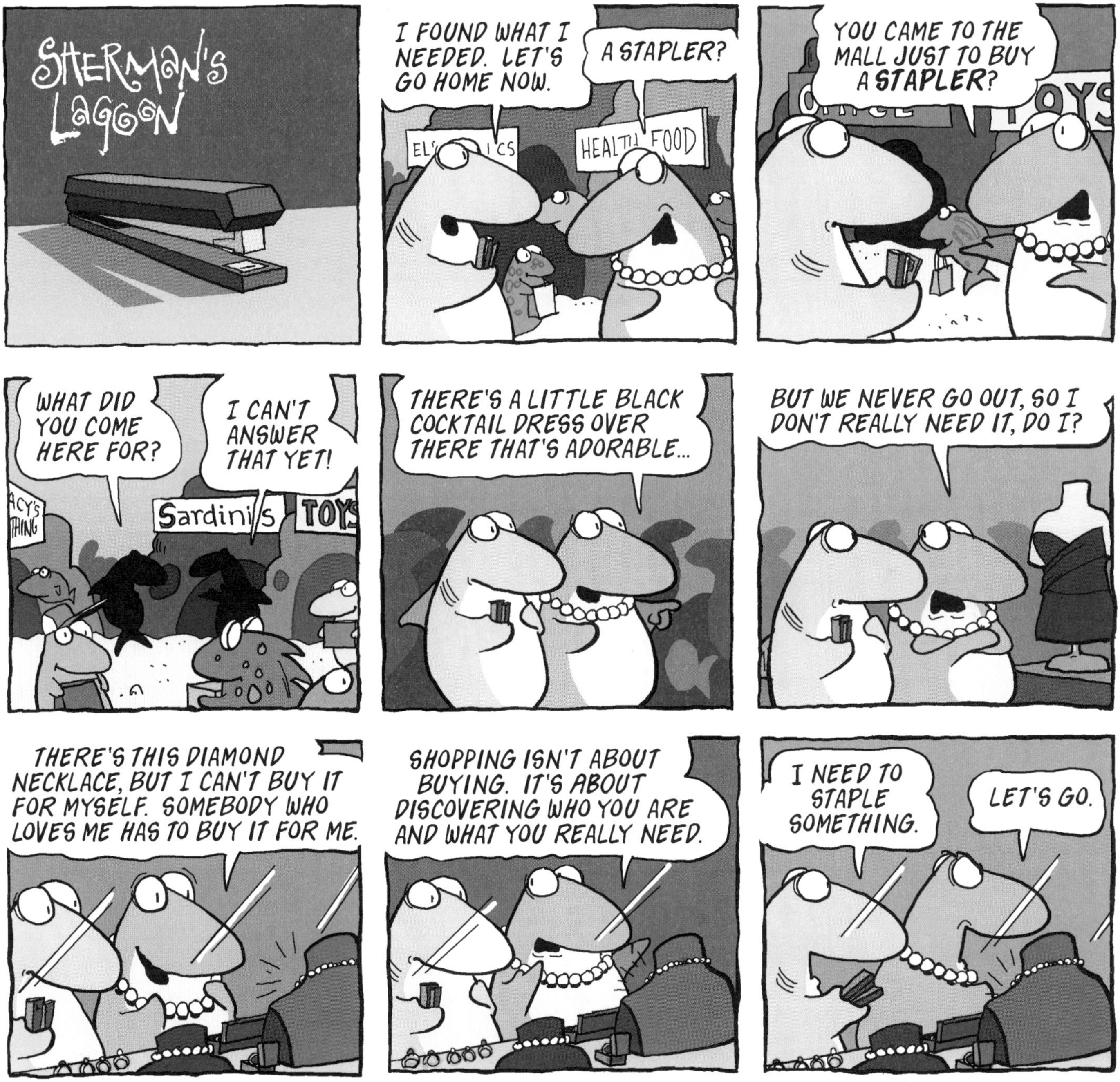
SHERMAN'S LAGOON
I FOUND WHAT I NEEDED. LET'S GO HOME NOW.
A STAPLER?
YOU CAME TO THE MALL JUST TO BUY A STAPLER?
WHAT DID YOU COME HERE FOR?
I CAN'T ANSWER THAT YET!
THERE'S A LITTLE BLACK COCKTAIL DRESS OVER THERE THAT'S ADORABLE...
BUT WE NEVER GO OUT, SO I DON'T REALLY NEED IT, DO I?
THERE'S THIS DIAMOND NECKLACE, BUT I CAN'T BUY IT FOR MYSELF. SOMEBODY WHO LOVES ME HAS TO BUY IT FOR ME.
SHOPPING ISN'T ABOUT BUYING. IT'S ABOUT DISCOVERING WHO YOU ARE AND WHAT YOU REALLY NEED.
I NEED TO STAPLE SOMETHING.
LET'S GO.

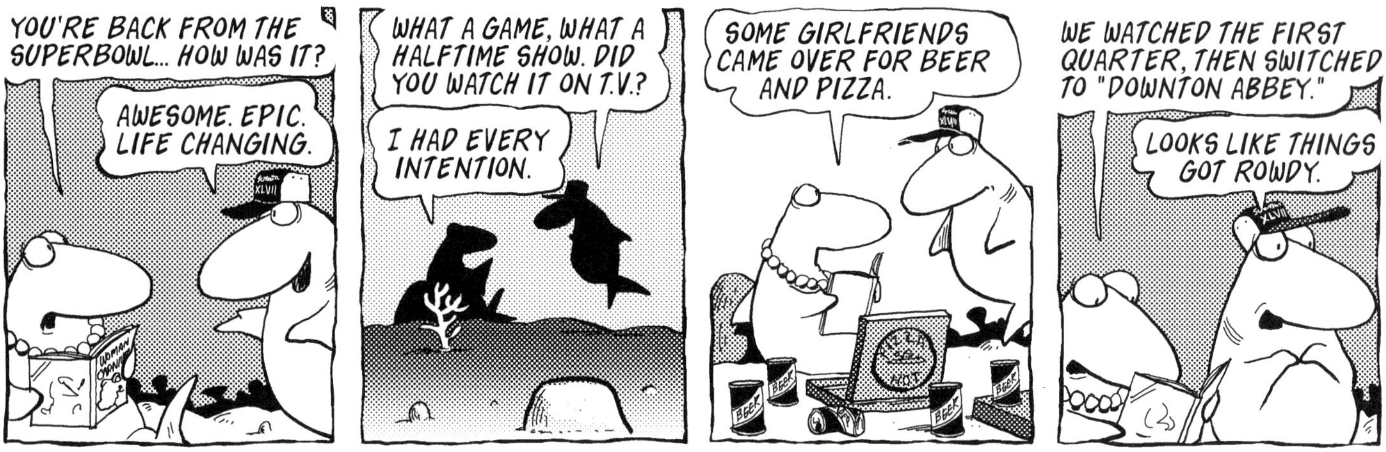
YOU'RE BACK FROM THE SUPERBOWL... HOW WAS IT?
AWESOME. EPIC. LIFE CHANGING.
WHAT A GAME, WHAT A HALFTIME SHOW. DID YOU WATCH IT ON T.V.?
I HAD EVERY INTENTION.
SOME GIRLFRIENDS CAME OVER FOR BEER AND PIZZA.
WE WATCHED THE FIRST QUARTER, THEN SWITCHED TO "DOWNTON ABBEY."
LOOKS LIKE THINGS GOT ROWDY.

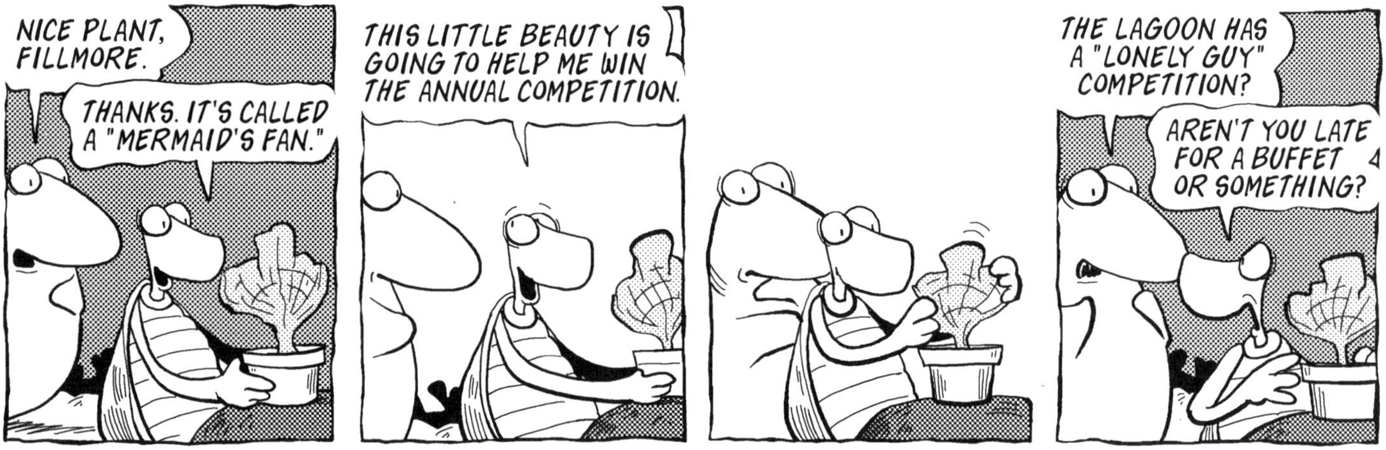
NICE PLANT, FILLMORE.
THANKS. IT'S CALLED A "MERMAID'S FAN."
THIS LITTLE BEAUTY IS GOING TO HELP ME WIN THE ANNUAL COMPETITION.
THE LAGOON HAS A "LONELY GUY" COMPETITION?
AREN'T YOU LATE FOR A BUFFET OR SOMETHING?

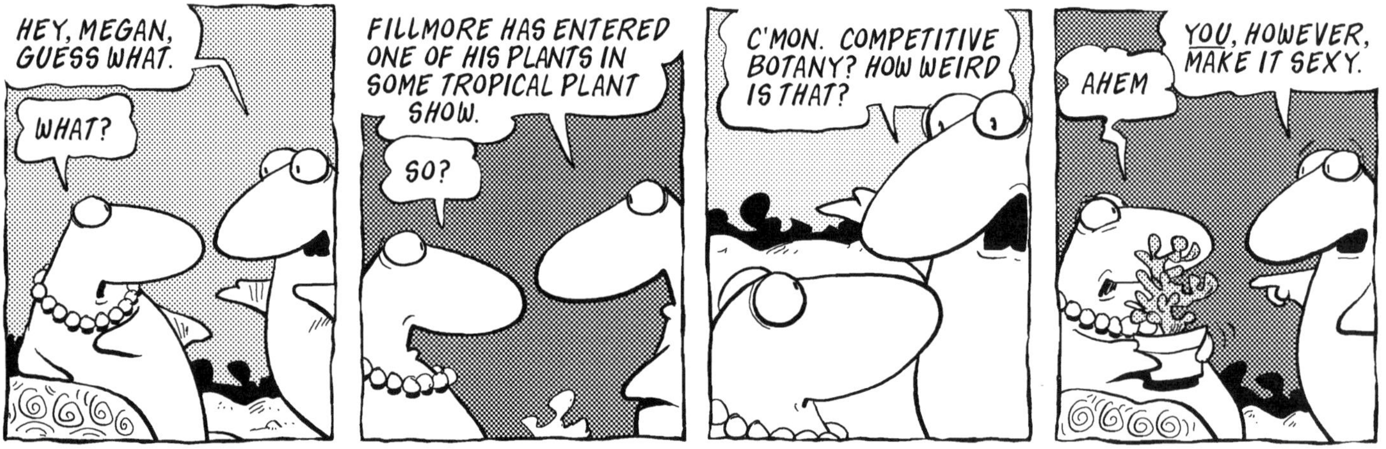
HEY, MEGAN, GUESS WHAT.
WHAT?
FILLMORE HAS ENTERED ONE OF HIS PLANTS IN SOME TROPICAL PLANT SHOW.
SO?
C'MON. COMPETITIVE BOTANY? HOW WEIRD IS THAT?
AHEM
YOU, HOWEVER, MAKE IT SEXY.

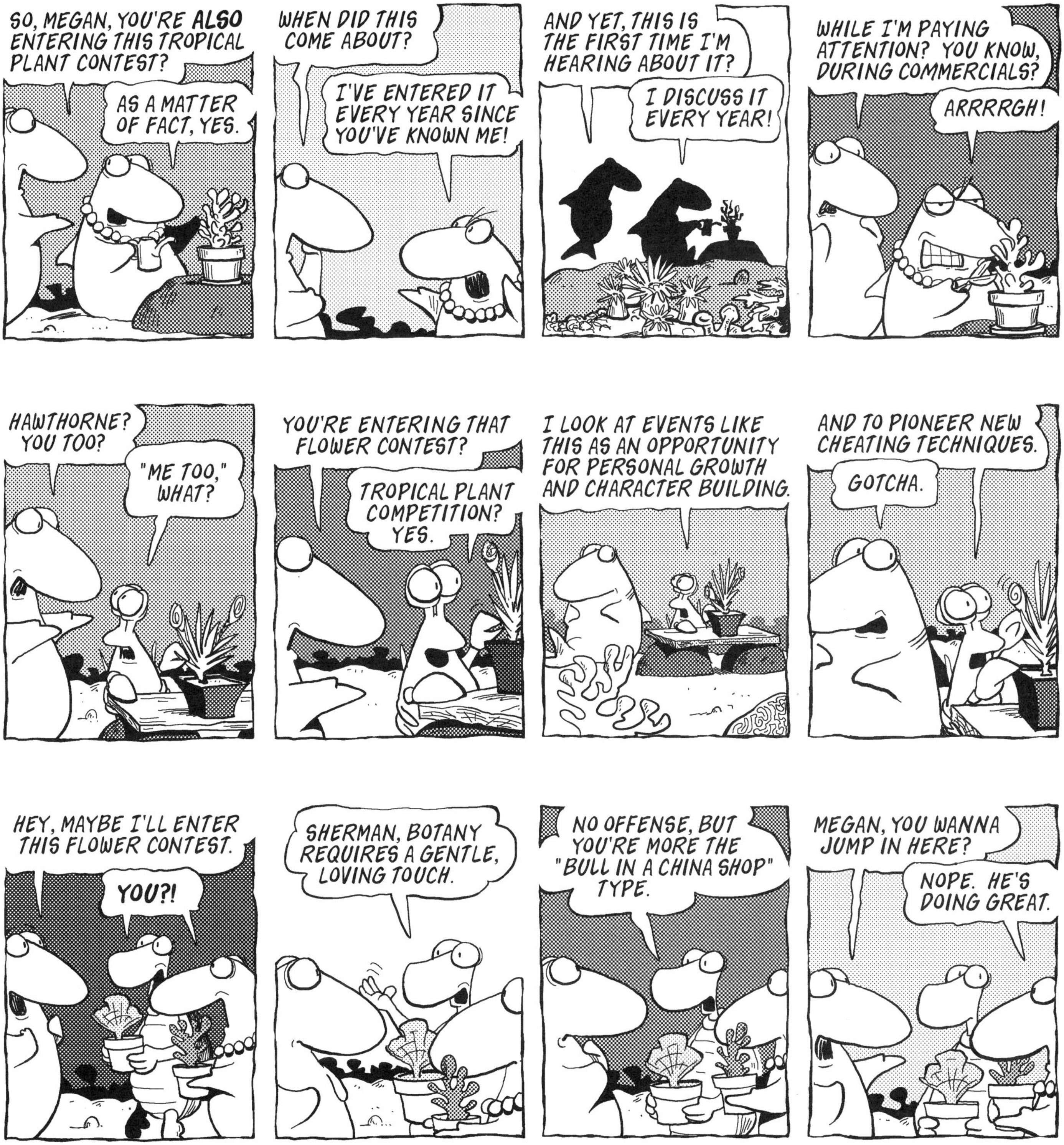
SO, MEGAN, YOU'RE ALSO ENTERING THIS TROPICAL PLANT CONTEST?
AS A MATTER OF FACT, YES.
WHEN DID THIS COME ABOUT?
I'VE ENTERED IT EVERY YEAR SINCE YOU'VE KNOWN ME!
AND YET, THIS IS THE FIRST TIME I'M HEARING ABOUT IT?
I DISCUSS IT EVERY YEAR!
WHILE I'M PAYING ATTENTION? YOU KNOW, DURING COMMERCIALS?
ARRRRGH!
HAWTHORNE? YOU TOO?
"ME TOO," WHAT?
YOU'RE ENTERING THAT FLOWER CONTEST?
TROPICAL PLANT COMPETITION? YES.
I LOOK AT EVENTS LIKE THIS AS AN OPPORTUNITY FOR PERSONAL GROWTH AND CHARACTER BUILDING.
AND TO PIONEER NEW CHEATING TECHNIQUES.
GOTCHA.
HEY, MAYBE I'LL ENTER THIS FLOWER CONTEST.
YOU?!
SHERMAN, BOTANY REQUIRES A GENTLE, LOVING TOUCH.
NO OFFENSE, BUT YOU'RE MORE THE "BULL IN A CHINA SHOP" TYPE.
MEGAN, YOU WANNA JUMP IN HERE?
NOPE. HE'S DOING GREAT.

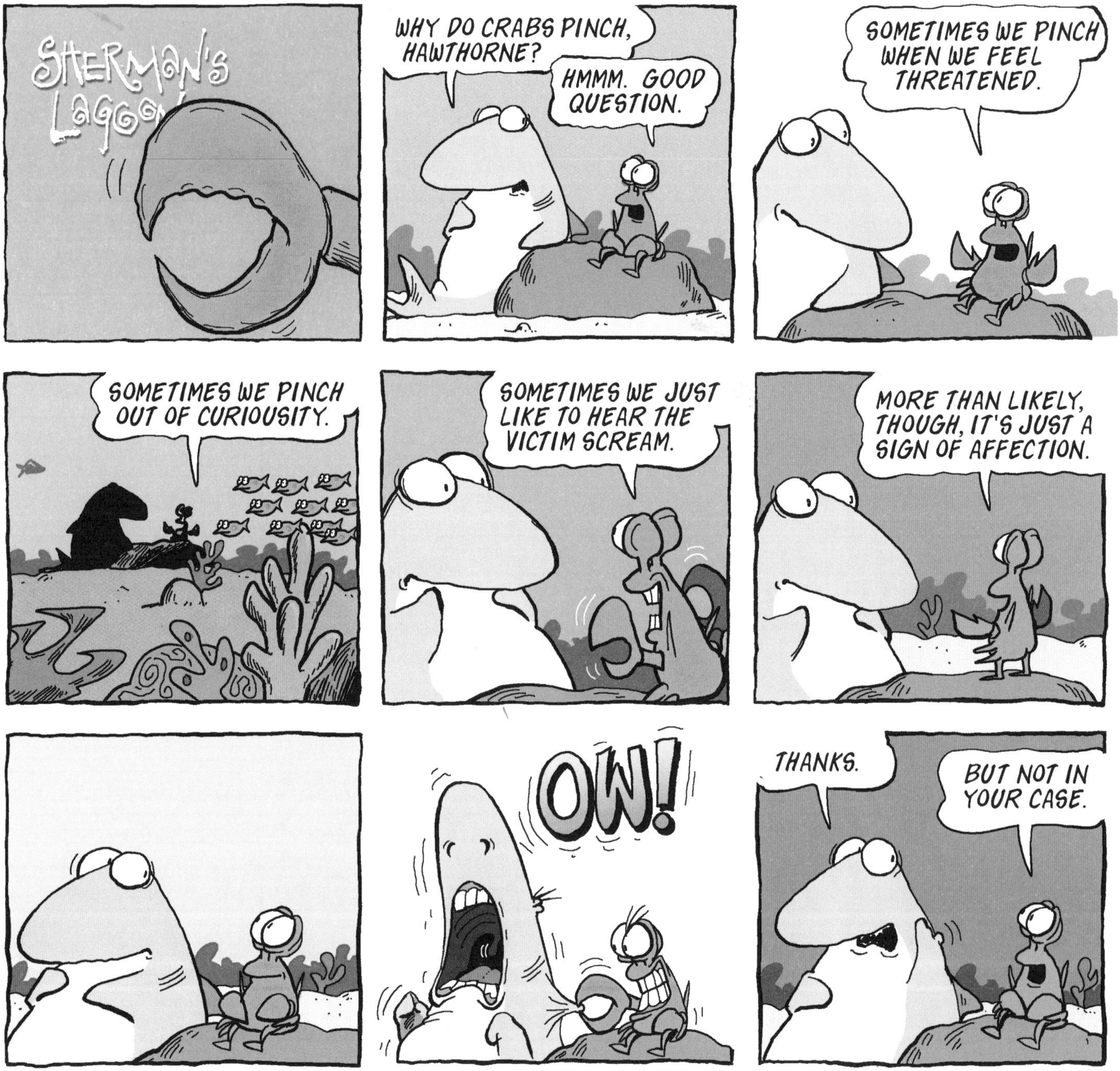

SHERMAN'S LAGOON
WHY DO CRABS PINCH, HAWTHORNE?
HMMM. GOOD QUESTION.
SOMETIMES WE PINCH WHEN WE FEEL THREATENED.
SOMETIMES WE PINCH OUT OF CURIOUSITY.
SOMETIMES WE JUST LIKE TO HEAR THE VICTIM SCREAM.
MORE THAN LIKELY, THOUGH, IT'S JUST A SIGN OF AFFECTION.
OW!
THANKS.
BUT NOT IN YOUR CASE.

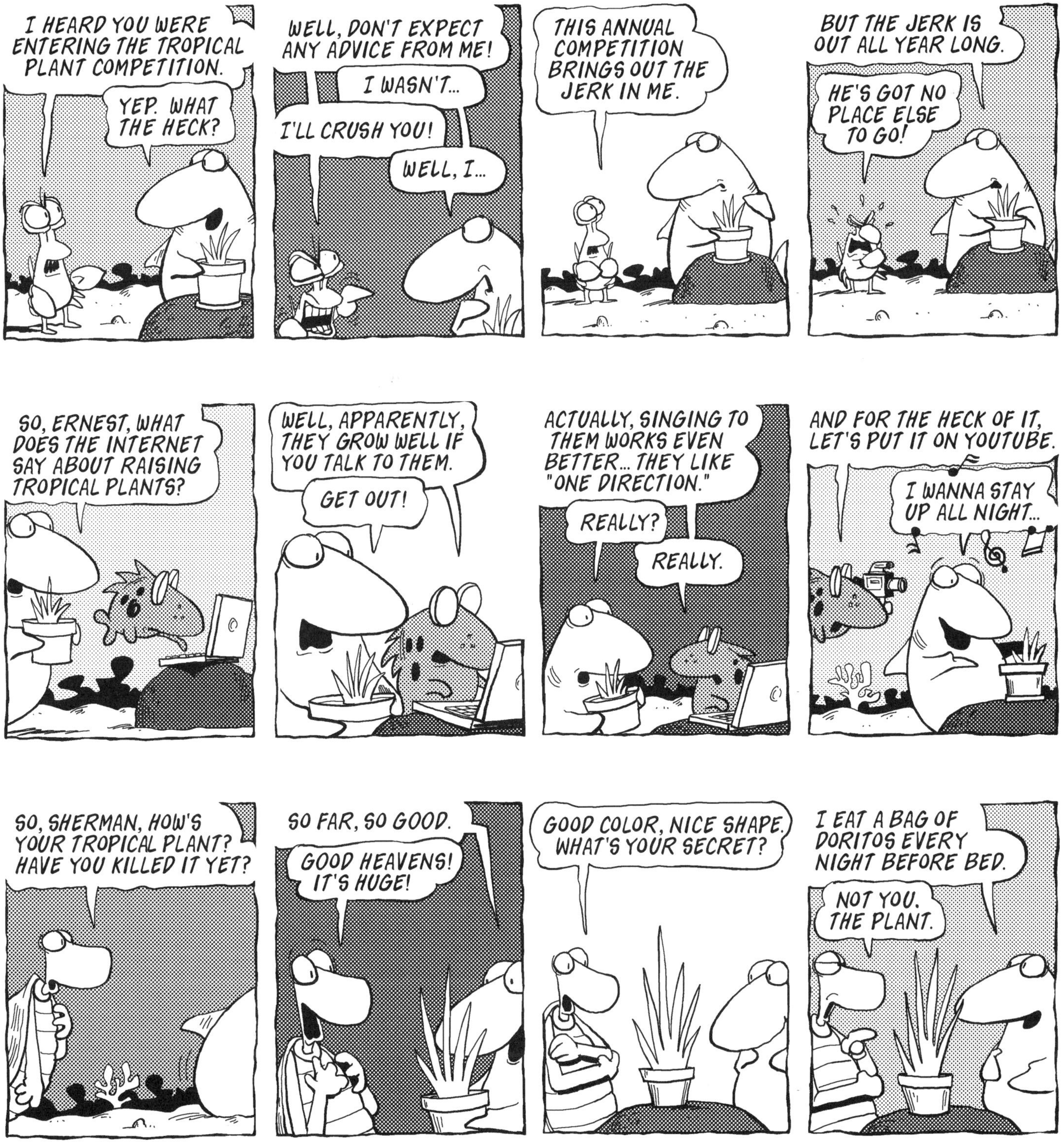
I HEARD YOU WERE ENTERING THE TROPICAL PLANT COMPETITION.
YEP. WHAT THE HECK?
WELL, DON'T EXPECT ANY ADVICE FROM ME!
I WASN'T...
I'LL CRUSH YOU!
WELL, I...
THIS ANNUAL COMPETITION BRINGS OUT THE JERK IN ME.
BUT THE JERK IS OUT ALL YEAR LONG.
HE'S GOT NO PLACE ELSE TO GO!
SO, ERNEST, WHAT DOES THE INTERNET SAY ABOUT RAISING TROPICAL PLANTS?
WELL, APPARENTLY, THEY GROW WELL IF YOU TALK TO THEM.
GET OUT!
ACTUALLY, SINGING TO THEM WORKS EVEN BETTER... THEY LIKE "ONE DIRECTION."
REALLY?
REALLY.
AND FOR THE HECK OF IT, LET'S PUT IT ON YOUTUBE.
I WANNA STAY UP ALL NIGHT...
SO, SHERMAN, HOW'S YOUR TROPICAL PLANT? HAVE YOU KILLED IT YET?
SO FAR, SO GOOD.
GOOD HEAVENS! IT'S HUGE!
GOOD COLOR, NICE SHAPE. WHAT'S YOUR SECRET?
I EAT A BAG OF DORITOS EVERY NIGHT BEFORE BED.
NOT YOU. THE PLANT.

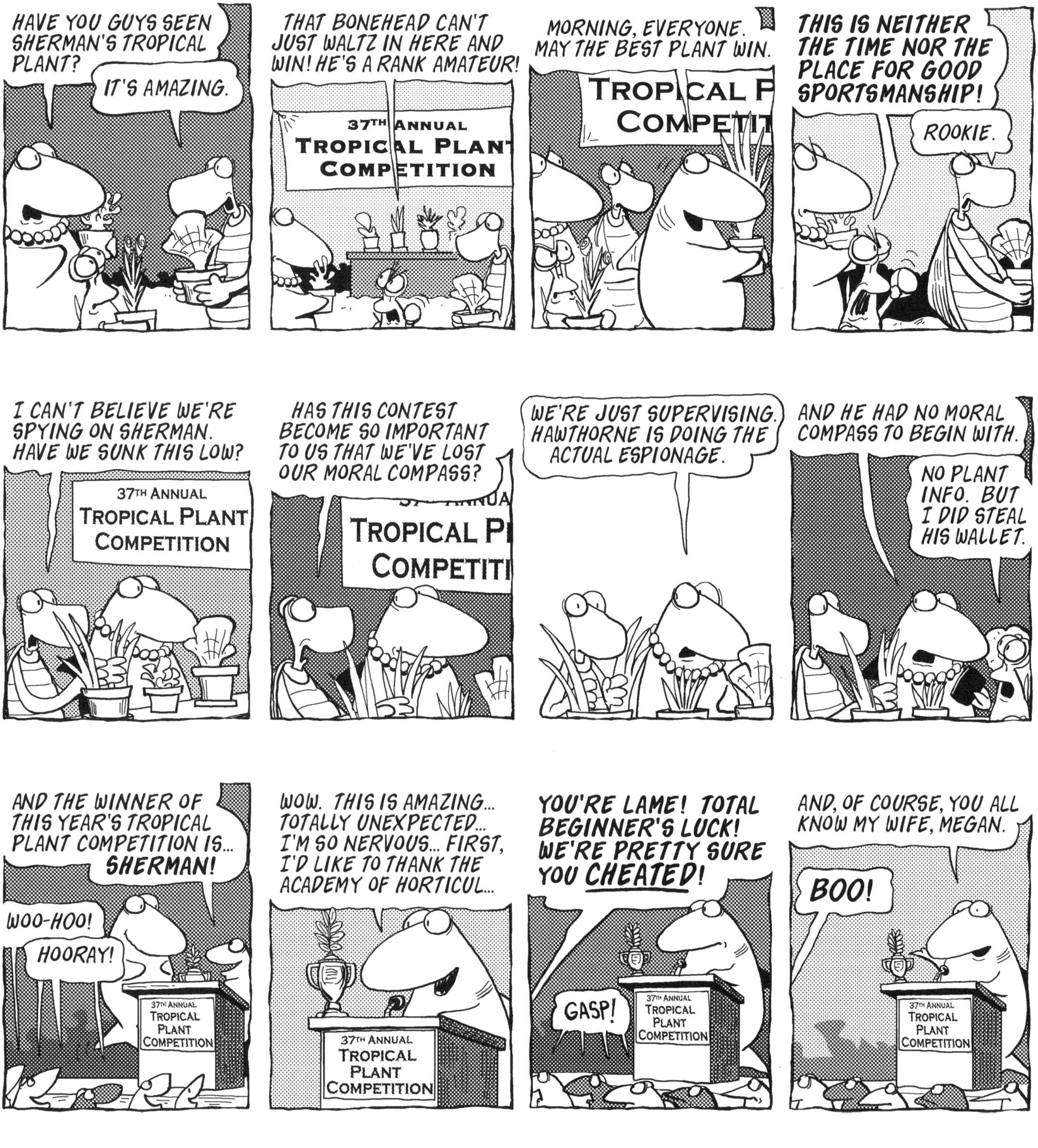
HAVE YOU GUYS SEEN SHERMAN'S TROPICAL PLANT?
IT'S AMAZING.
THAT BONEHEAD CAN'T JUST WALTZ IN HERE AND WIN! HE'S A RANK AMATEUR!
37TH ANNUAL TROPICAL PLANT COMPETITION
MORNING, EVERYONE. MAY THE BEST PLANT WIN.
THIS IS NEITHER THE TIME NOR THE PLACE FOR GOOD SPORTSMANSHIP!
ROOKIE.
I CAN'T BELIEVE WE'RE SPYING ON SHERMAN. HAVE WE SUNK THIS LOW?
37TH ANNUAL TROPICAL PLANT COMPETITION
HAS THIS CONTEST BECOME SO IMPORTANT TO US THAT WE'VE LOST OUR MORAL COMPASS?
WE'RE JUST SUPERVISING. HAWTHORNE IS DOING THE ACTUAL ESPIONAGE.
AND HE HAD NO MORAL COMPASS TO BEGIN WITH.
NO PLANT INFO. BUT I DID STEAL HIS WALLET.
AND THE WINNER OF THIS YEAR'S TROPICAL PLANT COMPETITION IS... SHERMAN!
WOO-HOO!
HOORAY!
37TH ANNUAL TROPICAL PLANT COMPETITION
WOW. THIS IS AMAZING... TOTALLY UNEXPECTED... I'M SO NERVOUS... FIRST, I'D LIKE TO THANK THE ACADEMY OF HORTICUL...
37TH ANNUAL TROPICAL PLANT COMPETITION
YOU'RE LAME! TOTAL BEGINNER'S LUCK! WE'RE PRETTY SURE YOU CHEATED!
GASP!
37TH ANNUAL TROPICAL PLANT COMPETITION
AND, OF COURSE, YOU ALL KNOW MY WIFE, MEGAN.
BOO!
37TH ANNUAL TROPICAL PLANT COMPETITION

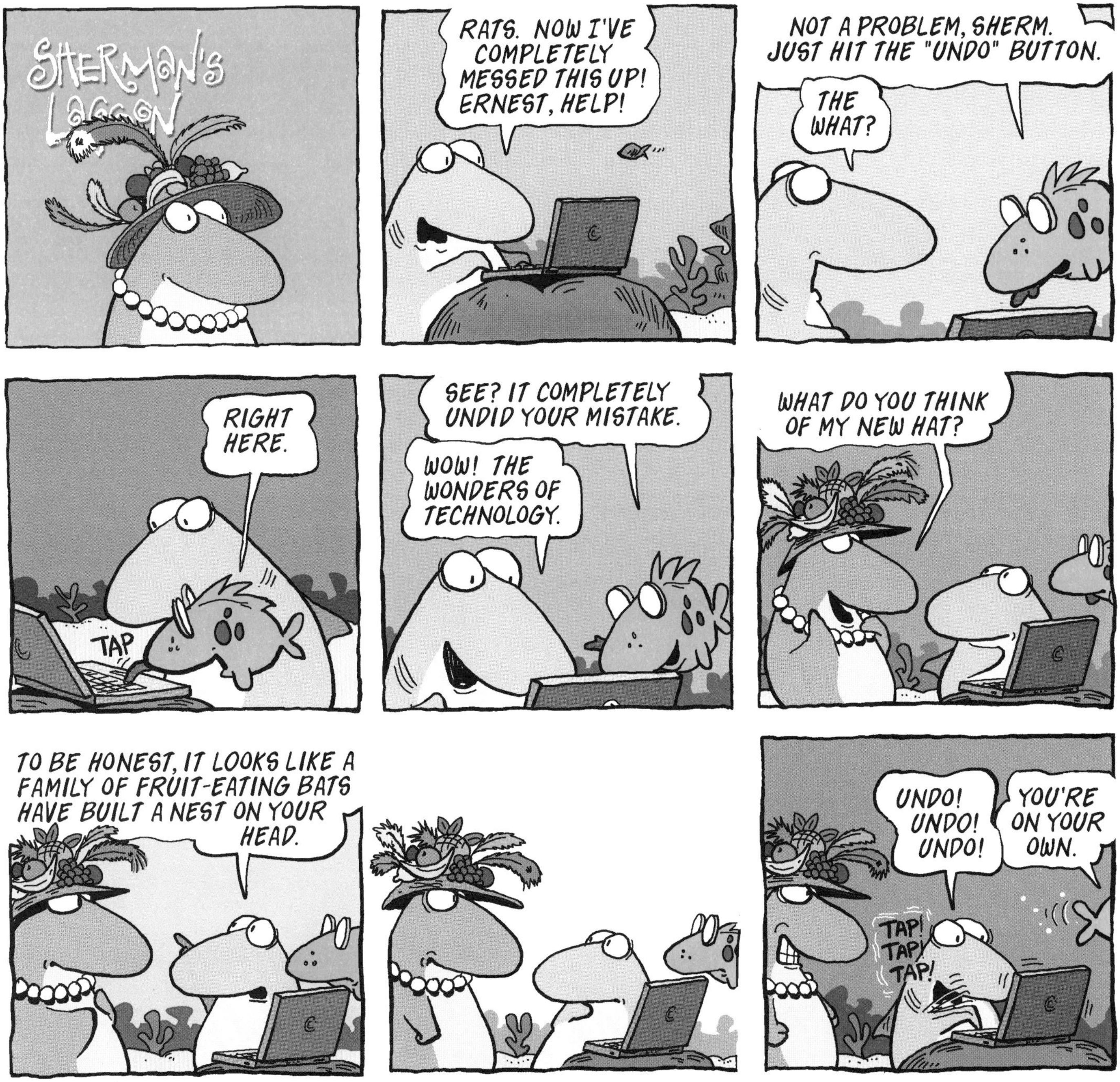
SHERMAN'S LAGOON
RATS. NOW I'VE COMPLETELY MESSED THIS UP! ERNEST, HELP!
NOT A PROBLEM, SHERM. JUST HIT THE "UNDO" BUTTON.
THE WHAT?
RIGHT HERE.
TAP
SEE? IT COMPLETELY UNDID YOUR MISTAKE.
WOW! THE WONDERS OF TECHNOLOGY.
WHAT DO YOU THINK OF MY NEW HAT?
TO BE HONEST, IT LOOKS LIKE A FAMILY OF FRUIT-EATING BATS HAVE BUILT A NEST ON YOUR HEAD.
UNDO! UNDO! UNDO!
YOU'RE ON YOUR OWN.
TAP! TAP! TAP!

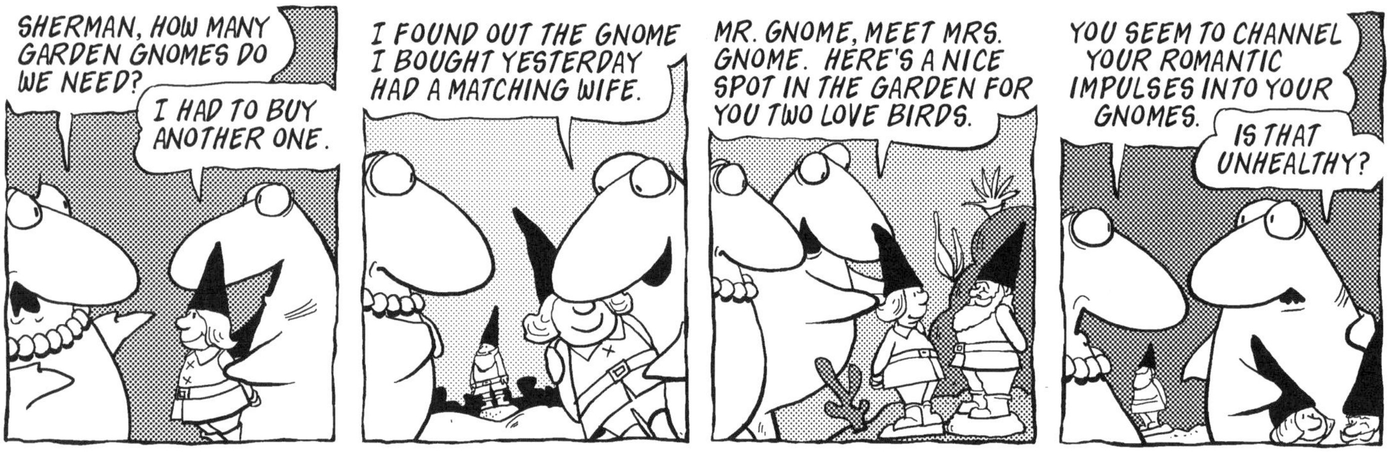
SHERMAN, HOW MANY GARDEN GNOMES DO WE NEED?
I HAD TO BUY ANOTHER ONE.
I FOUND OUT THE GNOME I BOUGHT YESTERDAY HAD A MATCHING WIFE.
MR. GNOME, MEET MRS. GNOME. HERE'S A NICE SPOT IN THE GARDEN FOR YOU TWO LOVE BIRDS.
YOU SEEM TO CHANNEL YOUR ROMANTIC IMPULSES INTO YOUR GNOMES.
IS THAT UNHEALTHY?

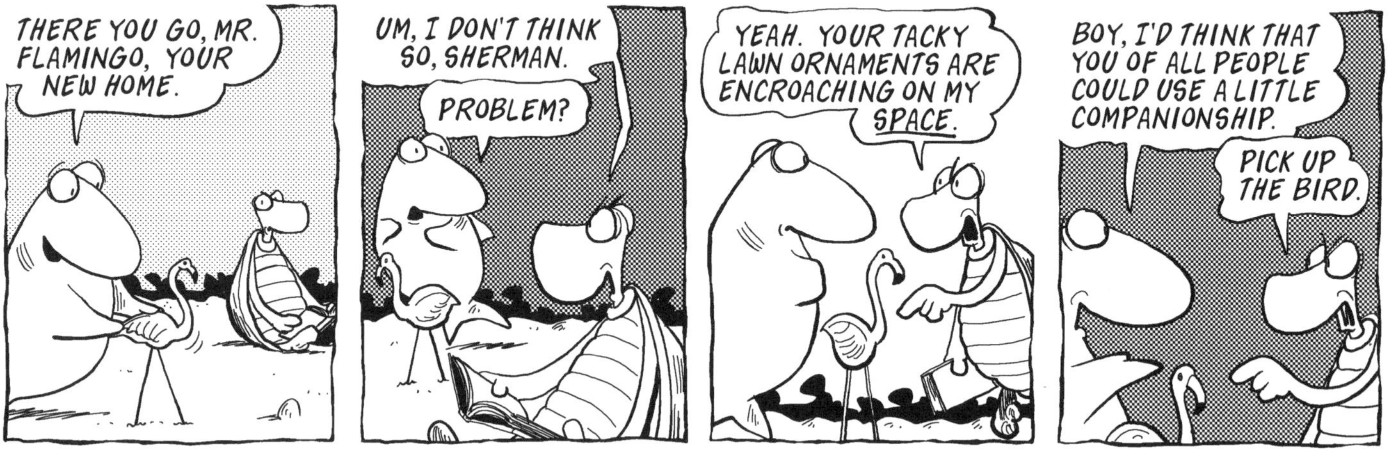
THERE YOU GO, MR. FLAMINGO, YOUR NEW HOME.
UM, I DON'T THINK SO, SHERMAN.
PROBLEM?
YEAH. YOUR TACKY LAWN ORNAMENTS ARE ENCROACHING ON MY SPACE.
BOY, I'D THINK THAT YOU OF ALL PEOPLE COULD USE A LITTLE COMPANIONSHIP.
PICK UP THE BIRD.

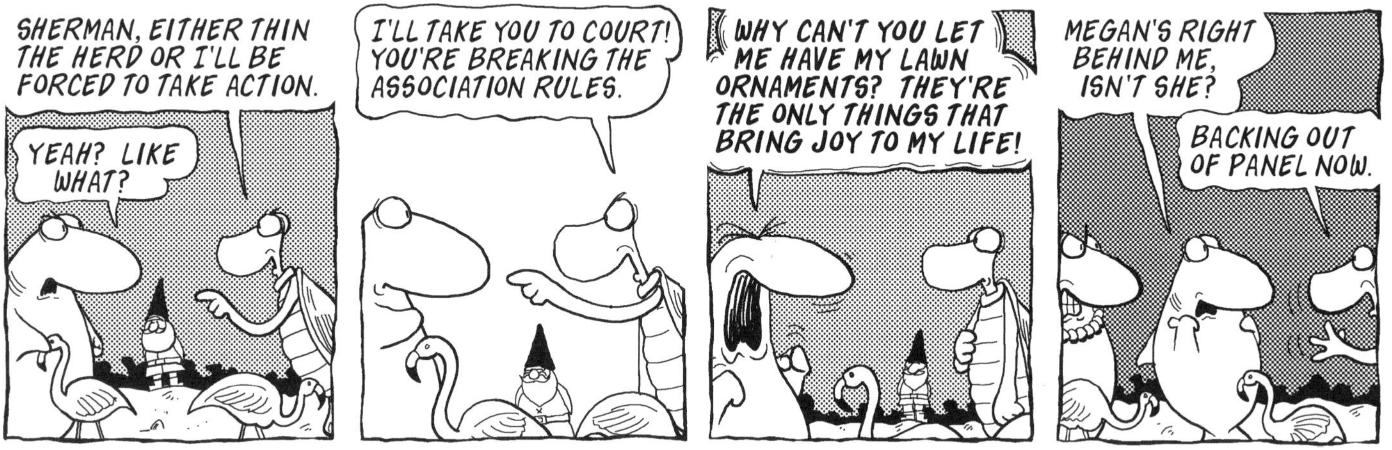
SHERMAN, EITHER THIN THE HERD OR I'LL BE FORCED TO TAKE ACTION.
YEAH? LIKE WHAT?
I'LL TAKE YOU TO COURT! YOU'RE BREAKING THE ASSOCIATION RULES.
WHY CAN'T YOU LET ME HAVE MY LAWN ORNAMENTS? THEY'RE THE ONLY THINGS THAT BRING JOY TO MY LIFE!
MEGAN'S RIGHT BEHIND ME, ISN'T SHE?
BACKING OUT OF PANEL NOW.

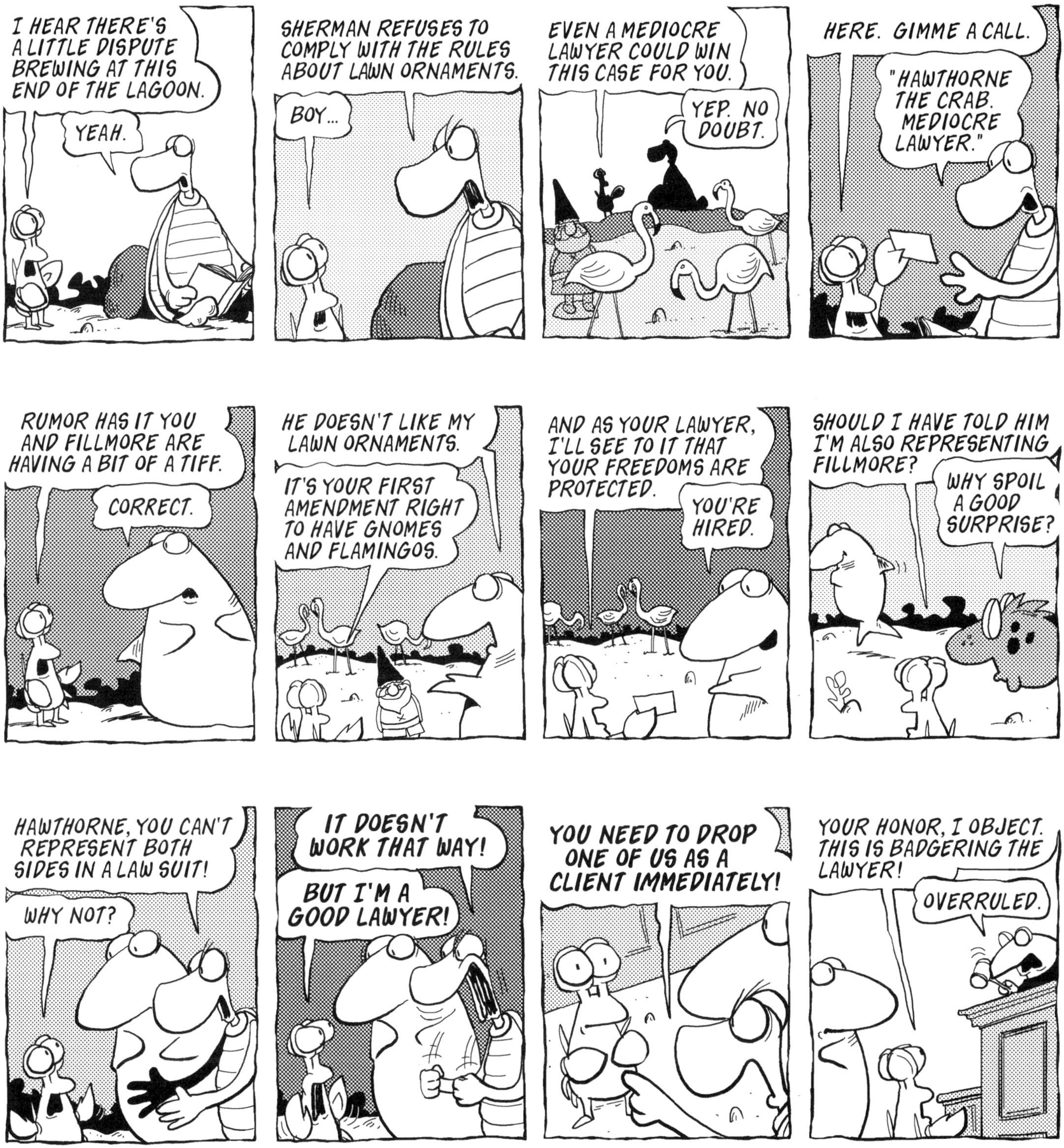
I HEAR THERE'S A LITTLE DISPUTE BREWING AT THIS END OF THE LAGOON.
YEAH.
SHERMAN REFUSES TO COMPLY WITH THE RULES ABOUT LAWN ORNAMENTS.
BOY...
EVEN A MEDIOCRE LAWYER COULD WIN THIS CASE FOR YOU.
YEP. NO DOUBT.
HERE. GIMME A CALL.
"HAWTHORNE THE CRAB. MEDIOCRE LAWYER."
RUMOR HAS IT YOU AND FILLMORE ARE HAVING A BIT OF A TIFF.
CORRECT.
HE DOESN'T LIKE MY LAWN ORNAMENTS.
IT'S YOUR FIRST AMENDMENT RIGHT TO HAVE GNOMES AND FLAMINGOS.
AND AS YOUR LAWYER, I'LL SEE TO IT THAT YOUR FREEDOMS ARE PROTECTED.
YOU'RE HIRED.
SHOULD I HAVE TOLD HIM I'M ALSO REPRESENTING FILLMORE?
WHY SPOIL A GOOD SURPRISE?
HAWTHORNE, YOU CAN'T REPRESENT BOTH SIDES IN A LAW SUIT!
WHY NOT?
IT DOESN'T WORK THAT WAY!
BUT I'M A GOOD LAWYER!
YOU NEED TO DROP ONE OF US AS A CLIENT IMMEDIATELY!
YOUR HONOR, I OBJECT. THIS IS BADGERING THE LAWYER!
OVERRULED.

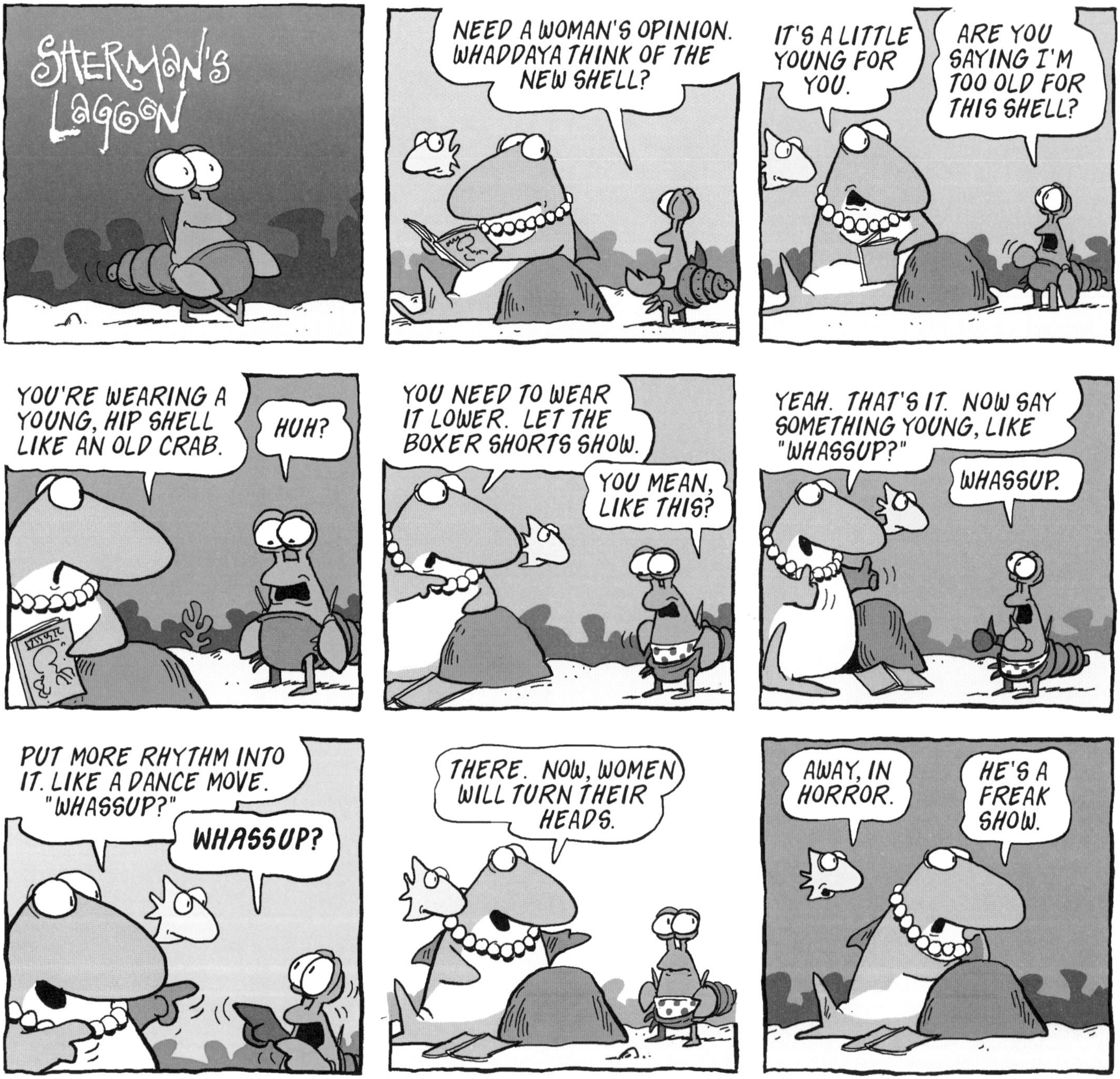
SHERMAN'S LAGOON
NEED A WOMAN'S OPINION. WHADDAYA THINK OF THE NEW SHELL?
IT'S A LITTLE YOUNG FOR YOU.
ARE YOU SAYING I'M TOO OLD FOR THIS SHELL?
YOU'RE WEARING A YOUNG, HIP SHELL LIKE AN OLD CRAB.
HUH?
YOU NEED TO WEAR IT LOWER. LET THE BOXER SHORTS SHOW.
YOU MEAN, LIKE THIS?
YEAH. THAT'S IT. NOW SAY SOMETHING YOUNG, LIKE "WHASSUP?"
WHASSUP.
PUT MORE RHYTHM INTO IT. LIKE A DANCE MOVE. "WHASSUP?"
WHASSUP?
THERE. NOW, WOMEN WILL TURN THEIR HEADS.
AWAY, IN HORROR.
HE'S A FREAK SHOW.

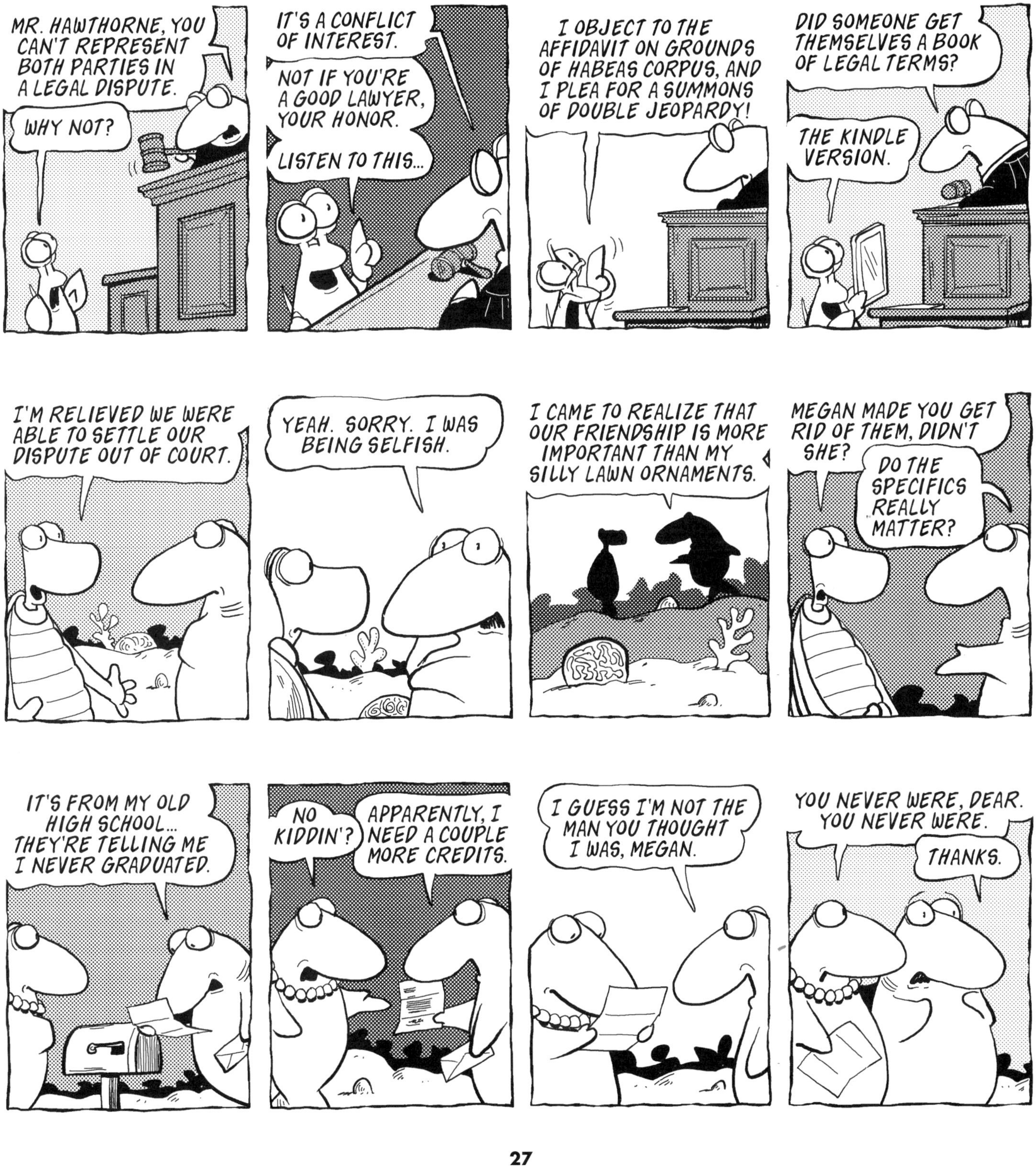
MR. HAWTHORNE, YOU CAN'T REPRESENT BOTH PARTIES IN A LEGAL DISPUTE.
WHY NOT?
IT'S A CONFLICT OF INTEREST.
NOT IF YOU'RE A GOOD LAWYER, YOUR HONOR.
LISTEN TO THIS...
I OBJECT TO THE AFFIDAVIT ON GROUNDS OF HABEAS CORPUS, AND I PLEA FOR A SUMMONS OF DOUBLE JEOPARDY!
DID SOMEONE GET THEMSELVES A BOOK OF LEGAL TERMS?
THE KINDLE VERSION.
I'M RELIEVED WE WERE ABLE TO SETTLE OUR DISPUTE OUT OF COURT.
YEAH. SORRY. I WAS BEING SELFISH.
I CAME TO REALIZE THAT OUR FRIENDSHIP IS MORE IMPORTANT THAN MY SILLY LAWN ORNAMENTS.
MEGAN MADE YOU GET RID OF THEM, DIDN'T SHE?
DO THE SPECIFICS REALLY MATTER?
IT'S FROM MY OLD HIGH SCHOOL... THEY'RE TELLING ME I NEVER GRADUATED.
NO KIDDIN'?
APPARENTLY, I NEED A COUPLE MORE CREDITS.
I GUESS I'M NOT THE MAN YOU THOUGHT I WAS, MEGAN.
YOU NEVER WERE, DEAR. YOU NEVER WERE.
THANKS.

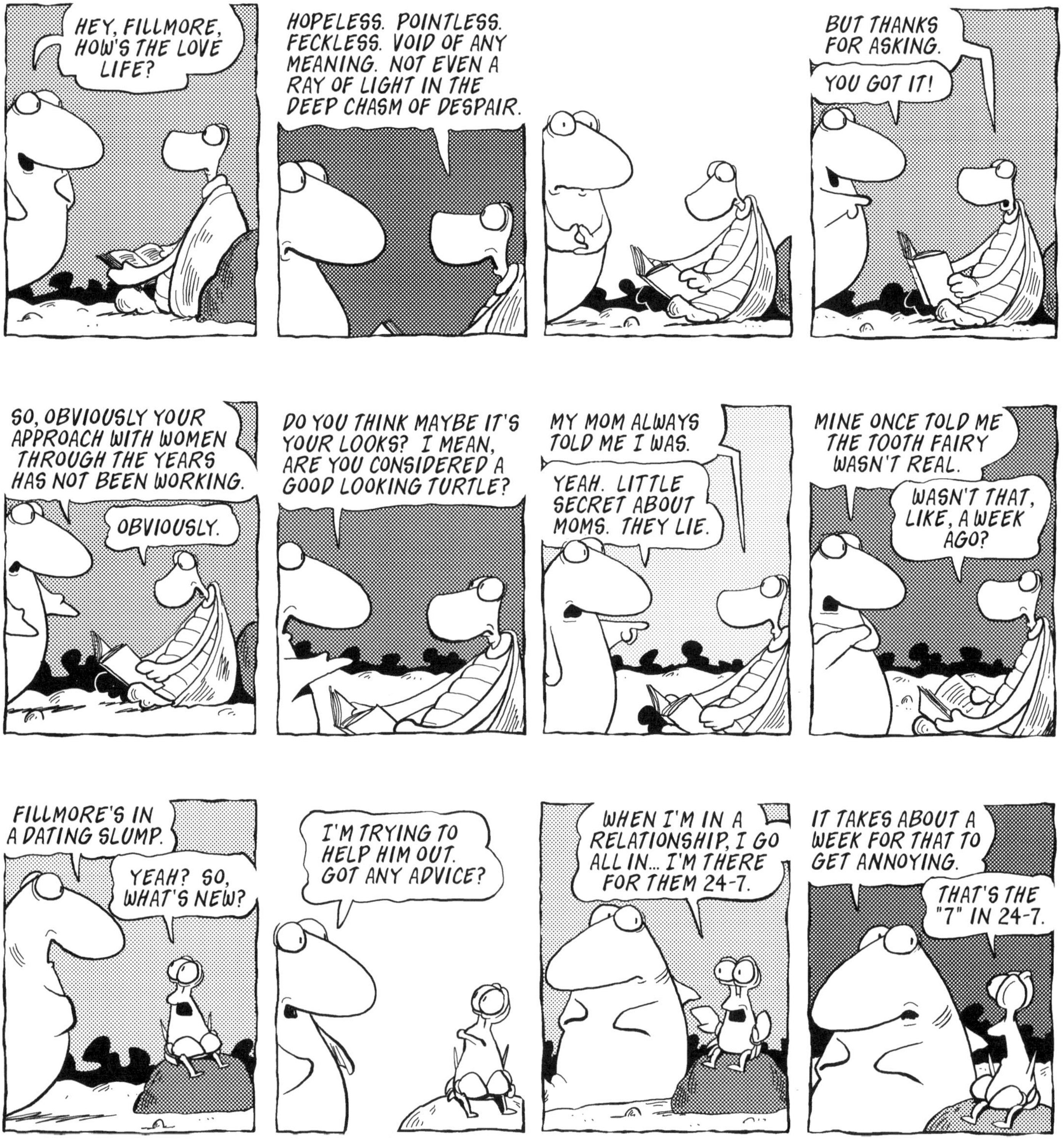
HEY, FILLMORE, HOW'S THE LOVE LIFE?
HOPELESS. POINTLESS. FECKLESS. VOID OF ANY MEANING. NOT EVEN A RAY OF LIGHT IN THE DEEP CHASM OF DESPAIR.
BUT THANKS FOR ASKING.
YOU GOT IT!
SO, OBVIOUSLY YOUR APPROACH WITH WOMEN THROUGH THE YEARS HAS NOT BEEN WORKING.
OBVIOUSLY.
DO YOU THINK MAYBE IT'S YOUR LOOKS? I MEAN, ARE YOU CONSIDERED A GOOD LOOKING TURTLE?
MY MOM ALWAYS TOLD ME I WAS.
YEAH. LITTLE SECRET ABOUT MOMS. THEY LIE.
MINE ONCE TOLD ME THE TOOTH FAIRY WASN'T REAL.
WASN'T THAT, LIKE, A WEEK AGO?
FILLMORE'S IN A DATING SLUMP.
YEAH? SO, WHAT'S NEW?
I'M TRYING TO HELP HIM OUT. GOT ANY ADVICE?
WHEN I'M IN A RELATIONSHIP, I GO ALL IN... I'M THERE FOR THEM 24-7.
IT TAKES ABOUT A WEEK FOR THAT TO GET ANNOYING.
THAT'S THE "7" IN 24-7.

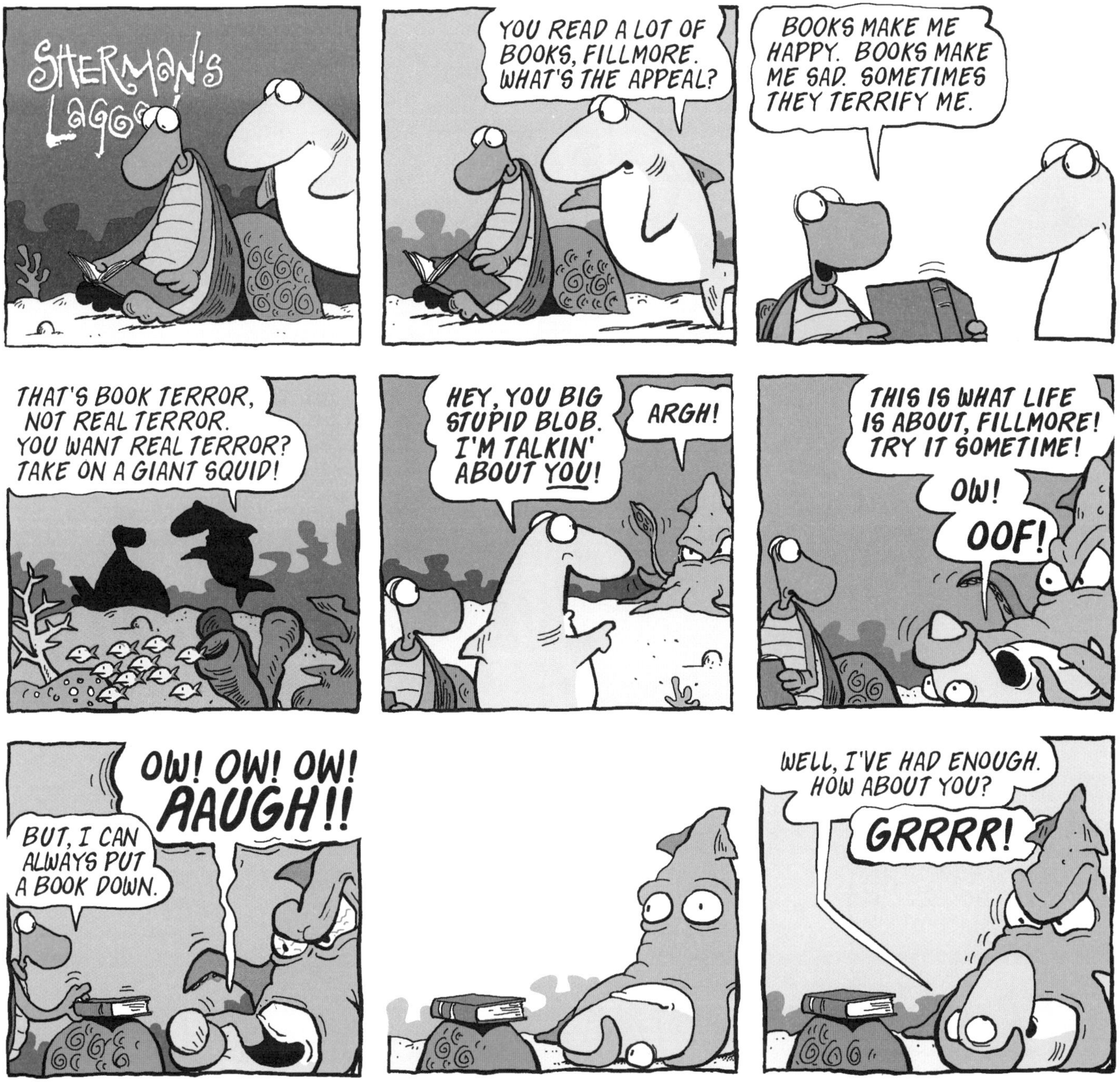
SHERMAN'S LAGOON
YOU READ A LOT OF BOOKS, FILLMORE. WHAT'S THE APPEAL?
BOOKS MAKE ME HAPPY. BOOKS MAKE ME SAD. SOMETIMES THEY TERRIFY ME.
THAT'S BOOK TERROR, NOT REAL TERROR. YOU WANT REAL TERROR? TAKE ON A GIANT SQUID!
HEY, YOU BIG STUPID BLOB. I'M TALKIN' ABOUT YOU!
ARGH!
THIS IS WHAT LIFE IS ABOUT, FILLMORE! TRY IT SOMETIME!
OW!
OOF!
OW! OW! OW! AAUGH!!
BUT, I CAN ALWAYS PUT A BOOK DOWN.
WELL, I'VE HAD ENOUGH. HOW ABOUT YOU?
GRRRR!

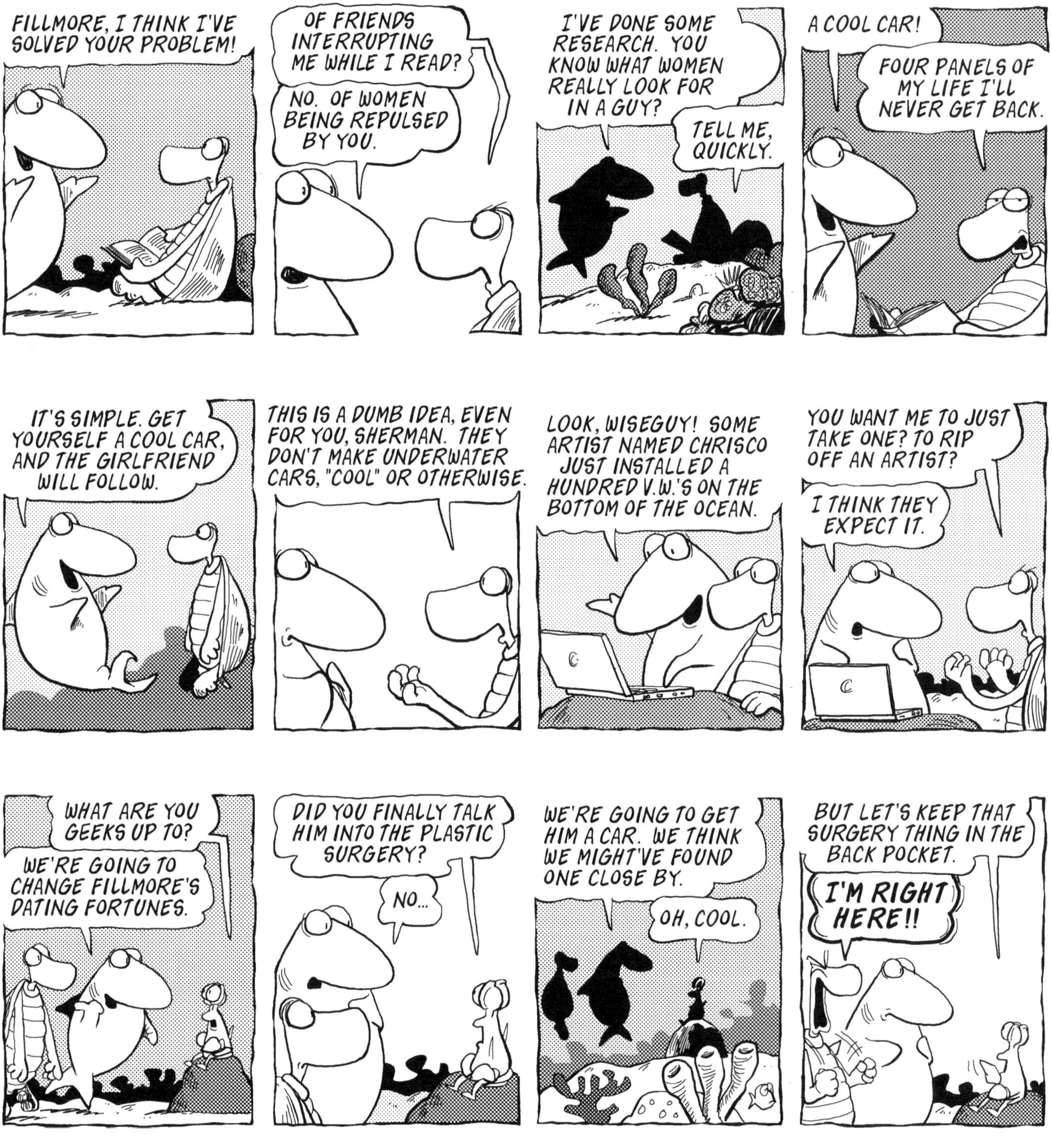
FILLMORE, I THINK I'VE SOLVED YOUR PROBLEM!
OF FRIENDS INTERRUPTING ME WHILE I READ?
NO. OF WOMEN BEING REPULSED BY YOU.
I'VE DONE SOME RESEARCH. YOU KNOW WHAT WOMEN REALLY LOOK FOR IN A GUY?
TELL ME, QUICKLY.
A COOL CAR!
FOUR PANELS OF MY LIFE I'LL NEVER GET BACK.
IT'S SIMPLE. GET YOURSELF A COOL CAR, AND THE GIRLFRIEND WILL FOLLOW.
THIS IS A DUMB IDEA, EVEN FOR YOU, SHERMAN. THEY DON'T MAKE UNDERWATER CARS, "COOL" OR OTHERWISE.
LOOK, WISEGUY! SOME ARTIST NAMED CHRISCO JUST INSTALLED A HUNDRED V.W.'S ON THE BOTTOM OF THE OCEAN.
YOU WANT ME TO JUST TAKE ONE? TO RIP OFF AN ARTIST?
I THINK THEY EXPECT IT.
WHAT ARE YOU GEEKS UP TO?
WE'RE GOING TO CHANGE FILLMORE'S DATING FORTUNES.
DID YOU FINALLY TALK HIM INTO THE PLASTIC SURGERY?
NO...
WE'RE GOING TO GET HIM A CAR. WE THINK WE MIGHT'VE FOUND ONE CLOSE BY.
OH, COOL.
BUT LET'S KEEP THAT SURGERY THING IN THE BACK POCKET.
I'M RIGHT HERE!!

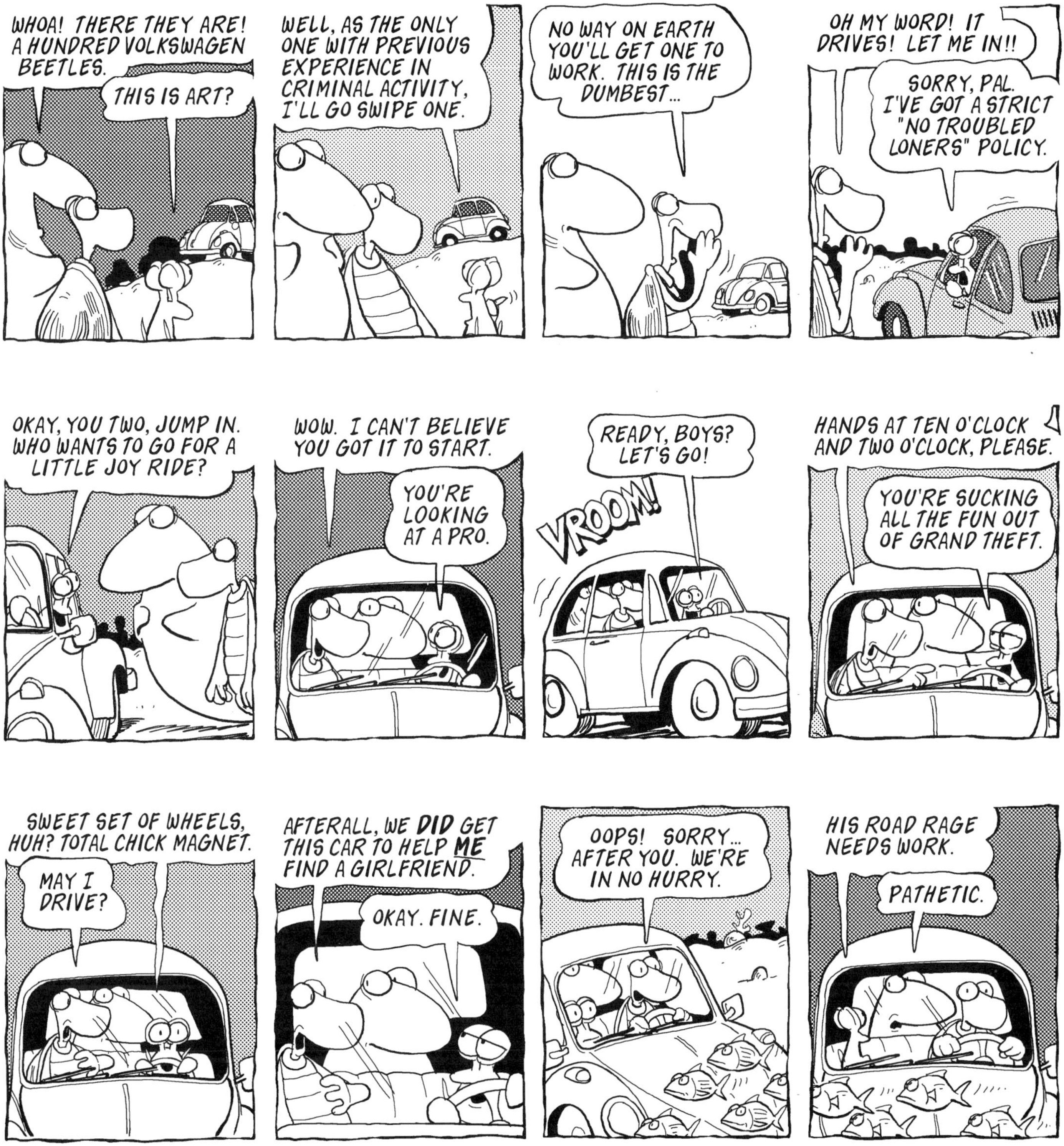
WHOA! THERE THEY ARE! A HUNDRED VOLKSWAGEN BEETLES.
THIS IS ART?
WELL, AS THE ONLY ONE WITH PREVIOUS EXPERIENCE IN CRIMINAL ACTIVITY, I'LL GO SWIPE ONE.
NO WAY ON EARTH YOU'LL GET ONE TO WORK. THIS IS THE DUMBEST...
OH MY WORD! IT DRIVES! LET ME IN!!
SORRY, PAL. I'VE GOT A STRICT "NO TROUBLED LONERS" POLICY.
OKAY, YOU TWO, JUMP IN. WHO WANTS TO GO FOR A LITTLE JOY RIDE?
WOW. I CAN'T BELIEVE YOU GOT IT TO START.
YOU'RE LOOKING AT A PRO.
VROOM!
READY, BOYS? LET'S GO!
HANDS AT TEN O'CLOCK AND TWO O'CLOCK, PLEASE.
YOU'RE SUCKING ALL THE FUN OUT OF GRAND THEFT.
SWEET SET OF WHEELS, HUH? TOTAL CHICK MAGNET.
MAY I DRIVE?
AFTERALL, WE DID GET THIS CAR TO HELP ME FIND A GIRLFRIEND.
OKAY. FINE.
OOPS! SORRY... AFTER YOU. WE'RE IN NO HURRY.
HIS ROAD RAGE NEEDS WORK.
PATHETIC.

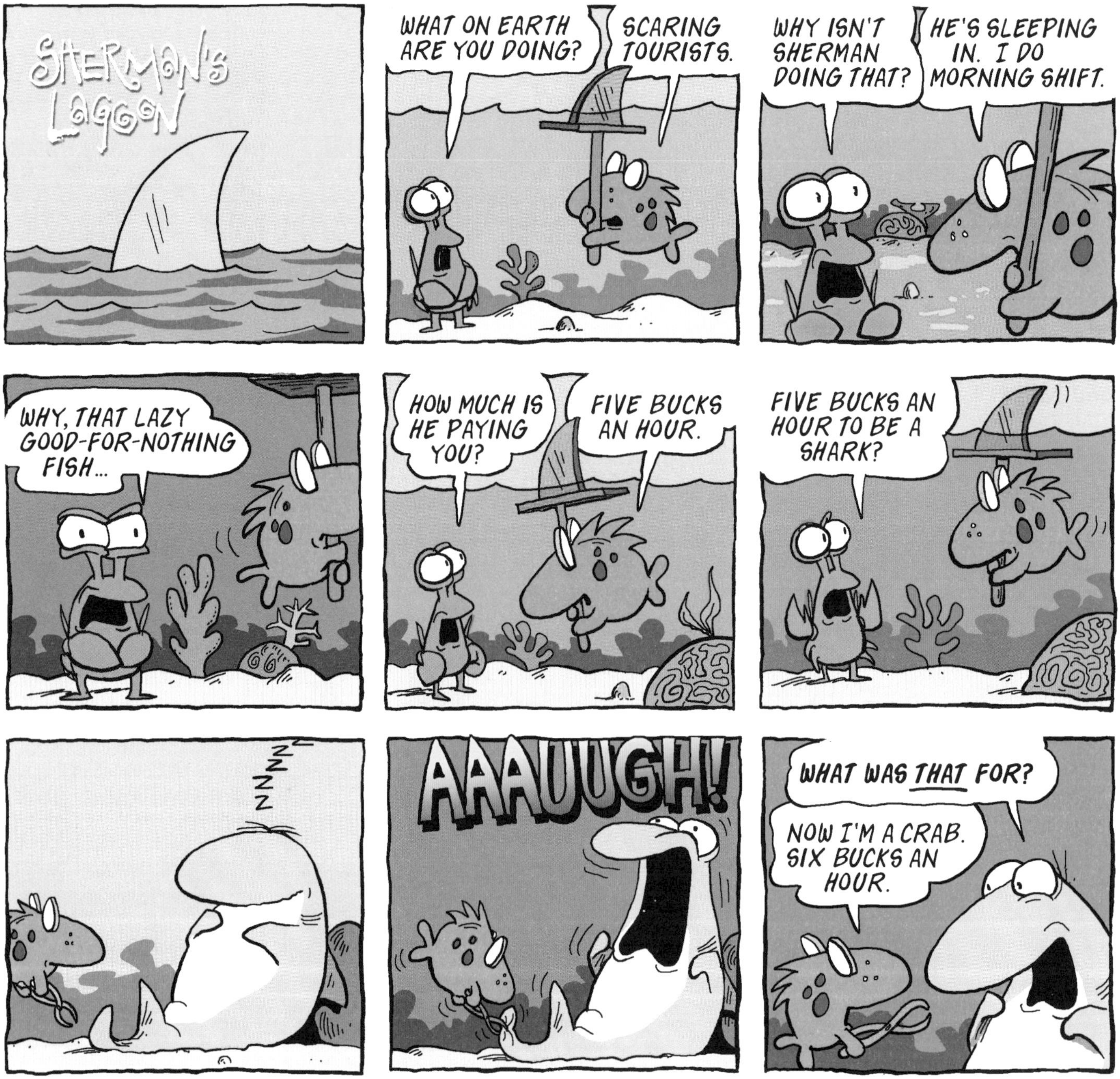
SHERMAN'S LAGOON
WHAT ON EARTH ARE YOU DOING?
SCARING TOURISTS.
WHY ISN'T SHERMAN DOING THAT?
HE'S SLEEPING IN. I DO MORNING SHIFT.
WHY, THAT LAZY GOOD-FOR-NOTHING FISH...
HOW MUCH IS HE PAYING YOU?
FIVE BUCKS AN HOUR.
FIVE BUCKS AN HOUR TO BE A SHARK?
Z Z Z Z
AAAUUGH!
WHAT WAS THAT FOR?
NOW I'M A CRAB. SIX BUCKS AN HOUR.

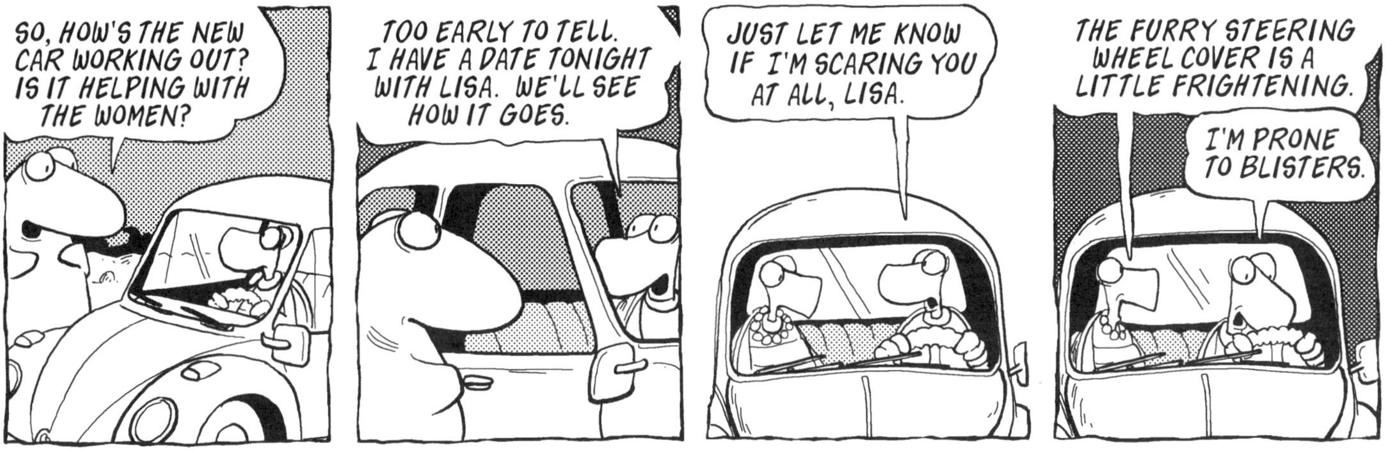
SO, HOW'S THE NEW CAR WORKING OUT? IS IT HELPING WITH THE WOMEN?
TOO EARLY TO TELL. I HAVE A DATE TONIGHT WITH LISA. WE'LL SEE HOW IT GOES.
JUST LET ME KNOW IF I'M SCARING YOU AT ALL, LISA.
THE FURRY STEERING WHEEL COVER IS A LITTLE FRIGHTENING.
I'M PRONE TO BLISTERS.

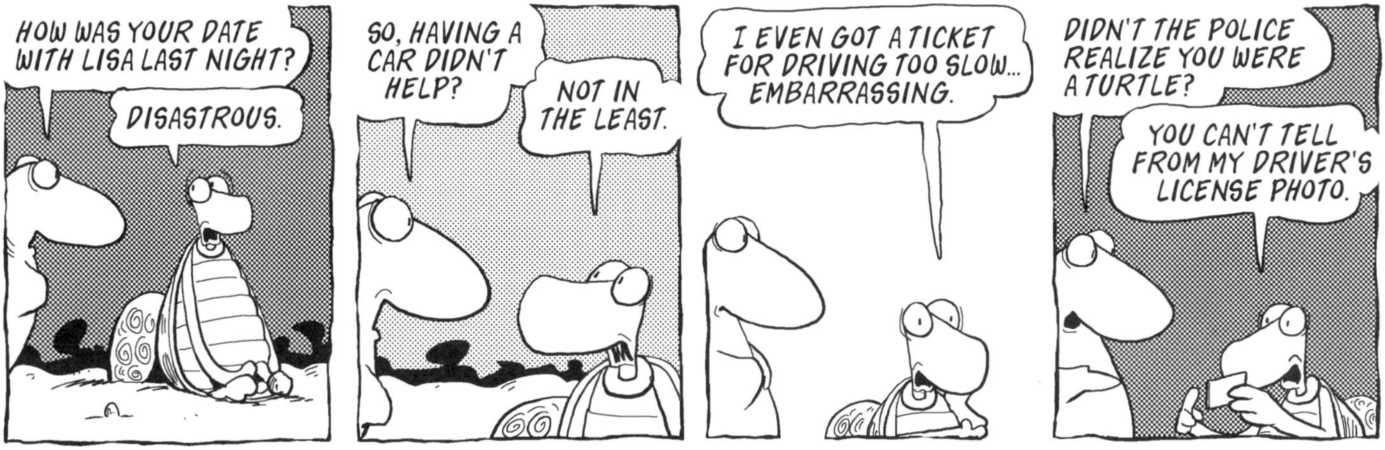
HOW WAS YOUR DATE WITH LISA LAST NIGHT?
DISASTROUS.
SO, HAVING A CAR DIDN'T HELP?
NOT IN THE LEAST.
I EVEN GOT A TICKET FOR DRIVING TOO SLOW... EMBARRASSING.
DIDN'T THE POLICE REALIZE YOU WERE A TURTLE?
YOU CAN'T TELL FROM MY DRIVER'S LICENSE PHOTO.

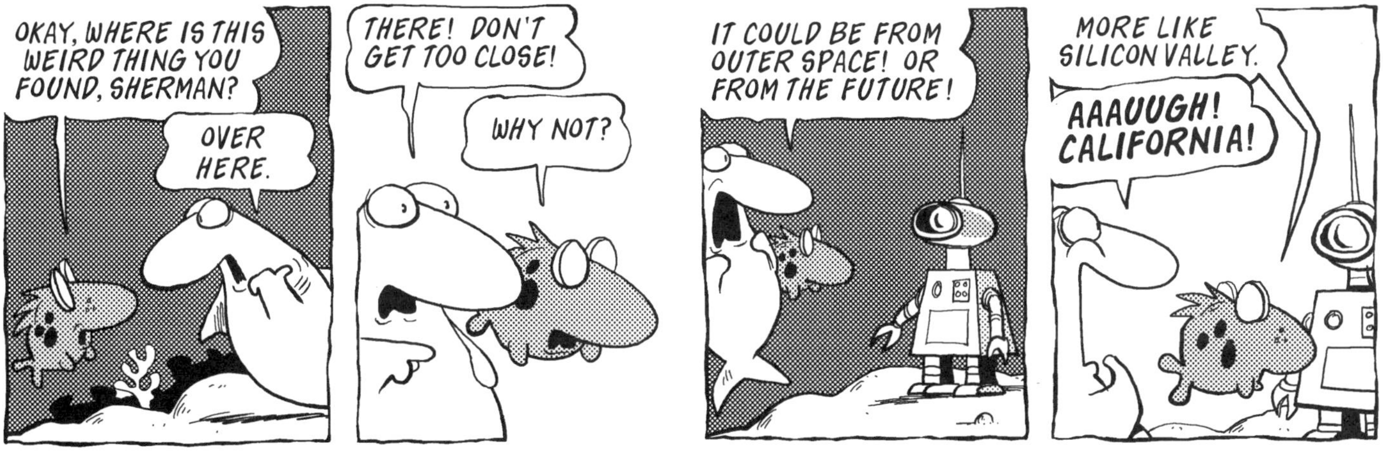
OKAY, WHERE IS THIS WEIRD THING YOU FOUND, SHERMAN?
OVER HERE.
THERE! DON'T GET TOO CLOSE!
WHY NOT?
IT COULD BE FROM OUTER SPACE! OR FROM THE FUTURE!
MORE LIKE SILICON VALLEY.
AAAUUGH! CALIFORNIA!

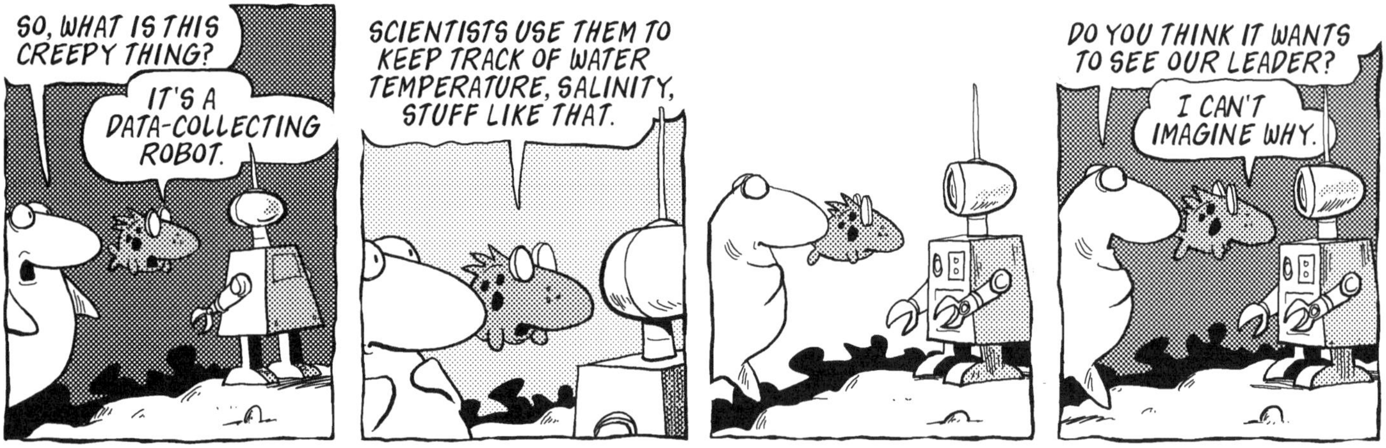
SO, WHAT IS THIS CREEPY THING?
IT'S A DATA-COLLECTING ROBOT.
SCIENTISTS USE THEM TO KEEP TRACK OF WATER TEMPERATURE, SALINITY, STUFF LIKE THAT.
DO YOU THINK IT WANTS TO SEE OUR LEADER?
I CAN'T IMAGINE WHY.

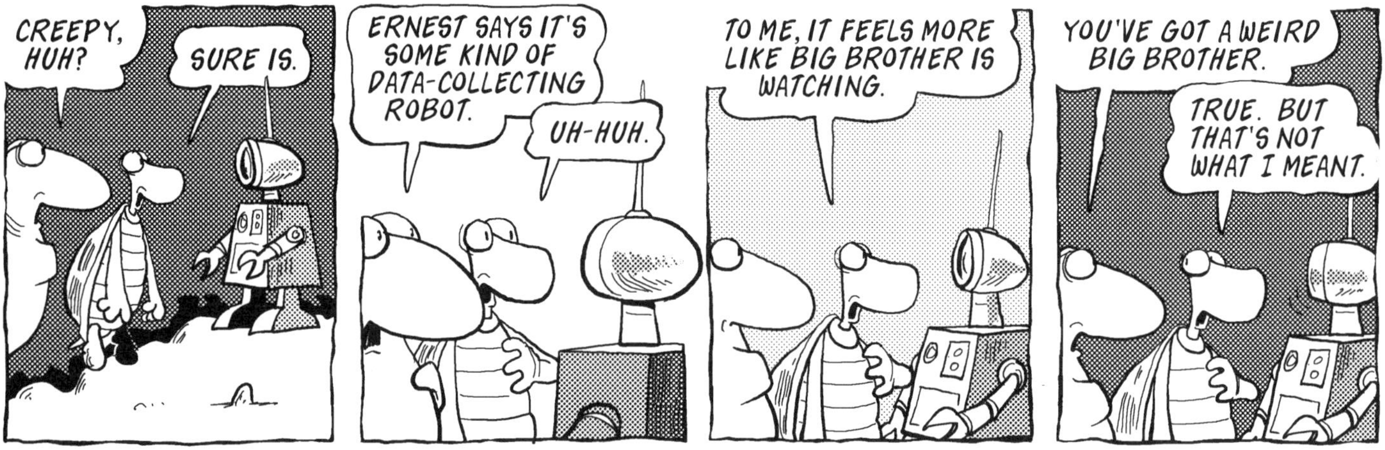
CREEPY, HUH?
SURE IS.
ERNEST SAYS IT'S SOME KIND OF DATA-COLLECTING ROBOT.
UH-HUH.
TO ME, IT FEELS MORE LIKE BIG BROTHER IS WATCHING.
YOU'VE GOT A WEIRD BIG BROTHER.
TRUE. BUT THAT'S NOT WHAT I MEANT.

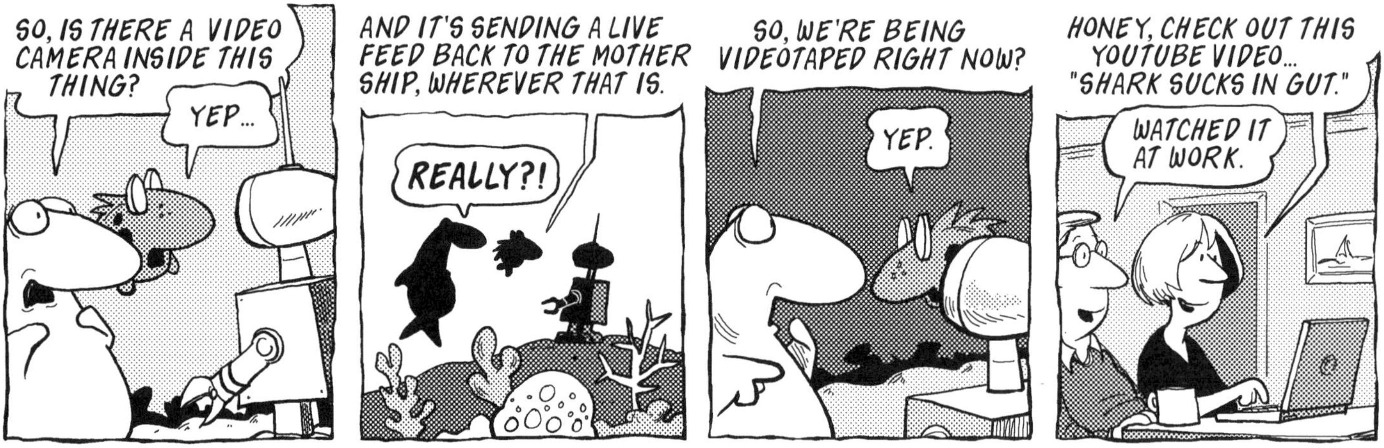
SO, IS THERE A VIDEO CAMERA INSIDE THIS THING?
YEP...
AND IT'S SENDING A LIVE FEED BACK TO THE MOTHER SHIP, WHEREVER THAT IS.
REALLY?!
SO, WE'RE BEING VIDEOTAPED RIGHT NOW?
YEP.
HONEY, CHECK OUT THIS YOUTUBE VIDEO... "SHARK SUCKS IN GUT."
WATCHED IT AT WORK.

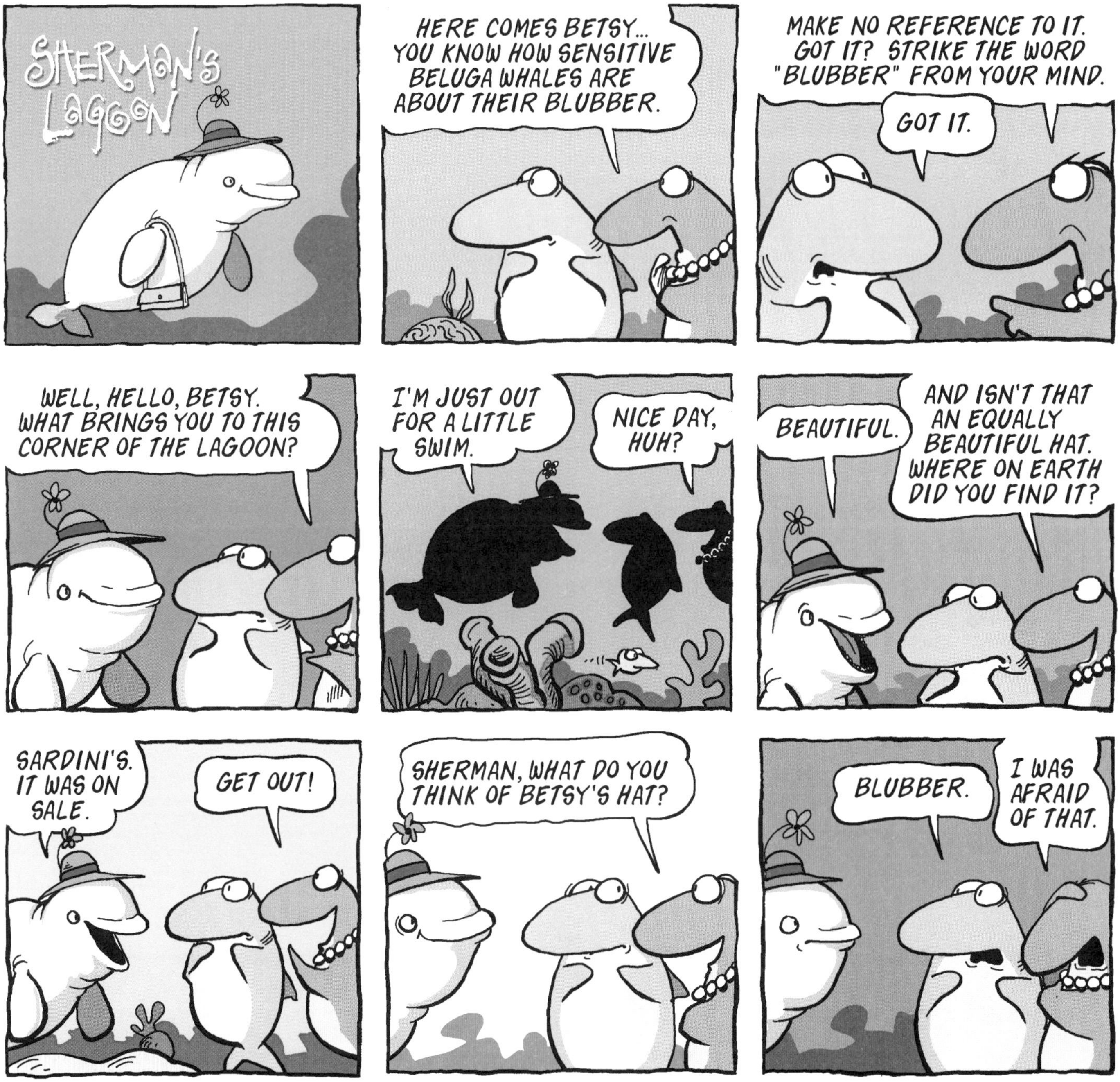

SHERMAN'S LAGOON
HERE COMES BETSY... YOU KNOW HOW SENSITIVE BELUGA WHALES ARE ABOUT THEIR BLUBBER.
MAKE NO REFERENCE TO IT. GOT IT? STRIKE THE WORD "BLUBBER" FROM YOUR MIND.
GOT IT.
WELL, HELLO, BETSY. WHAT BRINGS YOU TO THIS CORNER OF THE LAGOON?
I'M JUST OUT FOR A LITTLE SWIM.
NICE DAY, HUH?
BEAUTIFUL.
AND ISN'T THAT AN EQUALLY BEAUTIFUL HAT. WHERE ON EARTH DID YOU FIND IT?
SARDINI'S. IT WAS ON SALE.
GET OUT!
SHERMAN, WHAT DO YOU THINK OF BETSY'S HAT?
BLUBBER.
I WAS AFRAID OF THAT.

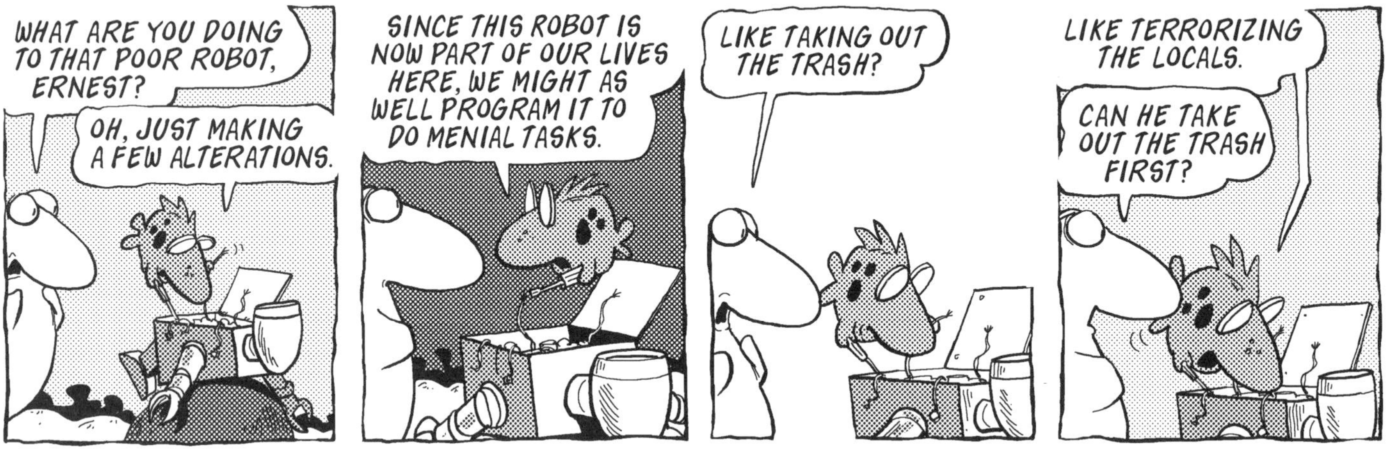
WHAT ARE YOU DOING TO THAT POOR ROBOT, ERNEST?
OH, JUST MAKING A FEW ALTERATIONS.
SINCE THIS ROBOT IS NOW PART OF OUR LIVES HERE, WE MIGHT AS WELL PROGRAM IT TO DO MENIAL TASKS.
LIKE TAKING OUT THE TRASH?
LIKE TERRORIZING THE LOCALS.
CAN HE TAKE OUT THE TRASH FIRST?

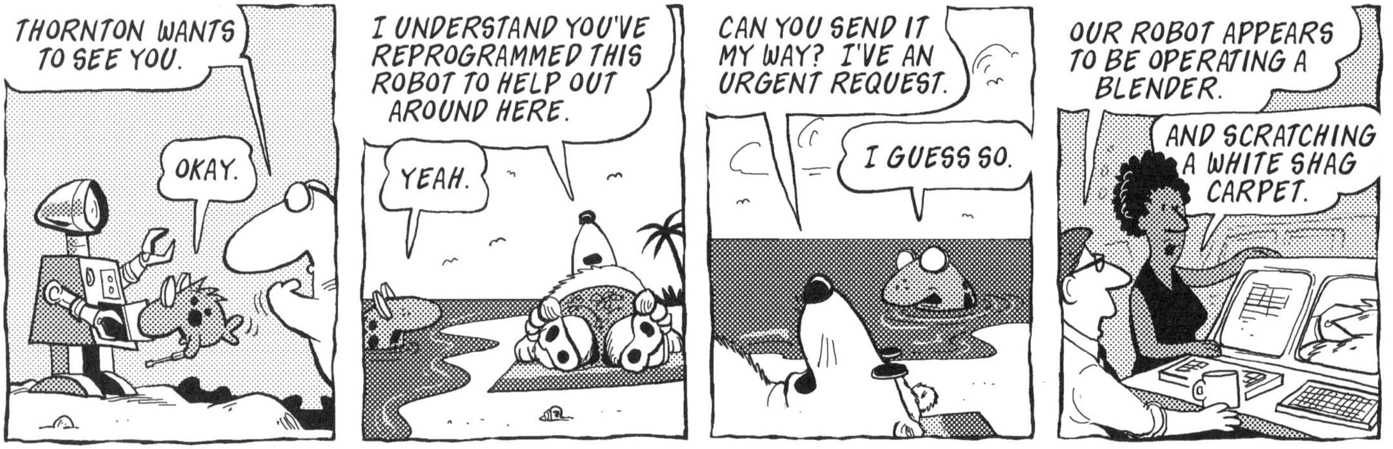
THORNTON WANTS TO SEE YOU.
OKAY.
I UNDERSTAND YOU'VE REPROGRAMMED THIS ROBOT TO HELP OUT AROUND HERE.
YEAH.
CAN YOU SEND IT MY WAY? I'VE AN URGENT REQUEST.
I GUESS SO.
OUR ROBOT APPEARS TO BE OPERATING A BLENDER.
AND SCRATCHING A WHITE SHAG CARPET.

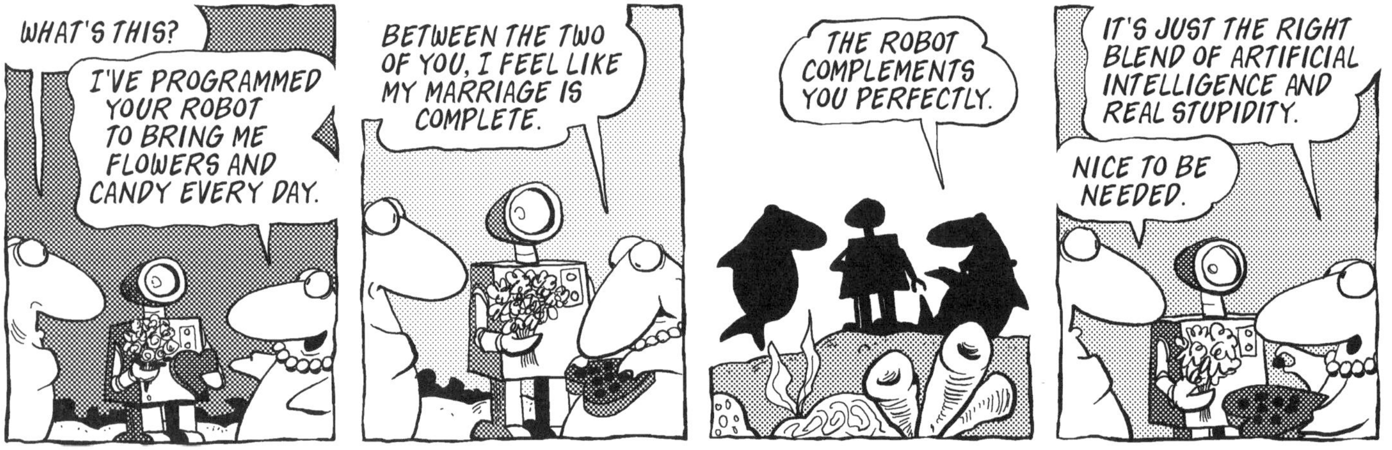
WHAT'S THIS?
I'VE PROGRAMMED YOUR ROBOT TO BRING ME FLOWERS AND CANDY EVERY DAY.
BETWEEN THE TWO OF YOU, I FEEL LIKE MY MARRIAGE IS COMPLETE.
THE ROBOT COMPLEMENTS YOU PERFECTLY.
IT'S JUST THE RIGHT BLEND OF ARTIFICIAL INTELLIGENCE AND REAL STUPIDITY.
NICE TO BE NEEDED.

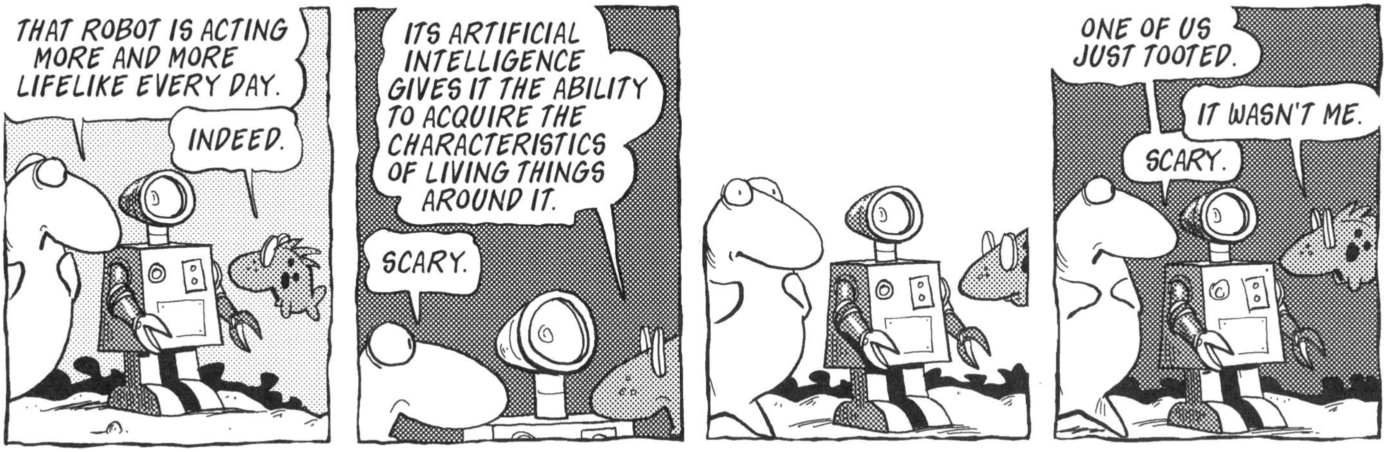
THAT ROBOT IS ACTING MORE AND MORE LIFELIKE EVERY DAY.
INDEED.
ITS ARTIFICIAL INTELLIGENCE GIVES IT THE ABILITY TO ACQUIRE THE CHARACTERISTICS OF LIVING THINGS AROUND IT.
SCARY.
ONE OF US JUST TOOTED.
SCARY.
IT WASN'T ME.

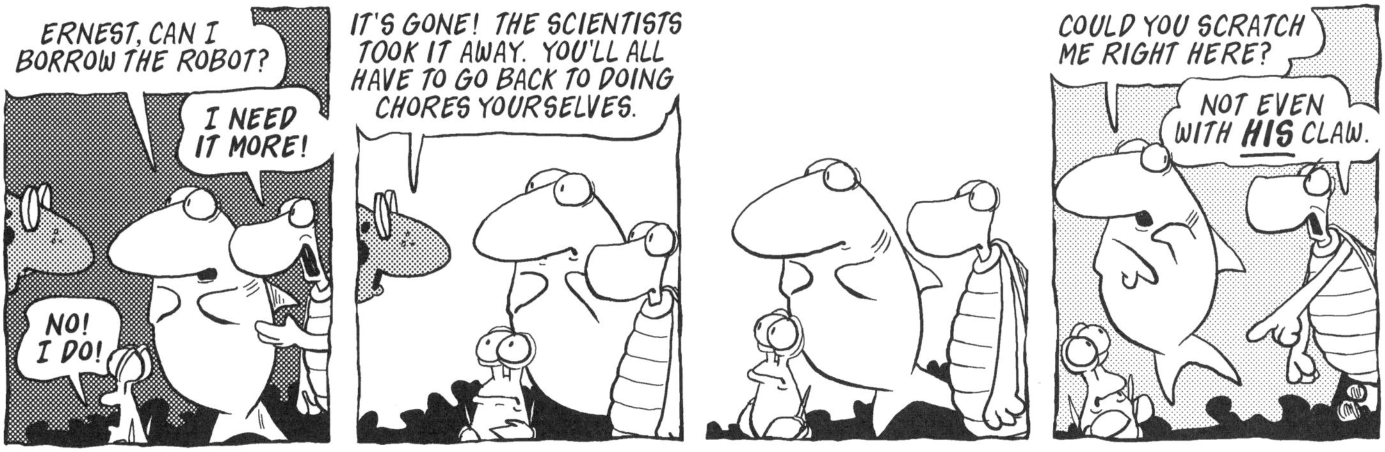
ERNEST, CAN I BORROW THE ROBOT?
I NEED IT MORE!
NO! I DO!
IT'S GONE! THE SCIENTISTS TOOK IT AWAY. YOU'LL ALL HAVE TO GO BACK TO DOING CHORES YOURSELVES.
COULD YOU SCRATCH ME RIGHT HERE?
NOT EVEN WITH HIS CLAW.

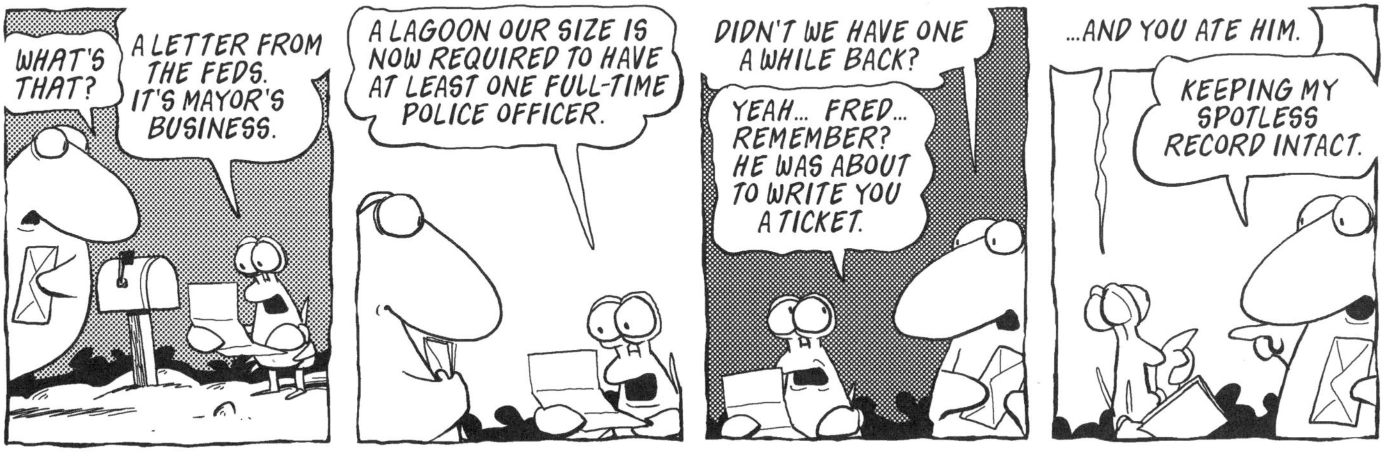
WHAT'S THAT?
A LETTER FROM THE FEDS. IT'S MAYOR'S BUSINESS.
A LAGOON OUR SIZE IS NOW REQUIRED TO HAVE AT LEAST ONE FULL-TIME POLICE OFFICER.
DIDN'T WE HAVE ONE A WHILE BACK?
YEAH... FRED... REMEMBER? HE WAS ABOUT TO WRITE YOU A TICKET.
...AND YOU ATE HIM.
KEEPING MY SPOTLESS RECORD INTACT.

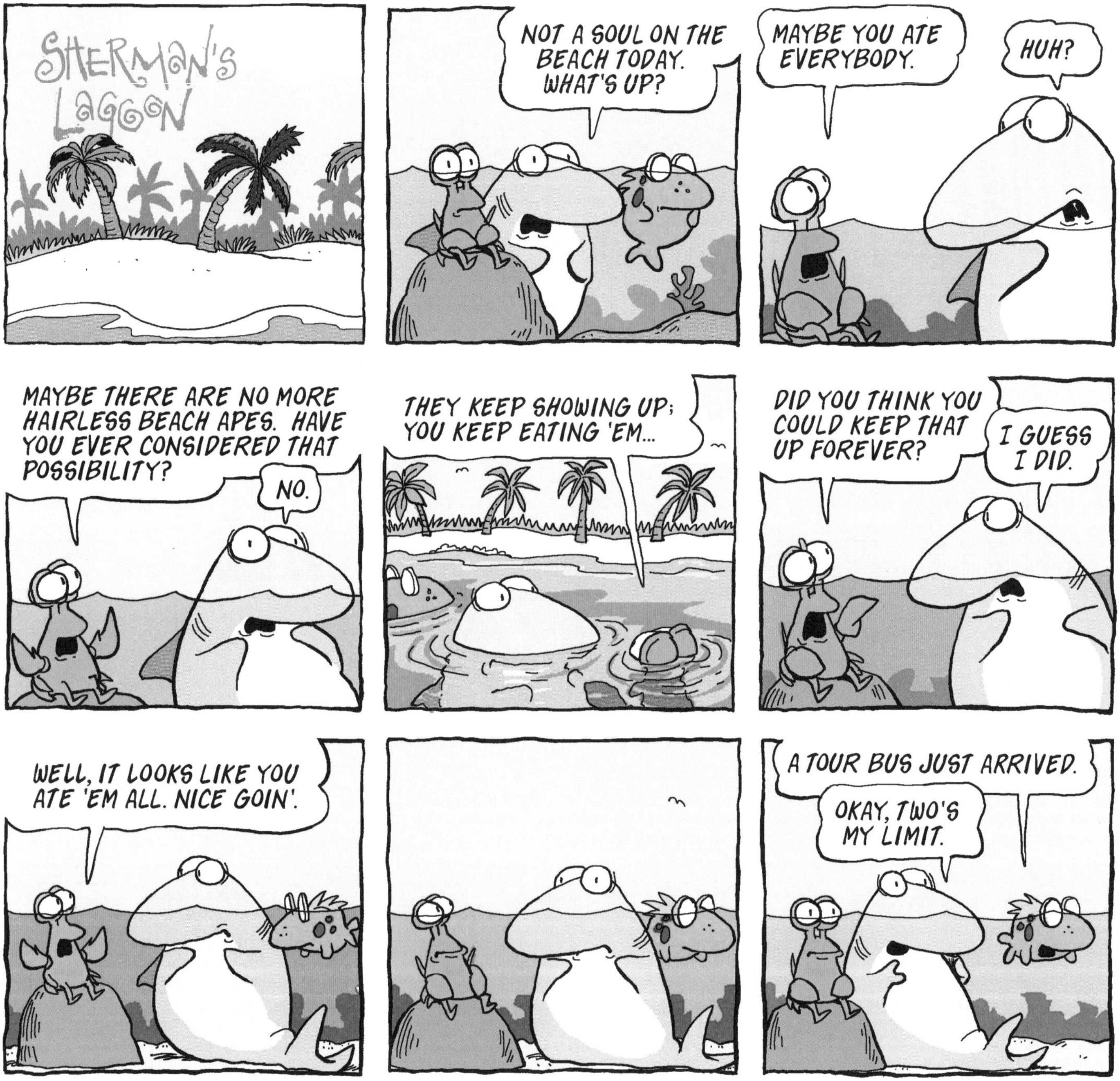
SHERMAN'S LAGOON
NOT A SOUL ON THE BEACH TODAY. WHAT'S UP?
MAYBE YOU ATE EVERYBODY.
HUH?
MAYBE THERE ARE NO MORE HAIRLESS BEACH APES. HAVE YOU EVER CONSIDERED THAT POSSIBILITY?
NO.
THEY KEEP SHOWING UP; YOU KEEP EATING 'EM...
DID YOU THINK YOU COULD KEEP THAT UP FOREVER?
I GUESS I DID.
WELL, IT LOOKS LIKE YOU ATE 'EM ALL. NICE GOIN'.
A TOUR BUS JUST ARRIVED.
OKAY, TWO'S MY LIMIT.

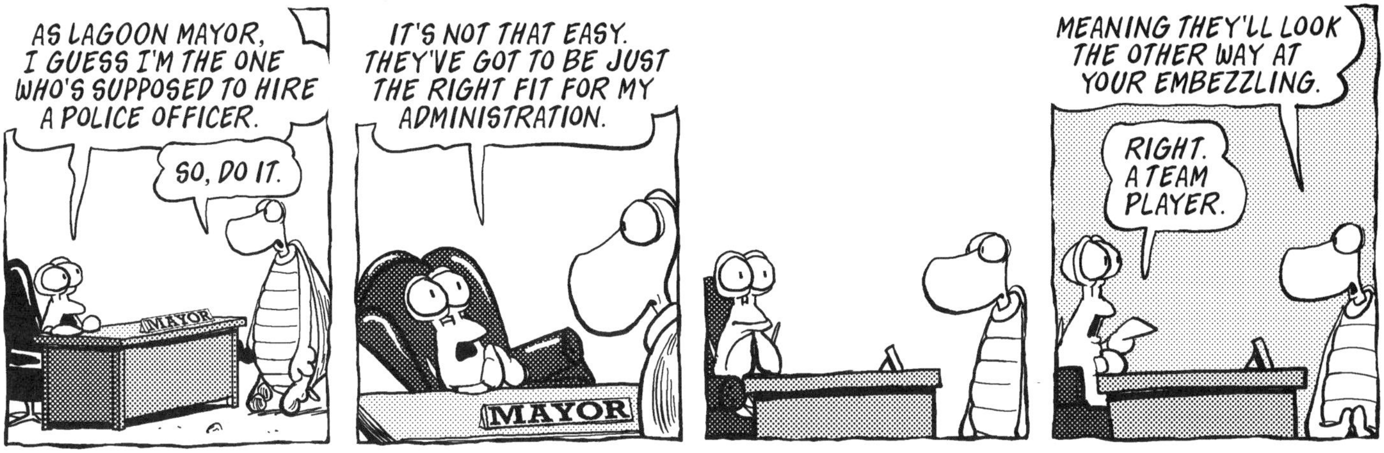
AS LAGOON MAYOR, I GUESS I'M THE ONE WHO'S SUPPOSED TO HIRE A POLICE OFFICER.
SO, DO IT.
IT'S NOT THAT EASY. THEY'VE GOT TO BE JUST THE RIGHT FIT FOR MY ADMINISTRATION.
MAYOR
MEANING THEY'LL LOOK THE OTHER WAY AT YOUR EMBEZZLING.
RIGHT. A TEAM PLAYER.

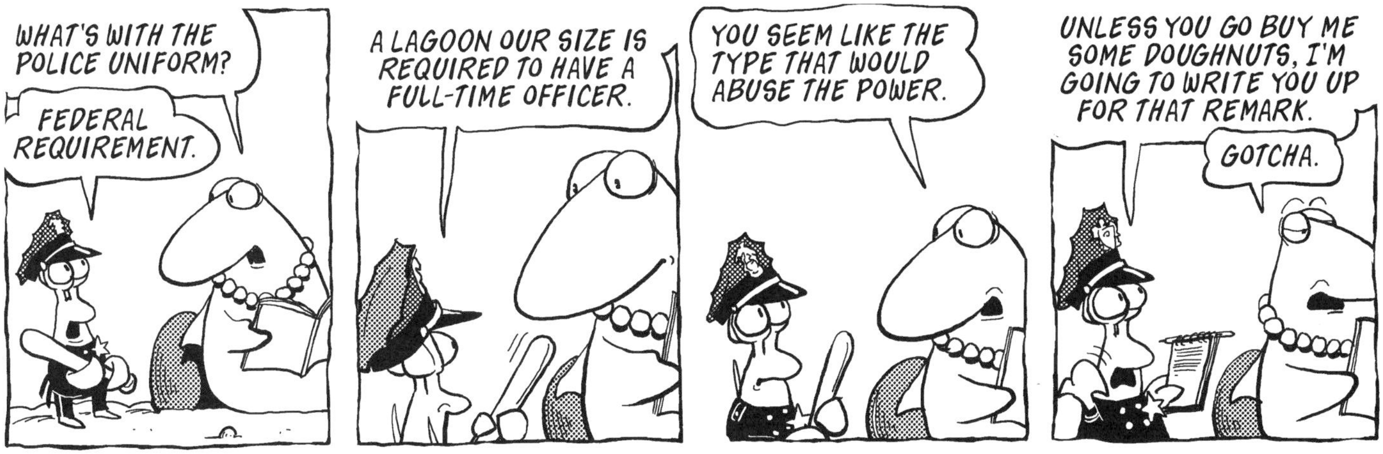
WHAT'S WITH THE POLICE UNIFORM?
FEDERAL REQUIREMENT.
A LAGOON OUR SIZE IS REQUIRED TO HAVE A FULL-TIME OFFICER.
YOU SEEM LIKE THE TYPE THAT WOULD ABUSE THE POWER.
UNLESS YOU GO BUY ME SOME DOUGHNUTS, I'M GOING TO WRITE YOU UP FOR THAT REMARK.
GOTCHA.

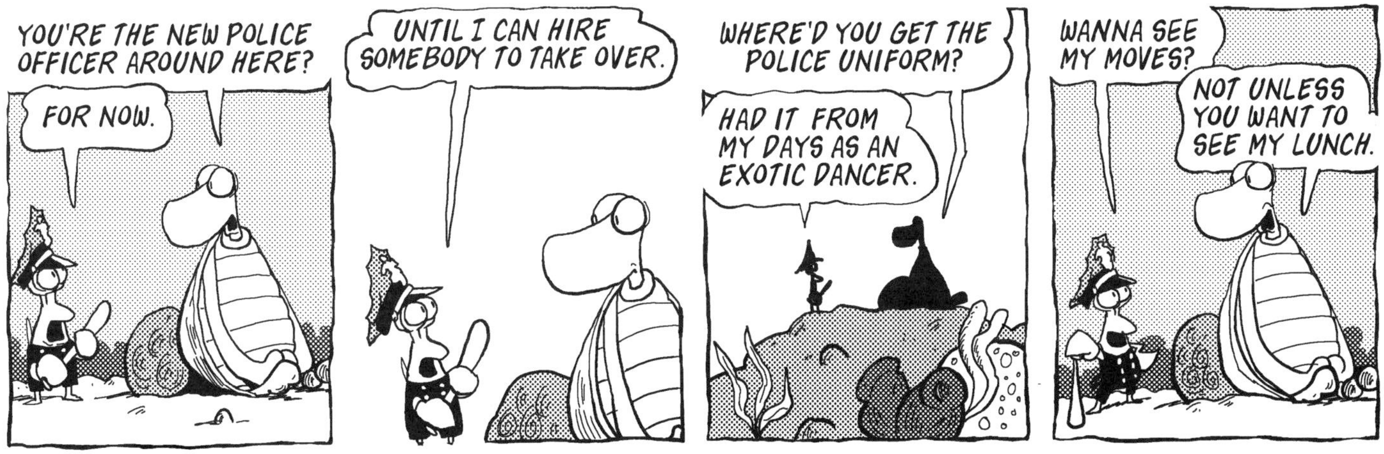
YOU'RE THE NEW POLICE OFFICER AROUND HERE?
FOR NOW.
UNTIL I CAN HIRE SOMEBODY TO TAKE OVER.
WHERE'D YOU GET THE POLICE UNIFORM?
HAD IT FROM MY DAYS AS AN EXOTIC DANCER.
WANNA SEE MY MOVES?
NOT UNLESS YOU WANT TO SEE MY LUNCH.

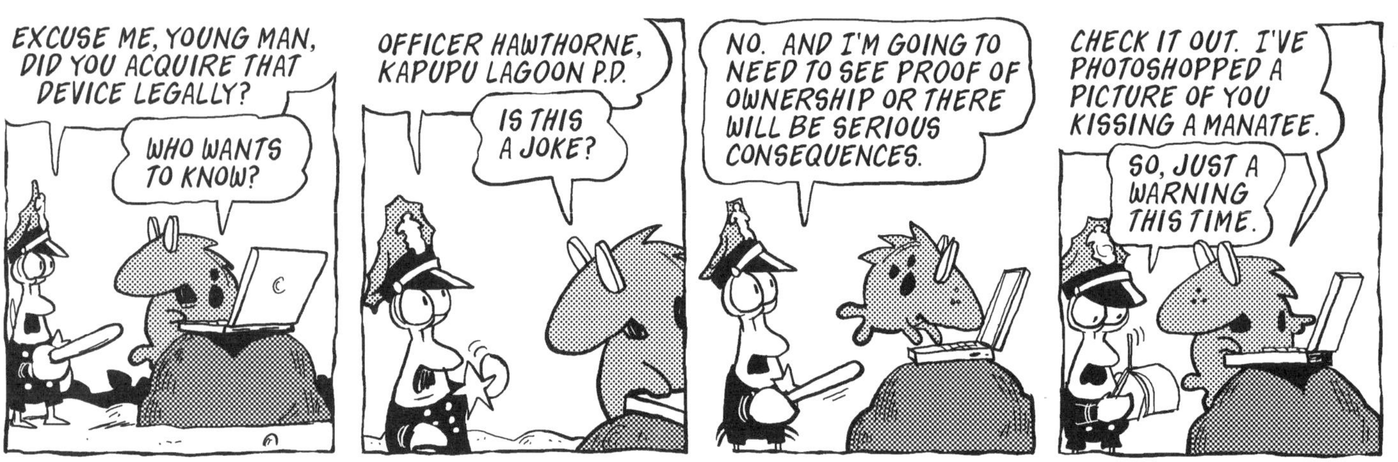
EXCUSE ME, YOUNG MAN, DID YOU ACQUIRE THAT DEVICE LEGALLY?
WHO WANTS TO KNOW?
OFFICER HAWTHORNE, KAPUPU LAGOON P.D.
IS THIS A JOKE?
NO. AND I'M GOING TO NEED TO SEE PROOF OF OWNERSHIP OR THERE WILL BE SERIOUS CONSEQUENCES.
CHECK IT OUT. I'VE PHOTOSHOPPED A PICTURE OF YOU KISSING A MANATEE.
SO, JUST A WARNING THIS TIME.

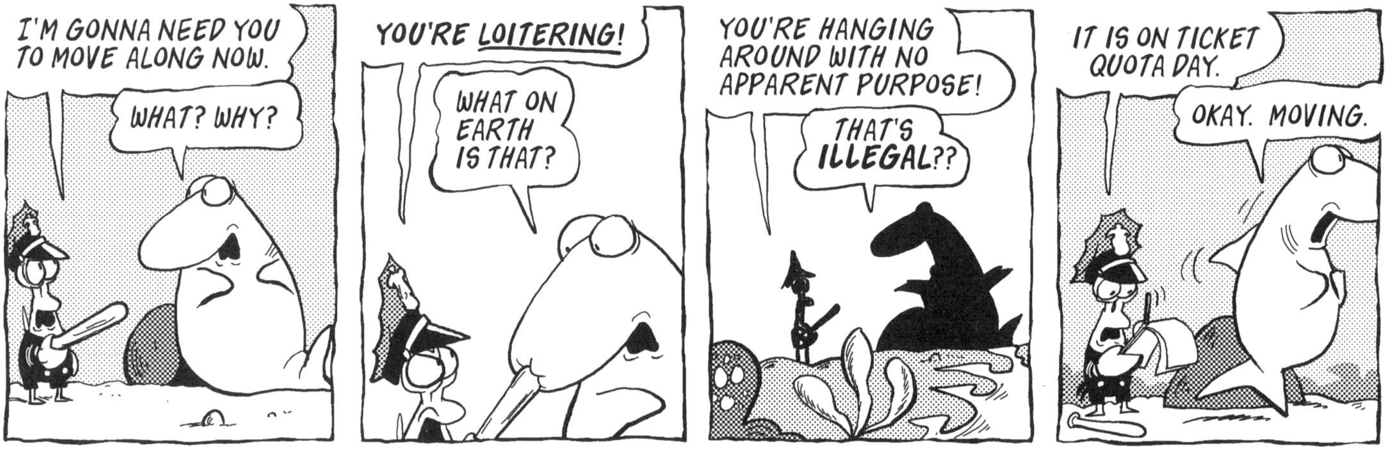
I'M GONNA NEED YOU TO MOVE ALONG NOW.
WHAT? WHY?
YOU'RE LOITERING!
WHAT ON EARTH IS THAT?
YOU'RE HANGING AROUND WITH NO APPARENT PURPOSE!
THAT'S ILLEGAL??
IT IS ON TICKET QUOTA DAY.
OKAY. MOVING.

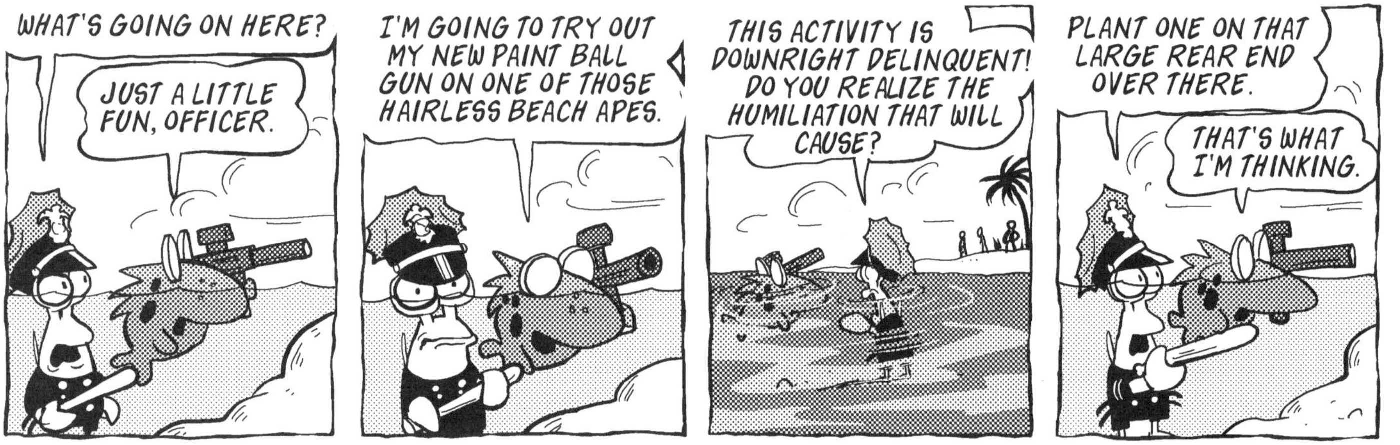
WHAT'S GOING ON HERE?
JUST A LITTLE FUN, OFFICER.
I'M GOING TO TRY OUT MY NEW PAINT BALL GUN ON ONE OF THOSE HAIRLESS BEACH APES.
THIS ACTIVITY IS DOWNRIGHT DELINQUENT! DO YOU REALIZE THE HUMILIATION THAT WILL CAUSE?
PLANT ONE ON THAT LARGE REAR END OVER THERE.
THAT'S WHAT I'M THINKING.

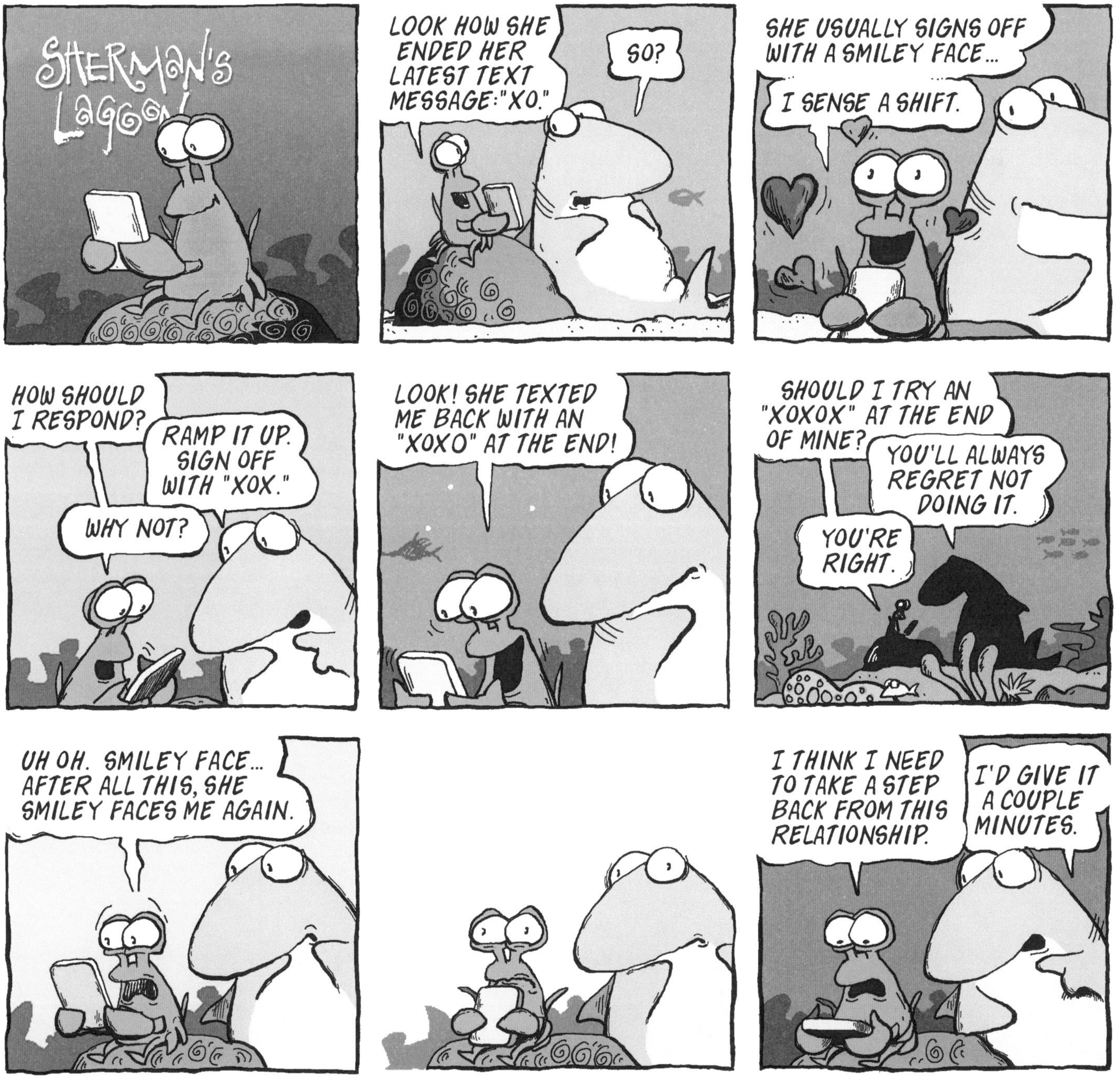
SHERMAN'S LAGOON
LOOK HOW SHE ENDED HER LATEST TEXT MESSAGE: "XO."
SO?
SHE USUALLY SIGNS OFF WITH A SMILEY FACE...
I SENSE A SHIFT.
HOW SHOULD I RESPOND?
RAMP IT UP. SIGN OFF WITH "XOX."
WHY NOT?
LOOK! SHE TEXTED ME BACK WITH AN "XOXO" AT THE END!
SHOULD I TRY AN "XOXOX" AT THE END OF MINE?
YOU'LL ALWAYS REGRET NOT DOING IT.
YOU'RE RIGHT.
UH OH. SMILEY FACE... AFTER ALL THIS, SHE SMILEY FACES ME AGAIN.
I THINK I NEED TO TAKE A STEP BACK FROM THIS RELATIONSHIP.
I'D GIVE IT A COUPLE MINUTES.

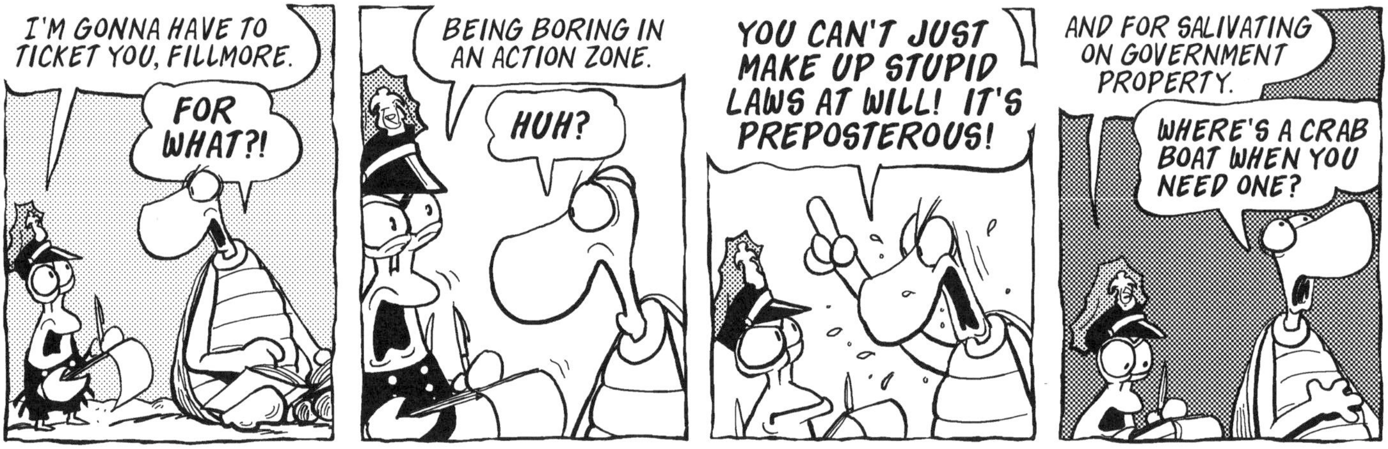
I'M GONNA HAVE TO TICKET YOU, FILLMORE.
FOR WHAT?!
BEING BORING IN AN ACTION ZONE.
HUH?
YOU CAN'T JUST MAKE UP STUPID LAWS AT WILL! IT'S PREPOSTEROUS!
AND FOR SALIVATING ON GOVERNMENT PROPERTY.
WHERE'S A CRAB BOAT WHEN YOU NEED ONE?

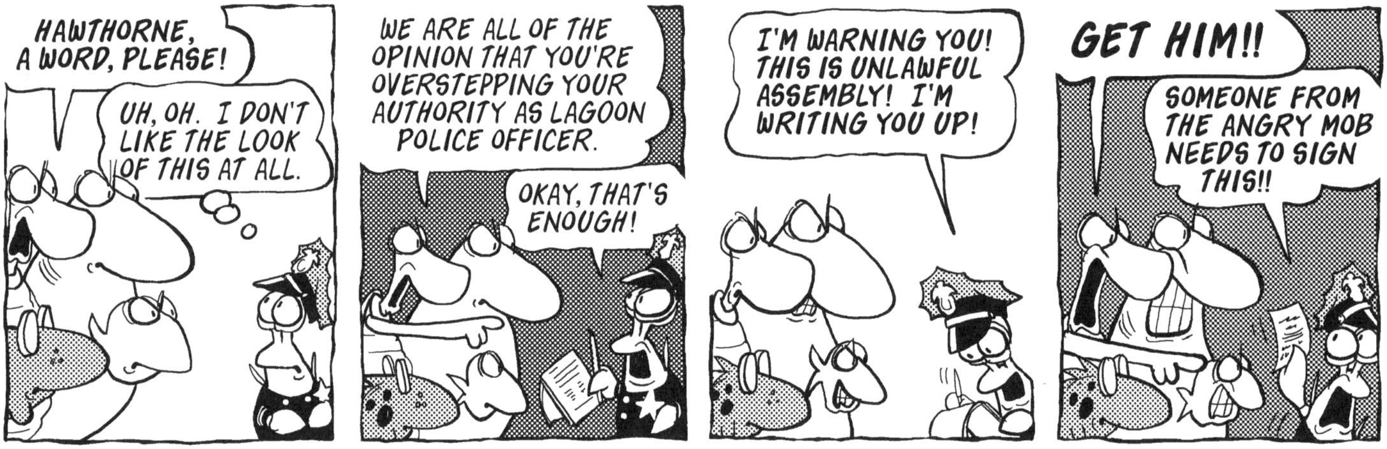
HAWTHORNE, A WORD, PLEASE!
UH, OH. I DON'T LIKE THE LOOK OF THIS AT ALL.
WE ARE ALL OF THE OPINION THAT YOU'RE OVERSTEPPING YOUR AUTHORITY AS LAGOON POLICE OFFICER.
OKAY, THAT'S ENOUGH!
I'M WARNING YOU! THIS IS UNLAWFUL ASSEMBLY! I'M WRITING YOU UP!
GET HIM!!
SOMEONE FROM THE ANGRY MOB NEEDS TO SIGN THIS!!

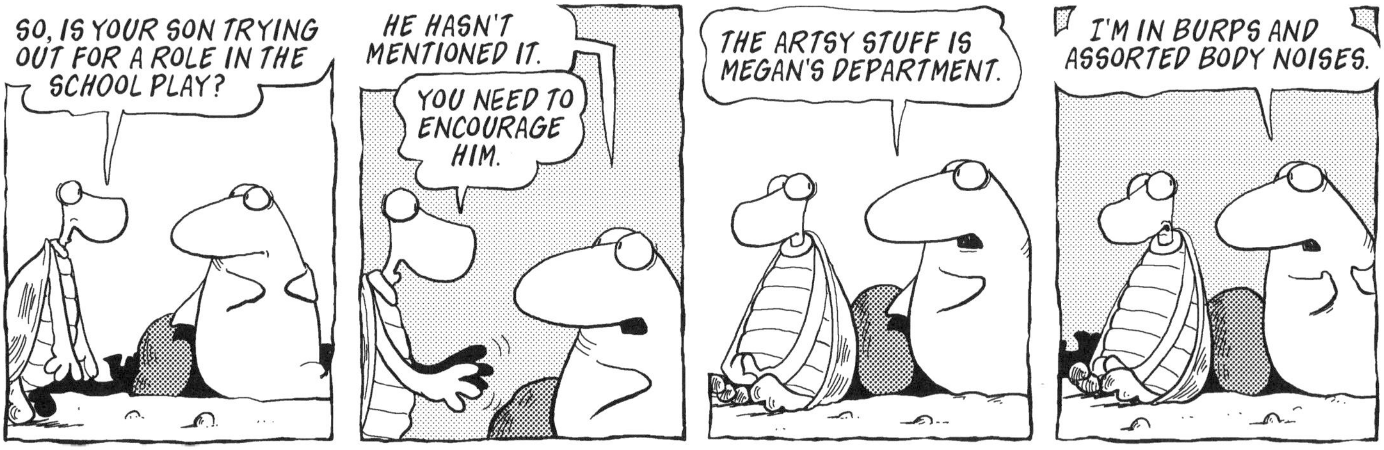
SO, IS YOUR SON TRYING OUT FOR A ROLE IN THE SCHOOL PLAY?
HE HASN'T MENTIONED IT.
YOU NEED TO ENCOURAGE HIM.
THE ARTSY STUFF IS MEGAN'S DEPARTMENT.
I'M IN BURPS AND ASSORTED BODY NOISES.

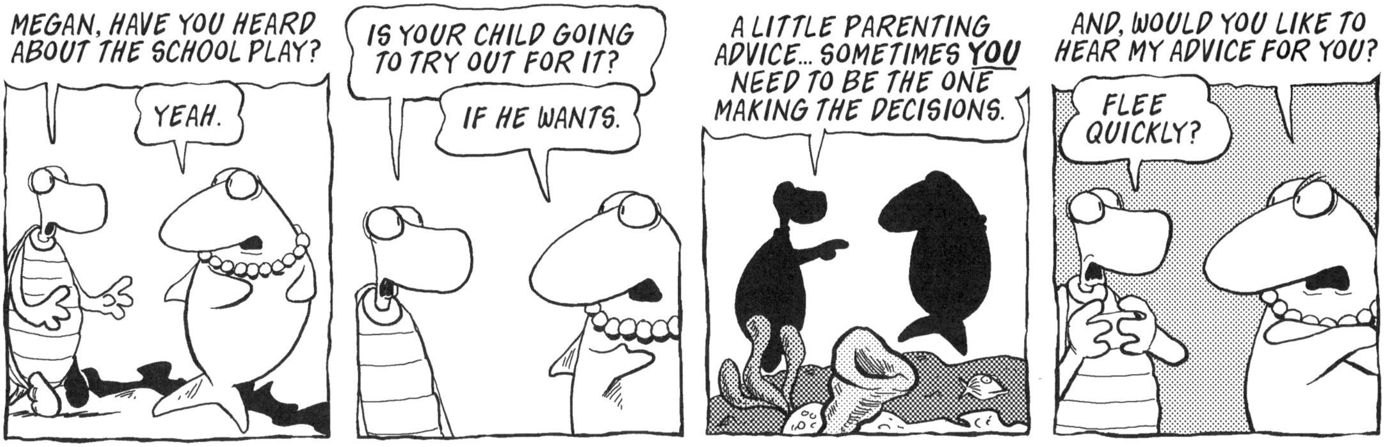
MEGAN, HAVE YOU HEARD ABOUT THE SCHOOL PLAY?
YEAH.
IS YOUR CHILD GOING TO TRY OUT FOR IT?
IF HE WANTS.
A LITTLE PARENTING ADVICE... SOMETIMES YOU NEED TO BE THE ONE MAKING THE DECISIONS.
AND, WOULD YOU LIKE TO HEAR MY ADVICE FOR YOU?
FLEE QUICKLY?

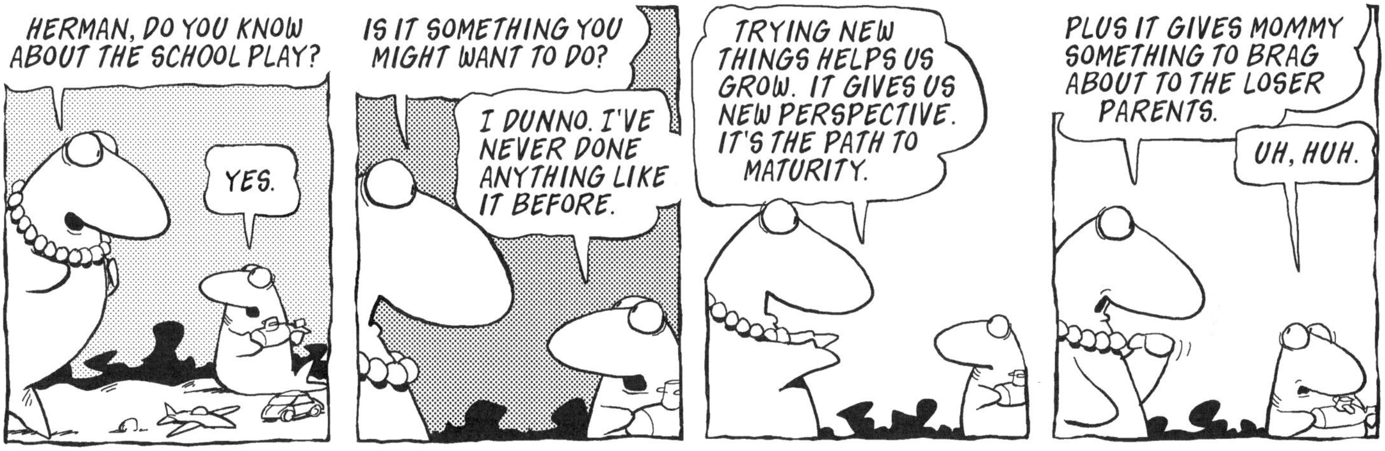
HERMAN, DO YOU KNOW ABOUT THE SCHOOL PLAY?
YES.
IS IT SOMETHING YOU MIGHT WANT TO DO?
I DUNNO. I'VE NEVER DONE ANYTHING LIKE IT BEFORE.
TRYING NEW THINGS HELPS US GROW. IT GIVES US NEW PERSPECTIVE. IT'S THE PATH TO MATURITY.
PLUS IT GIVES MOMMY SOMETHING TO BRAG ABOUT TO THE LOSER PARENTS.
UH, HUH.

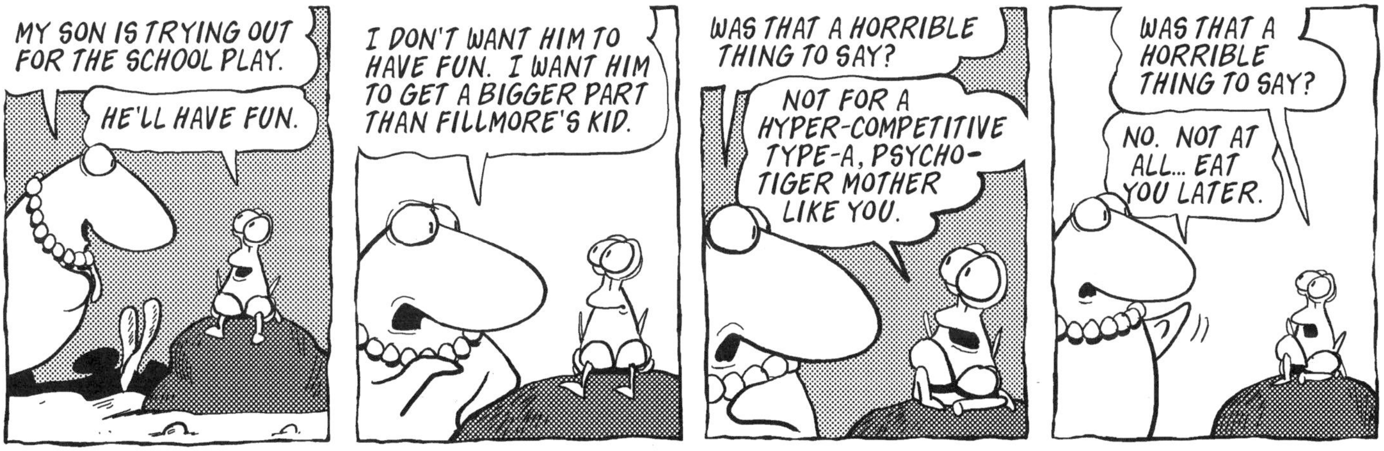
MY SON IS TRYING OUT FOR THE SCHOOL PLAY.
HE'LL HAVE FUN.
I DON'T WANT HIM TO HAVE FUN. I WANT HIM TO GET A BIGGER PART THAN FILLMORE'S KID.
WAS THAT A HORRIBLE THING TO SAY?
NOT FOR A HYPER-COMPETITIVE TYPE-A, PSYCHO-TIGER MOTHER LIKE YOU.
WAS THAT A HORRIBLE THING TO SAY?
NO. NOT AT ALL... EAT YOU LATER.

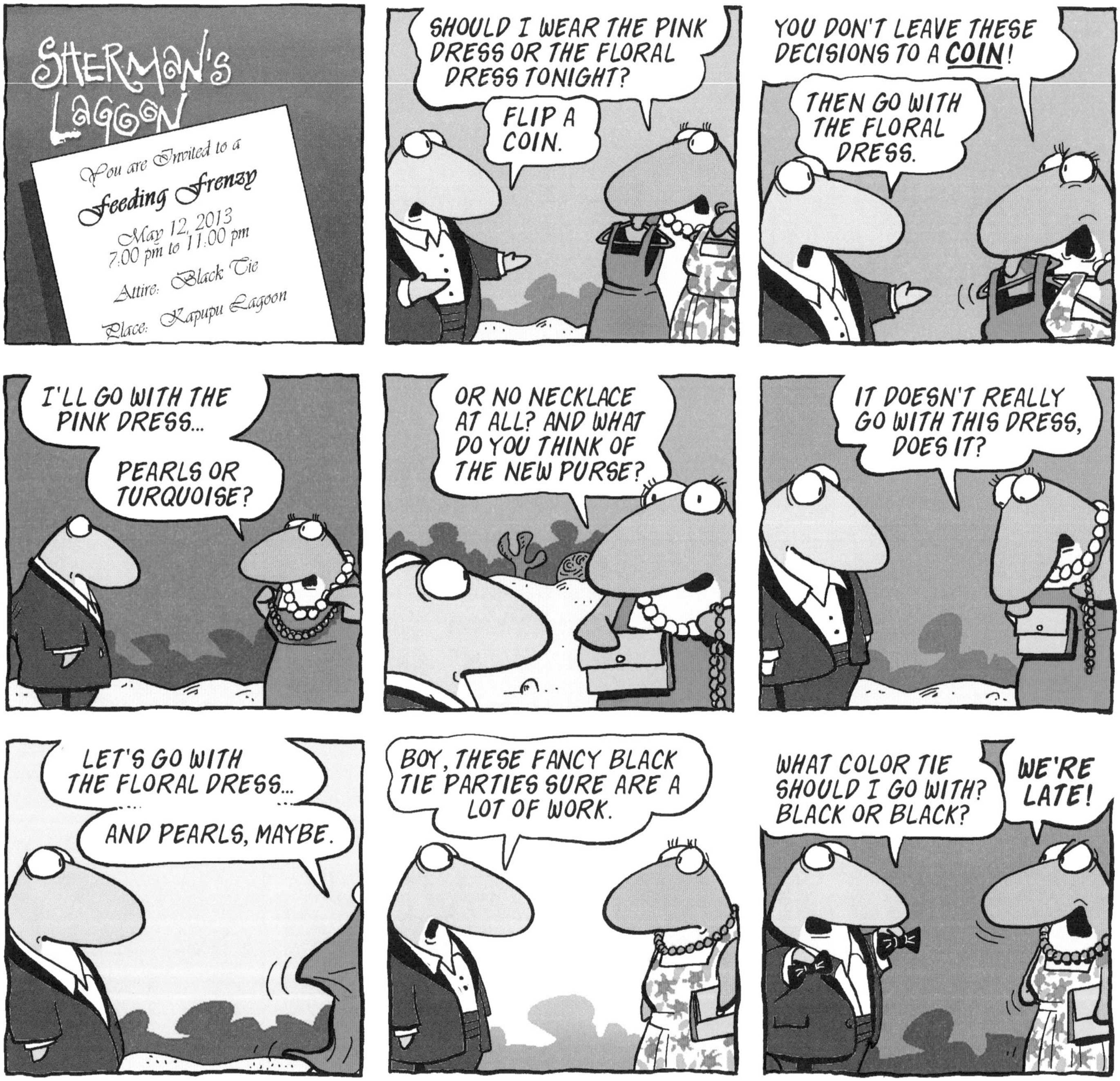
SHERMAN'S LAGOON
You are Invited to a
Feeding Frenzy
May 12, 2013
7:00 pm to 11:00 pm
Attire: Black Tie
Place: Kapupu Lagoon
SHOULD I WEAR THE PINK DRESS OR THE FLORAL DRESS TONIGHT?
FLIP A COIN.
YOU DON'T LEAVE THESE DECISIONS TO A COIN!
THEN GO WITH THE FLORAL DRESS.
I'LL GO WITH THE PINK DRESS...
PEARLS OR TURQUOISE?
OR NO NECKLACE AT ALL? AND WHAT DO YOU THINK OF THE NEW PURSE?
IT DOESN'T REALLY GO WITH THIS DRESS, DOES IT?
LET'S GO WITH THE FLORAL DRESS...
AND PEARLS, MAYBE.
BOY, THESE FANCY BLACK TIE PARTIES SURE ARE A LOT OF WORK.
WHAT COLOR TIE SHOULD I GO WITH? BLACK OR BLACK?
WE'RE LATE!

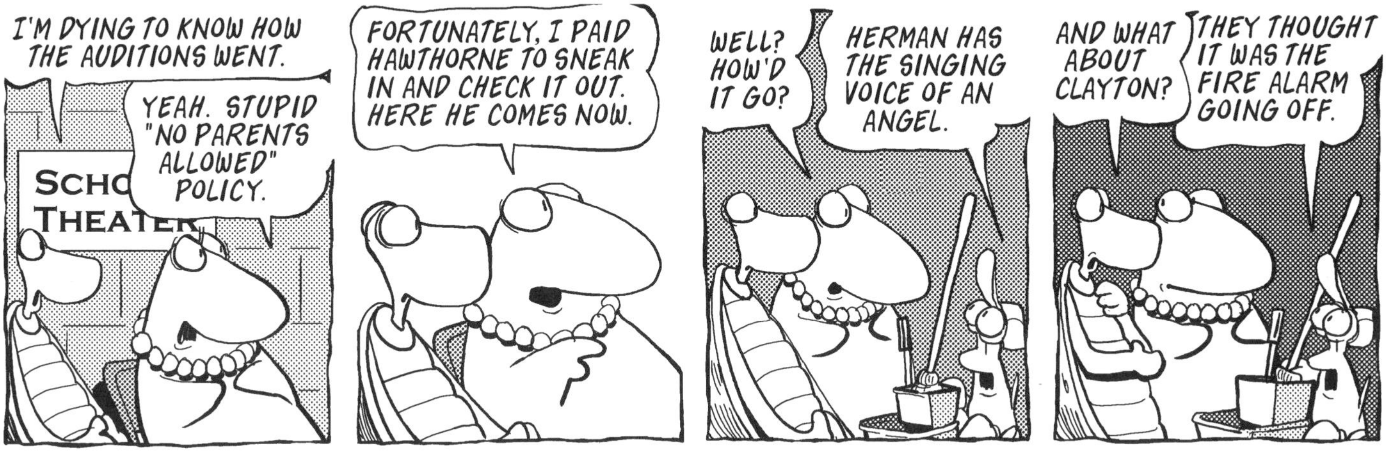
I'M DYING TO KNOW HOW THE AUDITIONS WENT.
YEAH. STUPID "NO PARENTS ALLOWED" POLICY.
SCHO THEATER
FORTUNATELY, I PAID HAWTHORNE TO SNEAK IN AND CHECK IT OUT. HERE HE COMES NOW.
WELL? HOW'D IT GO?
HERMAN HAS THE SINGING VOICE OF AN ANGEL.
AND WHAT ABOUT CLAYTON?
THEY THOUGHT IT WAS THE FIRE ALARM GOING OFF.

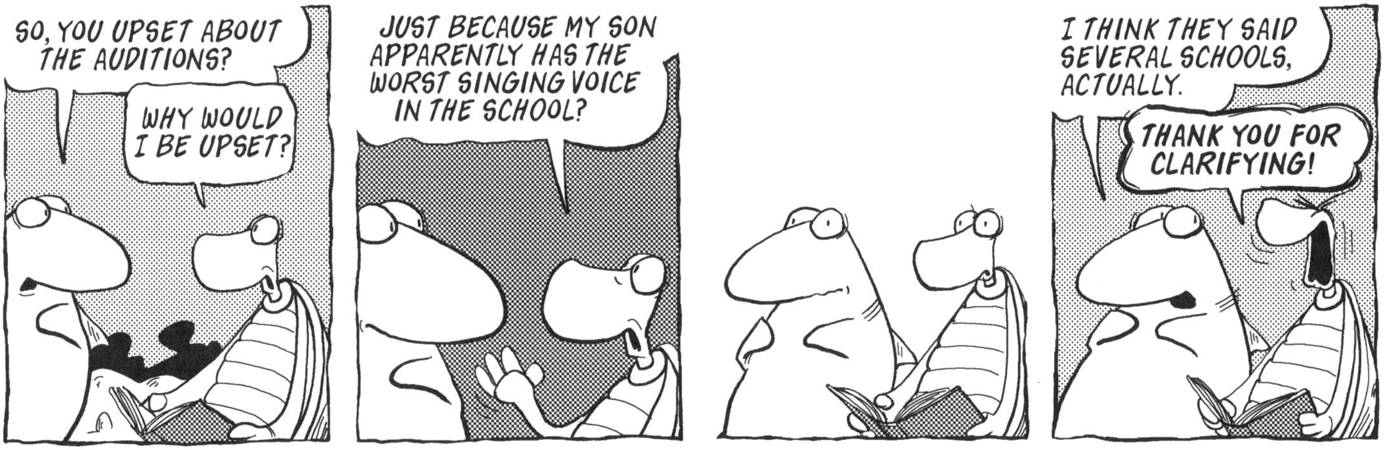
SO, YOU UPSET ABOUT THE AUDITIONS?
WHY WOULD I BE UPSET?
JUST BECAUSE MY SON APPARENTLY HAS THE WORST SINGING VOICE IN THE SCHOOL?
I THINK THEY SAID SEVERAL SCHOOLS, ACTUALLY.
THANK YOU FOR CLARIFYING!

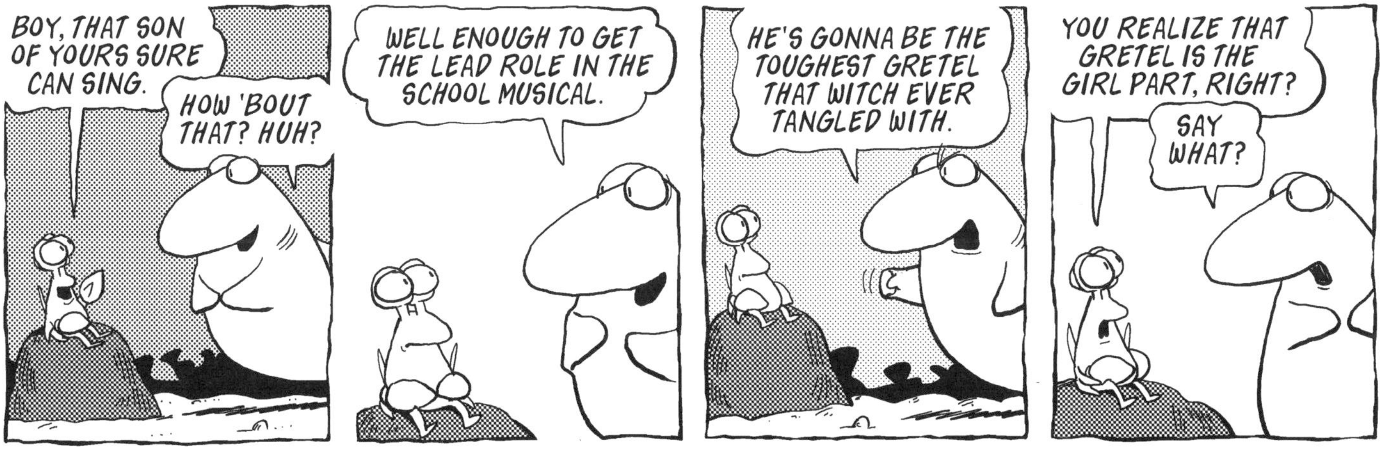
BOY, THAT SON OF YOURS SURE CAN SING.
HOW 'BOUT THAT? HUH?
WELL ENOUGH TO GET THE LEAD ROLE IN THE SCHOOL MUSICAL.
HE'S GONNA BE THE TOUGHEST GRETEL THAT WITCH EVER TANGLED WITH.
YOU REALIZE THAT GRETEL IS THE GIRL PART, RIGHT?
SAY WHAT?

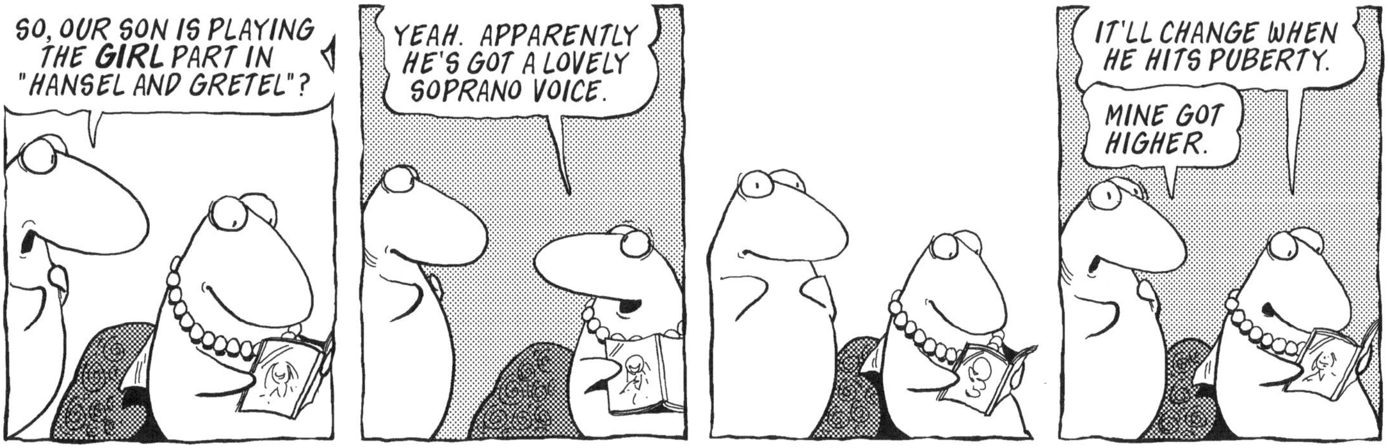
SO, OUR SON IS PLAYING THE GIRL PART IN "HANSEL AND GRETEL"?
YEAH. APPARENTLY HE'S GOT A LOVELY SOPRANO VOICE.
IT'LL CHANGE WHEN HE HITS PUBERTY.
MINE GOT HIGHER.

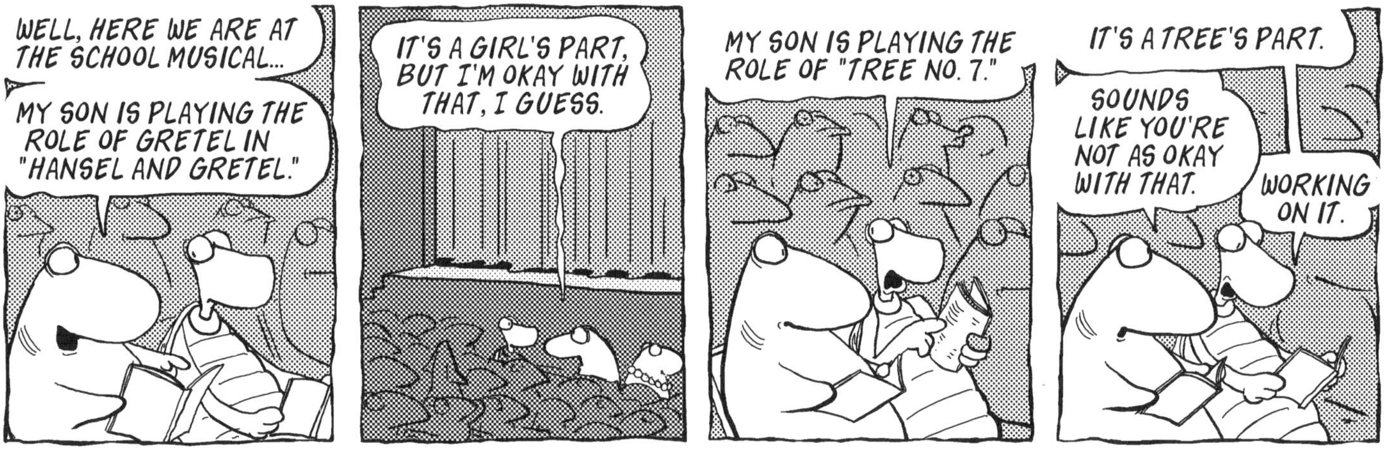
WELL, HERE WE ARE AT THE SCHOOL MUSICAL...
MY SON IS PLAYING THE ROLE OF GRETEL IN "HANSEL AND GRETEL."
IT'S A GIRL'S PART, BUT I'M OKAY WITH THAT, I GUESS.
MY SON IS PLAYING THE ROLE OF "TREE NO. 7."
IT'S A TREE'S PART.
SOUNDS LIKE YOU'RE NOT AS OKAY WITH THAT.
WORKING ON IT.

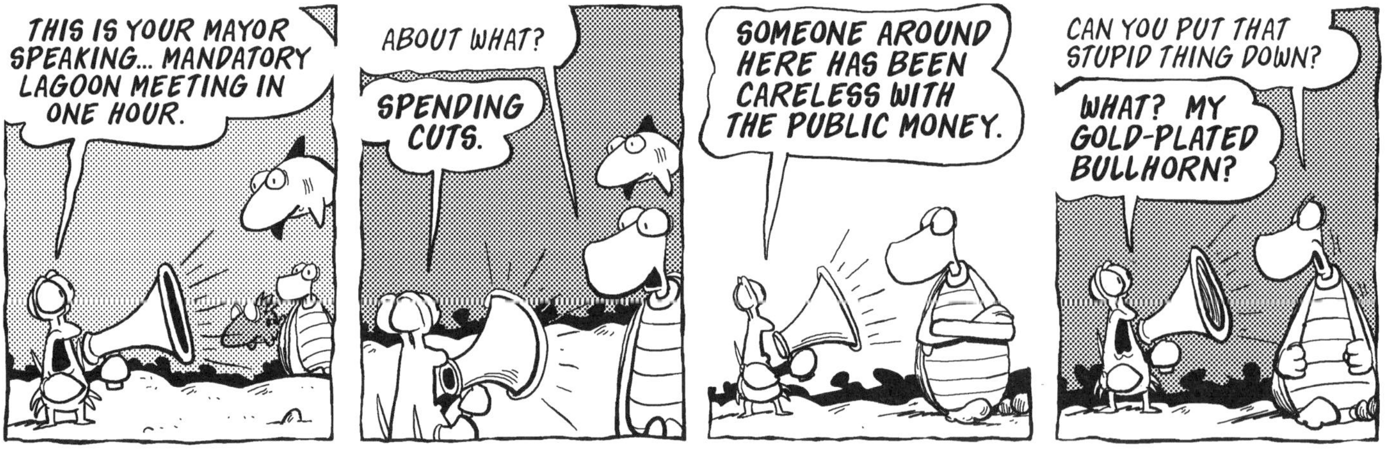
THIS IS YOUR MAYOR SPEAKING... MANDATORY LAGOON MEETING IN ONE HOUR.
ABOUT WHAT?
SPENDING CUTS.
SOMEONE AROUND HERE HAS BEEN CARELESS WITH THE PUBLIC MONEY.
CAN YOU PUT THAT STUPID THING DOWN?
WHAT? MY GOLD-PLATED BULLHORN?

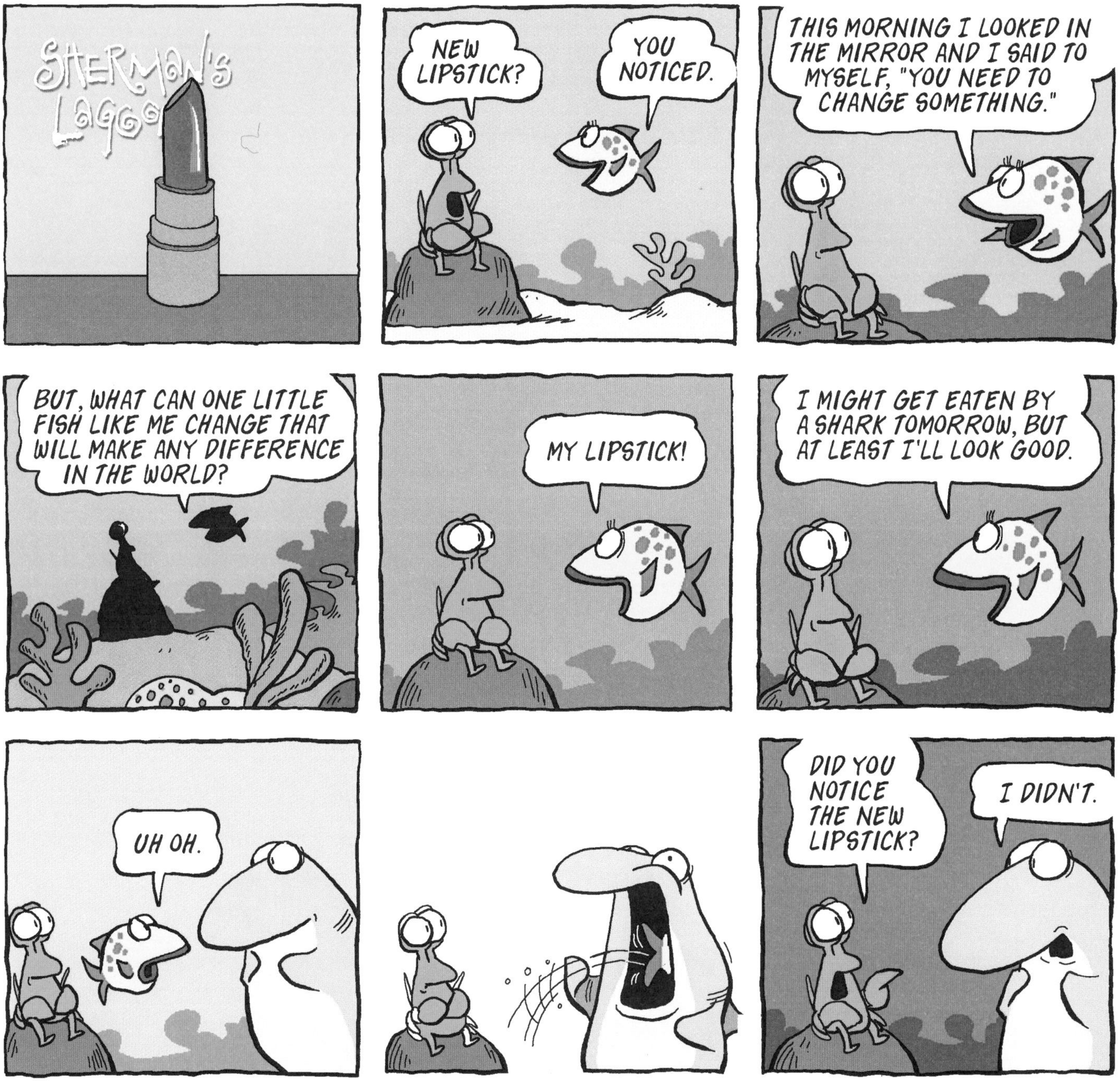
SHERMAN'S LAGOON
NEW LIPSTICK?
YOU NOTICED.
THIS MORNING I LOOKED IN THE MIRROR AND I SAID TO MYSELF, "YOU NEED TO CHANGE SOMETHING."
BUT, WHAT CAN ONE LITTLE FISH LIKE ME CHANGE THAT WILL MAKE ANY DIFFERENCE IN THE WORLD?
MY LIPSTICK!
I MIGHT GET EATEN BY A SHARK TOMORROW, BUT AT LEAST I'LL LOOK GOOD.
UH OH.
DID YOU NOTICE THE NEW LIPSTICK?
I DIDN'T.

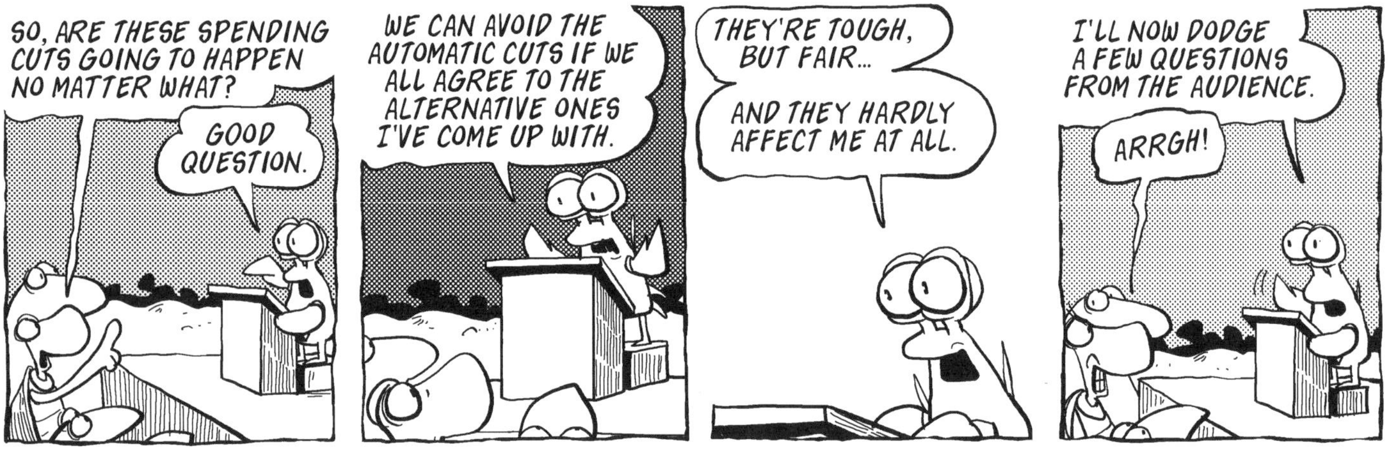
SO, ARE THESE SPENDING CUTS GOING TO HAPPEN NO MATTER WHAT?
GOOD QUESTION.
WE CAN AVOID THE AUTOMATIC CUTS IF WE ALL AGREE TO THE ALTERNATIVE ONES I'VE COME UP WITH.
THEY'RE TOUGH, BUT FAIR...
AND THEY HARDLY AFFECT ME AT ALL.
I'LL NOW DODGE A FEW QUESTIONS FROM THE AUDIENCE.
ARRGH!

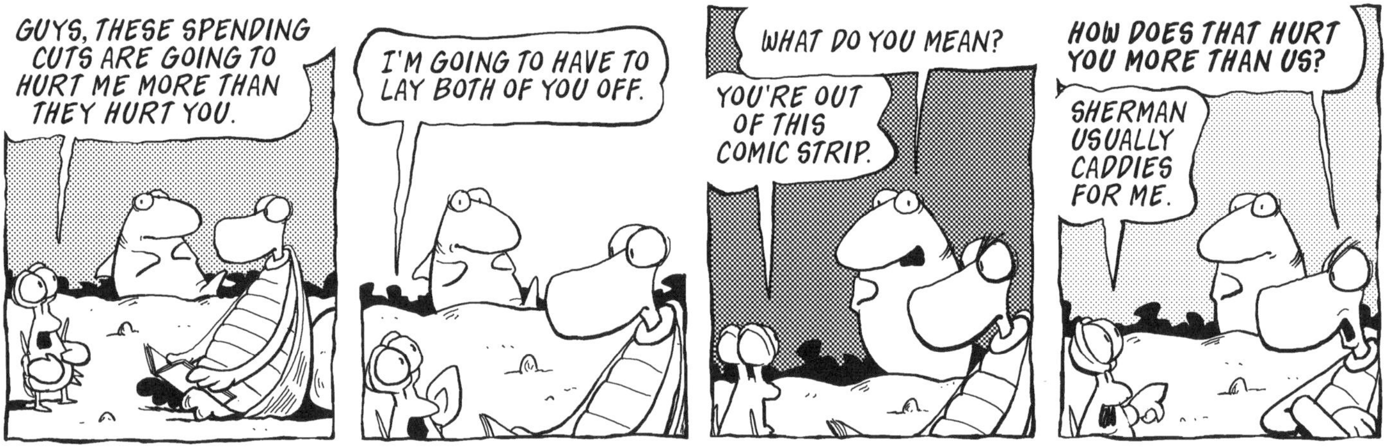
GUYS, THESE SPENDING CUTS ARE GOING TO HURT ME MORE THAN THEY HURT YOU.
I'M GOING TO HAVE TO LAY BOTH OF YOU OFF.
WHAT DO YOU MEAN?
YOU'RE OUT OF THIS COMIC STRIP.
HOW DOES THAT HURT YOU MORE THAN US?
SHERMAN USUALLY CADDIES FOR ME.

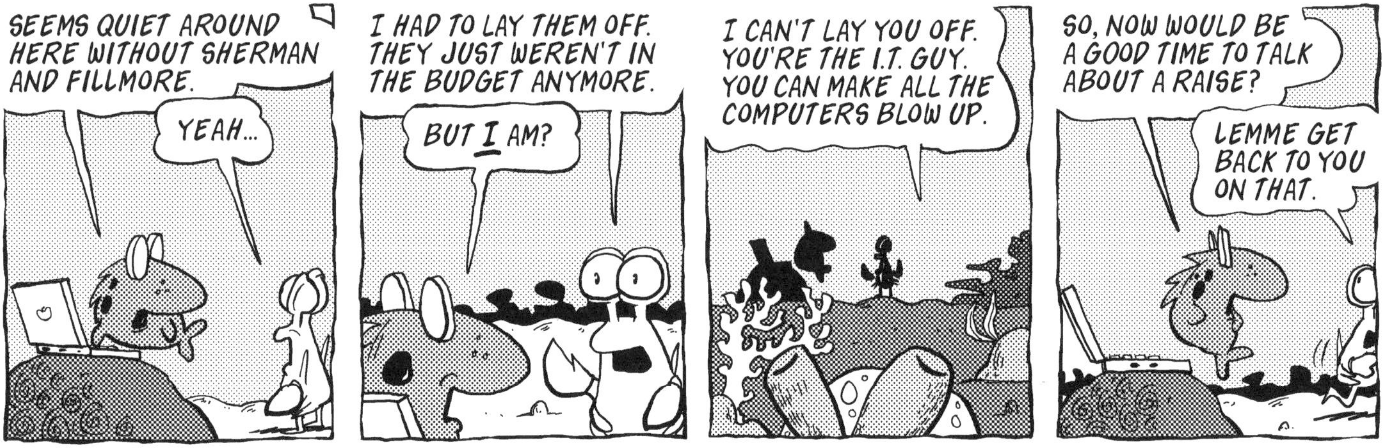
SEEMS QUIET AROUND HERE WITHOUT SHERMAN AND FILLMORE.
YEAH...
I HAD TO LAY THEM OFF. THEY JUST WEREN'T IN THE BUDGET ANYMORE.
BUT I AM?
I CAN'T LAY YOU OFF. YOU'RE THE I.T. GUY. YOU CAN MAKE ALL THE COMPUTERS BLOW UP.
SO, NOW WOULD BE A GOOD TIME TO TALK ABOUT A RAISE?
LEMME GET BACK TO YOU ON THAT.

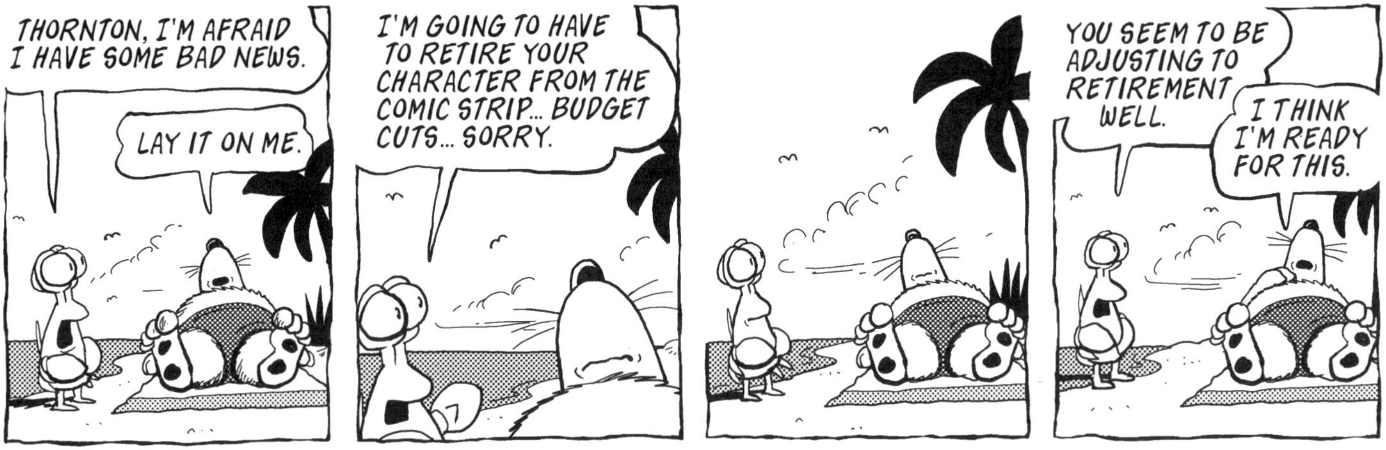
THORNTON, I'M AFRAID I HAVE SOME BAD NEWS.
LAY IT ON ME.
I'M GOING TO HAVE TO RETIRE YOUR CHARACTER FROM THE COMIC STRIP... BUDGET CUTS... SORRY.
YOU SEEM TO BE ADJUSTING TO RETIREMENT WELL.
I THINK I'M READY FOR THIS.

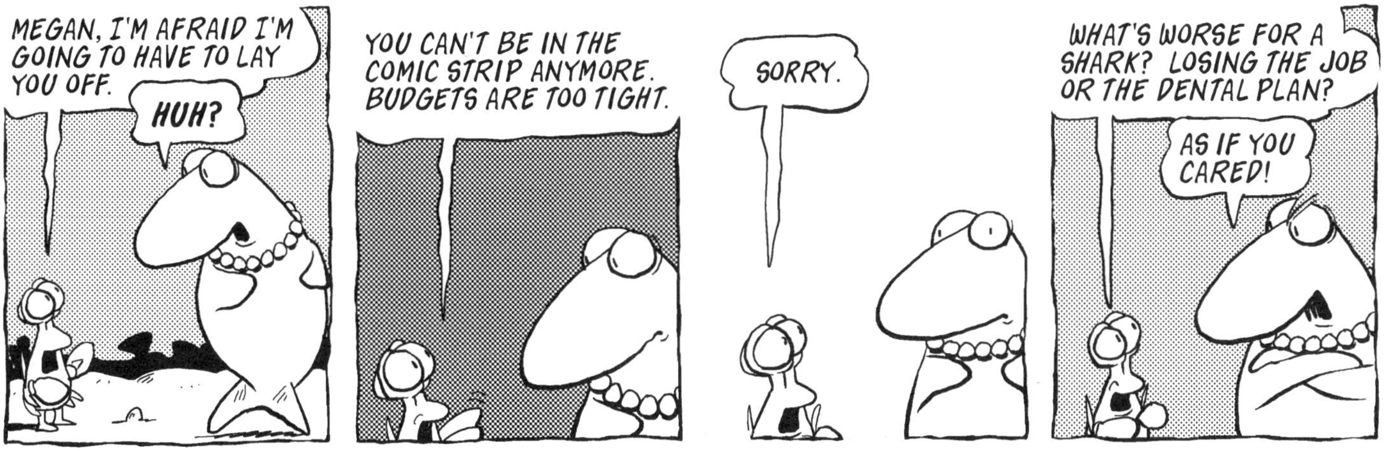
MEGAN, I'M AFRAID I'M GOING TO HAVE TO LAY YOU OFF.
HUH?
YOU CAN'T BE IN THE COMIC STRIP ANYMORE. BUDGETS ARE TOO TIGHT.
SORRY.
WHAT'S WORSE FOR A SHARK? LOSING THE JOB OR THE DENTAL PLAN?
AS IF YOU CARED!

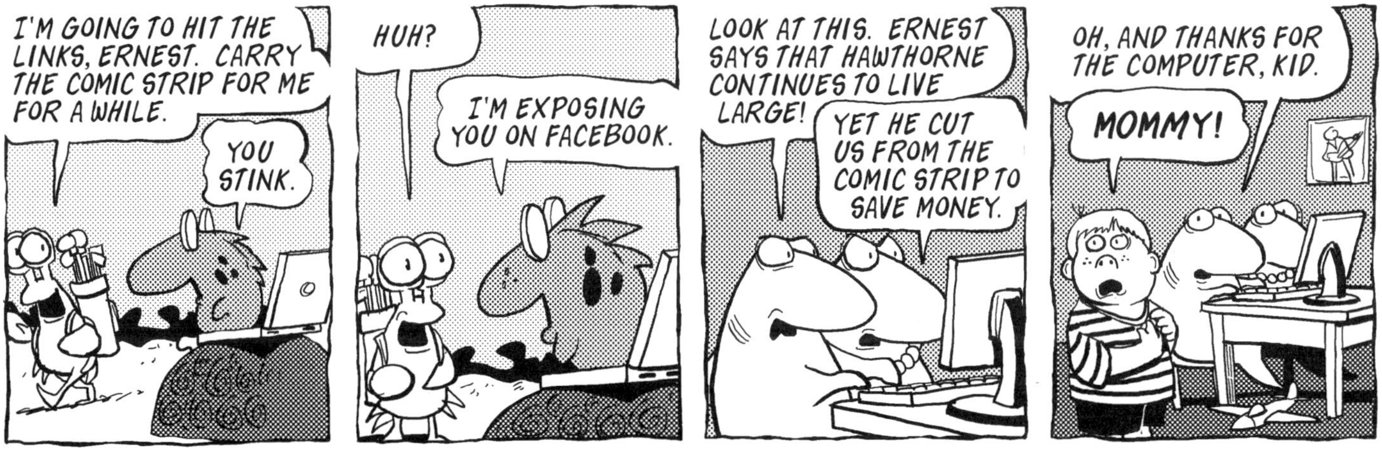
I'M GOING TO HIT THE LINKS, ERNEST. CARRY THE COMIC STRIP FOR ME FOR A WHILE.
YOU STINK.
HUH?
I'M EXPOSING YOU ON FACEBOOK.
LOOK AT THIS. ERNEST SAYS THAT HAWTHORNE CONTINUES TO LIVE LARGE!
YET HE CUT US FROM THE COMIC STRIP TO SAVE MONEY.
OH, AND THANKS FOR THE COMPUTER, KID.
MOMMY!

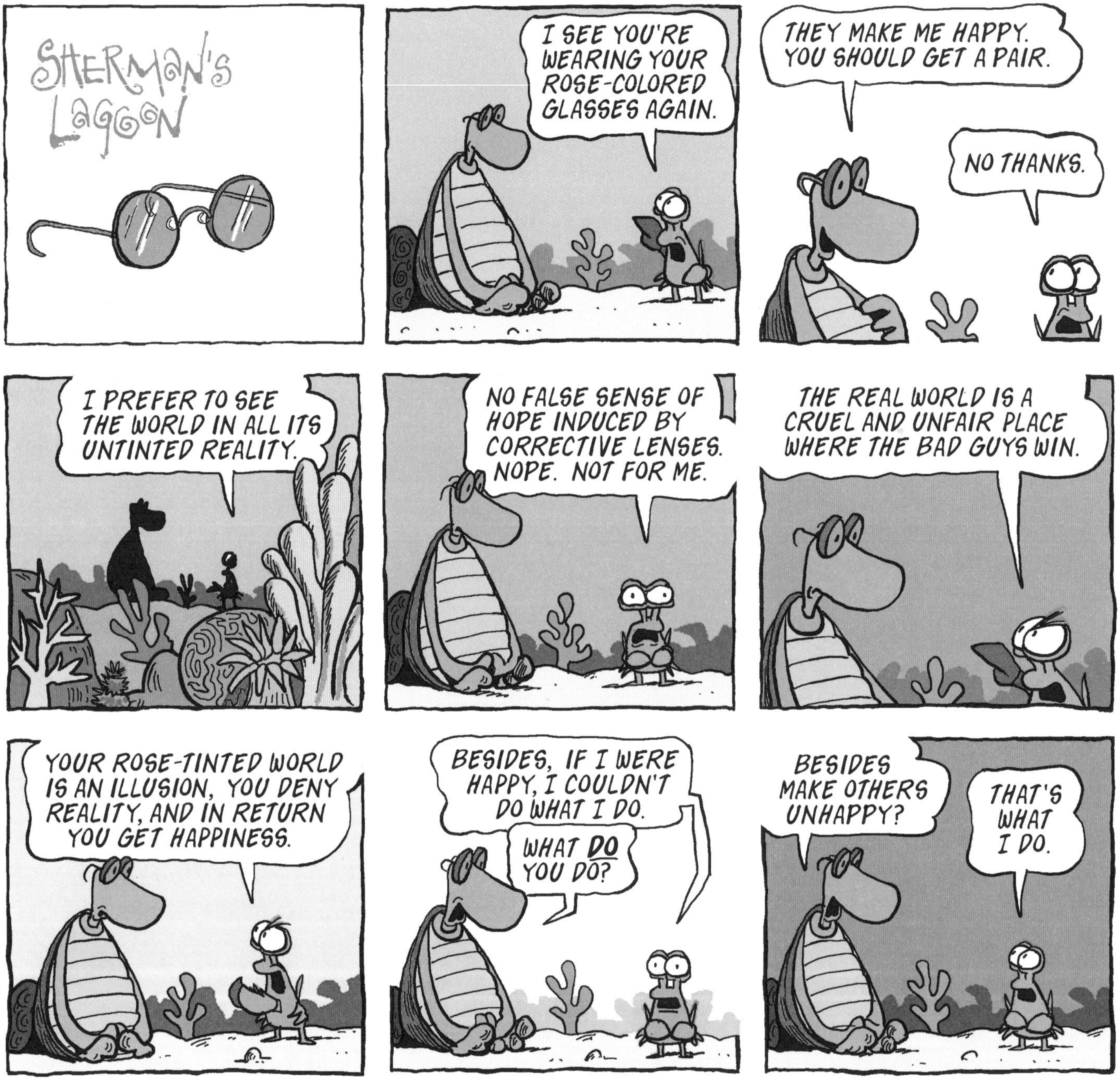
SHERMAN'S LAGOON
I SEE YOU'RE WEARING YOUR ROSE-COLORED GLASSES AGAIN.
THEY MAKE ME HAPPY. YOU SHOULD GET A PAIR.
NO THANKS.
I PREFER TO SEE THE WORLD IN ALL ITS UNTINTED REALITY.
NO FALSE SENSE OF HOPE INDUCED BY CORRECTIVE LENSES. NOPE. NOT FOR ME.
THE REAL WORLD IS A CRUEL AND UNFAIR PLACE WHERE THE BAD GUYS WIN.
YOUR ROSE-TINTED WORLD IS AN ILLUSION, YOU DENY REALITY, AND IN RETURN YOU GET HAPPINESS.
BESIDES, IF I WERE HAPPY, I COULDN'T DO WHAT I DO.
WHAT DO YOU DO?
BESIDES MAKE OTHERS UNHAPPY?
THAT'S WHAT I DO.

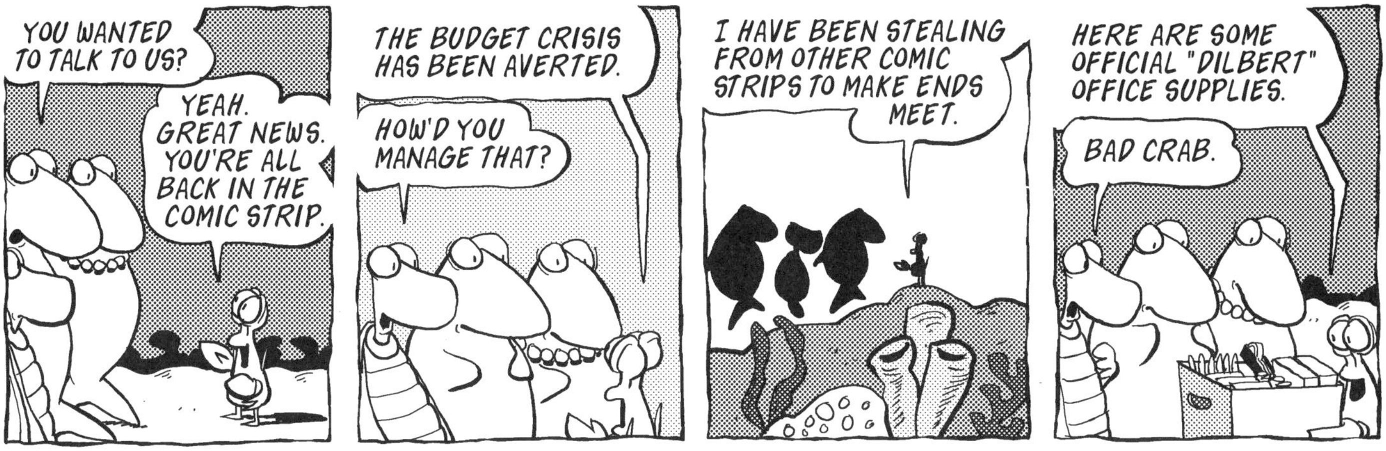
YOU WANTED TO TALK TO US?
YEAH. GREAT NEWS. YOU'RE ALL BACK IN THE COMIC STRIP.
THE BUDGET CRISIS HAS BEEN AVERTED.
HOW'D YOU MANAGE THAT?
I HAVE BEEN STEALING FROM OTHER COMIC STRIPS TO MAKE ENDS MEET.
HERE ARE SOME OFFICIAL "DILBERT" OFFICE SUPPLIES.
BAD CRAB.

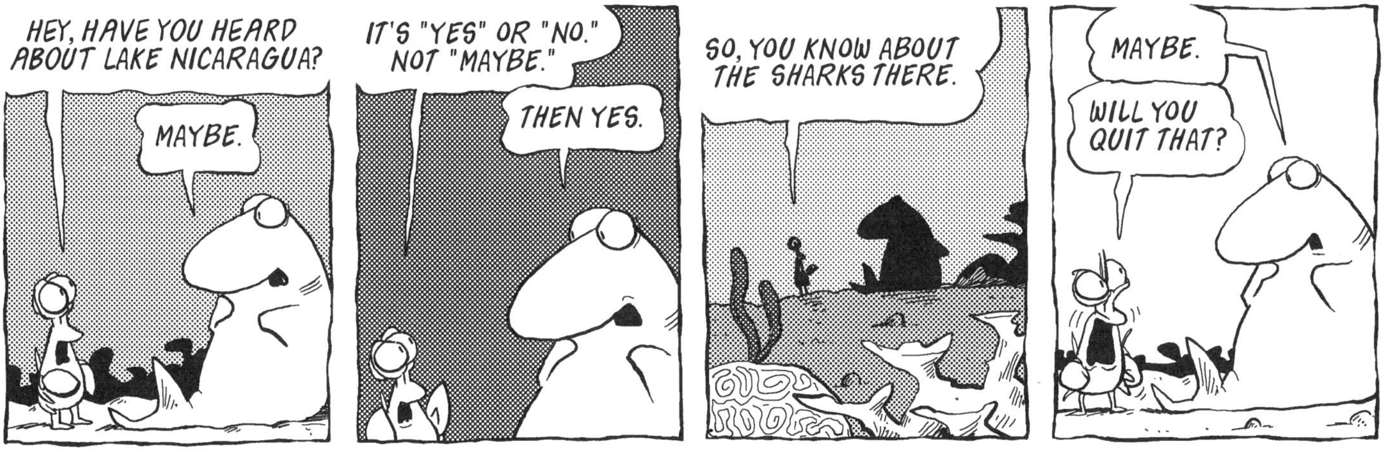
HEY, HAVE YOU HEARD ABOUT LAKE NICARAGUA?
MAYBE.
IT'S "YES" OR "NO." NOT "MAYBE."
THEN YES.
SO, YOU KNOW ABOUT THE SHARKS THERE.
MAYBE.
WILL YOU QUIT THAT?

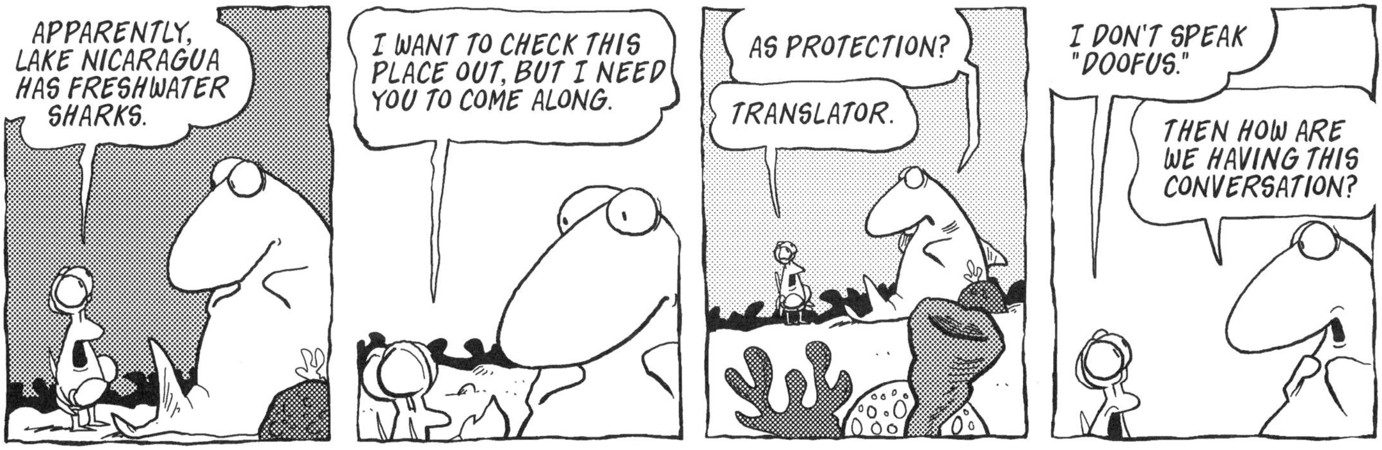
APPARENTLY, LAKE NICARAGUA HAS FRESHWATER SHARKS.
I WANT TO CHECK THIS PLACE OUT, BUT I NEED YOU TO COME ALONG.
AS PROTECTION?
TRANSLATOR.
I DON'T SPEAK "DOOFUS."
THEN HOW ARE WE HAVING THIS CONVERSATION?

ARE YOU READY TO HEAD TO LAKE NICARAGUA?

READY.

LET ME DIAL IT IN ON THE G.P.S. ...

NOT NECESSARY.

SHARKS HAVE AN INTERNAL G.P.S. ... IT'S A CERTAIN GUT FEELING I HAVE WHEN I TRAVEL.

THEN AGAIN, IT COULD BE THAT BREAKFAST BURRITO.

LET ME GET IN FRONT, PLEASE.

YOU KNOW WE SHARKS HAVE TO HAVE OUR DAILY FIX OF BLOOD. EVEN WHEN WE TRAVEL.

SOUNDS LIKE YOU HAVE A PROBLEM.

IT'S NOT A "PROBLEM."

NEEDING A DAILY FIX OF BLOOD IS A PROBLEM IN MY BOOK.

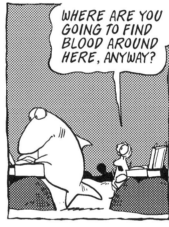

WHERE ARE YOU GOING TO FIND BLOOD AROUND HERE, ANYWAY?

I BROUGHT LITTLE AIRLINE BOTTLES.

YOU HAVE A PROBLEM.

WE FINALLY REACHED THE COAST OF NICARAGUA.

AND THIS MUST BE THE SAN JUAN RIVER.

YOU HAVE TO SWIM UP THIS RIVER, AGAINST THE RAPIDS WITH ALL YOUR MIGHT, IN ORDER TO REACH LAKE NICARAGUA.

BUT DON'T WORRY. WE'RE IN THIS TOGETHER. I'LL BE STRUGGLING RIGHT ALONG WITH YOU.

OOF!

OH, GREAT. THE MOVING SIDEWALK IS BROKEN.

DON'T WANNA... HEAR... ABOUT IT.

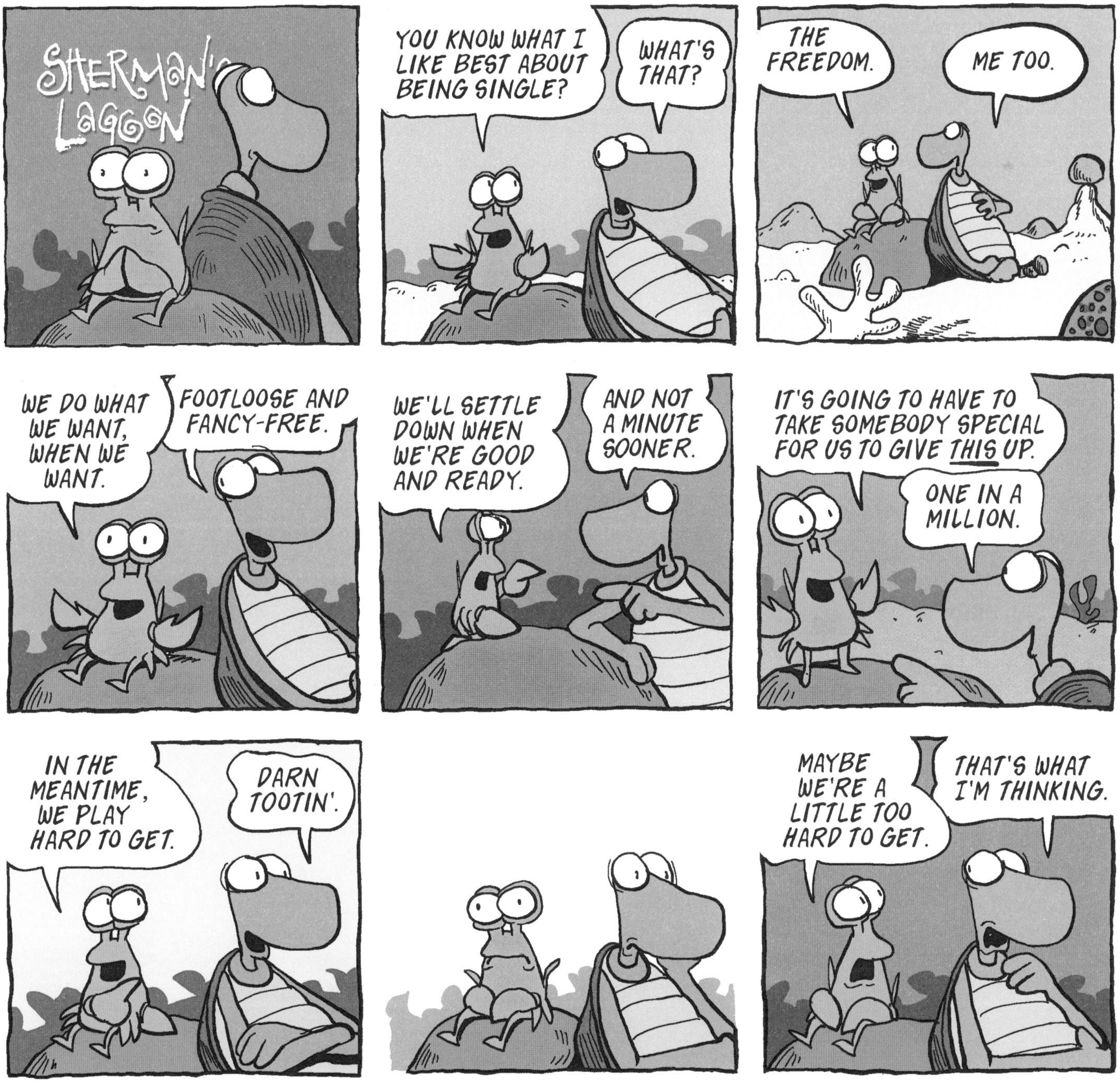
SHERMAN'S LAGOON
YOU KNOW WHAT I LIKE BEST ABOUT BEING SINGLE?
WHAT'S THAT?
THE FREEDOM.
ME TOO.
WE DO WHAT WE WANT, WHEN WE WANT.
FOOTLOOSE AND FANCY-FREE.
WE'LL SETTLE DOWN WHEN WE'RE GOOD AND READY.
AND NOT A MINUTE SOONER.
IT'S GOING TO HAVE TO TAKE SOMEBODY SPECIAL FOR US TO GIVE THIS UP.
ONE IN A MILLION.
IN THE MEANTIME, WE PLAY HARD TO GET.
DARN TOOTIN'.
MAYBE WE'RE A LITTLE TOO HARD TO GET.
THAT'S WHAT I'M THINKING.

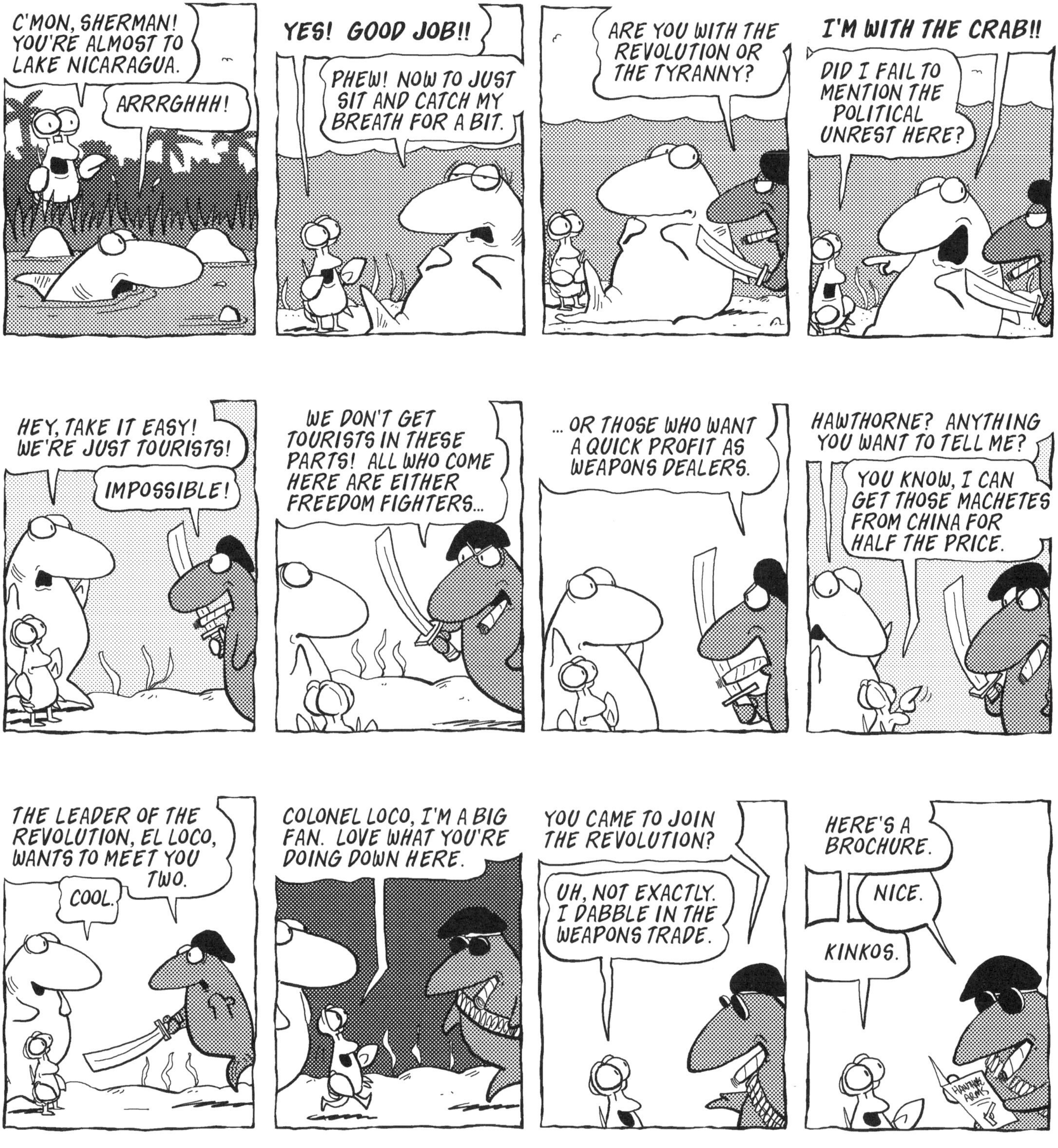

C'MON, SHERMAN! YOU'RE ALMOST TO LAKE NICARAGUA.
ARRRGHHH!
YES! GOOD JOB!!
PHEW! NOW TO JUST SIT AND CATCH MY BREATH FOR A BIT.
ARE YOU WITH THE REVOLUTION OR THE TYRANNY?
I'M WITH THE CRAB!!
DID I FAIL TO MENTION THE POLITICAL UNREST HERE?
HEY, TAKE IT EASY! WE'RE JUST TOURISTS!
IMPOSSIBLE!
WE DON'T GET TOURISTS IN THESE PARTS! ALL WHO COME HERE ARE EITHER FREEDOM FIGHTERS...
... OR THOSE WHO WANT A QUICK PROFIT AS WEAPONS DEALERS.
HAWTHORNE? ANYTHING YOU WANT TO TELL ME?
YOU KNOW, I CAN GET THOSE MACHETES FROM CHINA FOR HALF THE PRICE.
THE LEADER OF THE REVOLUTION, EL LOCO, WANTS TO MEET YOU TWO.
COOL.
COLONEL LOCO, I'M A BIG FAN. LOVE WHAT YOU'RE DOING DOWN HERE.
YOU CAME TO JOIN THE REVOLUTION?
UH, NOT EXACTLY. I DABBLE IN THE WEAPONS TRADE.
HERE'S A BROCHURE.
NICE.
KINKOS.

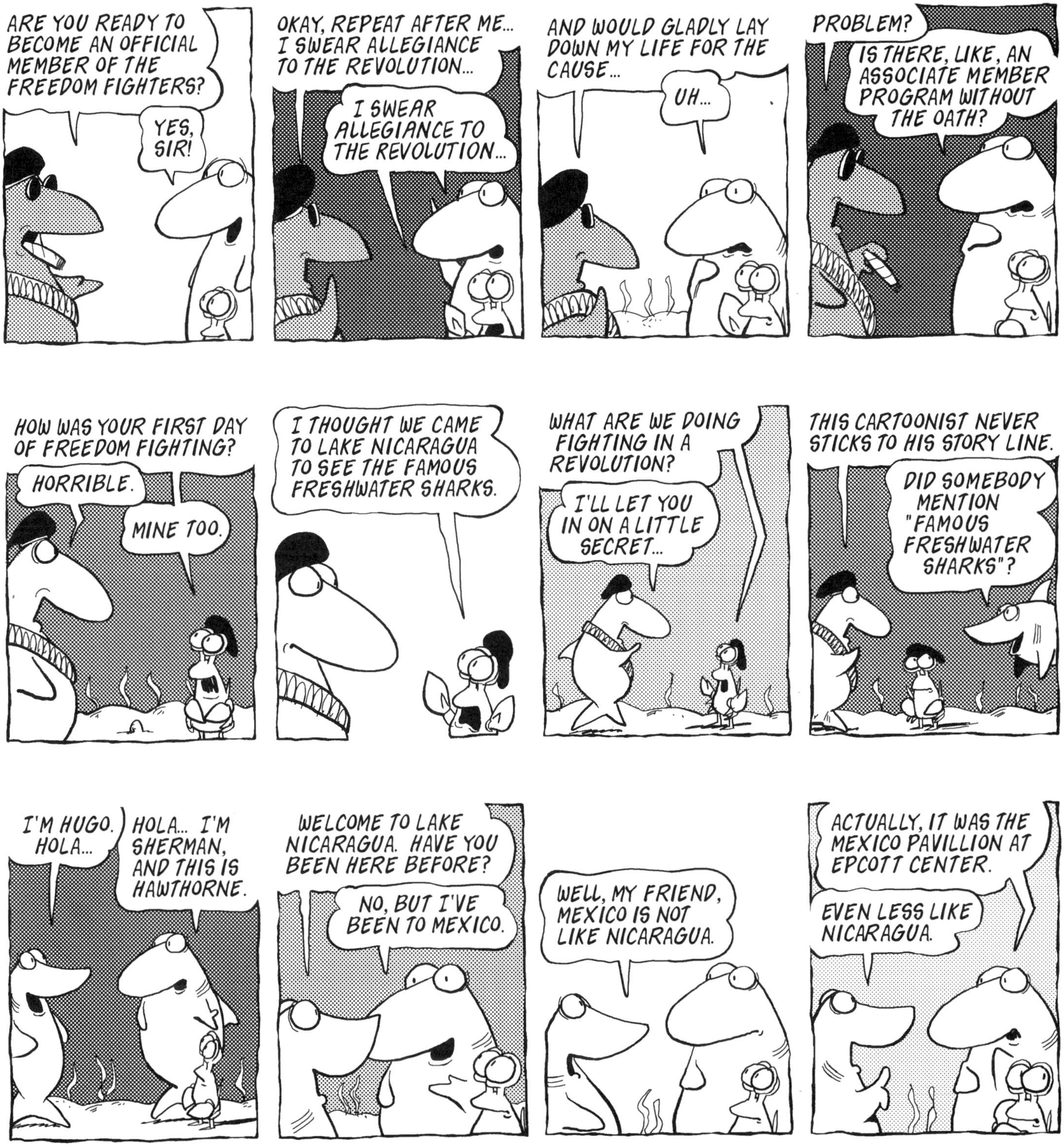
ARE YOU READY TO BECOME AN OFFICIAL MEMBER OF THE FREEDOM FIGHTERS?
YES, SIR!
OKAY, REPEAT AFTER ME... I SWEAR ALLEGIANCE TO THE REVOLUTION...
I SWEAR ALLEGIANCE TO THE REVOLUTION...
AND WOULD GLADLY LAY DOWN MY LIFE FOR THE CAUSE...
UH...
PROBLEM?
IS THERE, LIKE, AN ASSOCIATE MEMBER PROGRAM WITHOUT THE OATH?
HOW WAS YOUR FIRST DAY OF FREEDOM FIGHTING?
HORRIBLE.
MINE TOO.
I THOUGHT WE CAME TO LAKE NICARAGUA TO SEE THE FAMOUS FRESHWATER SHARKS.
WHAT ARE WE DOING FIGHTING IN A REVOLUTION?
I'LL LET YOU IN ON A LITTLE SECRET...
THIS CARTOONIST NEVER STICKS TO HIS STORY LINE.
DID SOMEBODY MENTION "FAMOUS FRESHWATER SHARKS"?
I'M HUGO. HOLA...
HOLA... I'M SHERMAN, AND THIS IS HAWTHORNE.
WELCOME TO LAKE NICARAGUA. HAVE YOU BEEN HERE BEFORE?
NO, BUT I'VE BEEN TO MEXICO.
WELL, MY FRIEND, MEXICO IS NOT LIKE NICARAGUA.
ACTUALLY, IT WAS THE MEXICO PAVILLION AT EPCOTT CENTER.
EVEN LESS LIKE NICARAGUA.

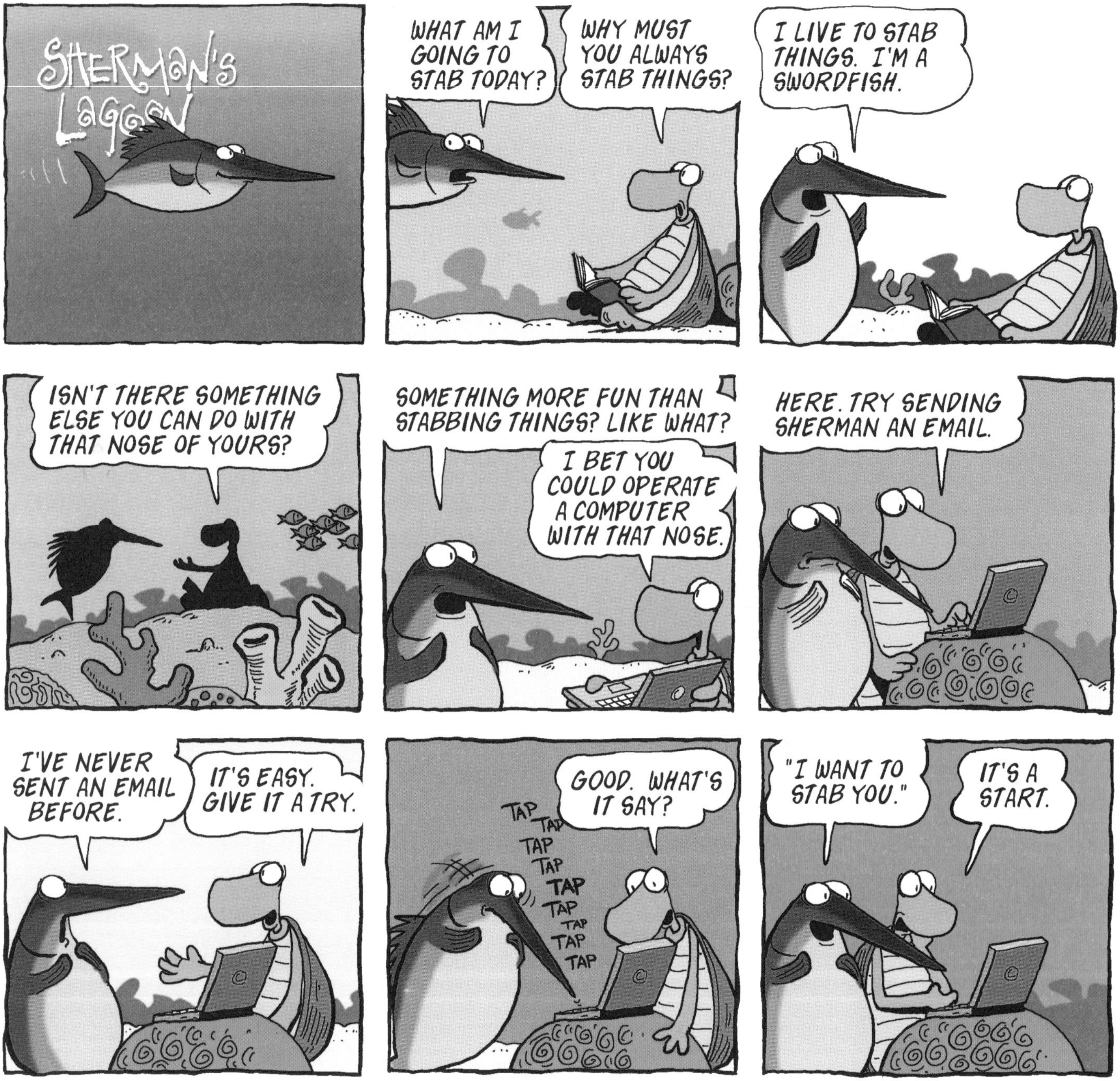
SHERMAN'S LAGOON
WHAT AM I GOING TO STAB TODAY?
WHY MUST YOU ALWAYS STAB THINGS?
I LIVE TO STAB THINGS. I'M A SWORDFISH.
ISN'T THERE SOMETHING ELSE YOU CAN DO WITH THAT NOSE OF YOURS?
SOMETHING MORE FUN THAN STABBING THINGS? LIKE WHAT?
I BET YOU COULD OPERATE A COMPUTER WITH THAT NOSE.
HERE. TRY SENDING SHERMAN AN EMAIL.
I'VE NEVER SENT AN EMAIL BEFORE.
IT'S EASY. GIVE IT A TRY.
TAP TAP TAP TAP TAP TAP TAP TAP TAP
GOOD. WHAT'S IT SAY?
"I WANT TO STAB YOU."
IT'S A START.

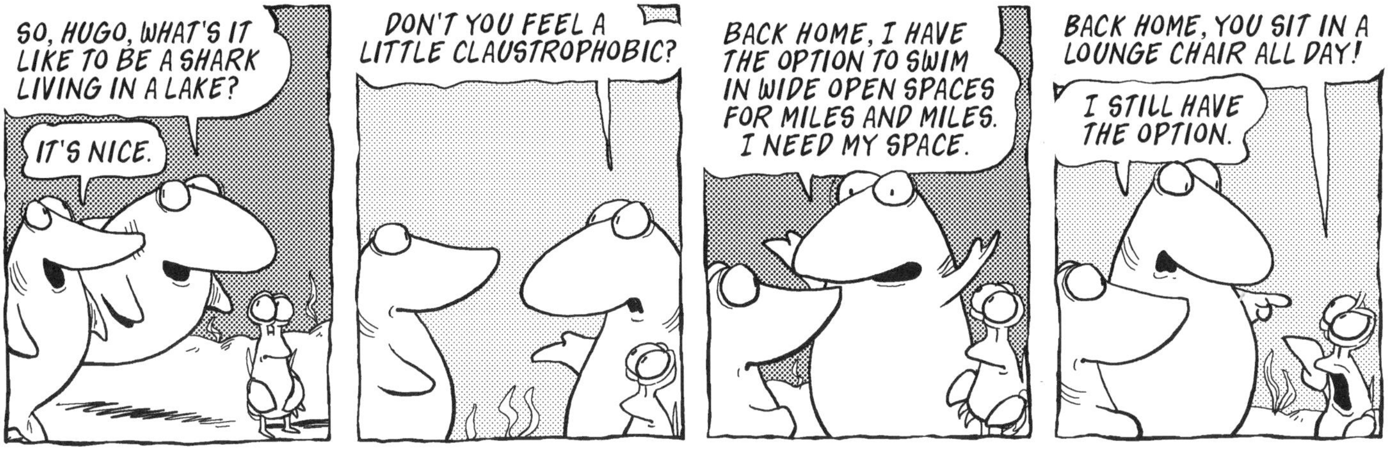
SO, HUGO, WHAT'S IT LIKE TO BE A SHARK LIVING IN A LAKE?
IT'S NICE.
DON'T YOU FEEL A LITTLE CLAUSTROPHOBIC?
BACK HOME, I HAVE THE OPTION TO SWIM IN WIDE OPEN SPACES FOR MILES AND MILES. I NEED MY SPACE.
BACK HOME, YOU SIT IN A LOUNGE CHAIR ALL DAY!
I STILL HAVE THE OPTION.

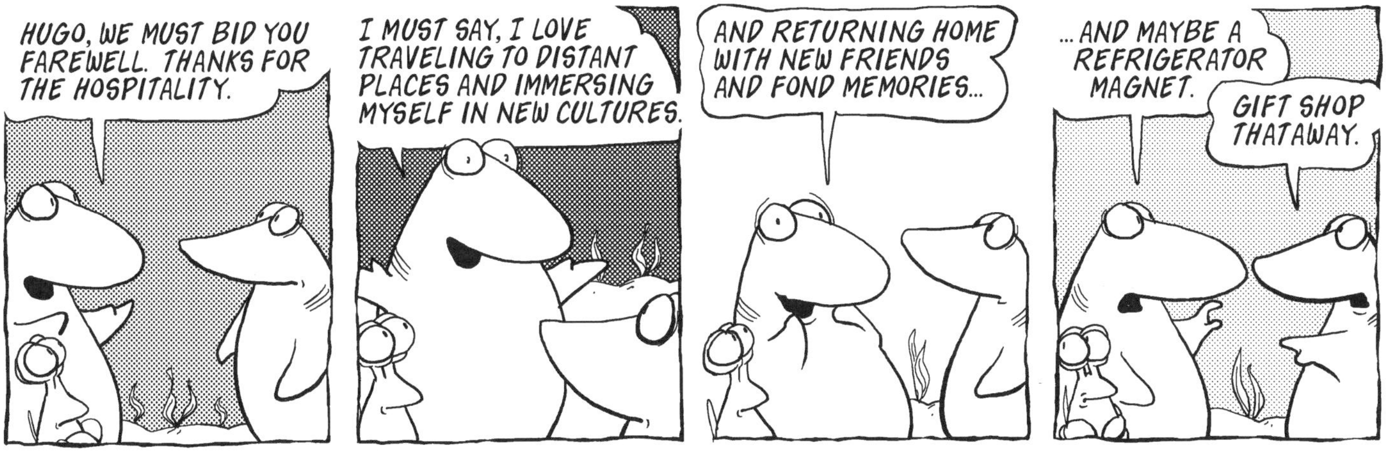
HUGO, WE MUST BID YOU FAREWELL. THANKS FOR THE HOSPITALITY.
I MUST SAY, I LOVE TRAVELING TO DISTANT PLACES AND IMMERSING MYSELF IN NEW CULTURES.
AND RETURNING HOME WITH NEW FRIENDS AND FOND MEMORIES...
...AND MAYBE A REFRIGERATOR MAGNET.
GIFT SHOP THATAWAY.

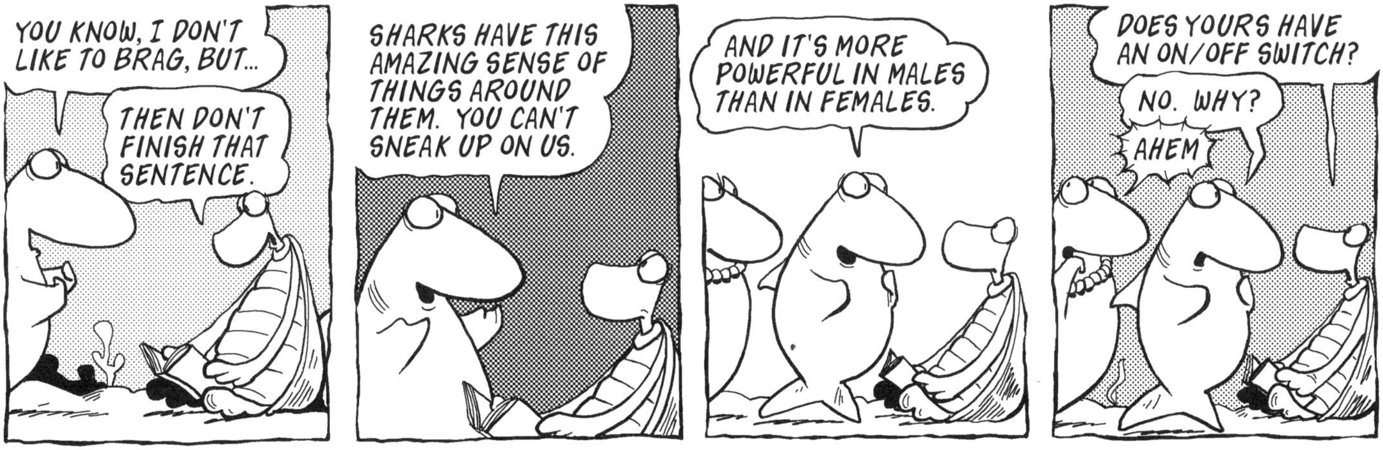
YOU KNOW, I DON'T LIKE TO BRAG, BUT...
THEN DON'T FINISH THAT SENTENCE.
SHARKS HAVE THIS AMAZING SENSE OF THINGS AROUND THEM. YOU CAN'T SNEAK UP ON US.
AND IT'S MORE POWERFUL IN MALES THAN IN FEMALES.
DOES YOURS HAVE AN ON/OFF SWITCH?
NO. WHY?
AHEM

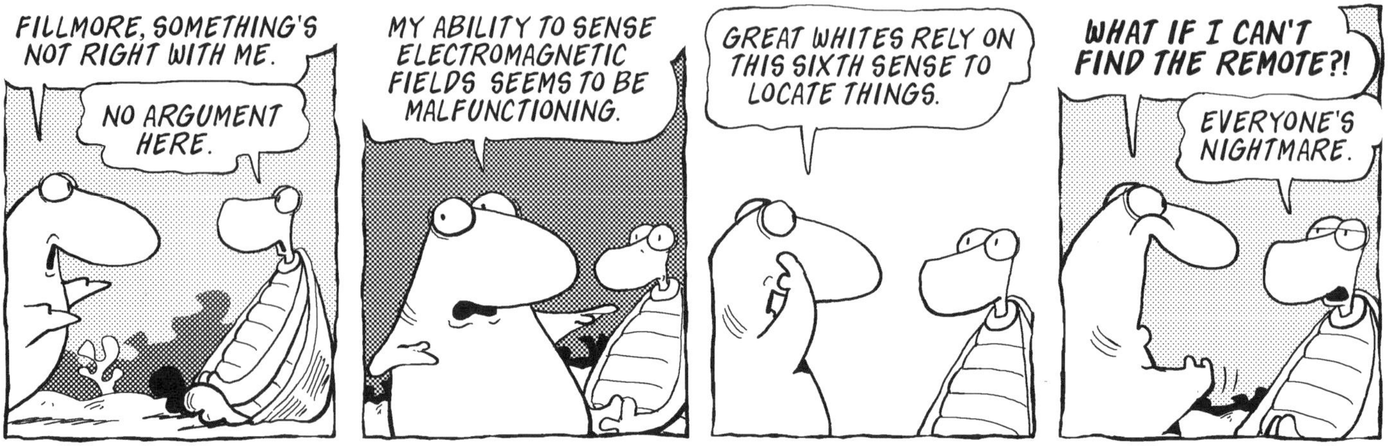
FILLMORE, SOMETHING'S NOT RIGHT WITH ME.
NO ARGUMENT HERE.
MY ABILITY TO SENSE ELECTROMAGNETIC FIELDS SEEMS TO BE MALFUNCTIONING.
GREAT WHITES RELY ON THIS SIXTH SENSE TO LOCATE THINGS.
WHAT IF I CAN'T FIND THE REMOTE?!
EVERYONE'S NIGHTMARE.

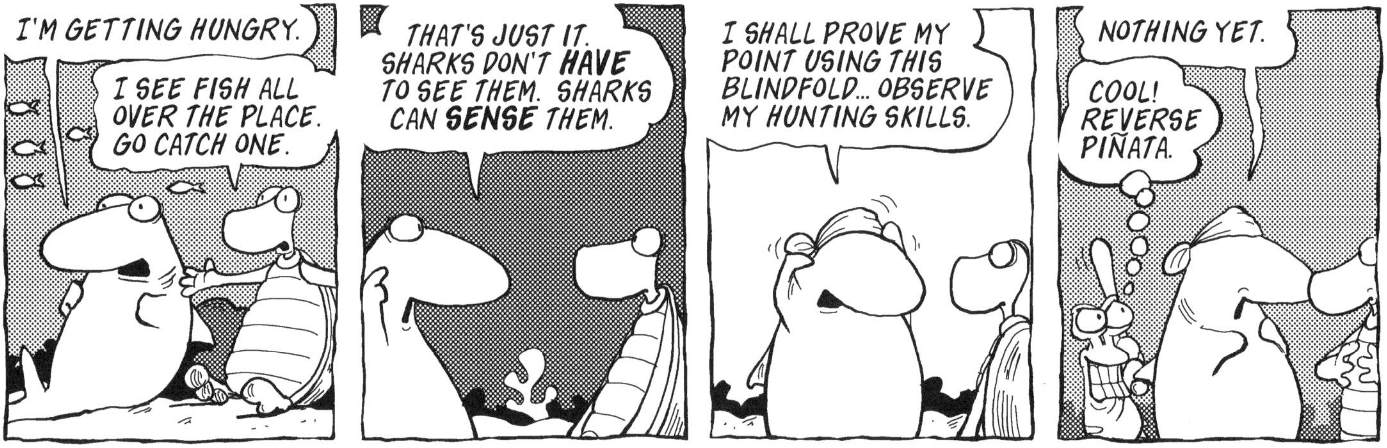
I'M GETTING HUNGRY.
I SEE FISH ALL OVER THE PLACE. GO CATCH ONE.
THAT'S JUST IT. SHARKS DON'T HAVE TO SEE THEM. SHARKS CAN SENSE THEM.
I SHALL PROVE MY POINT USING THIS BLINDFOLD... OBSERVE MY HUNTING SKILLS.
NOTHING YET.
COOL! REVERSE PIÑATA.

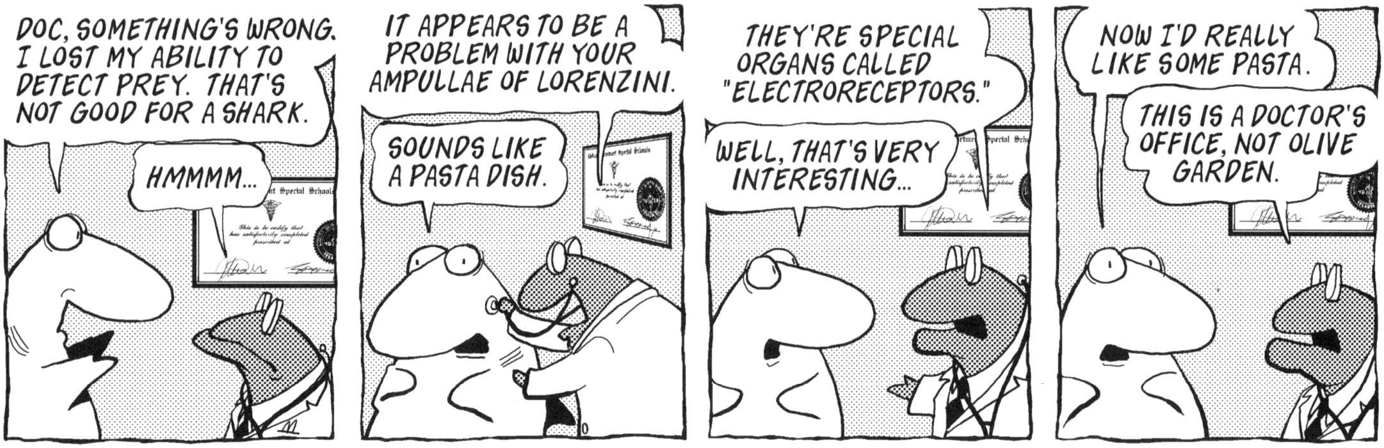
DOC, SOMETHING'S WRONG. I LOST MY ABILITY TO DETECT PREY. THAT'S NOT GOOD FOR A SHARK.
HMMMM...
IT APPEARS TO BE A PROBLEM WITH YOUR AMPULLAE OF LORENZINI.
SOUNDS LIKE A PASTA DISH.
THEY'RE SPECIAL ORGANS CALLED "ELECTRORECEPTORS."
WELL, THAT'S VERY INTERESTING...
NOW I'D REALLY LIKE SOME PASTA.
THIS IS A DOCTOR'S OFFICE, NOT OLIVE GARDEN.

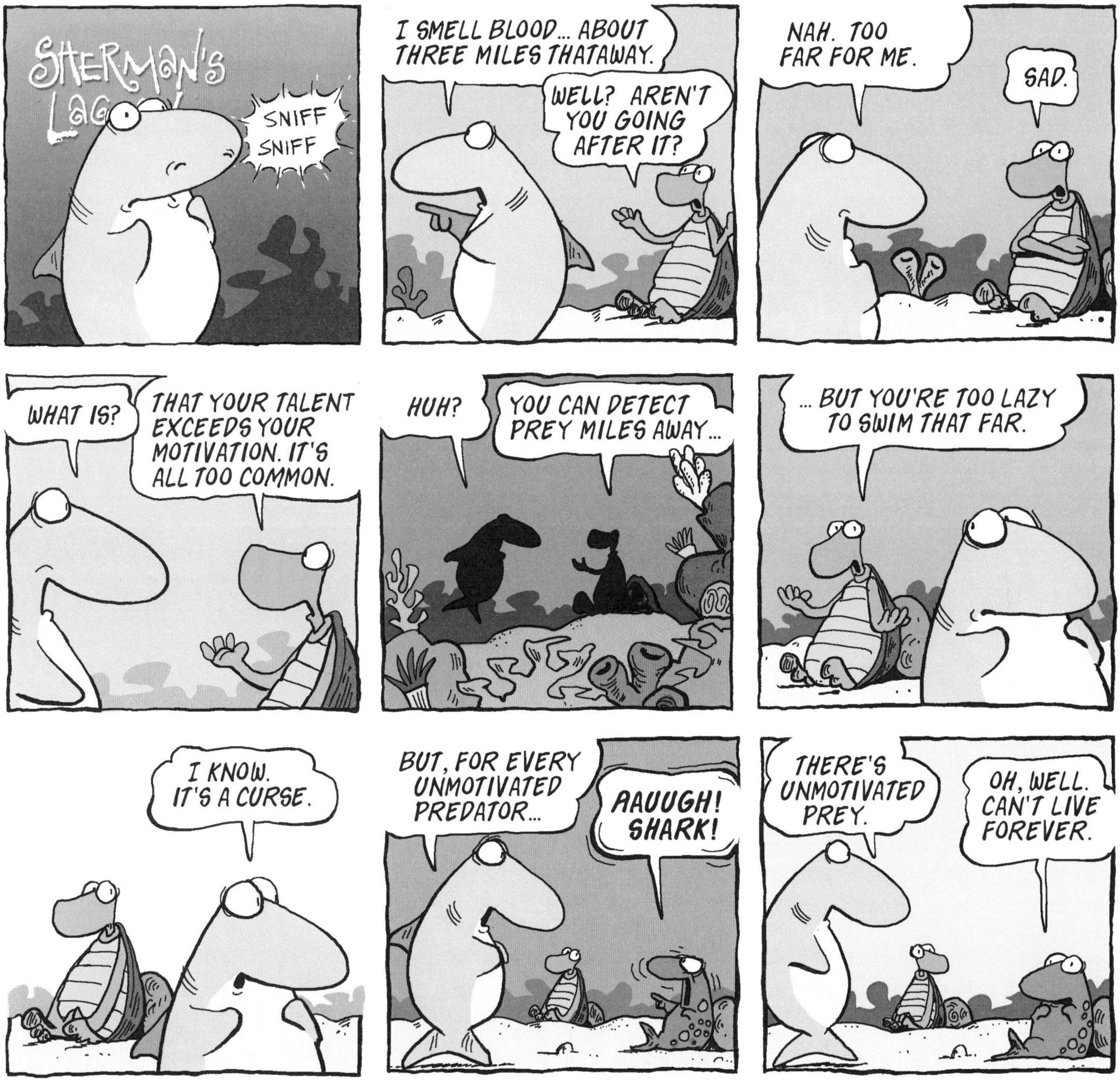
SHERMAN'S LAGOON
SNIFF SNIFF
I SMELL BLOOD... ABOUT THREE MILES THATAWAY.
WELL? AREN'T YOU GOING AFTER IT?
NAH. TOO FAR FOR ME.
SAD.
WHAT IS?
THAT YOUR TALENT EXCEEDS YOUR MOTIVATION. IT'S ALL TOO COMMON.
HUH?
YOU CAN DETECT PREY MILES AWAY...
... BUT YOU'RE TOO LAZY TO SWIM THAT FAR.
I KNOW. IT'S A CURSE.
BUT, FOR EVERY UNMOTIVATED PREDATOR...
AAUUGH! SHARK!
THERE'S UNMOTIVATED PREY.
OH, WELL. CAN'T LIVE FOREVER.

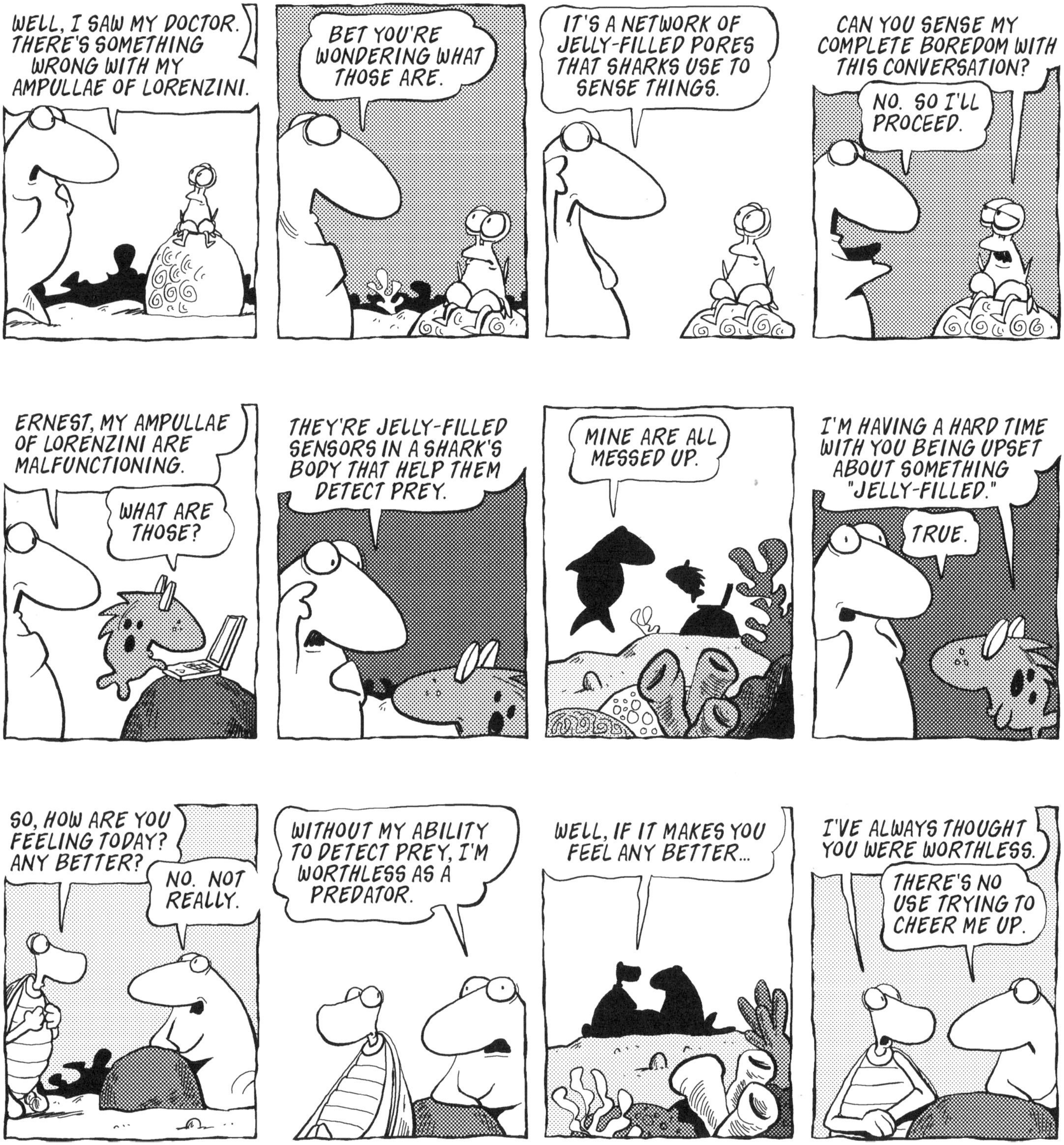
WELL, I SAW MY DOCTOR. THERE'S SOMETHING WRONG WITH MY AMPULLAE OF LORENZINI.
BET YOU'RE WONDERING WHAT THOSE ARE.
IT'S A NETWORK OF JELLY-FILLED PORES THAT SHARKS USE TO SENSE THINGS.
CAN YOU SENSE MY COMPLETE BOREDOM WITH THIS CONVERSATION?
NO. SO I'LL PROCEED.
ERNEST, MY AMPULLAE OF LORENZINI ARE MALFUNCTIONING.
WHAT ARE THOSE?
THEY'RE JELLY-FILLED SENSORS IN A SHARK'S BODY THAT HELP THEM DETECT PREY.
MINE ARE ALL MESSED UP.
I'M HAVING A HARD TIME WITH YOU BEING UPSET ABOUT SOMETHING "JELLY-FILLED."
TRUE.
SO, HOW ARE YOU FEELING TODAY? ANY BETTER?
NO. NOT REALLY.
WITHOUT MY ABILITY TO DETECT PREY, I'M WORTHLESS AS A PREDATOR.
WELL, IF IT MAKES YOU FEEL ANY BETTER...
I'VE ALWAYS THOUGHT YOU WERE WORTHLESS.
THERE'S NO USE TRYING TO CHEER ME UP.

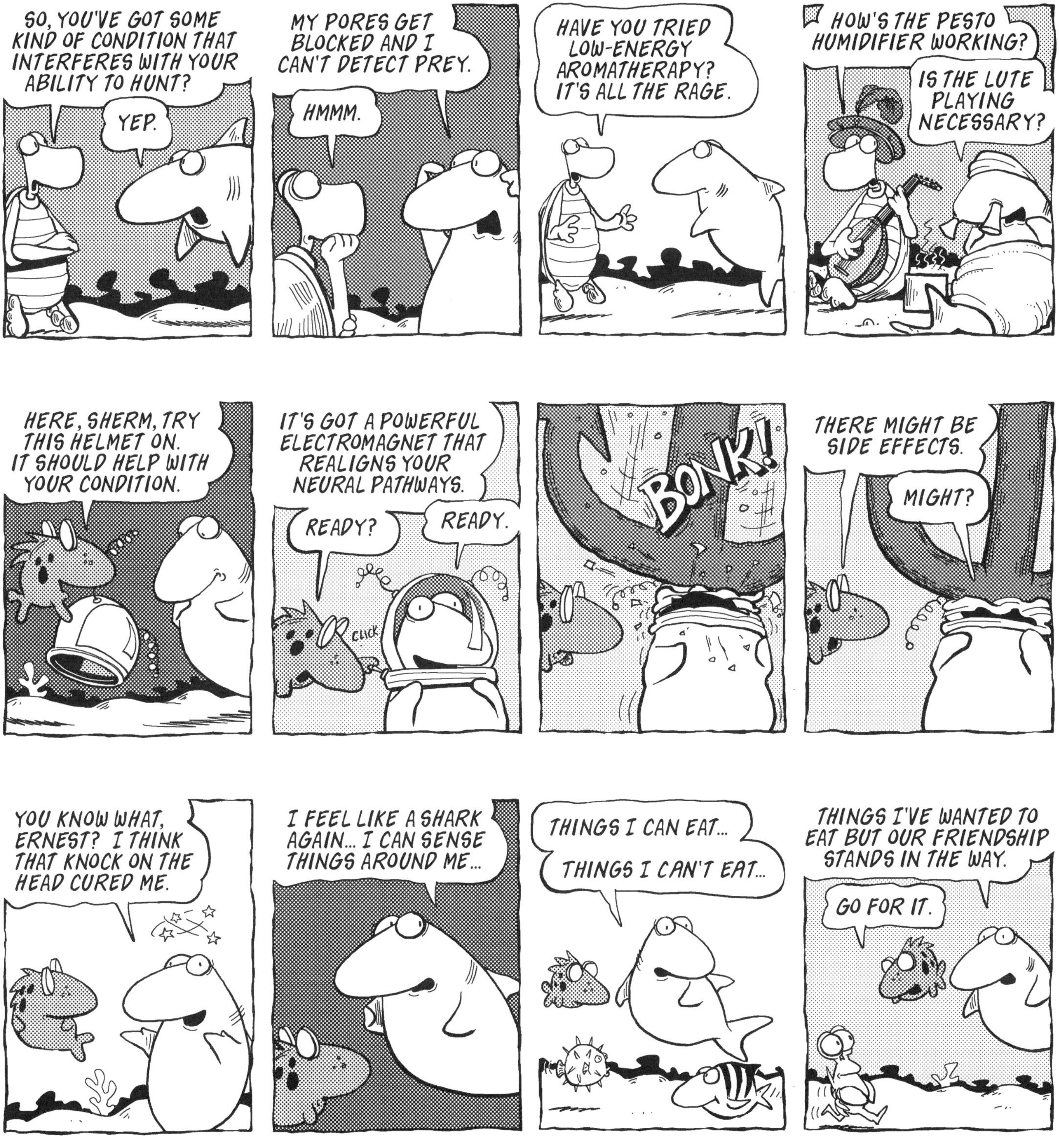
SO, YOU'VE GOT SOME KIND OF CONDITION THAT INTERFERES WITH YOUR ABILITY TO HUNT?
YEP.
MY PORES GET BLOCKED AND I CAN'T DETECT PREY.
HMMM.
HAVE YOU TRIED LOW-ENERGY AROMATHERAPY? IT'S ALL THE RAGE.
HOW'S THE PESTO HUMIDIFIER WORKING?
IS THE LUTE PLAYING NECESSARY?
HERE, SHERM, TRY THIS HELMET ON. IT SHOULD HELP WITH YOUR CONDITION.
IT'S GOT A POWERFUL ELECTROMAGNET THAT REALIGNS YOUR NEURAL PATHWAYS.
READY?
READY.
CLICK
BONK!
THERE MIGHT BE SIDE EFFECTS.
MIGHT?
YOU KNOW WHAT, ERNEST? I THINK THAT KNOCK ON THE HEAD CURED ME.
I FEEL LIKE A SHARK AGAIN... I CAN SENSE THINGS AROUND ME...
THINGS I CAN EAT...
THINGS I CAN'T EAT...
THINGS I'VE WANTED TO EAT BUT OUR FRIENDSHIP STANDS IN THE WAY.
GO FOR IT.

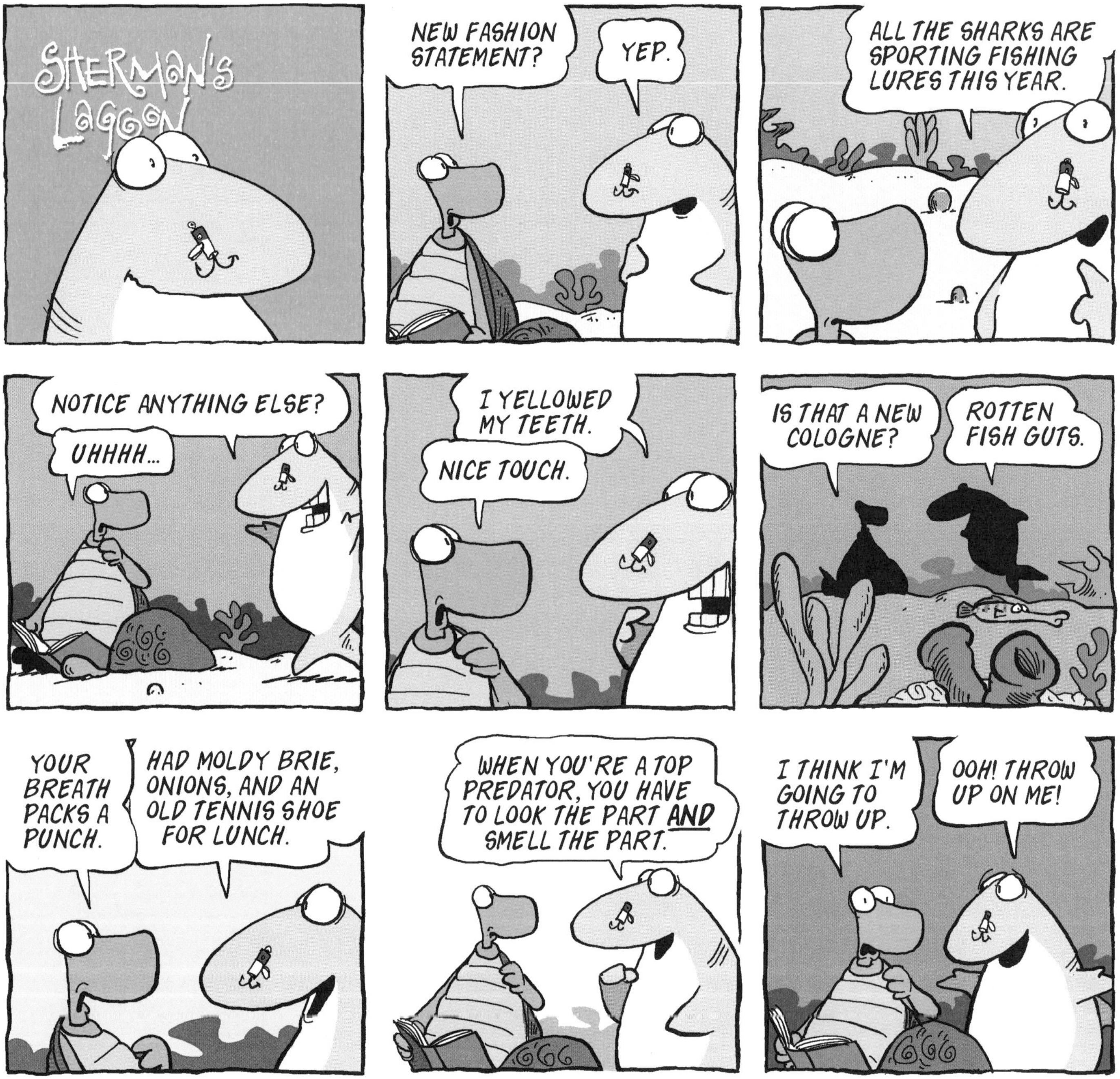
Sherman's Lagoon
NEW FASHION STATEMENT?
YEP.
ALL THE SHARKS ARE SPORTING FISHING LURES THIS YEAR.
NOTICE ANYTHING ELSE?
UHHHH...
I YELLOWED MY TEETH.
NICE TOUCH.
IS THAT A NEW COLOGNE?
ROTTEN FISH GUTS.
YOUR BREATH PACKS A PUNCH.
HAD MOLDY BRIE, ONIONS, AND AN OLD TENNIS SHOE FOR LUNCH.
WHEN YOU'RE A TOP PREDATOR, YOU HAVE TO LOOK THE PART AND SMELL THE PART.
I THINK I'M GOING TO THROW UP.
OOH! THROW UP ON ME!

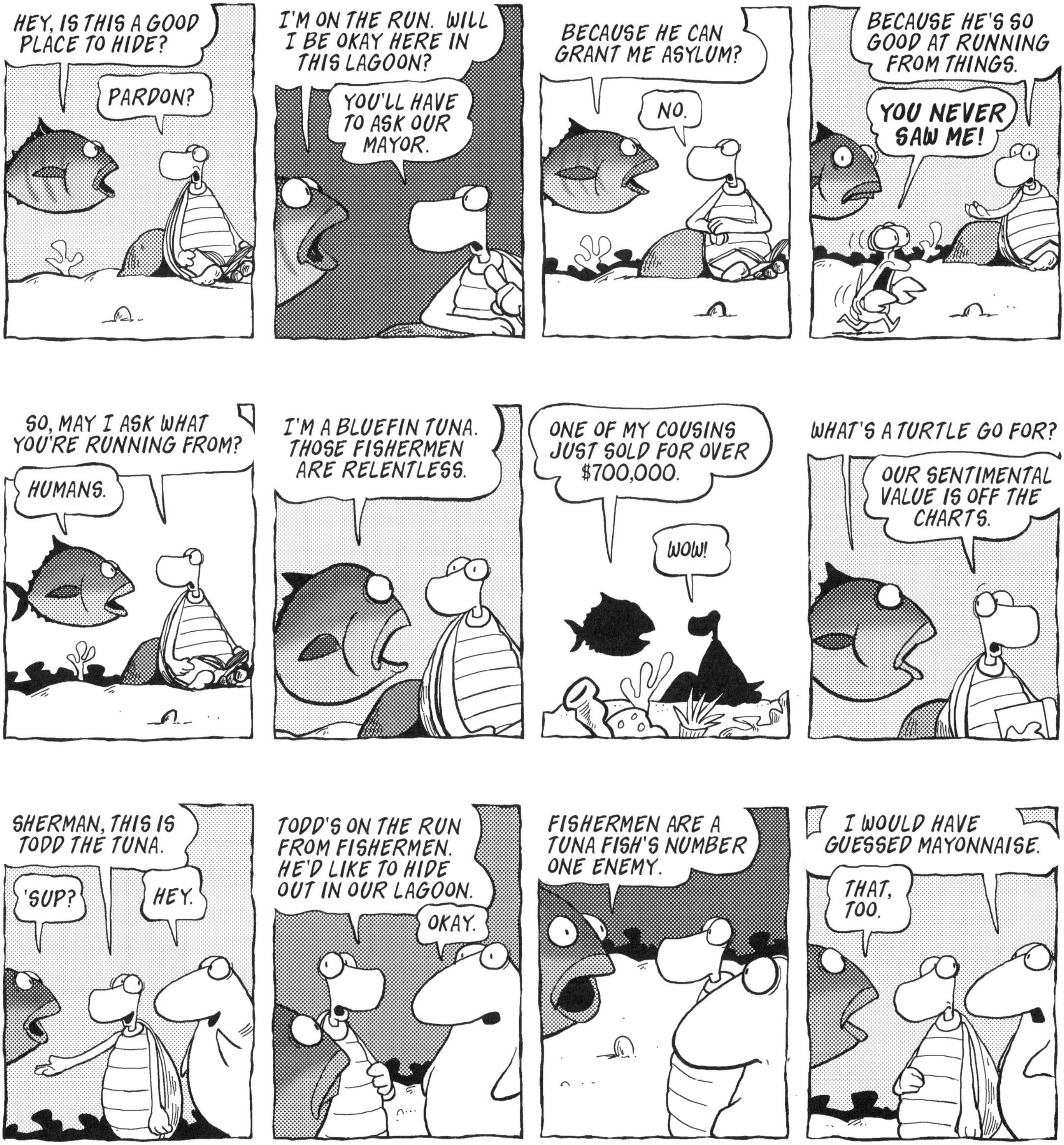
HEY, IS THIS A GOOD PLACE TO HIDE?
PARDON?
I'M ON THE RUN. WILL I BE OKAY HERE IN THIS LAGOON?
YOU'LL HAVE TO ASK OUR MAYOR.
BECAUSE HE CAN GRANT ME ASYLUM?
NO.
BECAUSE HE'S SO GOOD AT RUNNING FROM THINGS.
YOU NEVER SAW ME!
SO, MAY I ASK WHAT YOU'RE RUNNING FROM?
HUMANS.
I'M A BLUEFIN TUNA. THOSE FISHERMEN ARE RELENTLESS.
ONE OF MY COUSINS JUST SOLD FOR OVER $700,000.
WOW!
WHAT'S A TURTLE GO FOR?
OUR SENTIMENTAL VALUE IS OFF THE CHARTS.
SHERMAN, THIS IS TODD THE TUNA.
'SUP?
HEY.
TODD'S ON THE RUN FROM FISHERMEN. HE'D LIKE TO HIDE OUT IN OUR LAGOON.
OKAY.
FISHERMEN ARE A TUNA FISH'S NUMBER ONE ENEMY.
I WOULD HAVE GUESSED MAYONNAISE.
THAT, TOO.

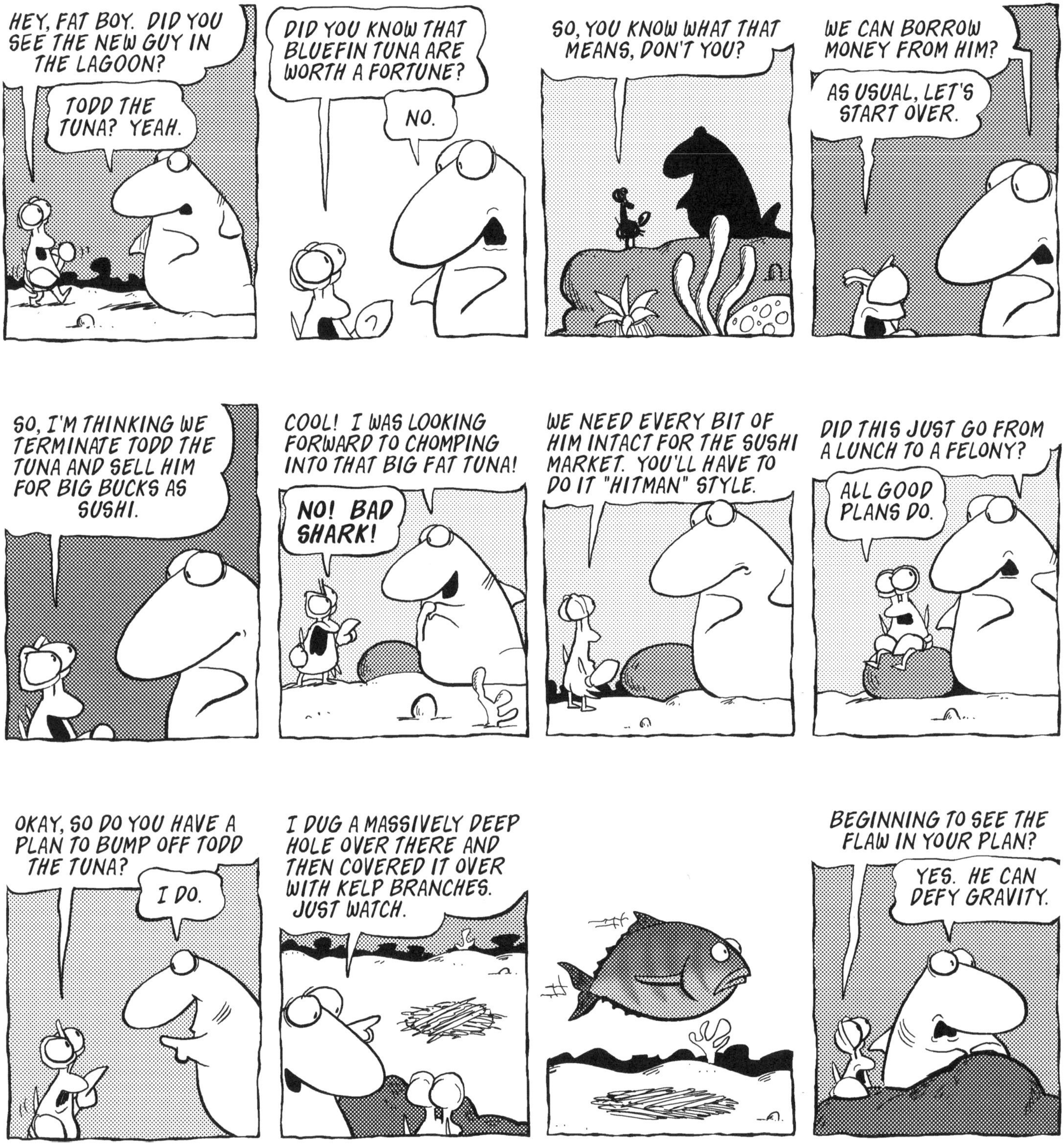
HEY, FAT BOY. DID YOU SEE THE NEW GUY IN THE LAGOON?
TODD THE TUNA? YEAH.
DID YOU KNOW THAT BLUEFIN TUNA ARE WORTH A FORTUNE?
NO.
SO, YOU KNOW WHAT THAT MEANS, DON'T YOU?
WE CAN BORROW MONEY FROM HIM?
AS USUAL, LET'S START OVER.
SO, I'M THINKING WE TERMINATE TODD THE TUNA AND SELL HIM FOR BIG BUCKS AS SUSHI.
COOL! I WAS LOOKING FORWARD TO CHOMPING INTO THAT BIG FAT TUNA!
NO! BAD SHARK!
WE NEED EVERY BIT OF HIM INTACT FOR THE SUSHI MARKET. YOU'LL HAVE TO DO IT "HITMAN" STYLE.
DID THIS JUST GO FROM A LUNCH TO A FELONY?
ALL GOOD PLANS DO.
OKAY, SO DO YOU HAVE A PLAN TO BUMP OFF TODD THE TUNA?
I DO.
I DUG A MASSIVELY DEEP HOLE OVER THERE AND THEN COVERED IT OVER WITH KELP BRANCHES. JUST WATCH.
BEGINNING TO SEE THE FLAW IN YOUR PLAN?
YES. HE CAN DEFY GRAVITY.

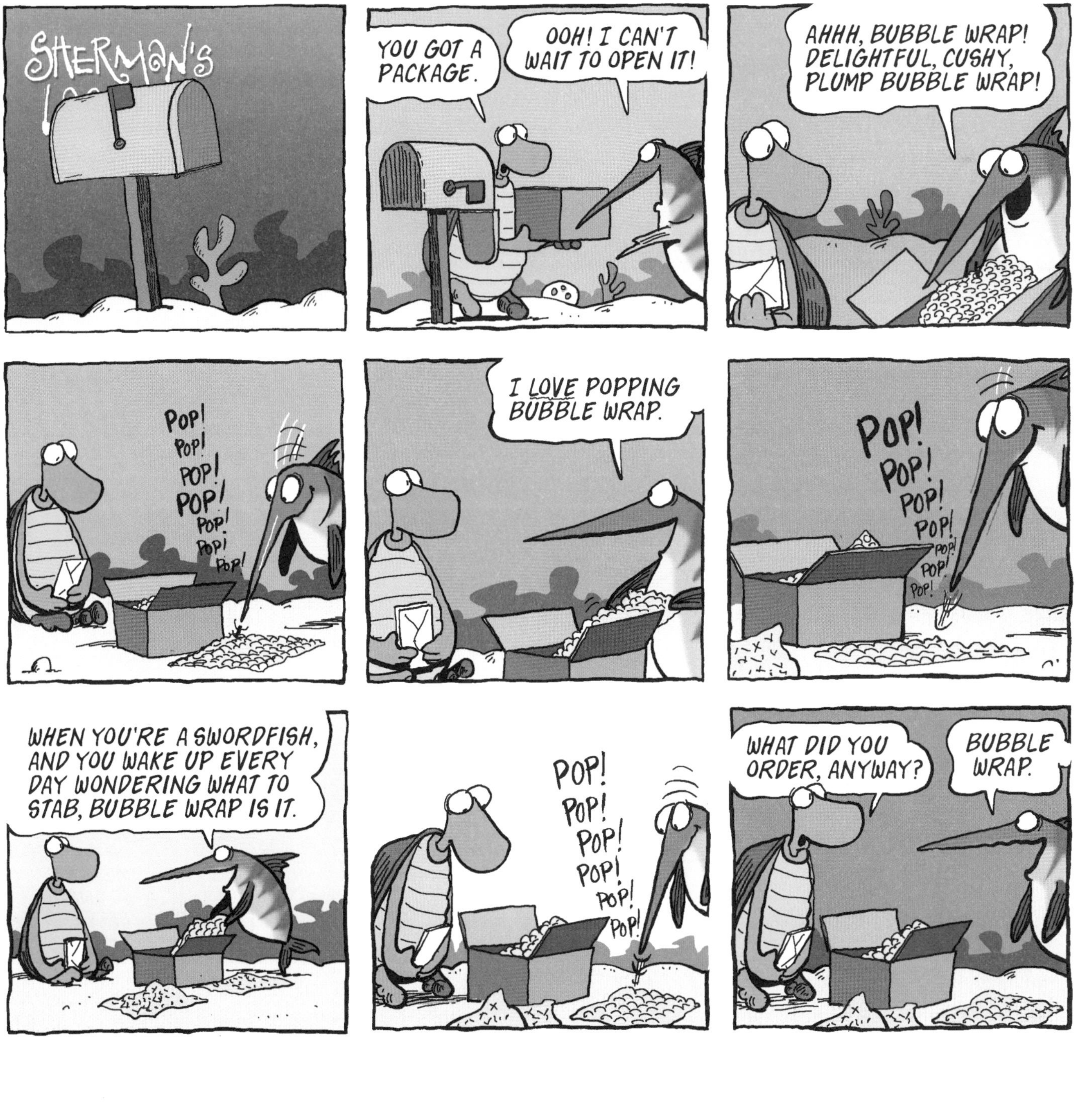
SHERMAN'S
YOU GOT A PACKAGE.
OOH! I CAN'T WAIT TO OPEN IT!
AHHH, BUBBLE WRAP! DELIGHTFUL, CUSHY, PLUMP BUBBLE WRAP!
POP! POP! POP! POP! POP! POP! POP!
I LOVE POPPING BUBBLE WRAP.
POP! POP! POP! POP! POP! POP! POP!
WHEN YOU'RE A SWORDFISH, AND YOU WAKE UP EVERY DAY WONDERING WHAT TO STAB, BUBBLE WRAP IS IT.
POP! POP! POP! POP! POP! POP!
WHAT DID YOU ORDER, ANYWAY?
BUBBLE WRAP.

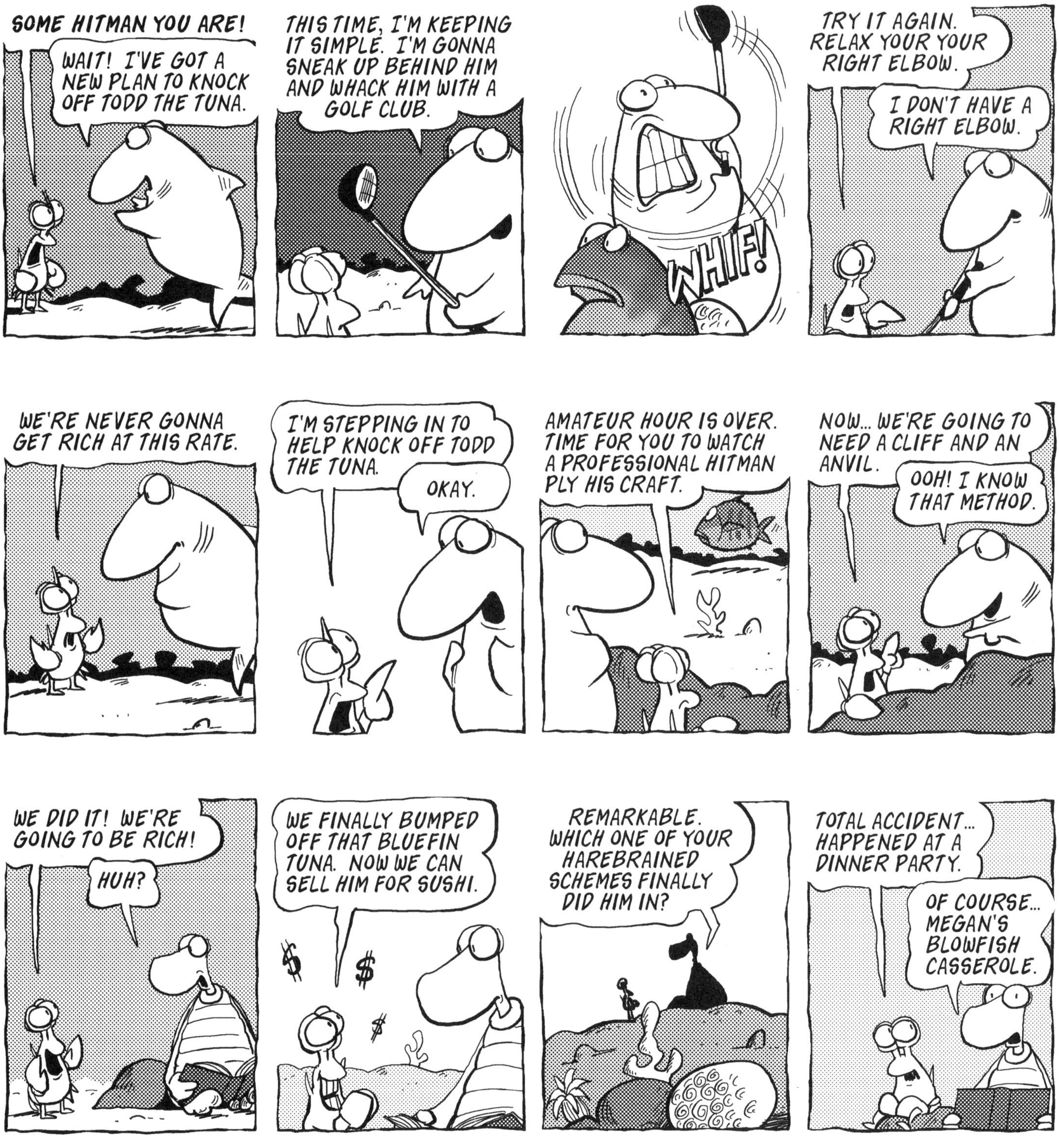
SOME HITMAN YOU ARE!
WAIT! I'VE GOT A NEW PLAN TO KNOCK OFF TODD THE TUNA.
THIS TIME, I'M KEEPING IT SIMPLE. I'M GONNA SNEAK UP BEHIND HIM AND WHACK HIM WITH A GOLF CLUB.
WHIF!
TRY IT AGAIN. RELAX YOUR YOUR RIGHT ELBOW.
I DON'T HAVE A RIGHT ELBOW.
WE'RE NEVER GONNA GET RICH AT THIS RATE.
I'M STEPPING IN TO HELP KNOCK OFF TODD THE TUNA.
OKAY.
AMATEUR HOUR IS OVER. TIME FOR YOU TO WATCH A PROFESSIONAL HITMAN PLY HIS CRAFT.
NOW... WE'RE GOING TO NEED A CLIFF AND AN ANVIL.
OOH! I KNOW THAT METHOD.
WE DID IT! WE'RE GOING TO BE RICH!
HUH?
WE FINALLY BUMPED OFF THAT BLUEFIN TUNA. NOW WE CAN SELL HIM FOR SUSHI.
REMARKABLE. WHICH ONE OF YOUR HAREBRAINED SCHEMES FINALLY DID HIM IN?
TOTAL ACCIDENT... HAPPENED AT A DINNER PARTY.
OF COURSE... MEGAN'S BLOWFISH CASSEROLE.

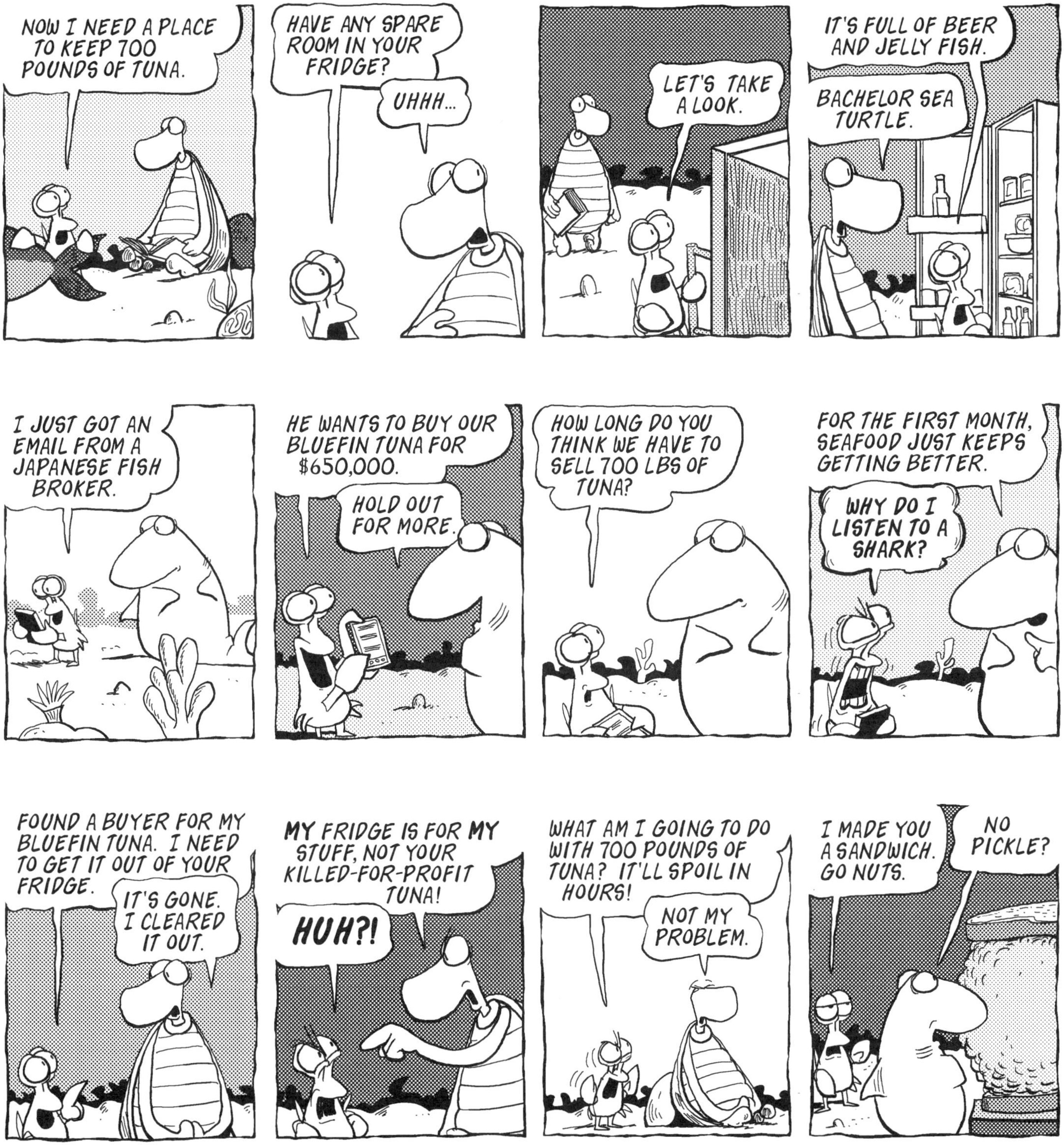
NOW I NEED A PLACE TO KEEP 700 POUNDS OF TUNA.
HAVE ANY SPARE ROOM IN YOUR FRIDGE?
UHHH...
LET'S TAKE A LOOK.
IT'S FULL OF BEER AND JELLY FISH.
BACHELOR SEA TURTLE.
I JUST GOT AN EMAIL FROM A JAPANESE FISH BROKER.
HE WANTS TO BUY OUR BLUEFIN TUNA FOR $650,000.
HOLD OUT FOR MORE.
HOW LONG DO YOU THINK WE HAVE TO SELL 700 LBS OF TUNA?
FOR THE FIRST MONTH, SEAFOOD JUST KEEPS GETTING BETTER.
WHY DO I LISTEN TO A SHARK?
FOUND A BUYER FOR MY BLUEFIN TUNA. I NEED TO GET IT OUT OF YOUR FRIDGE.
IT'S GONE. I CLEARED IT OUT.
MY FRIDGE IS FOR MY STUFF, NOT YOUR KILLED-FOR-PROFIT TUNA!
HUH?!
WHAT AM I GOING TO DO WITH 700 POUNDS OF TUNA? IT'LL SPOIL IN HOURS!
NOT MY PROBLEM.
I MADE YOU A SANDWICH. GO NUTS.
NO PICKLE?

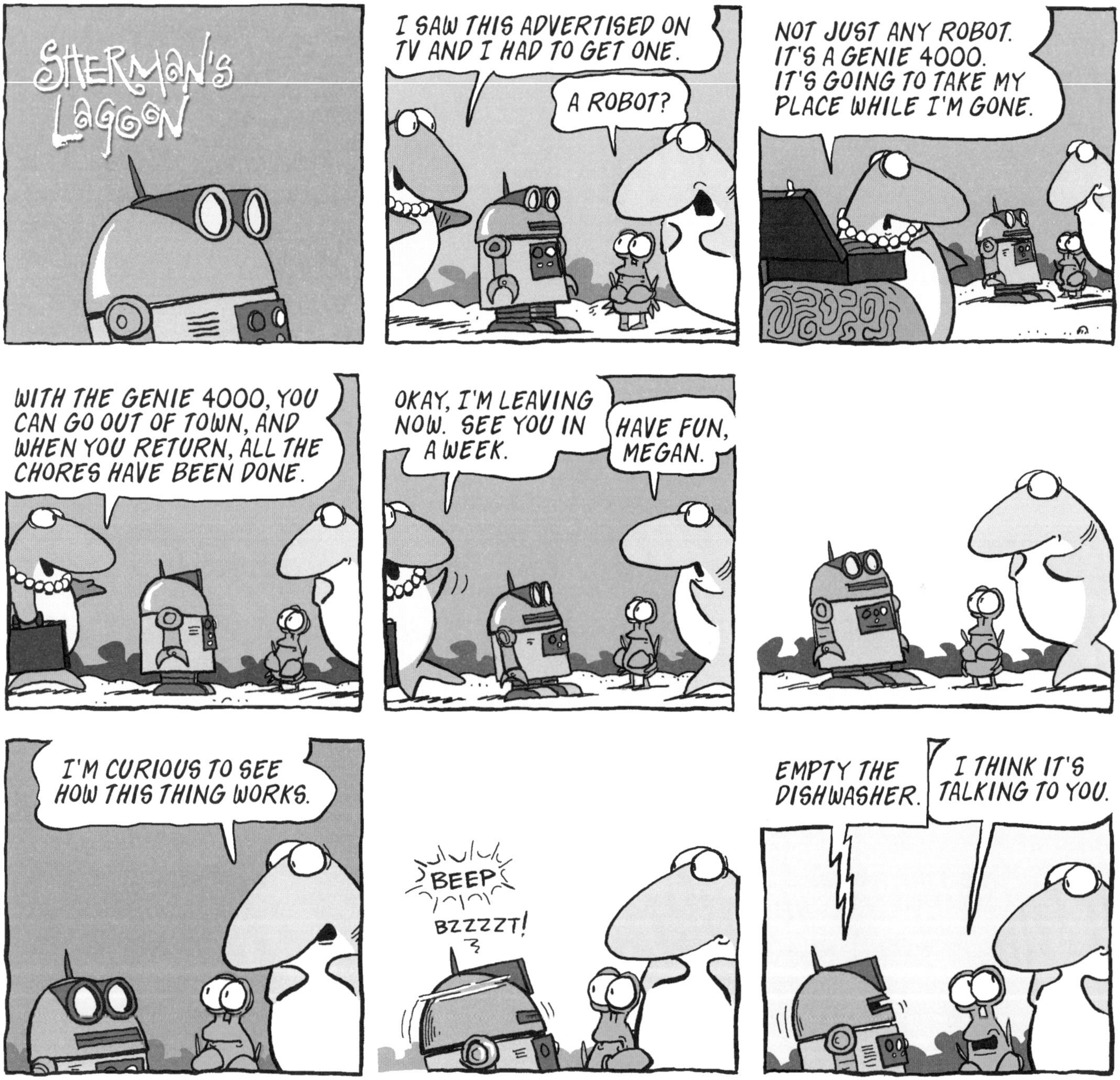
SHERMAN'S LAGOON
I SAW THIS ADVERTISED ON TV AND I HAD TO GET ONE.
A ROBOT?
NOT JUST ANY ROBOT. IT'S A GENIE 4000. IT'S GOING TO TAKE MY PLACE WHILE I'M GONE.
WITH THE GENIE 4000, YOU CAN GO OUT OF TOWN, AND WHEN YOU RETURN, ALL THE CHORES HAVE BEEN DONE.
OKAY, I'M LEAVING NOW. SEE YOU IN A WEEK.
HAVE FUN, MEGAN.
I'M CURIOUS TO SEE HOW THIS THING WORKS.
BEEP
BZZZZT!
EMPTY THE DISHWASHER.
I THINK IT'S TALKING TO YOU.

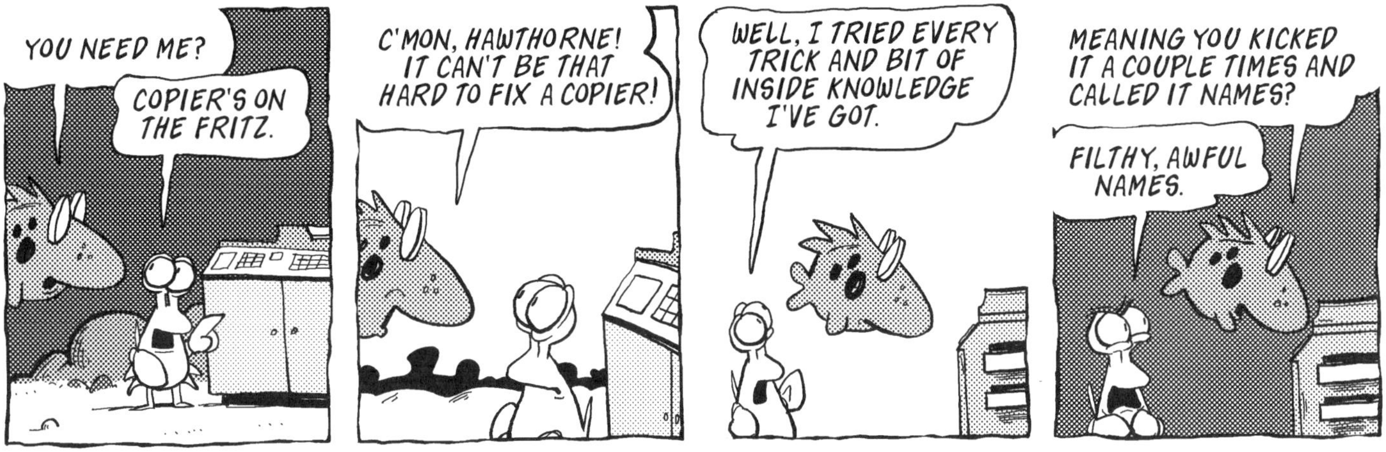
YOU NEED ME?
COPIER'S ON THE FRITZ.
C'MON, HAWTHORNE! IT CAN'T BE THAT HARD TO FIX A COPIER!
WELL, I TRIED EVERY TRICK AND BIT OF INSIDE KNOWLEDGE I'VE GOT.
MEANING YOU KICKED IT A COUPLE TIMES AND CALLED IT NAMES?
FILTHY, AWFUL NAMES.

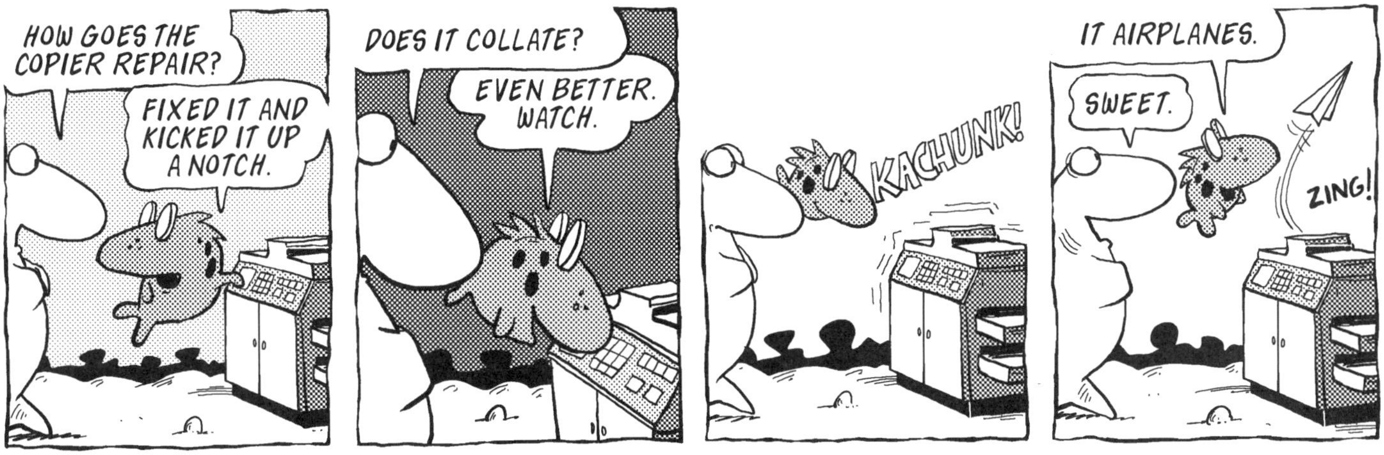
HOW GOES THE COPIER REPAIR?
FIXED IT AND KICKED IT UP A NOTCH.
DOES IT COLLATE?
EVEN BETTER. WATCH.
KACHUNK!
IT AIRPLANES.
SWEET.
ZING!

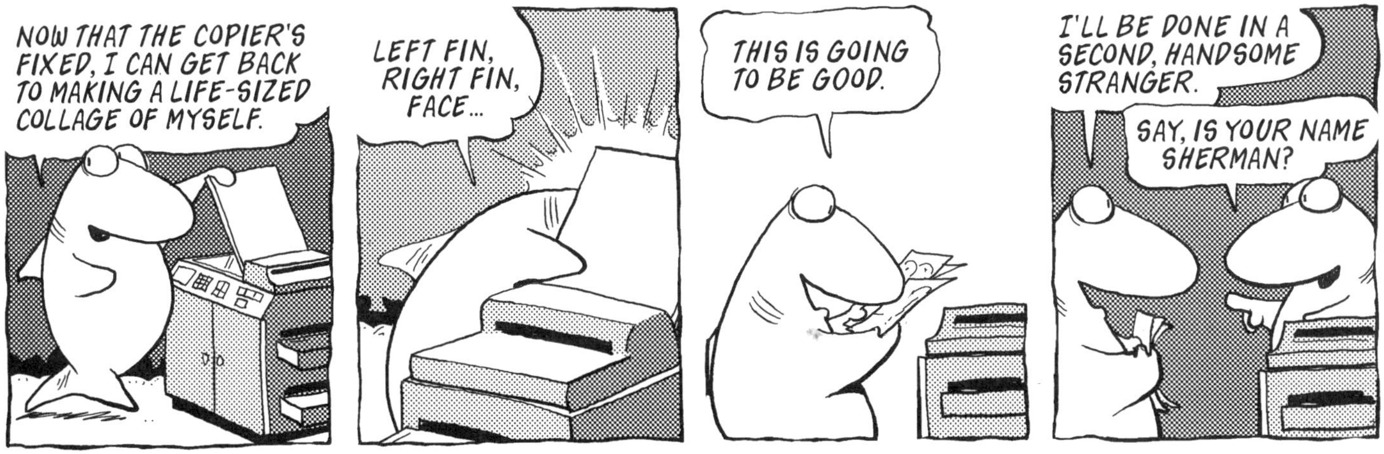
NOW THAT THE COPIER'S FIXED, I CAN GET BACK TO MAKING A LIFE-SIZED COLLAGE OF MYSELF.
LEFT FIN, RIGHT FIN, FACE...
THIS IS GOING TO BE GOOD.
I'LL BE DONE IN A SECOND, HANDSOME STRANGER.
SAY, IS YOUR NAME SHERMAN?

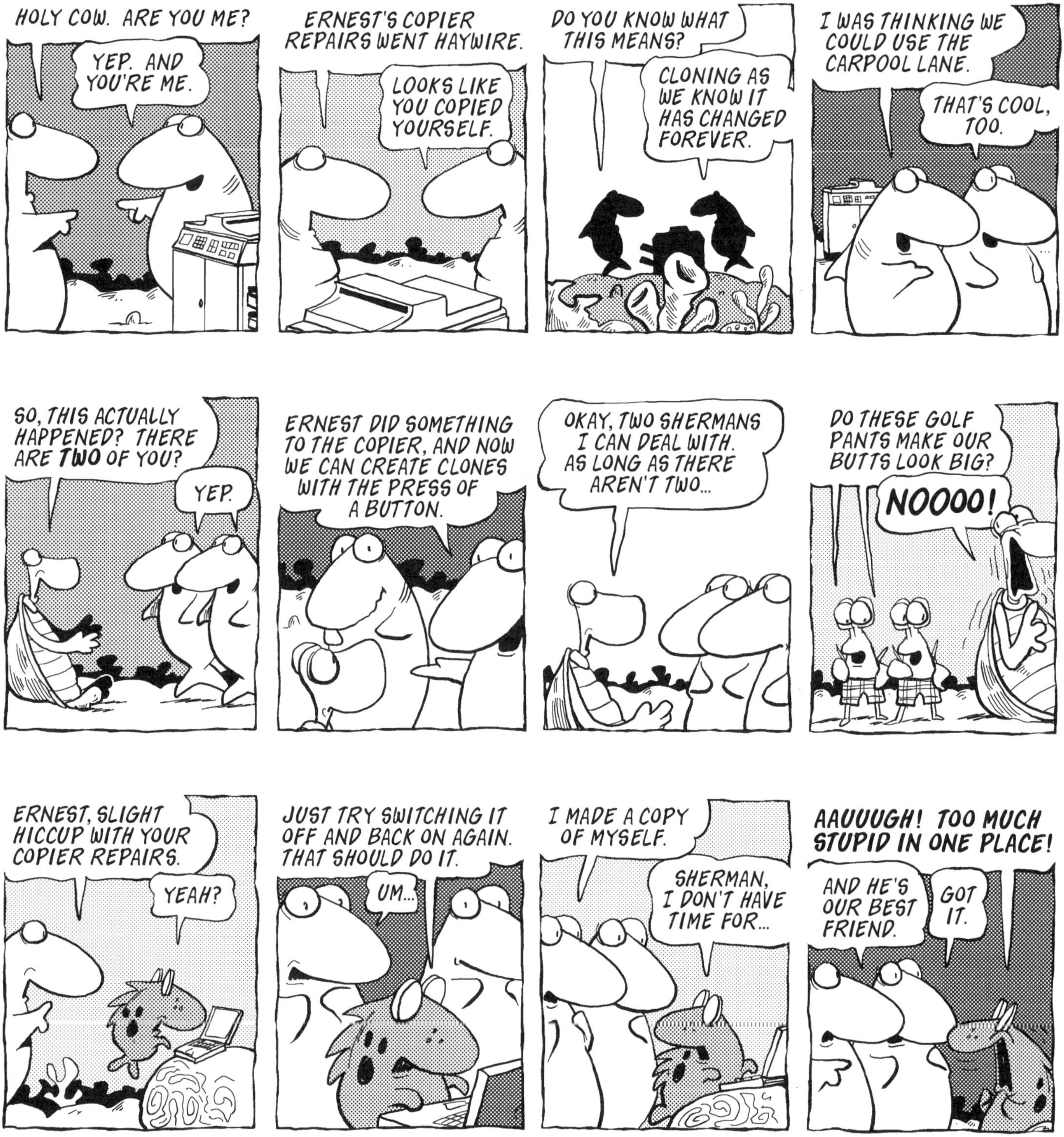
HOLY COW. ARE YOU ME?
YEP. AND YOU'RE ME.
ERNEST'S COPIER REPAIRS WENT HAYWIRE.
LOOKS LIKE YOU COPIED YOURSELF.
DO YOU KNOW WHAT THIS MEANS?
CLONING AS WE KNOW IT HAS CHANGED FOREVER.
I WAS THINKING WE COULD USE THE CARPOOL LANE.
THAT'S COOL, TOO.
SO, THIS ACTUALLY HAPPENED? THERE ARE **TWO** OF YOU?
YEP.
ERNEST DID SOMETHING TO THE COPIER, AND NOW WE CAN CREATE CLONES WITH THE PRESS OF A BUTTON.
OKAY, TWO SHERMANS I CAN DEAL WITH. AS LONG AS THERE AREN'T TWO...
DO THESE GOLF PANTS MAKE OUR BUTTS LOOK BIG?
NOOOO!
ERNEST, SLIGHT HICCUP WITH YOUR COPIER REPAIRS.
YEAH?
JUST TRY SWITCHING IT OFF AND BACK ON AGAIN. THAT SHOULD DO IT.
UM...
I MADE A COPY OF MYSELF.
SHERMAN, I DON'T HAVE TIME FOR...
AAUUUGH! TOO MUCH STUPID IN ONE PLACE!
AND HE'S OUR BEST FRIEND.
GOT IT.

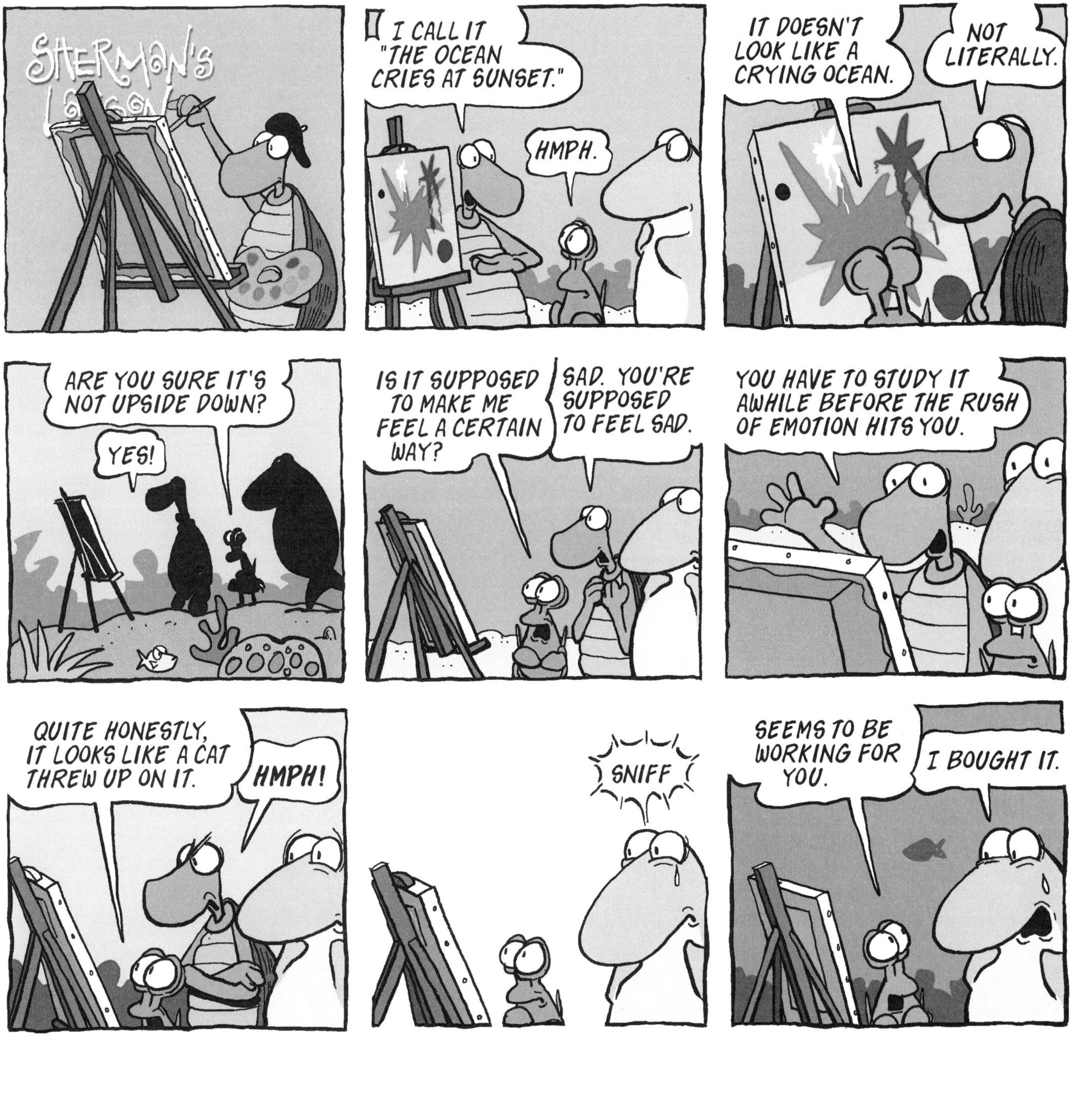
SHERMAN'S
I CALL IT "THE OCEAN CRIES AT SUNSET."
HMPH.
IT DOESN'T LOOK LIKE A CRYING OCEAN.
NOT LITERALLY.
ARE YOU SURE IT'S NOT UPSIDE DOWN?
YES!
IS IT SUPPOSED TO MAKE ME FEEL A CERTAIN WAY?
SAD. YOU'RE SUPPOSED TO FEEL SAD.
YOU HAVE TO STUDY IT AWHILE BEFORE THE RUSH OF EMOTION HITS YOU.
QUITE HONESTLY, IT LOOKS LIKE A CAT THREW UP ON IT.
HMPH!
SNIFF
SEEMS TO BE WORKING FOR YOU.
I BOUGHT IT.

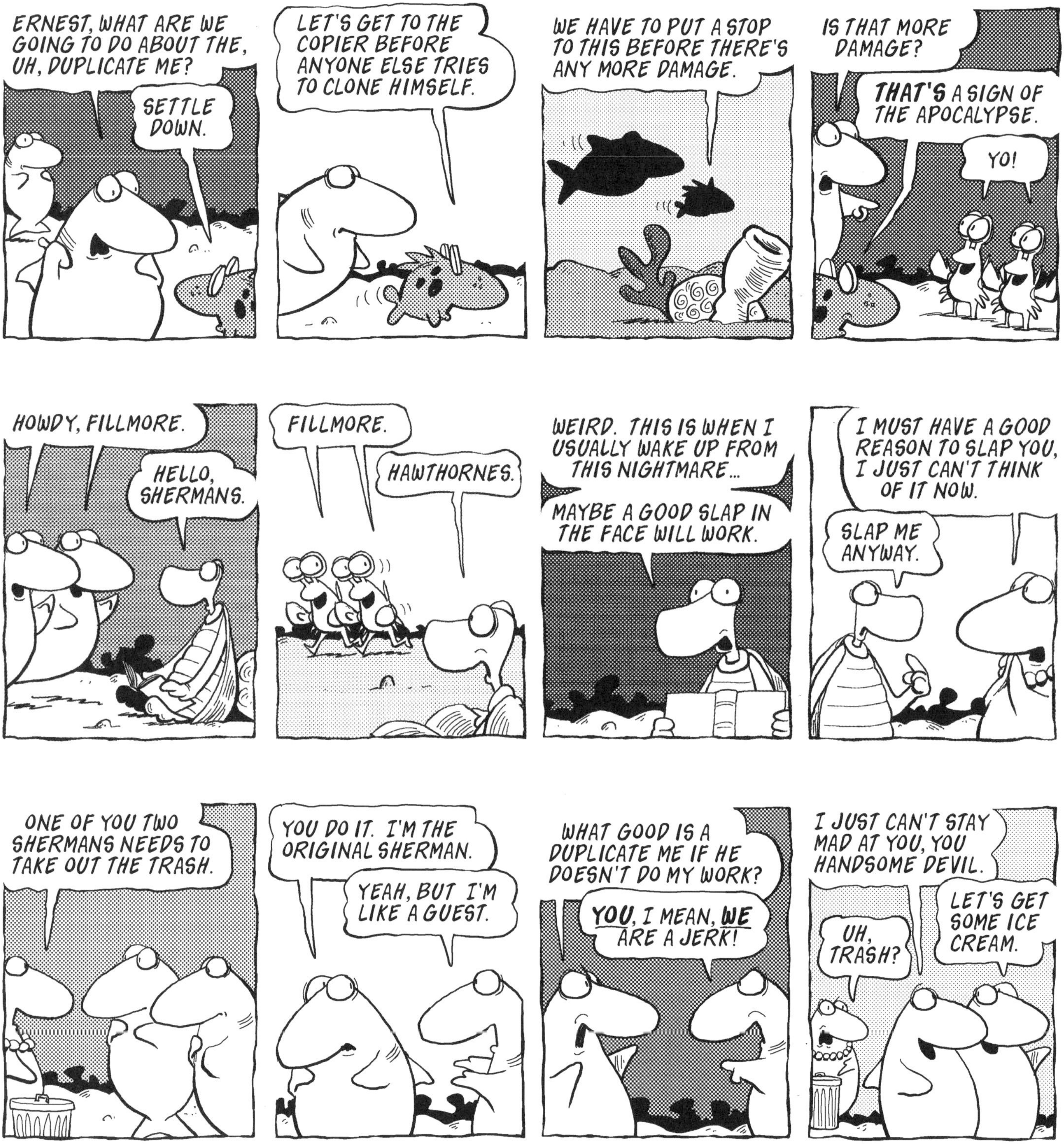
ERNEST, WHAT ARE WE GOING TO DO ABOUT THE, UH, DUPLICATE ME?
SETTLE DOWN.
LET'S GET TO THE COPIER BEFORE ANYONE ELSE TRIES TO CLONE HIMSELF.
WE HAVE TO PUT A STOP TO THIS BEFORE THERE'S ANY MORE DAMAGE.
IS THAT MORE DAMAGE?
THAT'S A SIGN OF THE APOCALYPSE.
YO!
HOWDY, FILLMORE.
HELLO, SHERMANS.
FILLMORE.
HAWTHORNES.
WEIRD. THIS IS WHEN I USUALLY WAKE UP FROM THIS NIGHTMARE...
MAYBE A GOOD SLAP IN THE FACE WILL WORK.
I MUST HAVE A GOOD REASON TO SLAP YOU, I JUST CAN'T THINK OF IT NOW.
SLAP ME ANYWAY.
ONE OF YOU TWO SHERMANS NEEDS TO TAKE OUT THE TRASH.
YOU DO IT. I'M THE ORIGINAL SHERMAN.
YEAH, BUT I'M LIKE A GUEST.
WHAT GOOD IS A DUPLICATE ME IF HE DOESN'T DO MY WORK?
YOU, I MEAN, WE ARE A JERK!
I JUST CAN'T STAY MAD AT YOU, YOU HANDSOME DEVIL.
UH, TRASH?
LET'S GET SOME ICE CREAM.

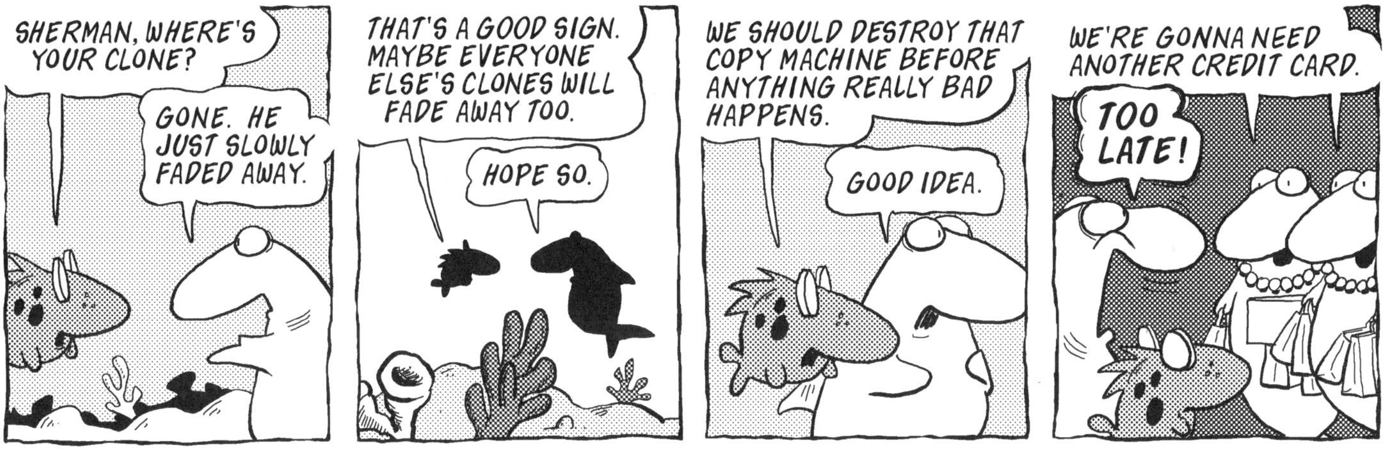
SHERMAN, WHERE'S YOUR CLONE?
GONE. HE JUST SLOWLY FADED AWAY.
THAT'S A GOOD SIGN. MAYBE EVERYONE ELSE'S CLONES WILL FADE AWAY TOO.
HOPE SO.
WE SHOULD DESTROY THAT COPY MACHINE BEFORE ANYTHING REALLY BAD HAPPENS.
GOOD IDEA.
WE'RE GONNA NEED ANOTHER CREDIT CARD.
TOO LATE!

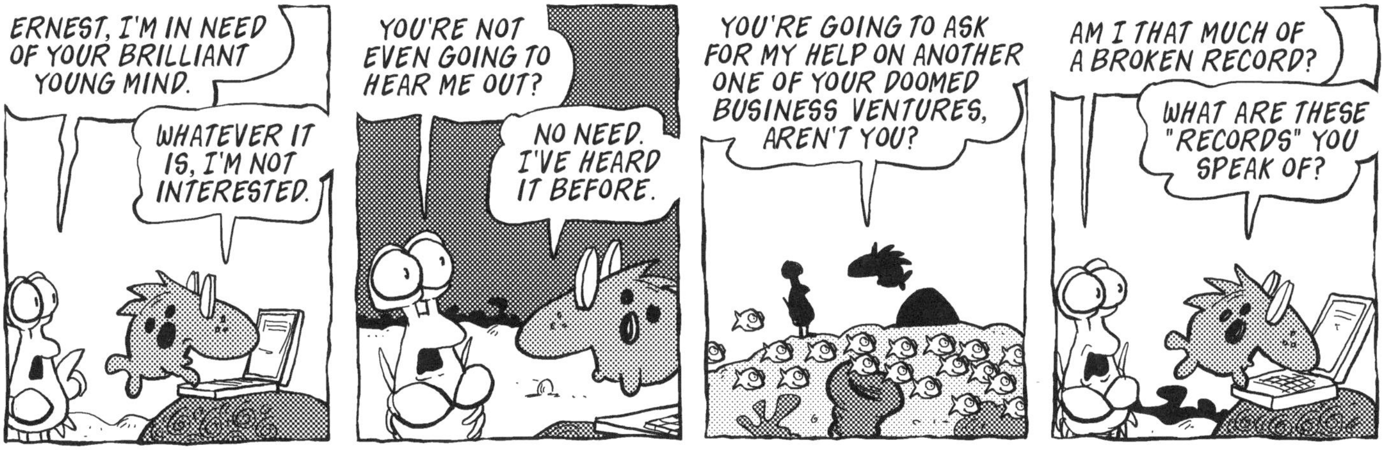
ERNEST, I'M IN NEED OF YOUR BRILLIANT YOUNG MIND.
WHATEVER IT IS, I'M NOT INTERESTED.
YOU'RE NOT EVEN GOING TO HEAR ME OUT?
NO NEED. I'VE HEARD IT BEFORE.
YOU'RE GOING TO ASK FOR MY HELP ON ANOTHER ONE OF YOUR DOOMED BUSINESS VENTURES, AREN'T YOU?
AM I THAT MUCH OF A BROKEN RECORD?
WHAT ARE THESE "RECORDS" YOU SPEAK OF?

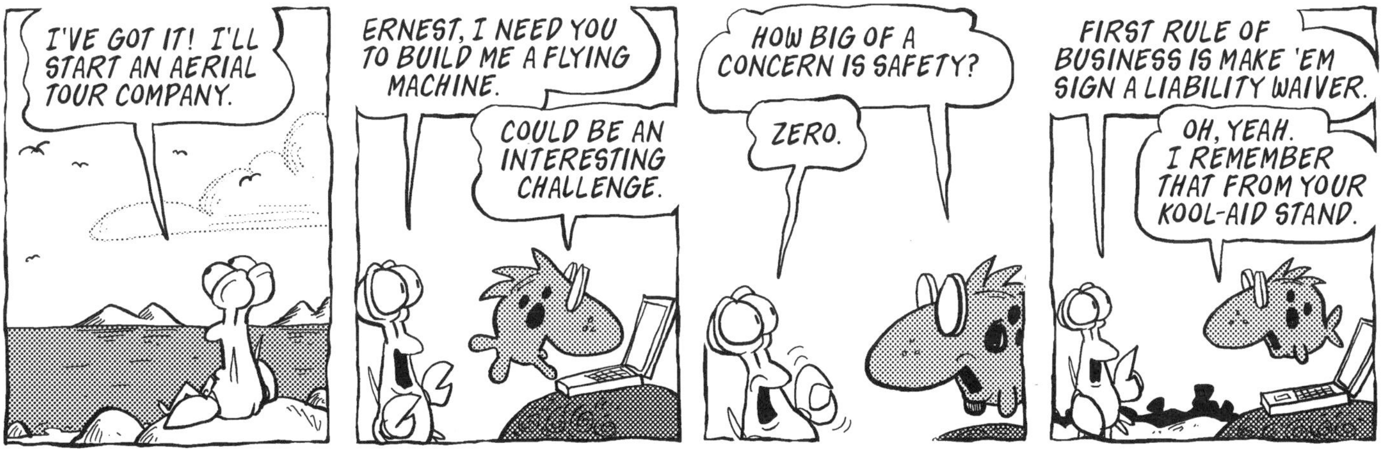
I'VE GOT IT! I'LL START AN AERIAL TOUR COMPANY.
ERNEST, I NEED YOU TO BUILD ME A FLYING MACHINE.
COULD BE AN INTERESTING CHALLENGE.
HOW BIG OF A CONCERN IS SAFETY?
ZERO.
FIRST RULE OF BUSINESS IS MAKE 'EM SIGN A LIABILITY WAIVER.
OH, YEAH. I REMEMBER THAT FROM YOUR KOOL-AID STAND.

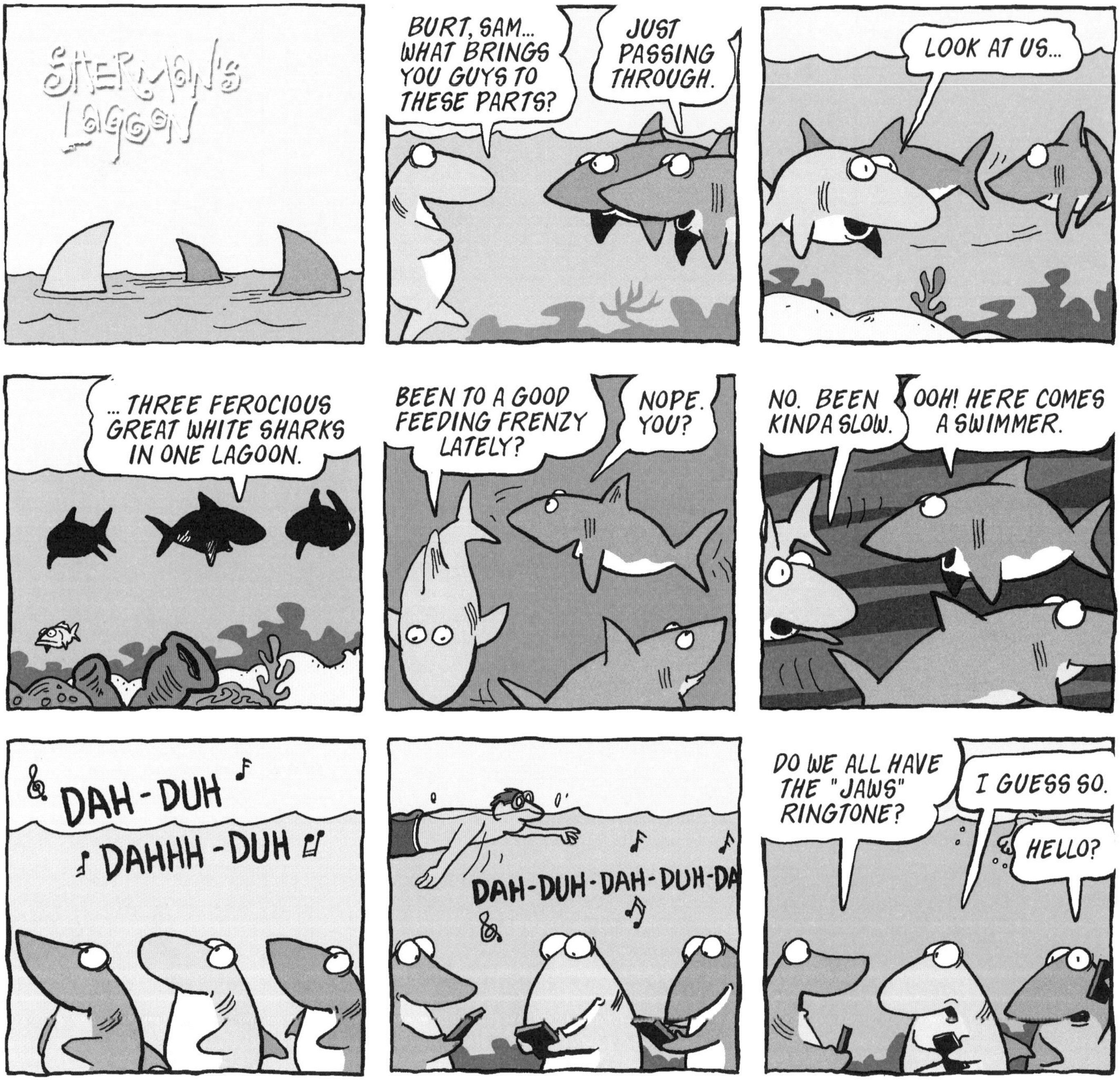
SHERMAN'S LAGOON
BURT, SAM... WHAT BRINGS YOU GUYS TO THESE PARTS?
JUST PASSING THROUGH.
LOOK AT US...
...THREE FEROCIOUS GREAT WHITE SHARKS IN ONE LAGOON.
BEEN TO A GOOD FEEDING FRENZY LATELY?
NOPE. YOU?
NO. BEEN KINDA SLOW.
OOH! HERE COMES A SWIMMER.
DAH-DUH
DAHHH-DUH
DAH-DUH-DAH-DUH-DA
DO WE ALL HAVE THE "JAWS" RINGTONE?
I GUESS SO.
HELLO?

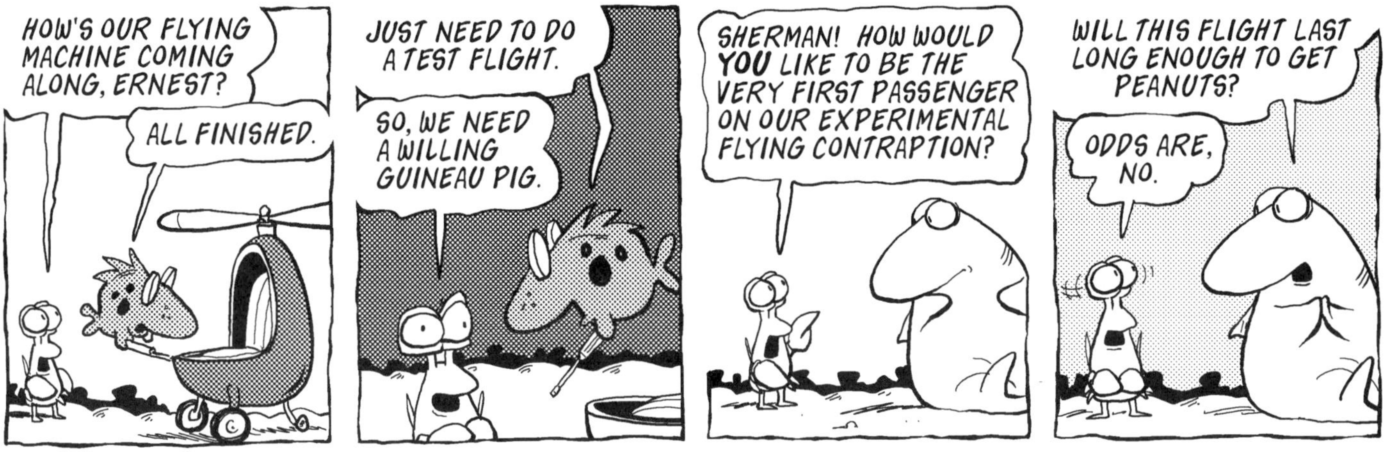
HOW'S OUR FLYING MACHINE COMING ALONG, ERNEST?
ALL FINISHED.
JUST NEED TO DO A TEST FLIGHT.
SO, WE NEED A WILLING GUINEAU PIG.
SHERMAN! HOW WOULD **YOU** LIKE TO BE THE VERY FIRST PASSENGER ON OUR EXPERIMENTAL FLYING CONTRAPTION?
WILL THIS FLIGHT LAST LONG ENOUGH TO GET PEANUTS?
ODDS ARE, NO.

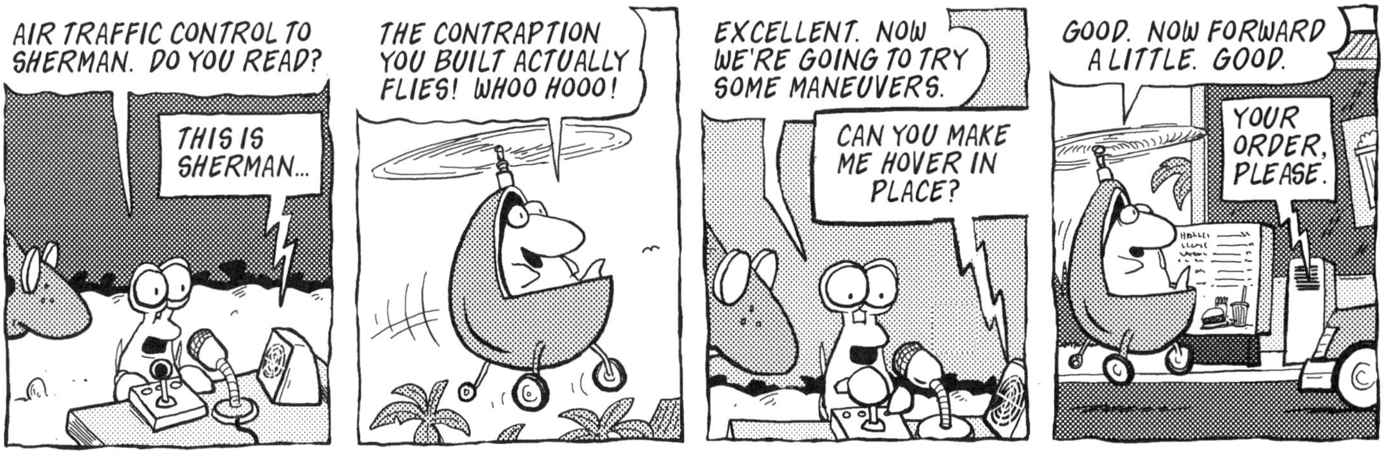
AIR TRAFFIC CONTROL TO SHERMAN. DO YOU READ?
THIS IS SHERMAN...
THE CONTRAPTION YOU BUILT ACTUALLY FLIES! WHOO HOOO!
EXCELLENT. NOW WE'RE GOING TO TRY SOME MANEUVERS.
CAN YOU MAKE ME HOVER IN PLACE?
GOOD. NOW FORWARD A LITTLE. GOOD.
YOUR ORDER, PLEASE.

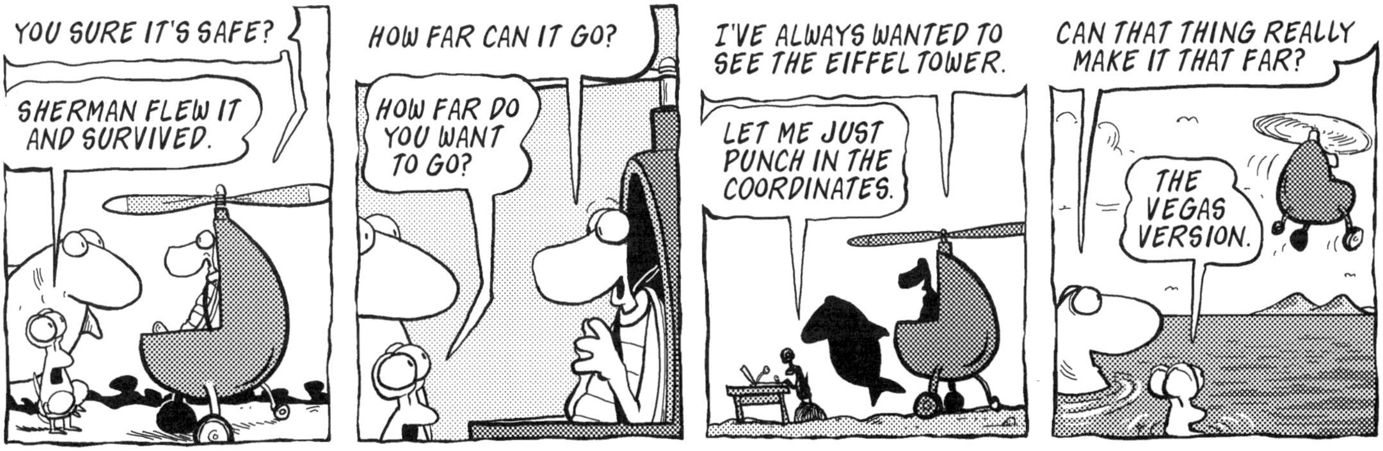
YOU SURE IT'S SAFE?
SHERMAN FLEW IT AND SURVIVED.
HOW FAR CAN IT GO?
HOW FAR DO YOU WANT TO GO?
I'VE ALWAYS WANTED TO SEE THE EIFFEL TOWER.
LET ME JUST PUNCH IN THE COORDINATES.
CAN THAT THING REALLY MAKE IT THAT FAR?
THE VEGAS VERSION.

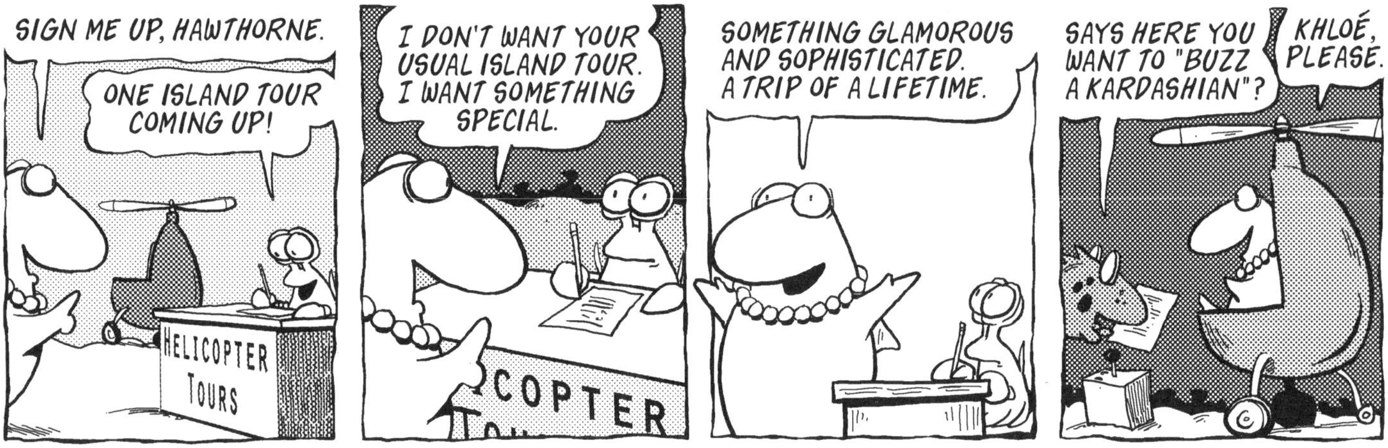
SIGN ME UP, HAWTHORNE.
ONE ISLAND TOUR COMING UP!
HELICOPTER TOURS
I DON'T WANT YOUR USUAL ISLAND TOUR. I WANT SOMETHING SPECIAL.
SOMETHING GLAMOROUS AND SOPHISTICATED. A TRIP OF A LIFETIME.
SAYS HERE YOU WANT TO "BUZZ A KARDASHIAN"?
KHLOÉ, PLEASE.

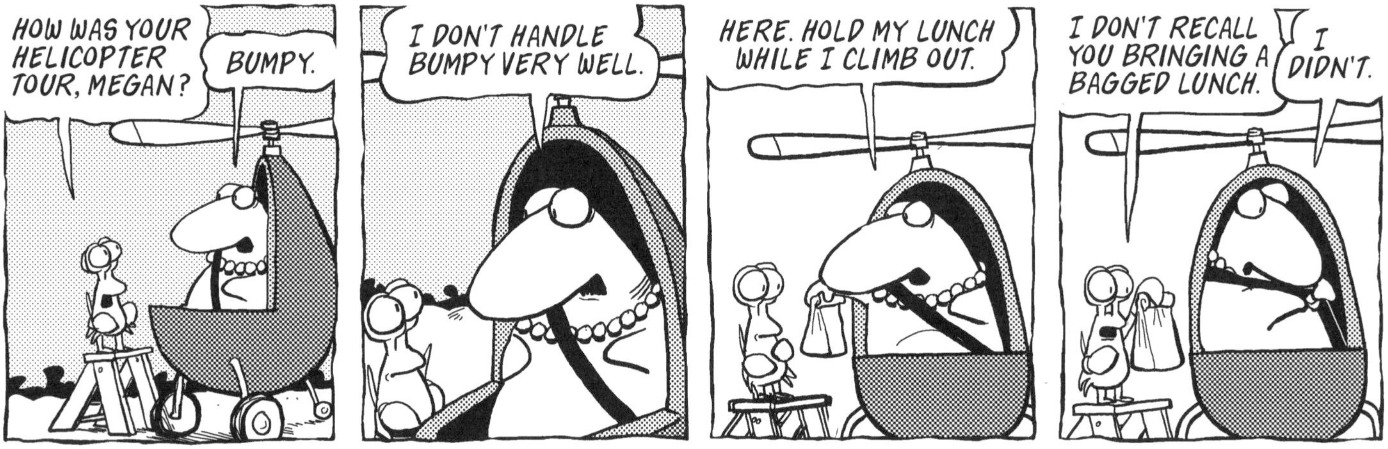
HOW WAS YOUR HELICOPTER TOUR, MEGAN?
BUMPY.
I DON'T HANDLE BUMPY VERY WELL.
HERE. HOLD MY LUNCH WHILE I CLIMB OUT.
I DON'T RECALL YOU BRINGING A BAGGED LUNCH.
I DIDN'T.

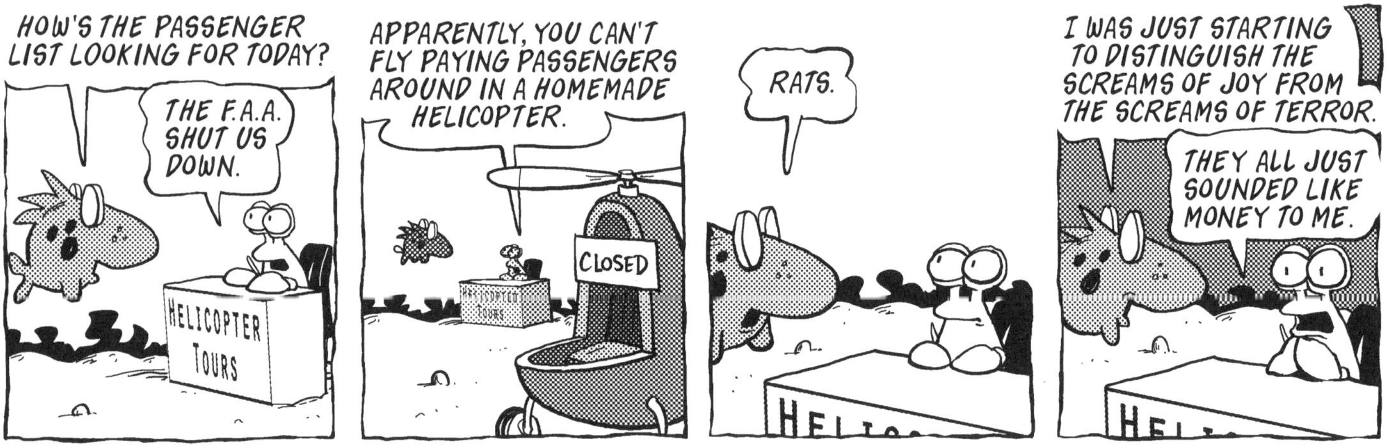
HOW'S THE PASSENGER LIST LOOKING FOR TODAY?
THE F.A.A. SHUT US DOWN.
HELICOPTER TOURS
APPARENTLY, YOU CAN'T FLY PAYING PASSENGERS AROUND IN A HOMEMADE HELICOPTER.
CLOSED
RATS.
I WAS JUST STARTING TO DISTINGUISH THE SCREAMS OF JOY FROM THE SCREAMS OF TERROR.
THEY ALL JUST SOUNDED LIKE MONEY TO ME.

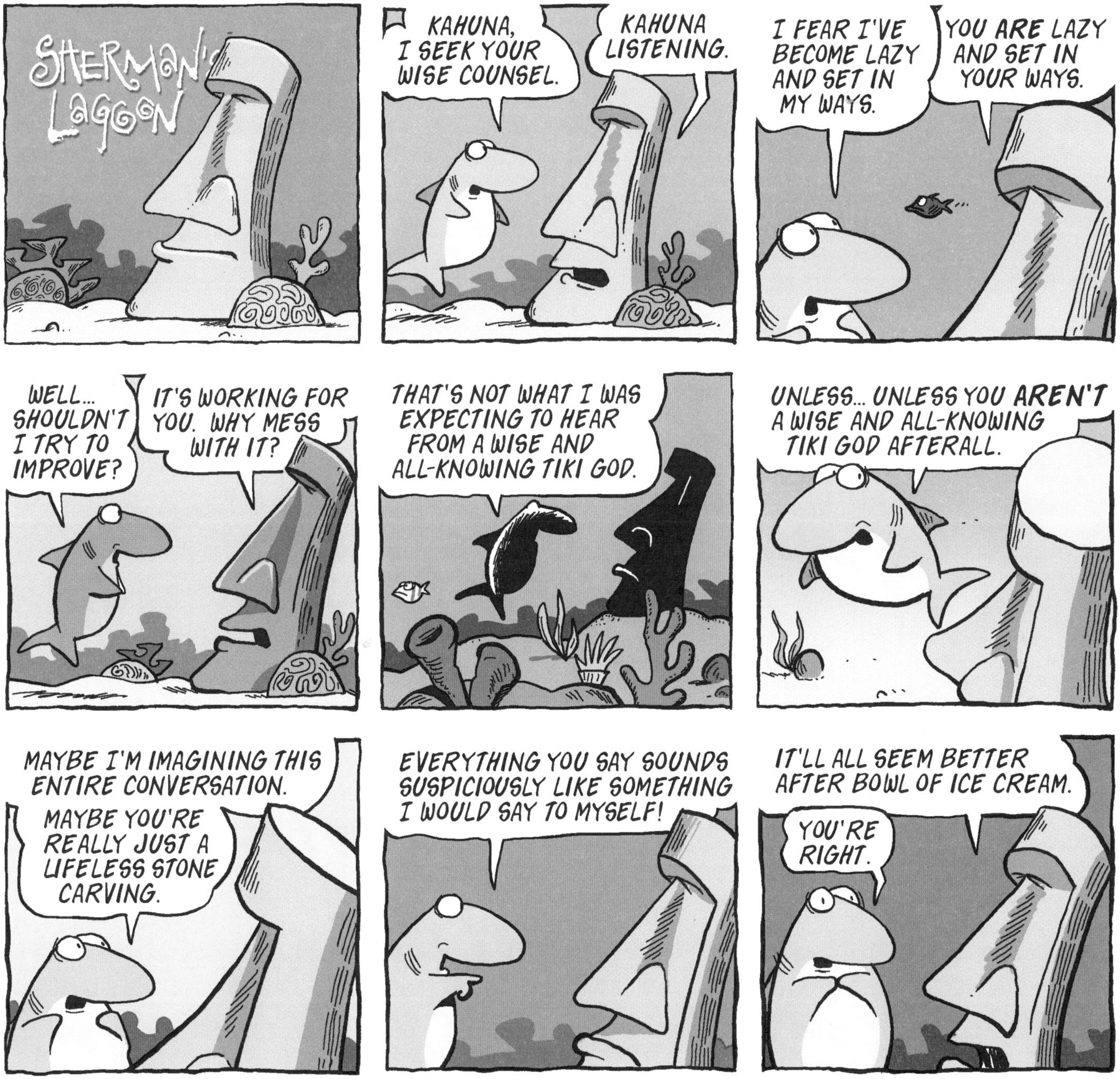
SHERMAN'S LAGOON
KAHUNA, I SEEK YOUR WISE COUNSEL.
KAHUNA LISTENING.
I FEAR I'VE BECOME LAZY AND SET IN MY WAYS.
YOU ARE LAZY AND SET IN YOUR WAYS.
WELL... SHOULDN'T I TRY TO IMPROVE?
IT'S WORKING FOR YOU. WHY MESS WITH IT?
THAT'S NOT WHAT I WAS EXPECTING TO HEAR FROM A WISE AND ALL-KNOWING TIKI GOD.
UNLESS... UNLESS YOU AREN'T A WISE AND ALL-KNOWING TIKI GOD AFTERALL.
MAYBE I'M IMAGINING THIS ENTIRE CONVERSATION.
MAYBE YOU'RE REALLY JUST A LIFELESS STONE CARVING.
EVERYTHING YOU SAY SOUNDS SUSPICIOUSLY LIKE SOMETHING I WOULD SAY TO MYSELF!
IT'LL ALL SEEM BETTER AFTER BOWL OF ICE CREAM.
YOU'RE RIGHT.

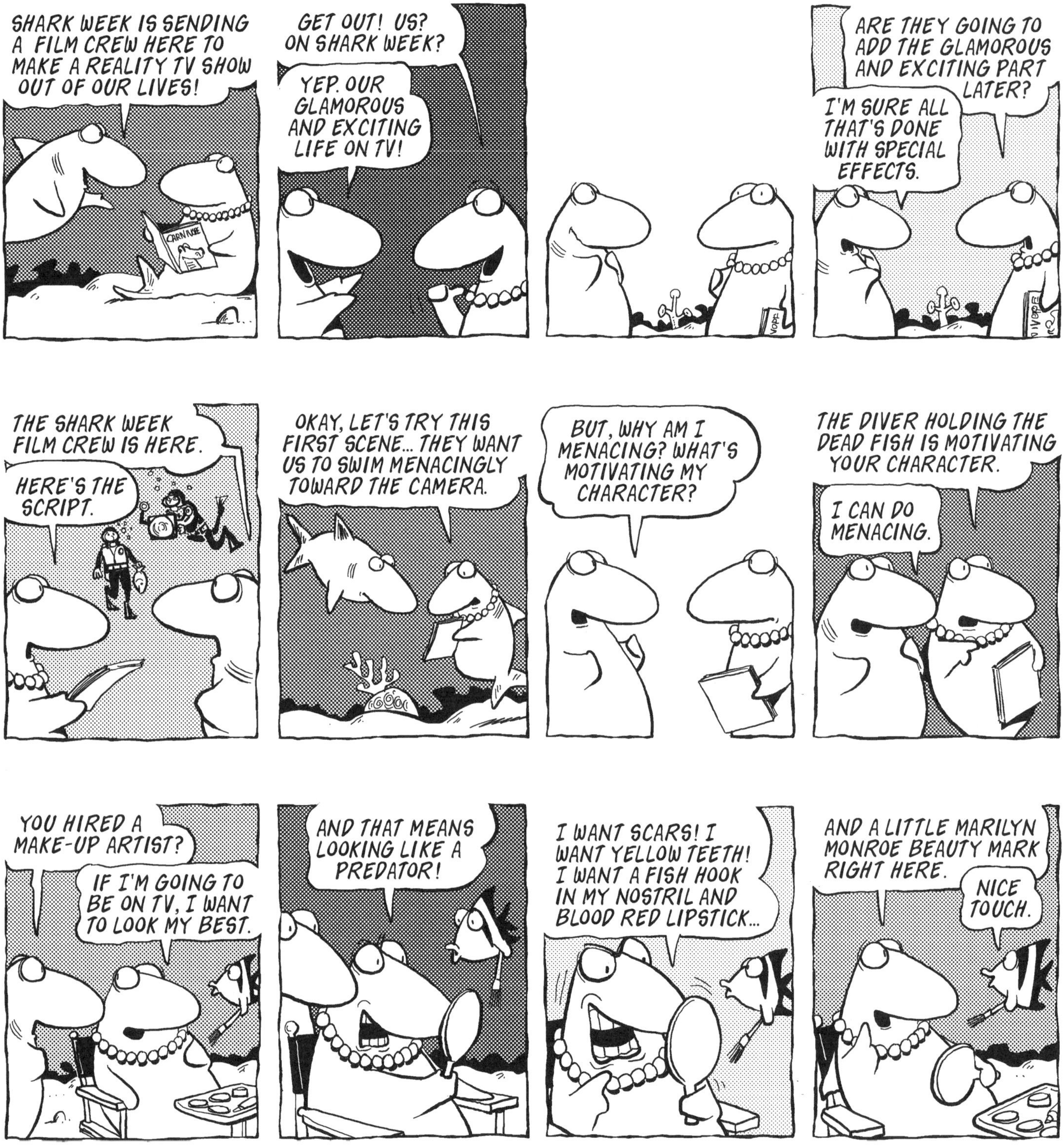
SHARK WEEK IS SENDING A FILM CREW HERE TO MAKE A REALITY TV SHOW OUT OF OUR LIVES!
GET OUT! US? ON SHARK WEEK?
YEP. OUR GLAMOROUS AND EXCITING LIFE ON TV!
ARE THEY GOING TO ADD THE GLAMOROUS AND EXCITING PART LATER?
I'M SURE ALL THAT'S DONE WITH SPECIAL EFFECTS.
THE SHARK WEEK FILM CREW IS HERE.
HERE'S THE SCRIPT.
OKAY, LET'S TRY THIS FIRST SCENE... THEY WANT US TO SWIM MENACINGLY TOWARD THE CAMERA.
BUT, WHY AM I MENACING? WHAT'S MOTIVATING MY CHARACTER?
THE DIVER HOLDING THE DEAD FISH IS MOTIVATING YOUR CHARACTER.
I CAN DO MENACING.
YOU HIRED A MAKE-UP ARTIST?
IF I'M GOING TO BE ON TV, I WANT TO LOOK MY BEST.
AND THAT MEANS LOOKING LIKE A PREDATOR!
I WANT SCARS! I WANT YELLOW TEETH! I WANT A FISH HOOK IN MY NOSTRIL AND BLOOD RED LIPSTICK...
AND A LITTLE MARILYN MONROE BEAUTY MARK RIGHT HERE.
NICE TOUCH.

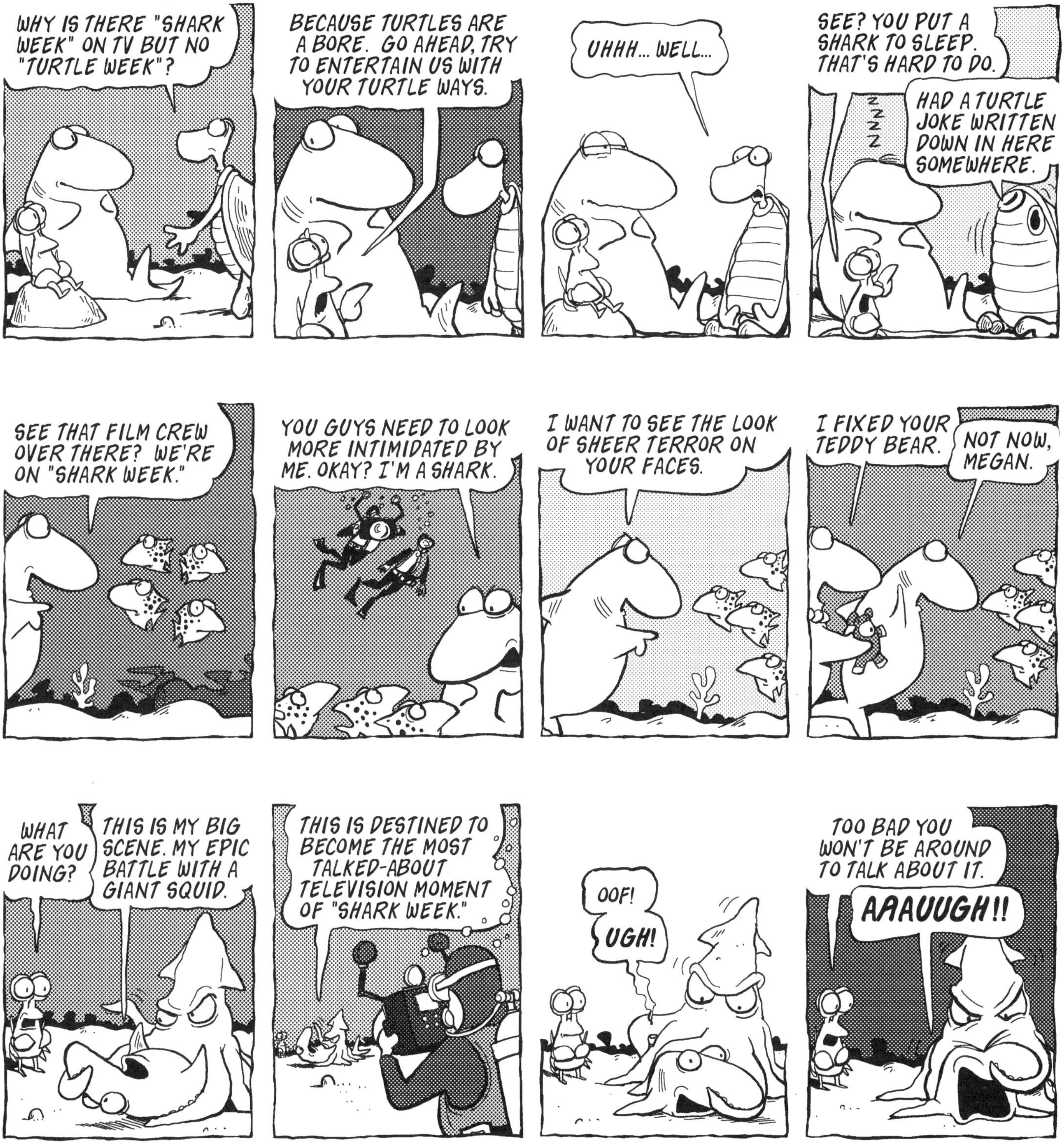
WHY IS THERE "SHARK WEEK" ON TV BUT NO "TURTLE WEEK"?
BECAUSE TURTLES ARE A BORE. GO AHEAD, TRY TO ENTERTAIN US WITH YOUR TURTLE WAYS.
UHHH... WELL...
SEE? YOU PUT A SHARK TO SLEEP. THAT'S HARD TO DO.
Z Z Z Z
HAD A TURTLE JOKE WRITTEN DOWN IN HERE SOMEWHERE.
SEE THAT FILM CREW OVER THERE? WE'RE ON "SHARK WEEK."
YOU GUYS NEED TO LOOK MORE INTIMIDATED BY ME. OKAY? I'M A SHARK.
I WANT TO SEE THE LOOK OF SHEER TERROR ON YOUR FACES.
I FIXED YOUR TEDDY BEAR.
NOT NOW, MEGAN.
WHAT ARE YOU DOING?
THIS IS MY BIG SCENE. MY EPIC BATTLE WITH A GIANT SQUID.
THIS IS DESTINED TO BECOME THE MOST TALKED-ABOUT TELEVISION MOMENT OF "SHARK WEEK."
OOF!
UGH!
TOO BAD YOU WON'T BE AROUND TO TALK ABOUT IT.
AAAUUGH!!

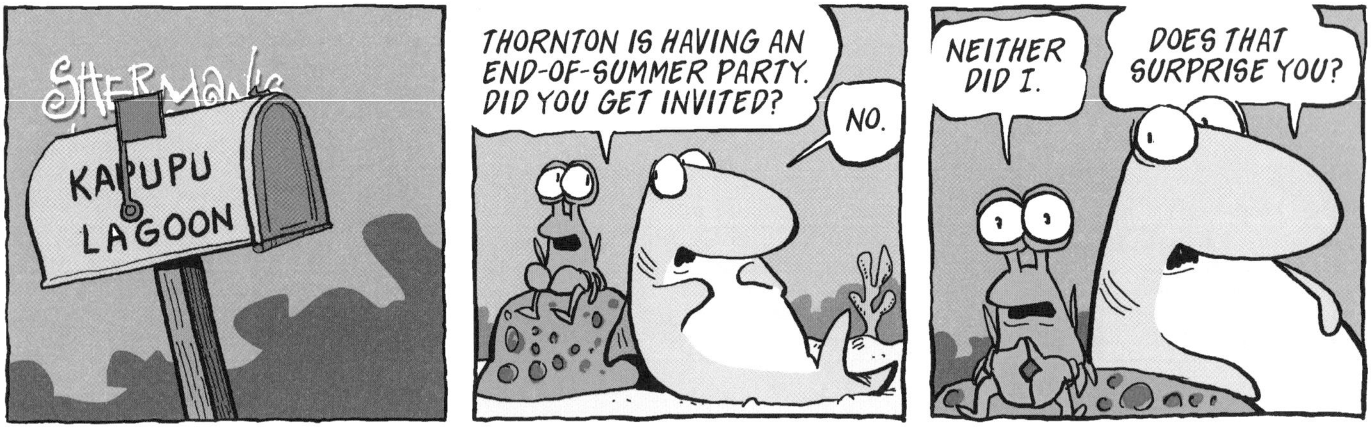
Sherman's
KAPUPU LAGOON
THORNTON IS HAVING AN END-OF-SUMMER PARTY. DID YOU GET INVITED?
NO.
NEITHER DID I.
DOES THAT SURPRISE YOU?

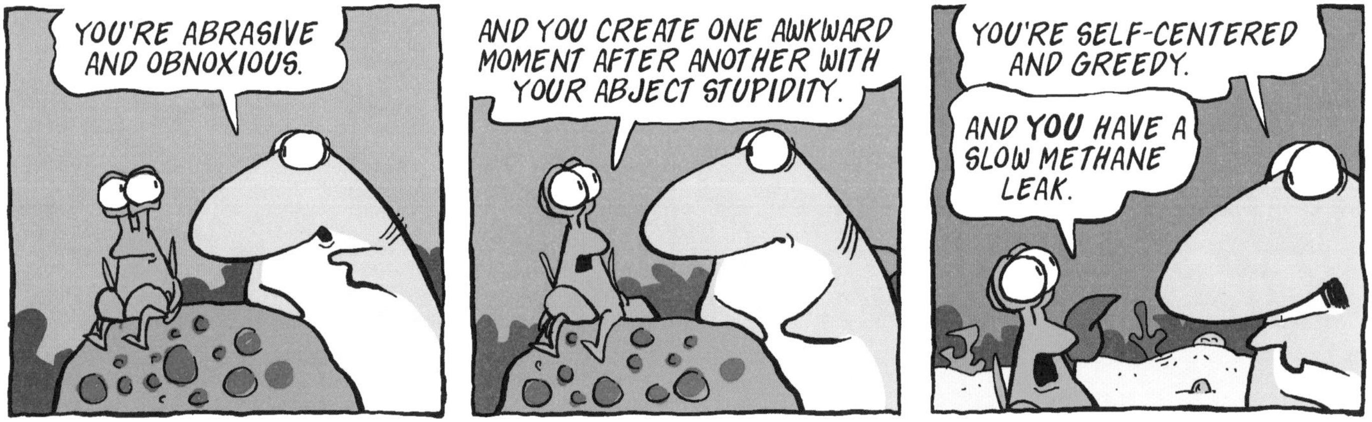
YOU'RE ABRASIVE AND OBNOXIOUS.
AND YOU CREATE ONE AWKWARD MOMENT AFTER ANOTHER WITH YOUR ABJECT STUPIDITY.
YOU'RE SELF-CENTERED AND GREEDY.
AND YOU HAVE A SLOW METHANE LEAK.

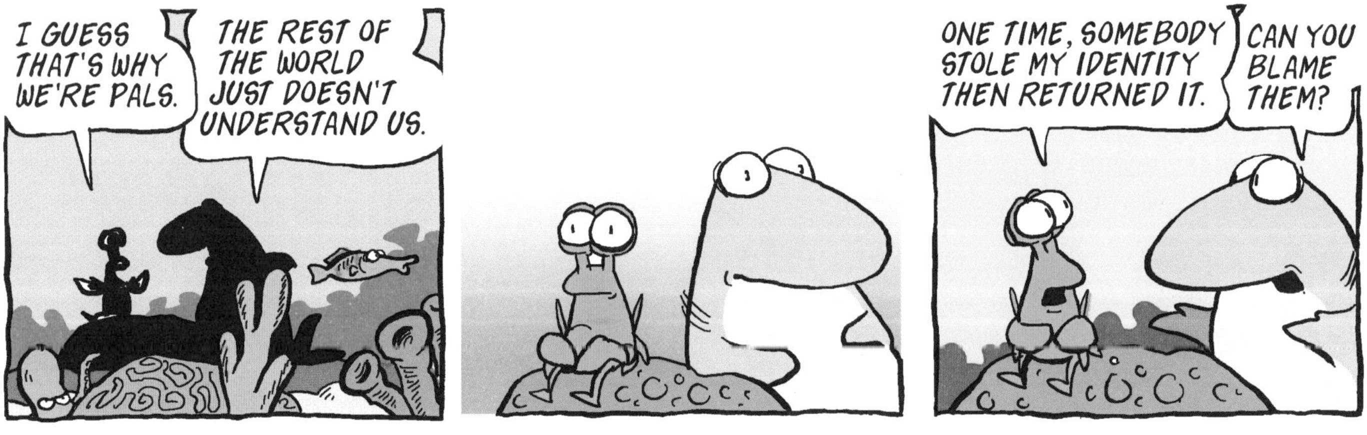
I GUESS THAT'S WHY WE'RE PALS.
THE REST OF THE WORLD JUST DOESN'T UNDERSTAND US.
ONE TIME, SOMEBODY STOLE MY IDENTITY THEN RETURNED IT.
CAN YOU BLAME THEM?

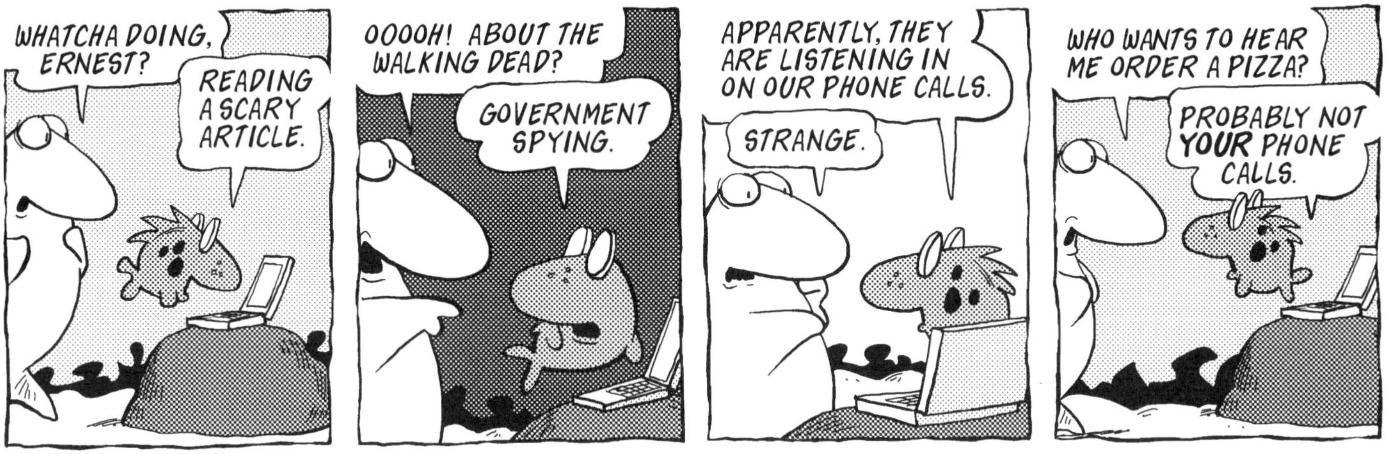
WHATCHA DOING, ERNEST?
READING A SCARY ARTICLE.
OOOOH! ABOUT THE WALKING DEAD?
GOVERNMENT SPYING.
APPARENTLY, THEY ARE LISTENING IN ON OUR PHONE CALLS.
STRANGE.
WHO WANTS TO HEAR ME ORDER A PIZZA?
PROBABLY NOT **YOUR** PHONE CALLS.

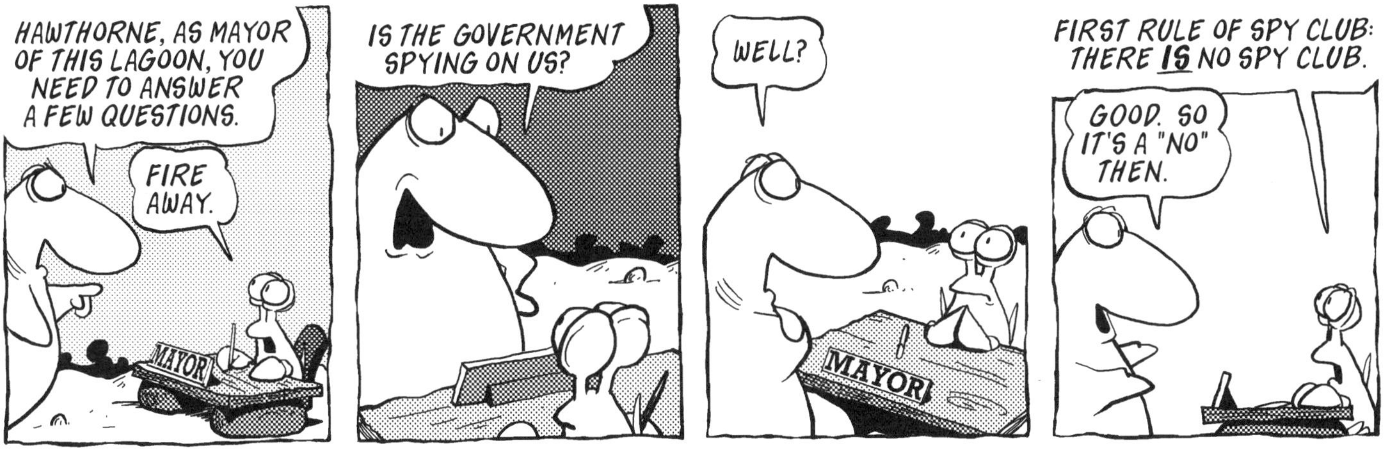
HAWTHORNE, AS MAYOR OF THIS LAGOON, YOU NEED TO ANSWER A FEW QUESTIONS.
FIRE AWAY.
MAYOR
IS THE GOVERNMENT SPYING ON US?
WELL?
MAYOR
FIRST RULE OF SPY CLUB: THERE IS NO SPY CLUB.
GOOD. SO IT'S A "NO" THEN.

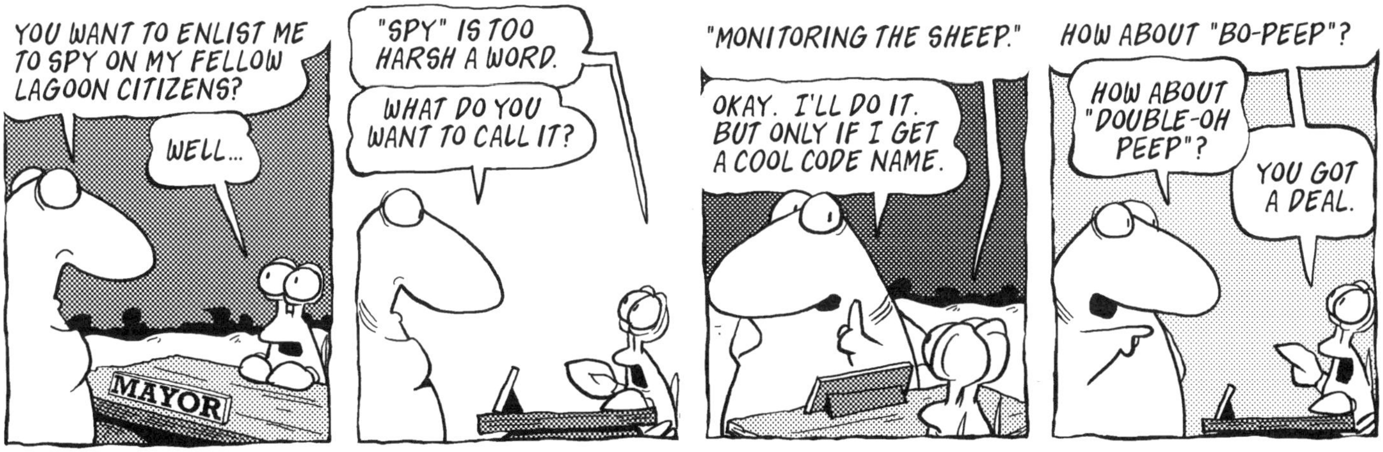
YOU WANT TO ENLIST ME TO SPY ON MY FELLOW LAGOON CITIZENS?
WELL...
MAYOR
"SPY" IS TOO HARSH A WORD.
WHAT DO YOU WANT TO CALL IT?
"MONITORING THE SHEEP."
OKAY. I'LL DO IT. BUT ONLY IF I GET A COOL CODE NAME.
HOW ABOUT "BO-PEEP"?
HOW ABOUT "DOUBLE-OH PEEP"?
YOU GOT A DEAL.

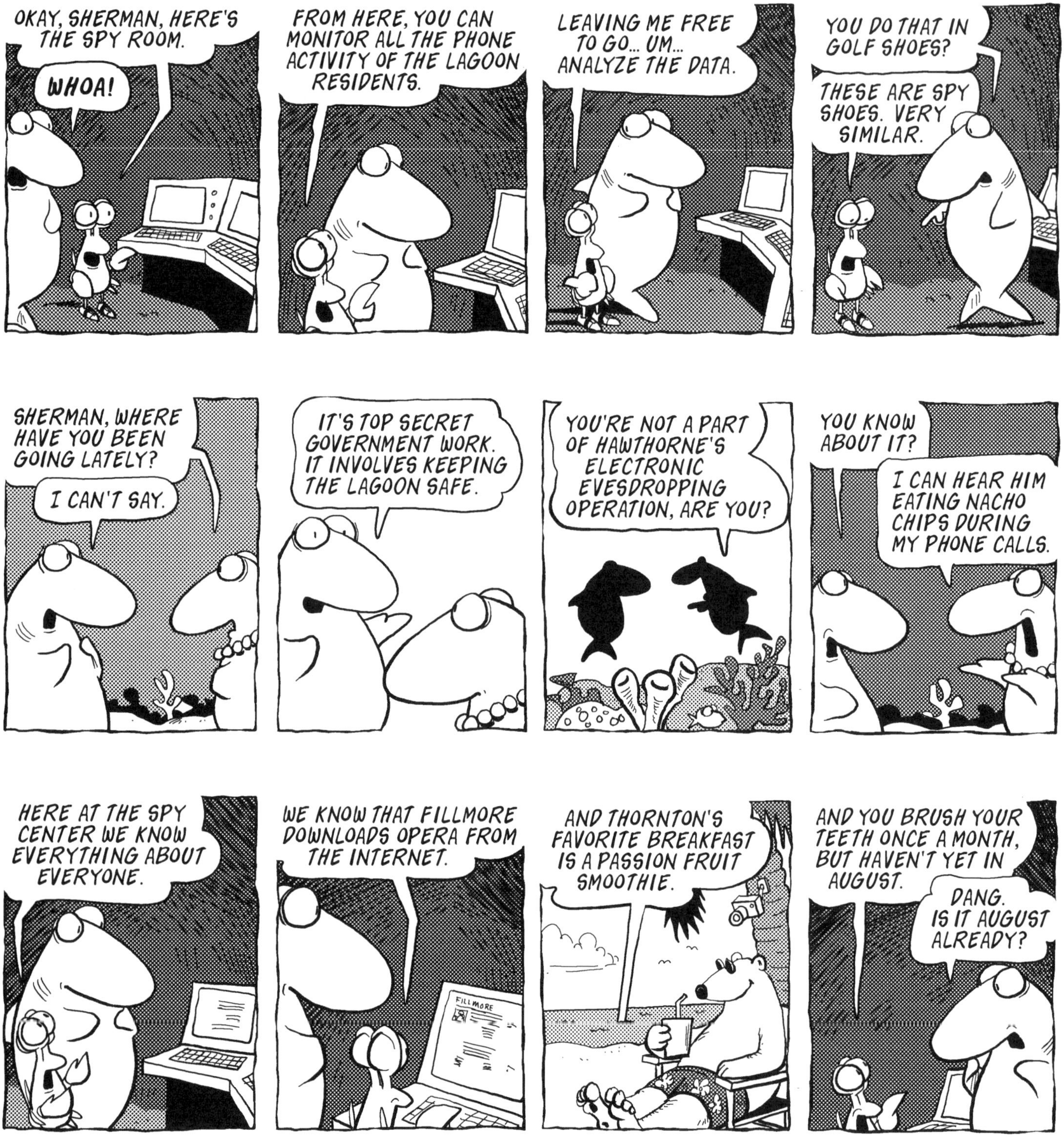
OKAY, SHERMAN, HERE'S THE SPY ROOM.
WHOA!
FROM HERE, YOU CAN MONITOR ALL THE PHONE ACTIVITY OF THE LAGOON RESIDENTS.
LEAVING ME FREE TO GO... UM... ANALYZE THE DATA.
YOU DO THAT IN GOLF SHOES?
THESE ARE SPY SHOES. VERY SIMILAR.
SHERMAN, WHERE HAVE YOU BEEN GOING LATELY?
I CAN'T SAY.
IT'S TOP SECRET GOVERNMENT WORK. IT INVOLVES KEEPING THE LAGOON SAFE.
YOU'RE NOT A PART OF HAWTHORNE'S ELECTRONIC EVESDROPPING OPERATION, ARE YOU?
YOU KNOW ABOUT IT?
I CAN HEAR HIM EATING NACHO CHIPS DURING MY PHONE CALLS.
HERE AT THE SPY CENTER WE KNOW EVERYTHING ABOUT EVERYONE.
WE KNOW THAT FILLMORE DOWNLOADS OPERA FROM THE INTERNET.
FILLMORE
AND THORNTON'S FAVORITE BREAKFAST IS A PASSION FRUIT SMOOTHIE.
AND YOU BRUSH YOUR TEETH ONCE A MONTH, BUT HAVEN'T YET IN AUGUST.
DANG. IS IT AUGUST ALREADY?

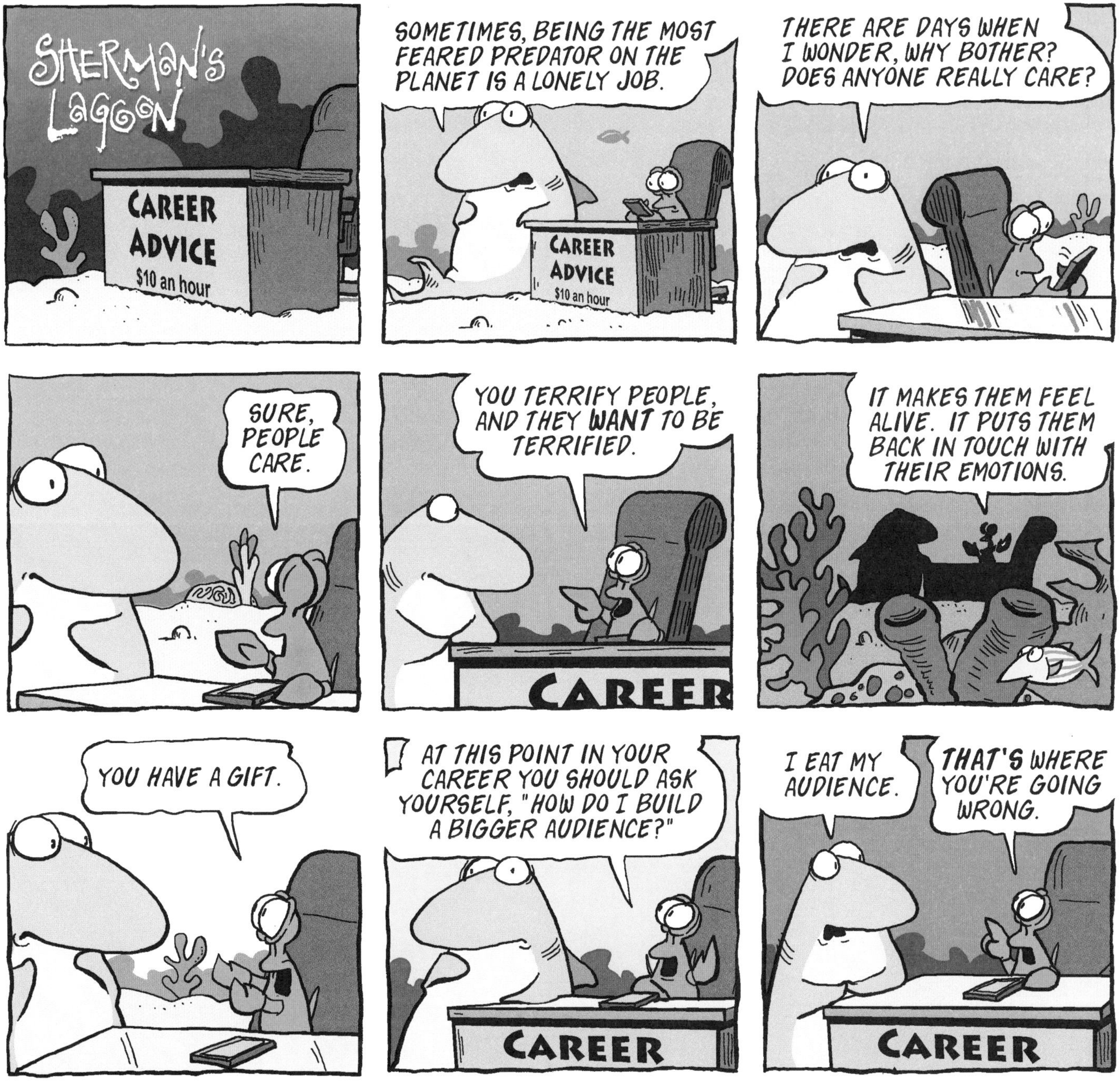
SHERMAN'S LAGOON
CAREER ADVICE
$10 an hour
SOMETIMES, BEING THE MOST FEARED PREDATOR ON THE PLANET IS A LONELY JOB.
CAREER ADVICE
$10 an hour
THERE ARE DAYS WHEN I WONDER, WHY BOTHER? DOES ANYONE REALLY CARE?
SURE, PEOPLE CARE.
YOU TERRIFY PEOPLE, AND THEY **WANT** TO BE TERRIFIED.
CAREER
IT MAKES THEM FEEL ALIVE. IT PUTS THEM BACK IN TOUCH WITH THEIR EMOTIONS.
YOU HAVE A GIFT.
AT THIS POINT IN YOUR CAREER YOU SHOULD ASK YOURSELF, "HOW DO I BUILD A BIGGER AUDIENCE?"
CAREER
I EAT MY AUDIENCE.
THAT'S WHERE YOU'RE GOING WRONG.
CAREER

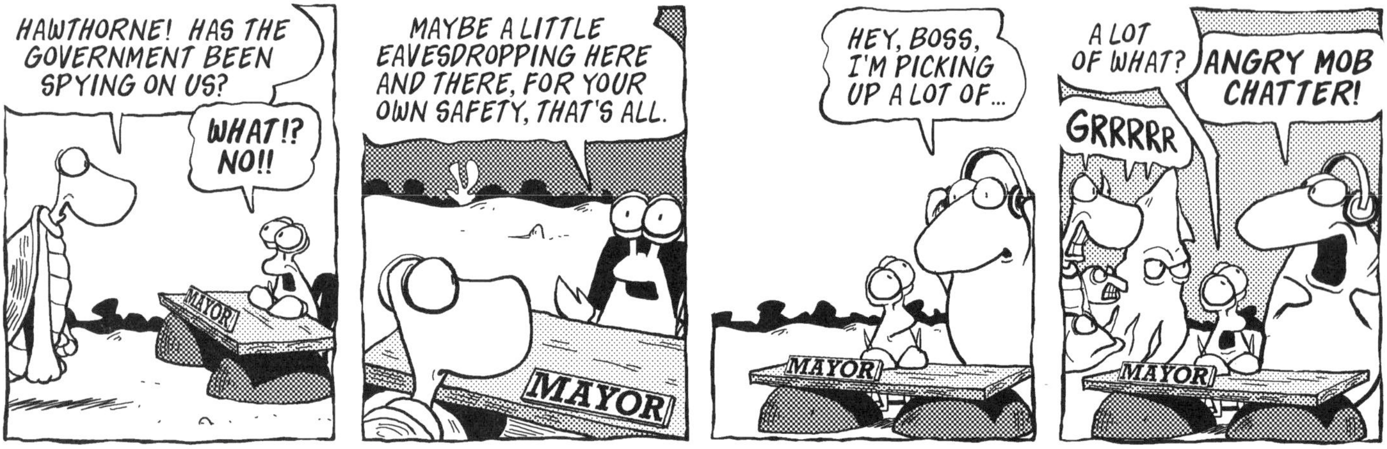
HAWTHORNE! HAS THE GOVERNMENT BEEN SPYING ON US?
WHAT!? NO!!
MAYOR
MAYBE A LITTLE EAVESDROPPING HERE AND THERE, FOR YOUR OWN SAFETY, THAT'S ALL.
MAYOR
HEY, BOSS, I'M PICKING UP A LOT OF...
MAYOR
A LOT OF WHAT?
ANGRY MOB CHATTER!
GRRRRR
MAYOR

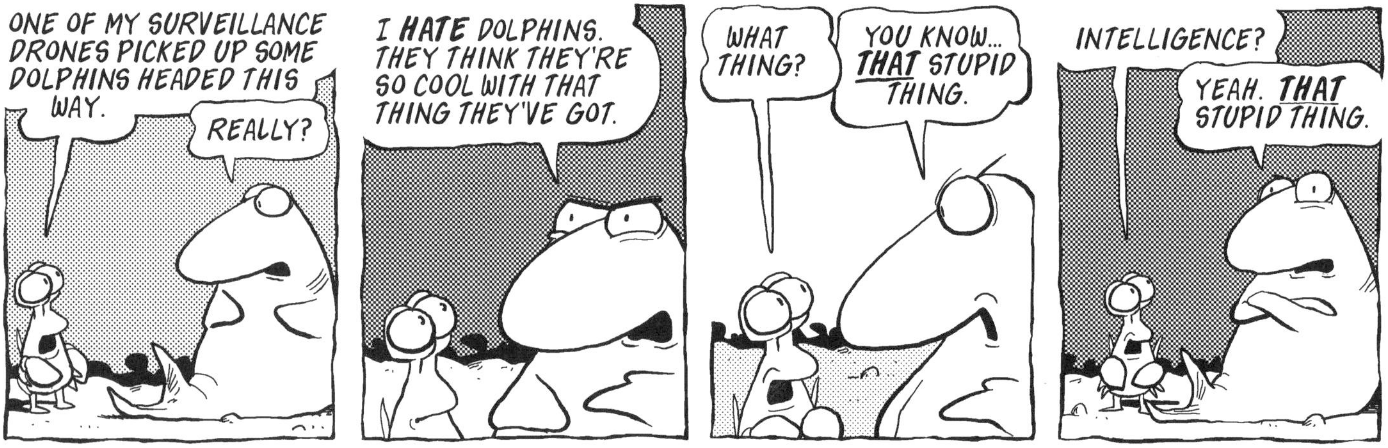
ONE OF MY SURVEILLANCE DRONES PICKED UP SOME DOLPHINS HEADED THIS WAY.
REALLY?
I HATE DOLPHINS. THEY THINK THEY'RE SO COOL WITH THAT THING THEY'VE GOT.
WHAT THING?
YOU KNOW... THAT STUPID THING.
INTELLIGENCE?
YEAH. THAT STUPID THING.

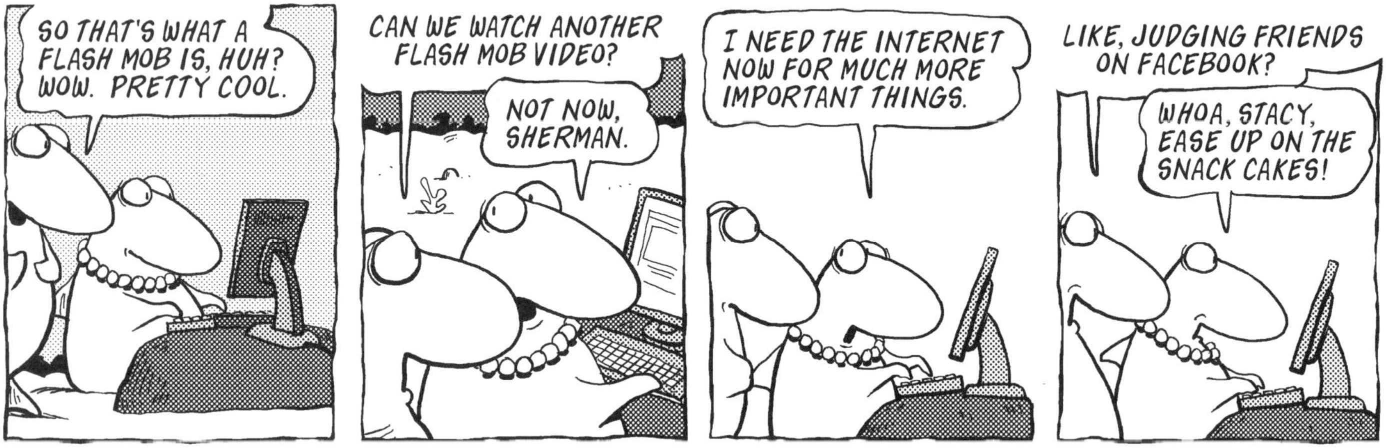
SO THAT'S WHAT A FLASH MOB IS, HUH? WOW. PRETTY COOL.
CAN WE WATCH ANOTHER FLASH MOB VIDEO?
NOT NOW, SHERMAN.
I NEED THE INTERNET NOW FOR MUCH MORE IMPORTANT THINGS.
LIKE, JUDGING FRIENDS ON FACEBOOK?
WHOA, STACY, EASE UP ON THE SNACK CAKES!

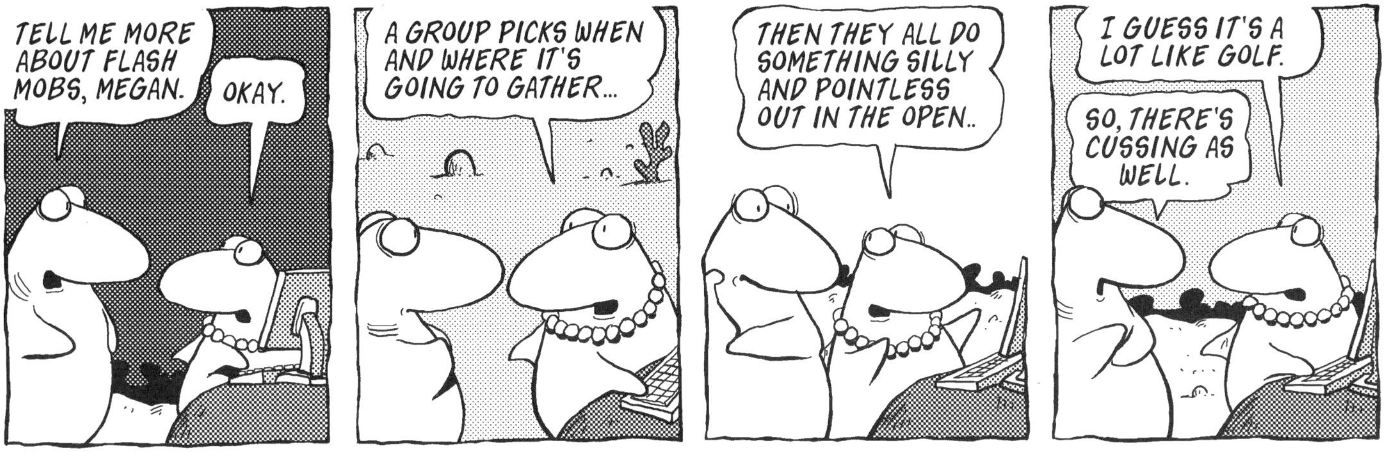
TELL ME MORE ABOUT FLASH MOBS, MEGAN.
OKAY.
A GROUP PICKS WHEN AND WHERE IT'S GOING TO GATHER...
THEN THEY ALL DO SOMETHING SILLY AND POINTLESS OUT IN THE OPEN..
I GUESS IT'S A LOT LIKE GOLF.
SO, THERE'S CUSSING AS WELL.

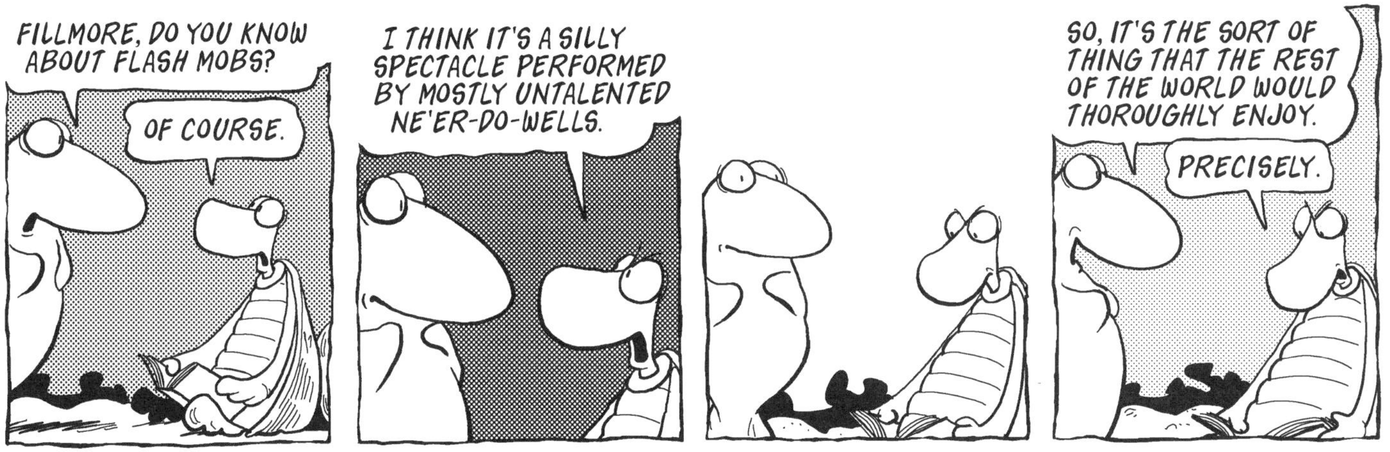
FILLMORE, DO YOU KNOW ABOUT FLASH MOBS?
OF COURSE.
I THINK IT'S A SILLY SPECTACLE PERFORMED BY MOSTLY UNTALENTED NE'ER-DO-WELLS.
SO, IT'S THE SORT OF THING THAT THE REST OF THE WORLD WOULD THOROUGHLY ENJOY.
PRECISELY.

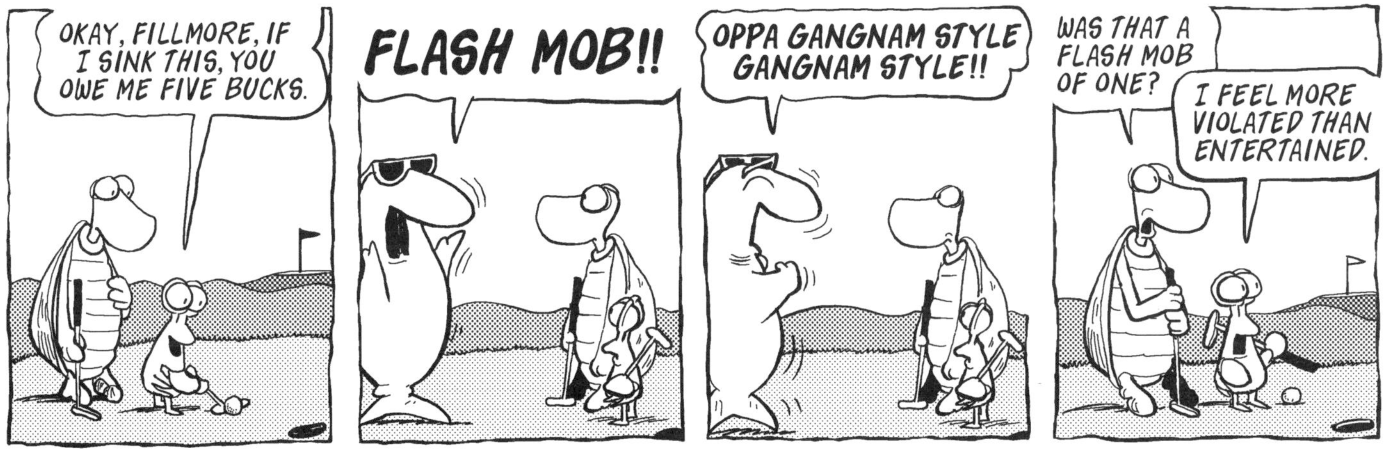
OKAY, FILLMORE, IF I SINK THIS, YOU OWE ME FIVE BUCKS.
FLASH MOB!!
OPPA GANGNAM STYLE GANGNAM STYLE!!
WAS THAT A FLASH MOB OF ONE?
I FEEL MORE VIOLATED THAN ENTERTAINED.

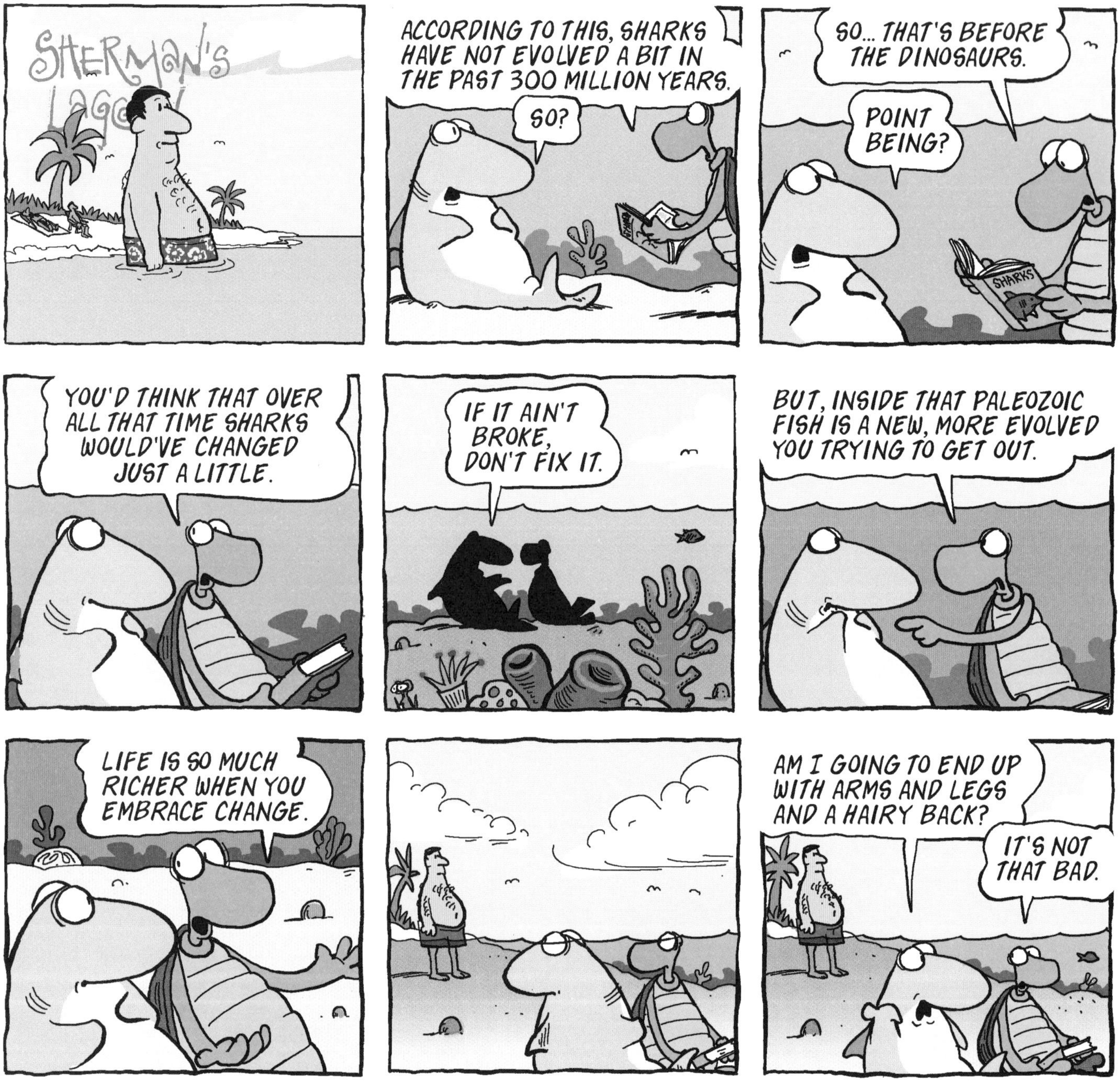
SHERMAN'S LAGOON
ACCORDING TO THIS, SHARKS HAVE NOT EVOLVED A BIT IN THE PAST 300 MILLION YEARS.
SO?
SO... THAT'S BEFORE THE DINOSAURS.
POINT BEING?
SHARKS
YOU'D THINK THAT OVER ALL THAT TIME SHARKS WOULD'VE CHANGED JUST A LITTLE.
IF IT AIN'T BROKE, DON'T FIX IT.
BUT, INSIDE THAT PALEOZOIC FISH IS A NEW, MORE EVOLVED YOU TRYING TO GET OUT.
LIFE IS SO MUCH RICHER WHEN YOU EMBRACE CHANGE.
AM I GOING TO END UP WITH ARMS AND LEGS AND A HAIRY BACK?
IT'S NOT THAT BAD.

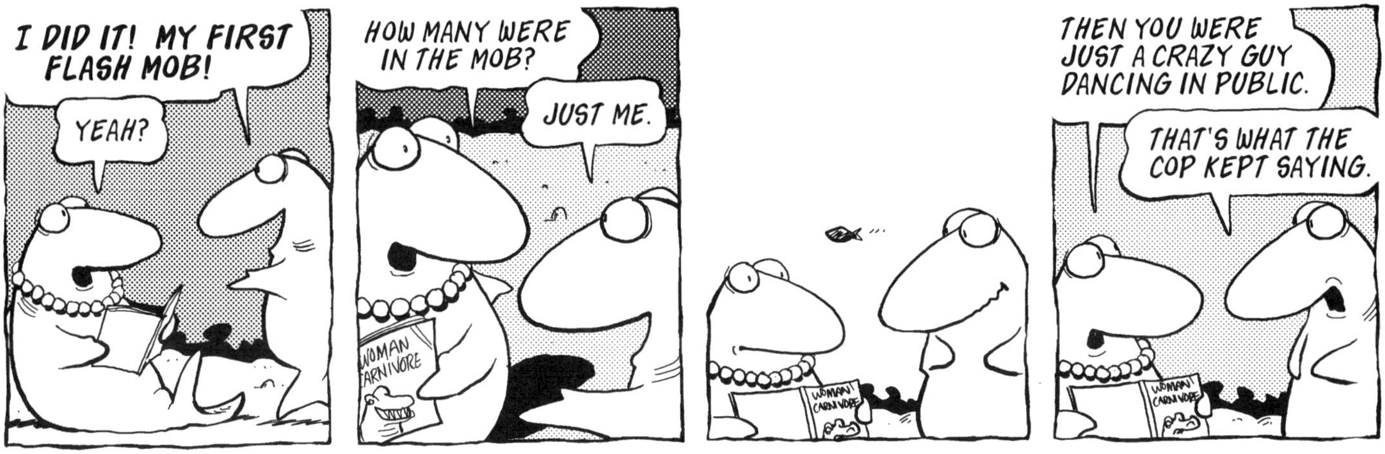
I DID IT! MY FIRST FLASH MOB!
YEAH?
HOW MANY WERE IN THE MOB?
JUST ME.
WOMAN CARNIVORE
THEN YOU WERE JUST A CRAZY GUY DANCING IN PUBLIC.
THAT'S WHAT THE COP KEPT SAYING.

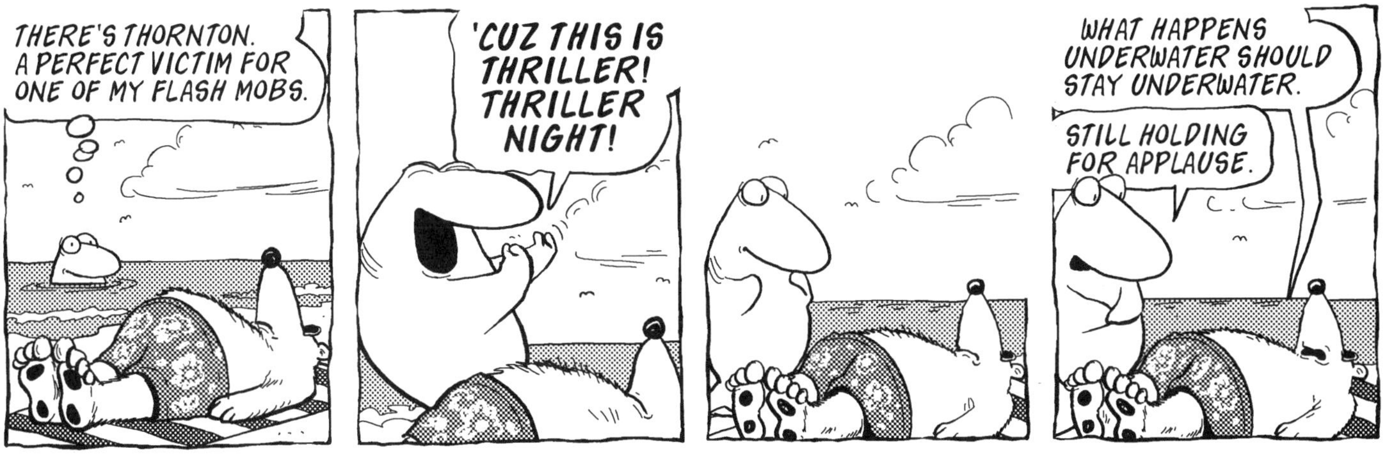
THERE'S THORNTON. A PERFECT VICTIM FOR ONE OF MY FLASH MOBS.
'CUZ THIS IS THRILLER! THRILLER NIGHT!
WHAT HAPPENS UNDERWATER SHOULD STAY UNDERWATER.
STILL HOLDING FOR APPLAUSE.

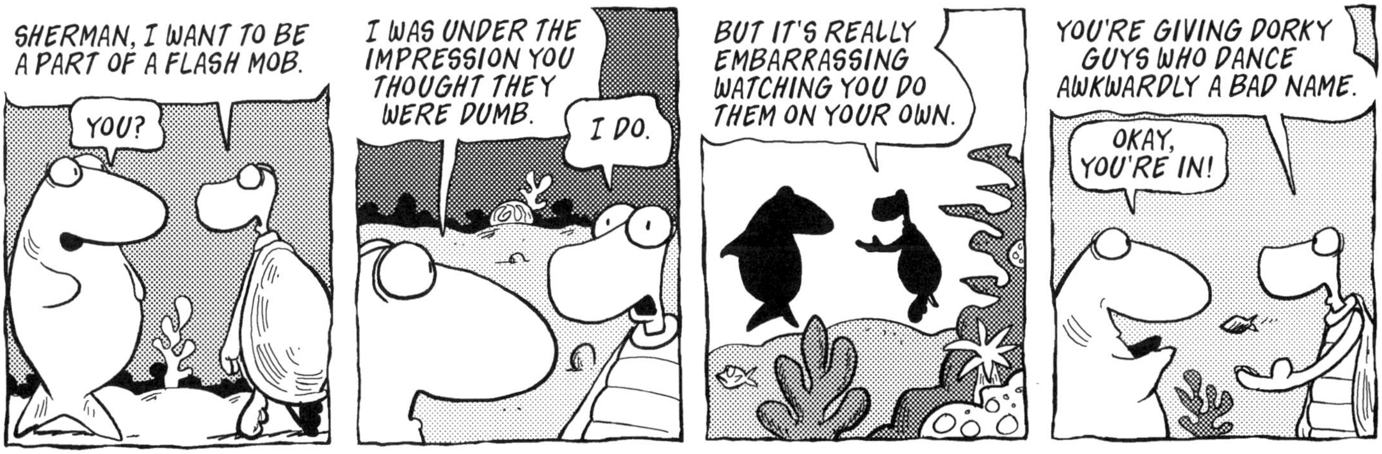
SHERMAN, I WANT TO BE A PART OF A FLASH MOB.
YOU?
I WAS UNDER THE IMPRESSION YOU THOUGHT THEY WERE DUMB.
I DO.
BUT IT'S REALLY EMBARRASSING WATCHING YOU DO THEM ON YOUR OWN.
YOU'RE GIVING DORKY GUYS WHO DANCE AWKWARDLY A BAD NAME.
OKAY, YOU'RE IN!

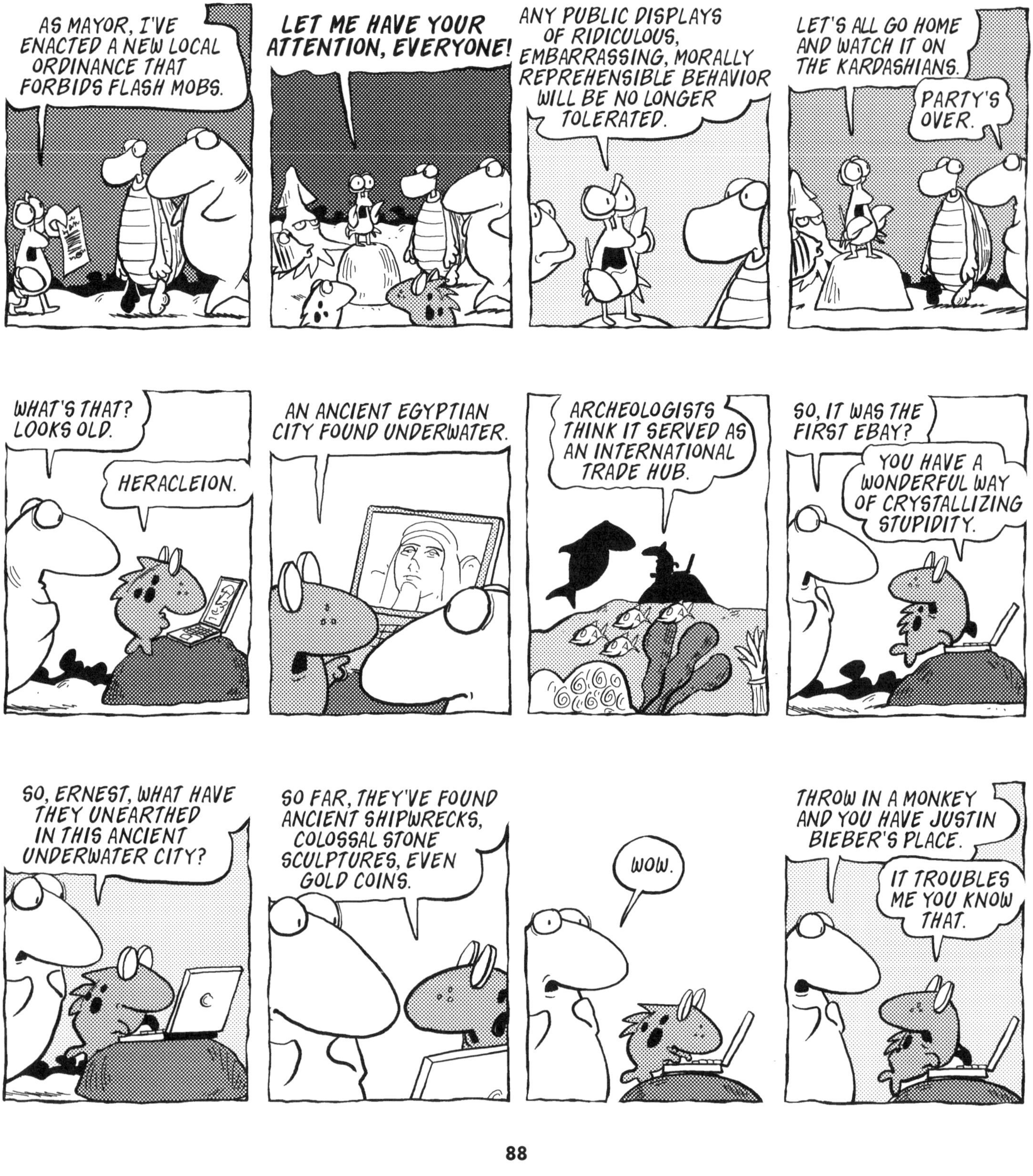
AS MAYOR, I'VE ENACTED A NEW LOCAL ORDINANCE THAT FORBIDS FLASH MOBS.
LET ME HAVE YOUR ATTENTION, EVERYONE!
ANY PUBLIC DISPLAYS OF RIDICULOUS, EMBARRASSING, MORALLY REPREHENSIBLE BEHAVIOR WILL BE NO LONGER TOLERATED.
LET'S ALL GO HOME AND WATCH IT ON THE KARDASHIANS.
PARTY'S OVER.
WHAT'S THAT? LOOKS OLD.
HERACLEION.
AN ANCIENT EGYPTIAN CITY FOUND UNDERWATER.
ARCHEOLOGISTS THINK IT SERVED AS AN INTERNATIONAL TRADE HUB.
SO, IT WAS THE FIRST EBAY?
YOU HAVE A WONDERFUL WAY OF CRYSTALLIZING STUPIDITY.
SO, ERNEST, WHAT HAVE THEY UNEARTHED IN THIS ANCIENT UNDERWATER CITY?
SO FAR, THEY'VE FOUND ANCIENT SHIPWRECKS, COLOSSAL STONE SCULPTURES, EVEN GOLD COINS.
WOW.
THROW IN A MONKEY AND YOU HAVE JUSTIN BIEBER'S PLACE.
IT TROUBLES ME YOU KNOW THAT.

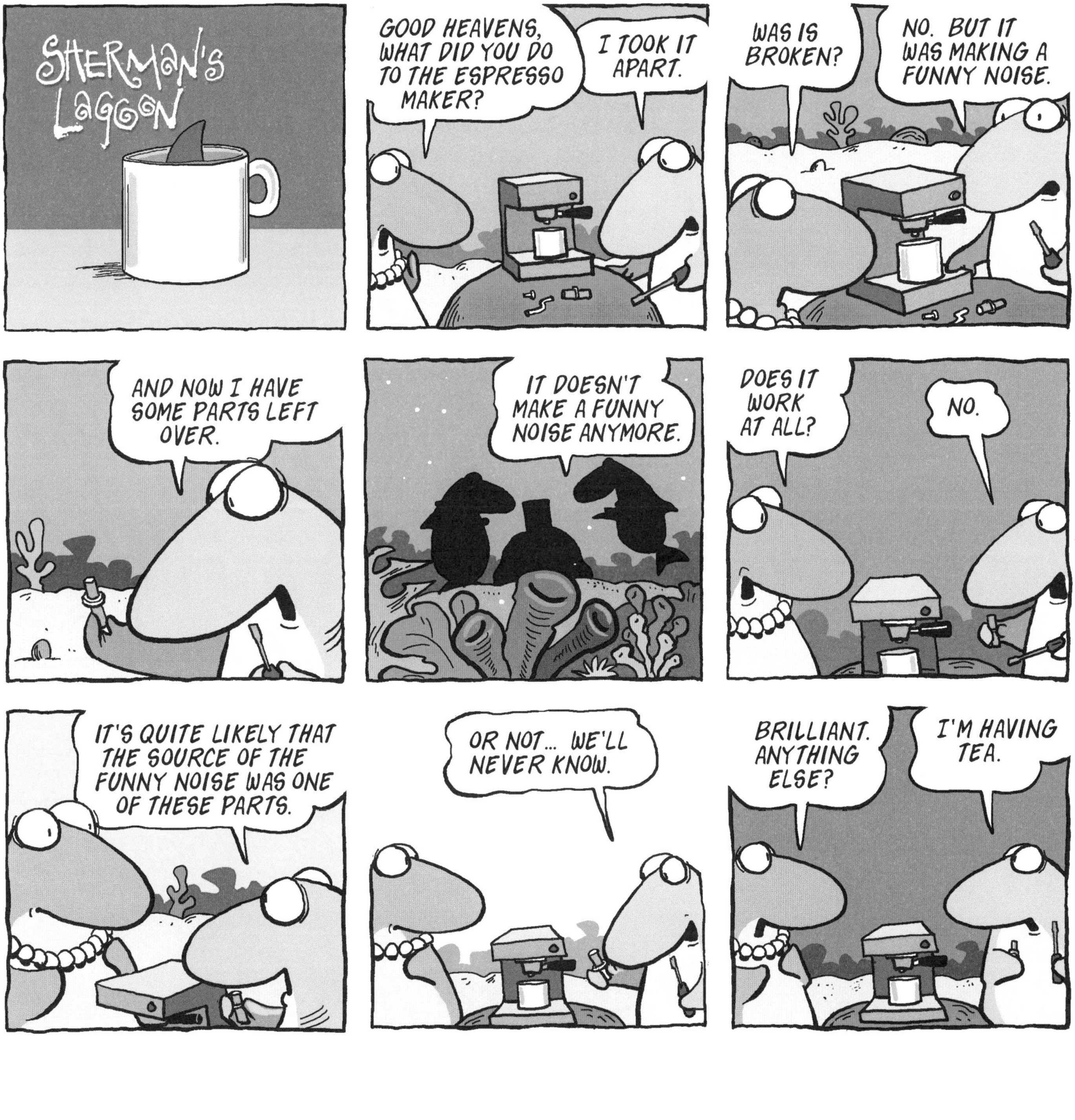
SHERMAN'S LAGOON
GOOD HEAVENS, WHAT DID YOU DO TO THE ESPRESSO MAKER?
I TOOK IT APART.
WAS IS BROKEN?
NO. BUT IT WAS MAKING A FUNNY NOISE.
AND NOW I HAVE SOME PARTS LEFT OVER.
IT DOESN'T MAKE A FUNNY NOISE ANYMORE.
DOES IT WORK AT ALL?
NO.
IT'S QUITE LIKELY THAT THE SOURCE OF THE FUNNY NOISE WAS ONE OF THESE PARTS.
OR NOT... WE'LL NEVER KNOW.
BRILLIANT. ANYTHING ELSE?
I'M HAVING TEA.

SHERMAN, I THINK WE SHOULD...

GO TO HERACLEION?

GET CAUGHT UP IN A WACKY, EXCITING ADVENTURE?

HAVE I BECOME THAT PREDICTABLE AT SUCH A YOUNG AGE?

NO. I GET THESE SCRIPTS IN ADVANCE.

CHEATER!

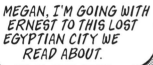

MEGAN, I'M GOING WITH ERNEST TO THIS LOST EGYPTIAN CITY WE READ ABOUT.

HOW WILL YOU KNOW WHERE IT IS?

WELL, IT'S NOT LOST ANYMORE.

ARCHEOLOGISTS ARE BUSILY EXCAVATING IT AS WE SPEAK.

THEN, WON'T YOU JUST BE IN THE WAY?

I CAN EITHER BE IN THE WAY **HERE** OR **THERE**.

GODSPEED.

SO, YOU'RE OFF TO EGYPT. BE CAREFUL.

WHY?

WHY? BECAUSE IT'S POLITICALLY UNSTABLE THERE AT THE MOMENT.

THERE ARE STREET PROTESTS, THERE ARE COUP ATTEMPTS.

IT'S DICEY.

DON'T YOU READ THE NEWSPAPER?

WELL, I READ THE COMICS. THAT'S HOW I FOUND OUT I WAS GOING.

IF YOU DRAW A STRAIGHT LINE BETWEEN OUR LAGOON AND EGYPT, HERE'S WHAT YOU GET...

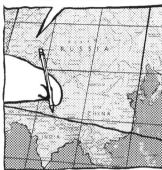

A PATH THAT TAKES US THROUGH THE FOOTHILLS OF THE HIMILAYAS.

THIS WOULD BE A VERY DIFFICULT JOURNEY FOR TWO TALKING FISH.

WHAT IF I DON'T TALK?

EASIER.

IT'S BEEN A LONG DAY OF TRAVELING. THIS IS PROBABLY A GOOD PLACE TO STOP FOR THE NIGHT.

WHAT'S THAT?

CHOCOLATE SYRUP.

IT'S A SHARK THING. WE NEVER BRUSH OUR TEETH. WE JUST GORGE ON CHOCOLATE EVERY NIGHT.

THEN ALL OUR TEETH FALL OUT, THEN WE GROW NEW ONES.

MIRACLE OF EVOLUTION.

WE MADE IT, SHERM. HERACLEION... THE ANCIENT UNDERWATER CITY.

YOU KNOW, WHEN YOU'RE IN THE PRESENCE OF SOMETHING REALLY OLD, THAT FEELING YOU GET?

THAT'S HOW I FEEL RIGHT NOW... LIKE, WOW. THIS STUFF HAS BEEN AROUND A LONG TIME.

I SORT OF FEEL IT AROUND YOU, BUT THIS IS DIFFERENT.

THANK YOU. I THINK.

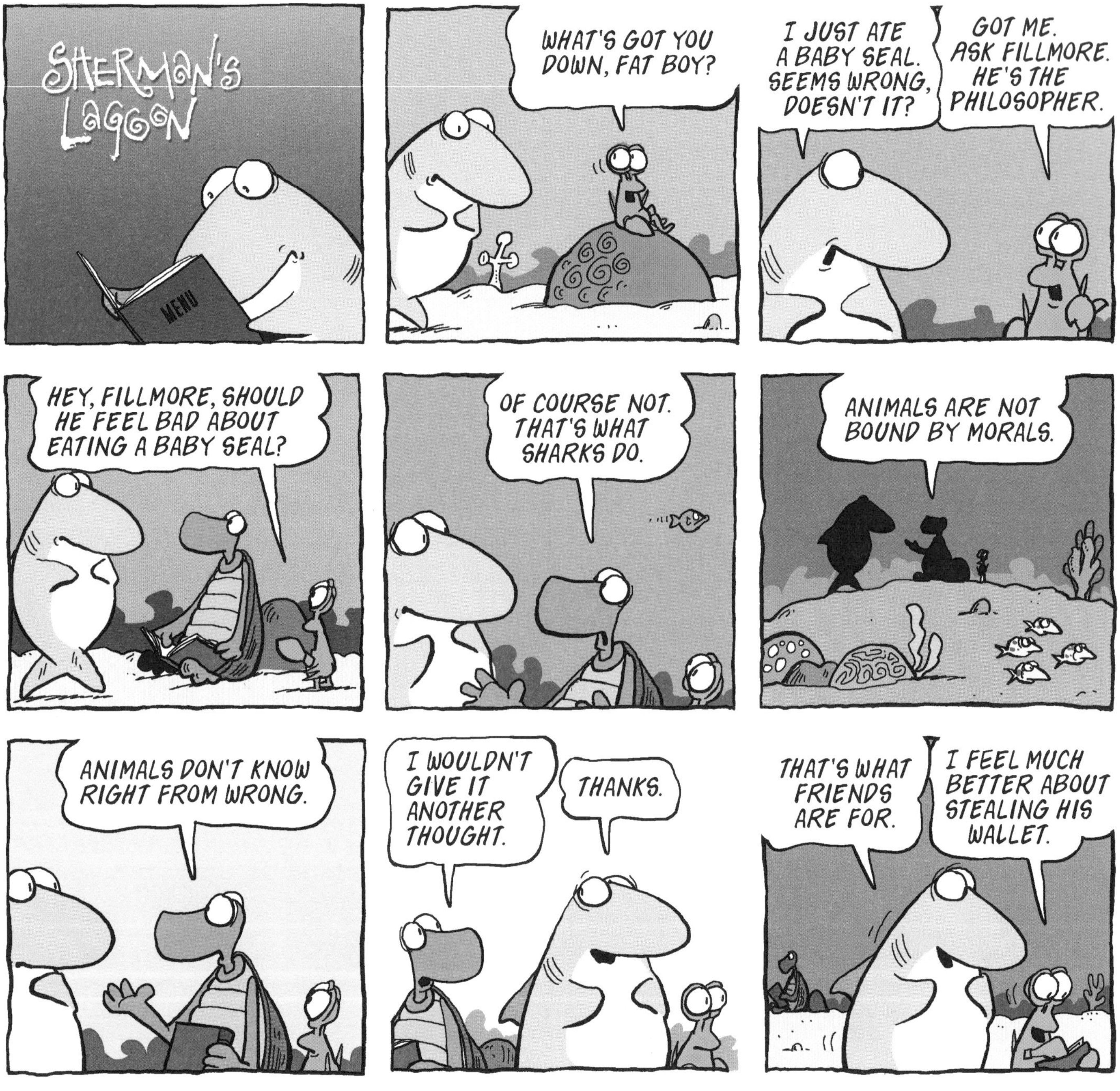
SHERMAN'S LAGOON
MENU
WHAT'S GOT YOU DOWN, FAT BOY?
I JUST ATE A BABY SEAL. SEEMS WRONG, DOESN'T IT?
GOT ME. ASK FILLMORE. HE'S THE PHILOSOPHER.
HEY, FILLMORE, SHOULD HE FEEL BAD ABOUT EATING A BABY SEAL?
OF COURSE NOT. THAT'S WHAT SHARKS DO.
ANIMALS ARE NOT BOUND BY MORALS.
ANIMALS DON'T KNOW RIGHT FROM WRONG.
I WOULDN'T GIVE IT ANOTHER THOUGHT.
THANKS.
THAT'S WHAT FRIENDS ARE FOR.
I FEEL MUCH BETTER ABOUT STEALING HIS WALLET.

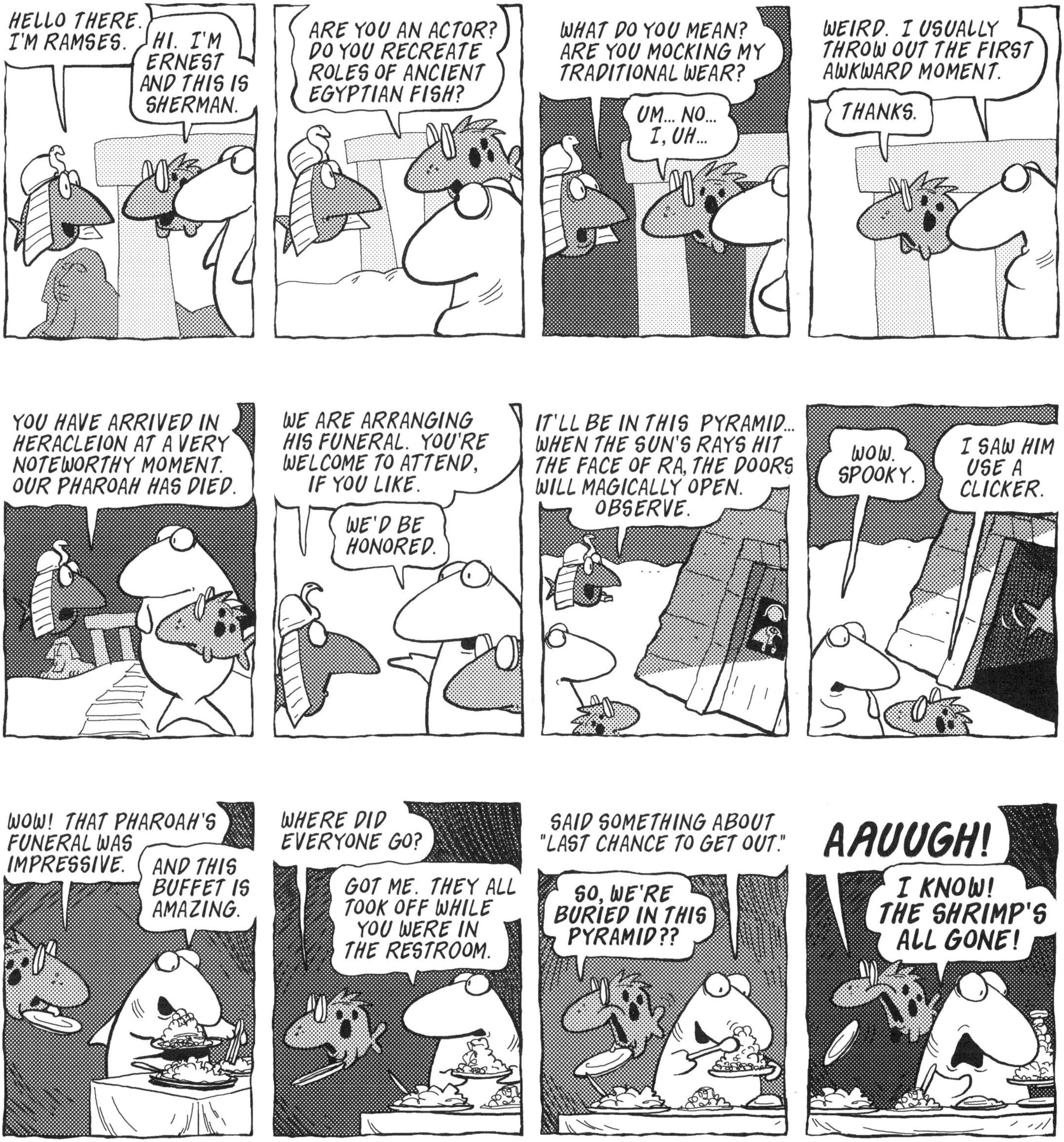
HELLO THERE. I'M RAMSES.
HI. I'M ERNEST AND THIS IS SHERMAN.
ARE YOU AN ACTOR? DO YOU RECREATE ROLES OF ANCIENT EGYPTIAN FISH?
WHAT DO YOU MEAN? ARE YOU MOCKING MY TRADITIONAL WEAR?
UM... NO... I, UH...
WEIRD. I USUALLY THROW OUT THE FIRST AWKWARD MOMENT.
THANKS.
YOU HAVE ARRIVED IN HERACLEION AT A VERY NOTEWORTHY MOMENT. OUR PHAROAH HAS DIED.
WE ARE ARRANGING HIS FUNERAL. YOU'RE WELCOME TO ATTEND, IF YOU LIKE.
WE'D BE HONORED.
IT'LL BE IN THIS PYRAMID... WHEN THE SUN'S RAYS HIT THE FACE OF RA, THE DOORS WILL MAGICALLY OPEN. OBSERVE.
WOW. SPOOKY.
I SAW HIM USE A CLICKER.
WOW! THAT PHAROAH'S FUNERAL WAS IMPRESSIVE.
AND THIS BUFFET IS AMAZING.
WHERE DID EVERYONE GO?
GOT ME. THEY ALL TOOK OFF WHILE YOU WERE IN THE RESTROOM.
SAID SOMETHING ABOUT "LAST CHANCE TO GET OUT."
SO, WE'RE BURIED IN THIS PYRAMID??
AAUUGH!
I KNOW! THE SHRIMP'S ALL GONE!

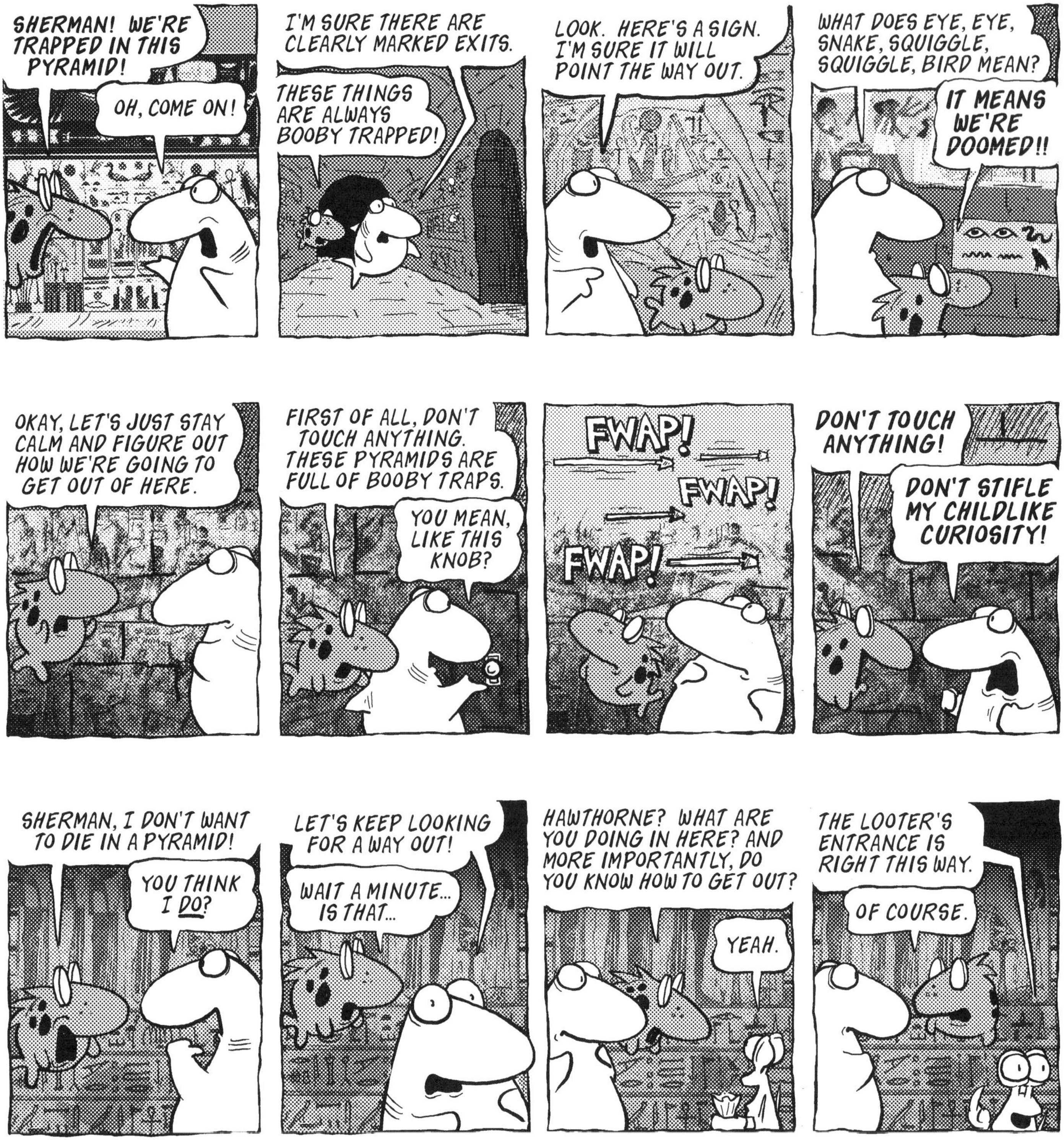
SHERMAN! WE'RE TRAPPED IN THIS PYRAMID!
OH, COME ON!
I'M SURE THERE ARE CLEARLY MARKED EXITS.
THESE THINGS ARE ALWAYS BOOBY TRAPPED!
LOOK. HERE'S A SIGN. I'M SURE IT WILL POINT THE WAY OUT.
WHAT DOES EYE, EYE, SNAKE, SQUIGGLE, SQUIGGLE, BIRD MEAN?
IT MEANS WE'RE DOOMED!!
OKAY, LET'S JUST STAY CALM AND FIGURE OUT HOW WE'RE GOING TO GET OUT OF HERE.
FIRST OF ALL, DON'T TOUCH ANYTHING. THESE PYRAMIDS ARE FULL OF BOOBY TRAPS.
YOU MEAN, LIKE THIS KNOB?
FWAP!
FWAP!
FWAP!
DON'T TOUCH ANYTHING!
DON'T STIFLE MY CHILDLIKE CURIOSITY!
SHERMAN, I DON'T WANT TO DIE IN A PYRAMID!
YOU THINK I DO?
LET'S KEEP LOOKING FOR A WAY OUT!
WAIT A MINUTE... IS THAT...
HAWTHORNE? WHAT ARE YOU DOING IN HERE? AND MORE IMPORTANTLY, DO YOU KNOW HOW TO GET OUT?
YEAH.
THE LOOTER'S ENTRANCE IS RIGHT THIS WAY.
OF COURSE.

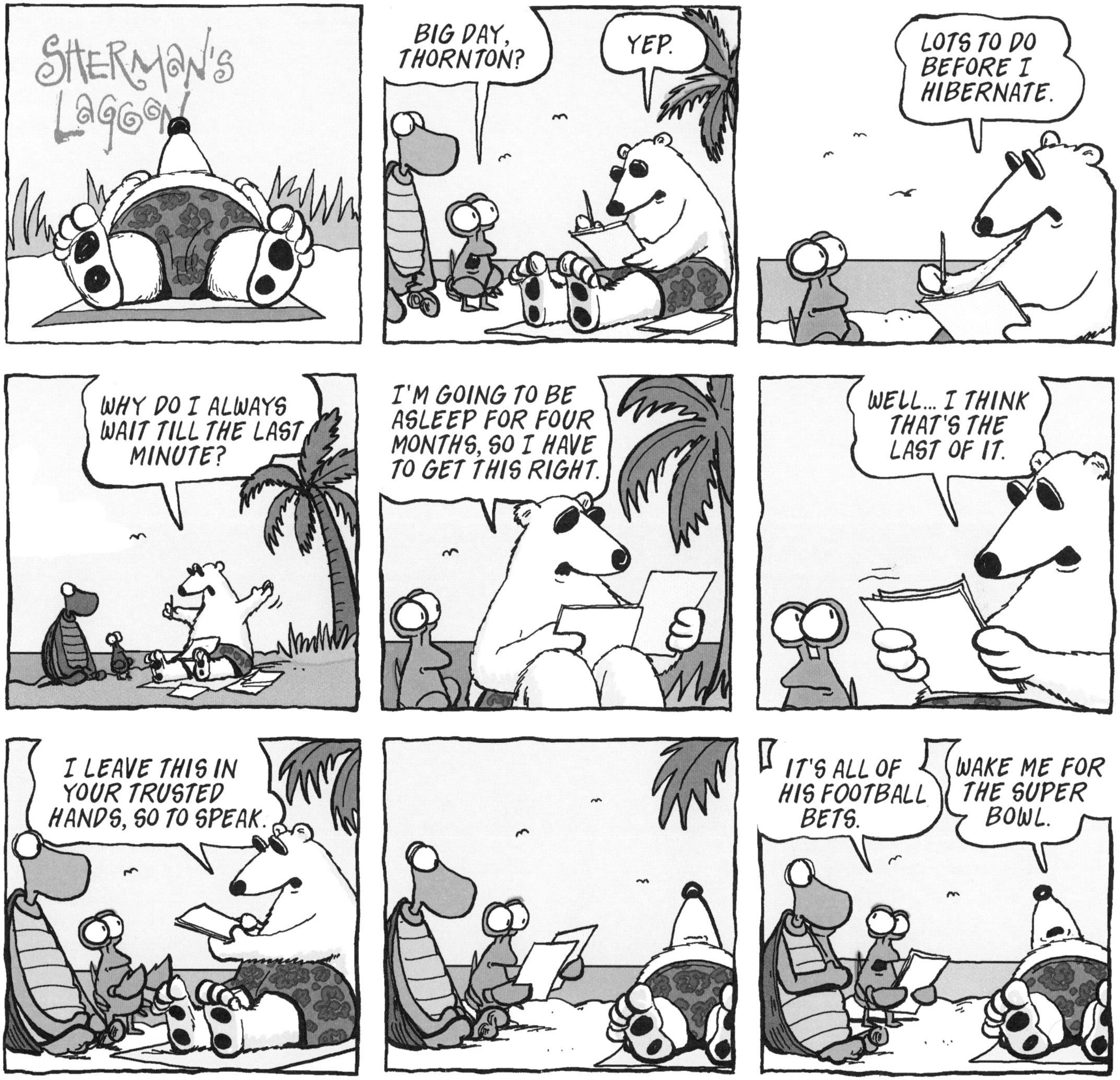
SHERMAN'S LAGOON
BIG DAY, THORNTON?
YEP.
LOTS TO DO BEFORE I HIBERNATE.
WHY DO I ALWAYS WAIT TILL THE LAST MINUTE?
I'M GOING TO BE ASLEEP FOR FOUR MONTHS, SO I HAVE TO GET THIS RIGHT.
WELL... I THINK THAT'S THE LAST OF IT.
I LEAVE THIS IN YOUR TRUSTED HANDS, SO TO SPEAK.
IT'S ALL OF HIS FOOTBALL BETS.
WAKE ME FOR THE SUPER BOWL.

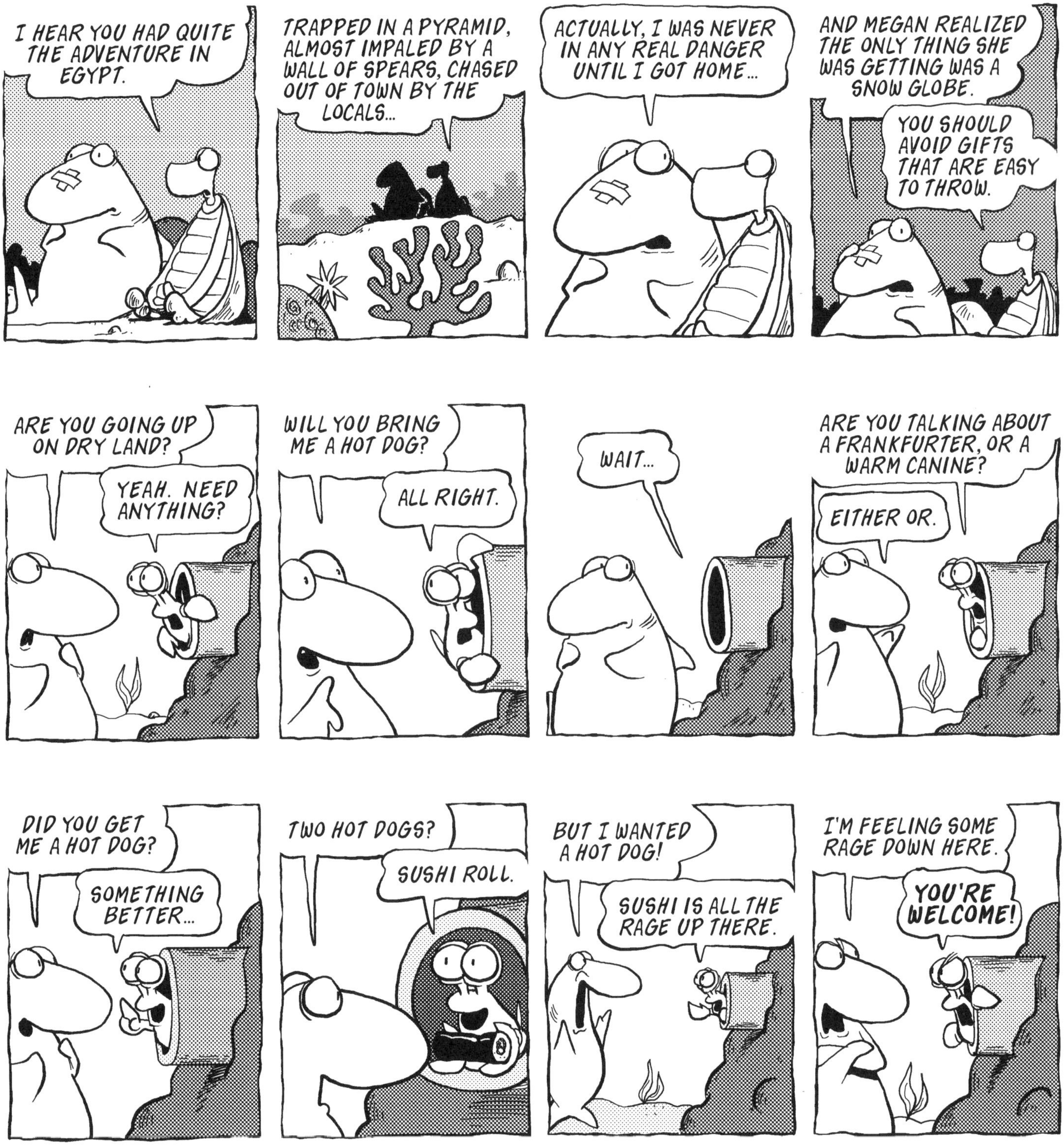
I HEAR YOU HAD QUITE THE ADVENTURE IN EGYPT.
TRAPPED IN A PYRAMID, ALMOST IMPALED BY A WALL OF SPEARS, CHASED OUT OF TOWN BY THE LOCALS...
ACTUALLY, I WAS NEVER IN ANY REAL DANGER UNTIL I GOT HOME...
AND MEGAN REALIZED THE ONLY THING SHE WAS GETTING WAS A SNOW GLOBE.
YOU SHOULD AVOID GIFTS THAT ARE EASY TO THROW.
ARE YOU GOING UP ON DRY LAND?
YEAH. NEED ANYTHING?
WILL YOU BRING ME A HOT DOG?
ALL RIGHT.
WAIT...
ARE YOU TALKING ABOUT A FRANKFURTER, OR A WARM CANINE?
EITHER OR.
DID YOU GET ME A HOT DOG?
SOMETHING BETTER...
TWO HOT DOGS?
SUSHI ROLL.
BUT I WANTED A HOT DOG!
SUSHI IS ALL THE RAGE UP THERE.
I'M FEELING SOME RAGE DOWN HERE.
YOU'RE WELCOME!

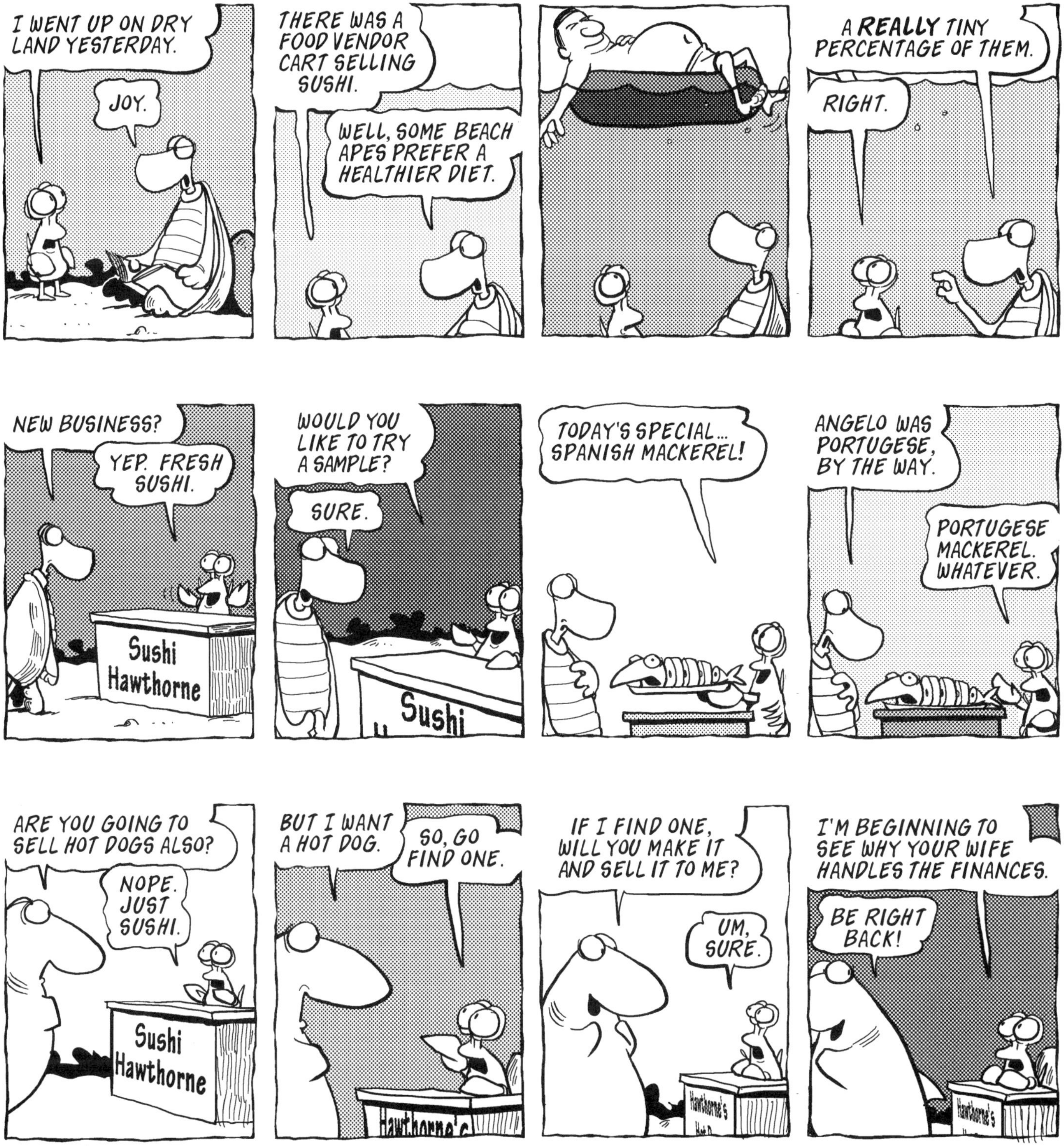
I WENT UP ON DRY LAND YESTERDAY.
JOY.
THERE WAS A FOOD VENDOR CART SELLING SUSHI.
WELL, SOME BEACH APES PREFER A HEALTHIER DIET.
A **REALLY** TINY PERCENTAGE OF THEM.
RIGHT.
NEW BUSINESS?
YEP. FRESH SUSHI.
Sushi Hawthorne
WOULD YOU LIKE TO TRY A SAMPLE?
SURE.
Sushi
TODAY'S SPECIAL... SPANISH MACKEREL!
ANGELO WAS PORTUGESE, BY THE WAY.
PORTUGESE MACKEREL. WHATEVER.
ARE YOU GOING TO SELL HOT DOGS ALSO?
NOPE. JUST SUSHI.
Sushi Hawthorne
BUT I WANT A HOT DOG.
SO, GO FIND ONE.
IF I FIND ONE, WILL YOU MAKE IT AND SELL IT TO ME?
UM, SURE.
Hawthorne's
I'M BEGINNING TO SEE WHY YOUR WIFE HANDLES THE FINANCES.
BE RIGHT BACK!
Hawthorne's

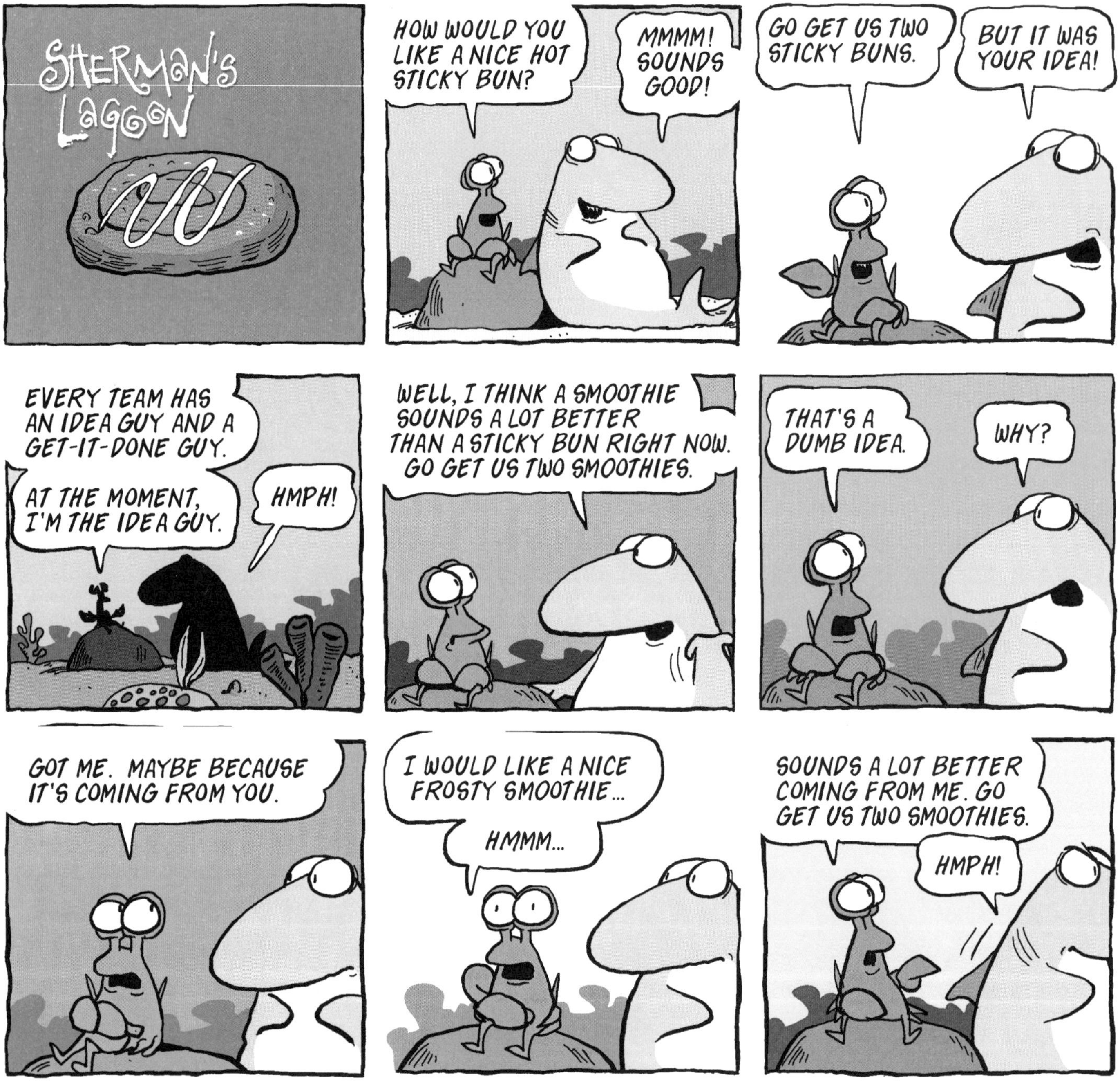
SHERMAN'S LAGOON
HOW WOULD YOU LIKE A NICE HOT STICKY BUN?
MMMM! SOUNDS GOOD!
GO GET US TWO STICKY BUNS.
BUT IT WAS YOUR IDEA!
EVERY TEAM HAS AN IDEA GUY AND A GET-IT-DONE GUY.
AT THE MOMENT, I'M THE IDEA GUY.
HMPH!
WELL, I THINK A SMOOTHIE SOUNDS A LOT BETTER THAN A STICKY BUN RIGHT NOW. GO GET US TWO SMOOTHIES.
THAT'S A DUMB IDEA.
WHY?
GOT ME. MAYBE BECAUSE IT'S COMING FROM YOU.
I WOULD LIKE A NICE FROSTY SMOOTHIE...
HMMM...
SOUNDS A LOT BETTER COMING FROM ME. GO GET US TWO SMOOTHIES.
HMPH!

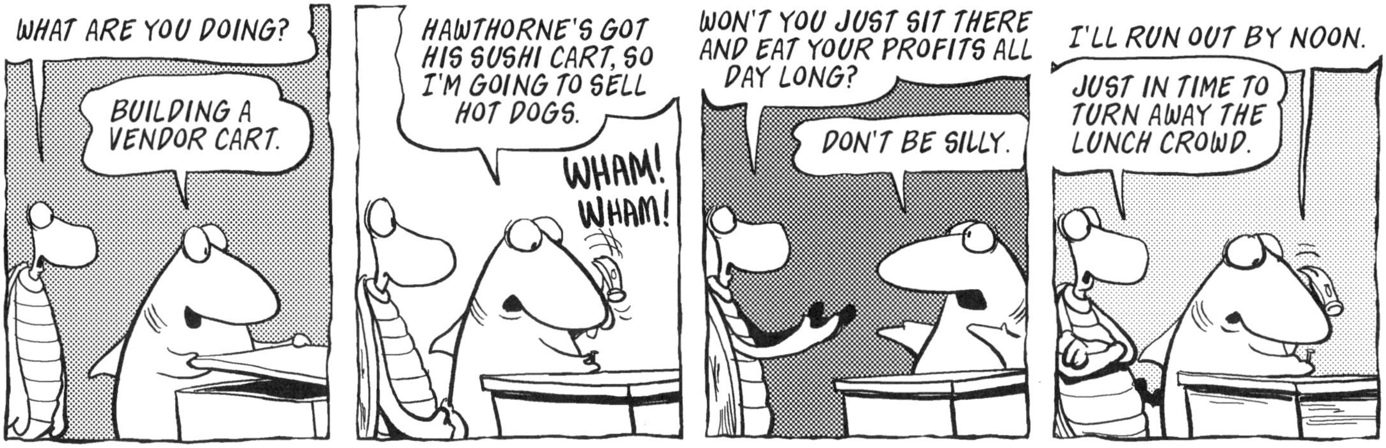
WHAT ARE YOU DOING?
BUILDING A VENDOR CART.
HAWTHORNE'S GOT HIS SUSHI CART, SO I'M GOING TO SELL HOT DOGS.
WHAM! WHAM!
WON'T YOU JUST SIT THERE AND EAT YOUR PROFITS ALL DAY LONG?
DON'T BE SILLY.
I'LL RUN OUT BY NOON.
JUST IN TIME TO TURN AWAY THE LUNCH CROWD.

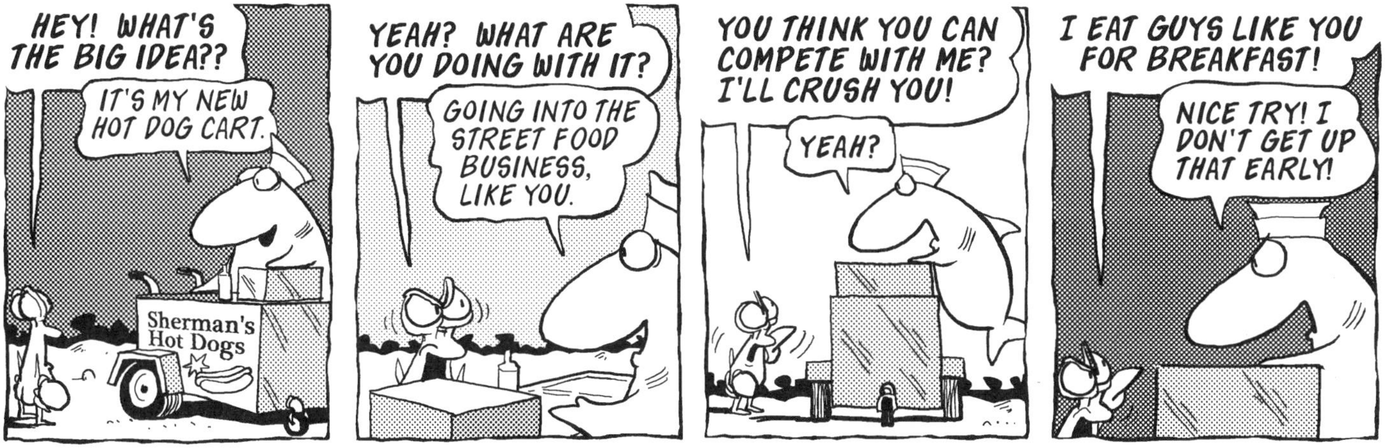
HEY! WHAT'S THE BIG IDEA??
IT'S MY NEW HOT DOG CART.
Sherman's Hot Dogs
YEAH? WHAT ARE YOU DOING WITH IT?
GOING INTO THE STREET FOOD BUSINESS, LIKE YOU.
YOU THINK YOU CAN COMPETE WITH ME? I'LL CRUSH YOU!
YEAH?
I EAT GUYS LIKE YOU FOR BREAKFAST!
NICE TRY! I DON'T GET UP THAT EARLY!

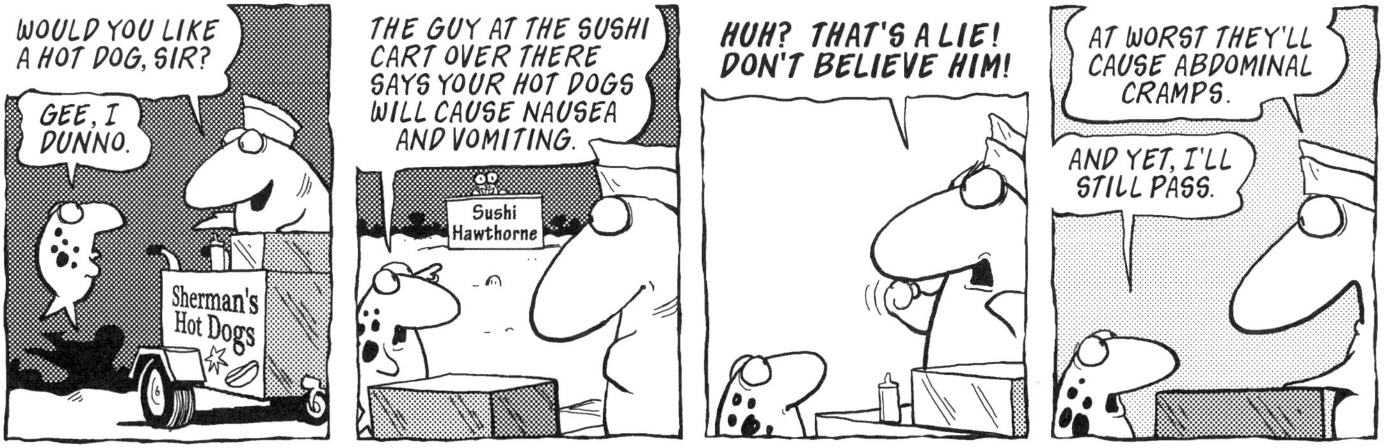
WOULD YOU LIKE A HOT DOG, SIR?
GEE, I DUNNO.
Sherman's Hot Dogs
THE GUY AT THE SUSHI CART OVER THERE SAYS YOUR HOT DOGS WILL CAUSE NAUSEA AND VOMITING.
Sushi Hawthorne
HUH? THAT'S A LIE! DON'T BELIEVE HIM!
AT WORST THEY'LL CAUSE ABDOMINAL CRAMPS.
AND YET, I'LL STILL PASS.

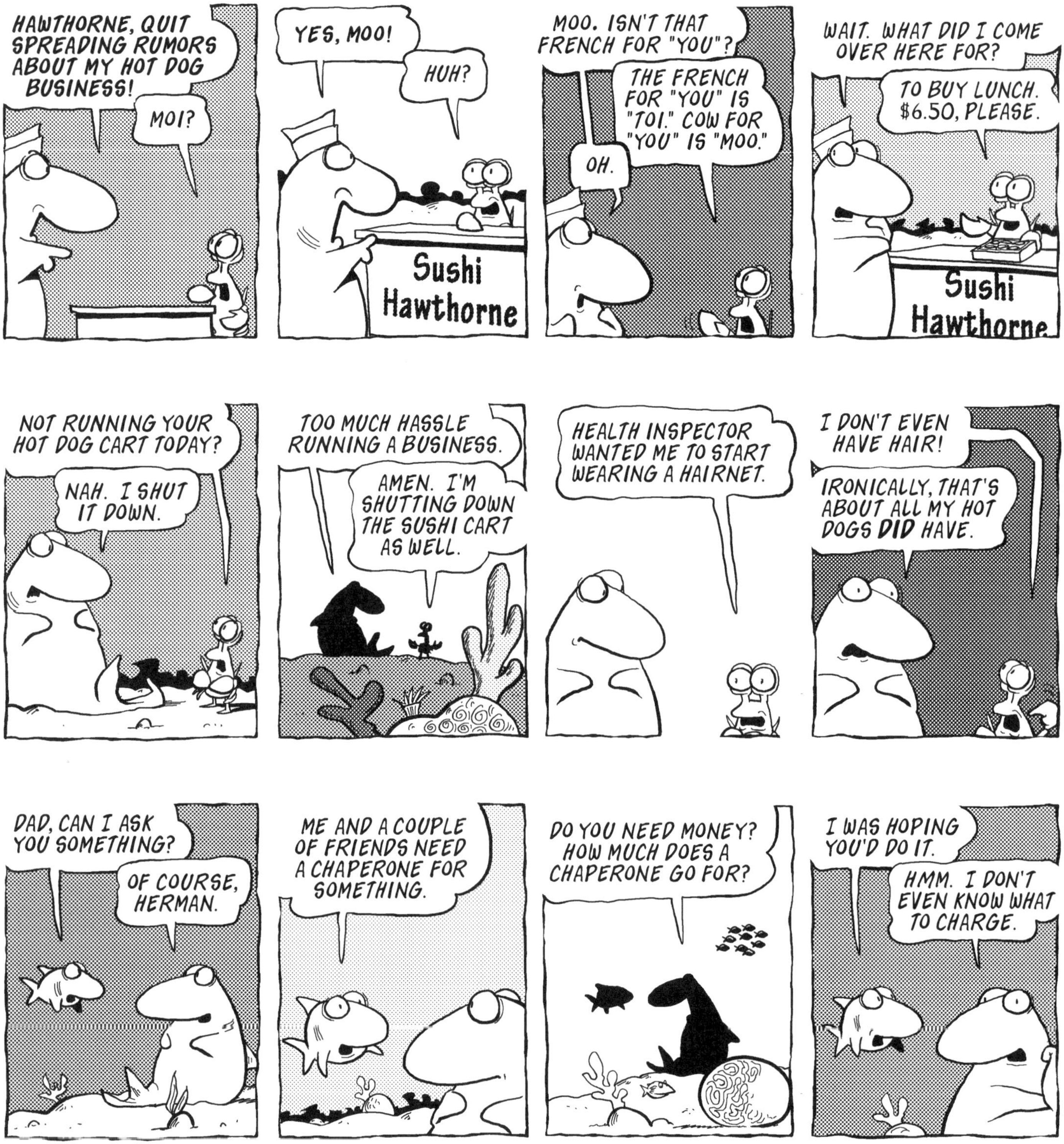
HAWTHORNE, QUIT SPREADING RUMORS ABOUT MY HOT DOG BUSINESS!
MOI?
YES, MOO!
HUH?
Sushi Hawthorne
MOO. ISN'T THAT FRENCH FOR "YOU"?
THE FRENCH FOR "YOU" IS "TOI." COW FOR "YOU" IS "MOO."
OH.
WAIT. WHAT DID I COME OVER HERE FOR?
TO BUY LUNCH. $6.50, PLEASE.
Sushi Hawthorne
NOT RUNNING YOUR HOT DOG CART TODAY?
NAH. I SHUT IT DOWN.
TOO MUCH HASSLE RUNNING A BUSINESS.
AMEN. I'M SHUTTING DOWN THE SUSHI CART AS WELL.
HEALTH INSPECTOR WANTED ME TO START WEARING A HAIRNET.
I DON'T EVEN HAVE HAIR!
IRONICALLY, THAT'S ABOUT ALL MY HOT DOGS DID HAVE.
DAD, CAN I ASK YOU SOMETHING?
OF COURSE, HERMAN.
ME AND A COUPLE OF FRIENDS NEED A CHAPERONE FOR SOMETHING.
DO YOU NEED MONEY? HOW MUCH DOES A CHAPERONE GO FOR?
I WAS HOPING YOU'D DO IT.
HMM. I DON'T EVEN KNOW WHAT TO CHARGE.

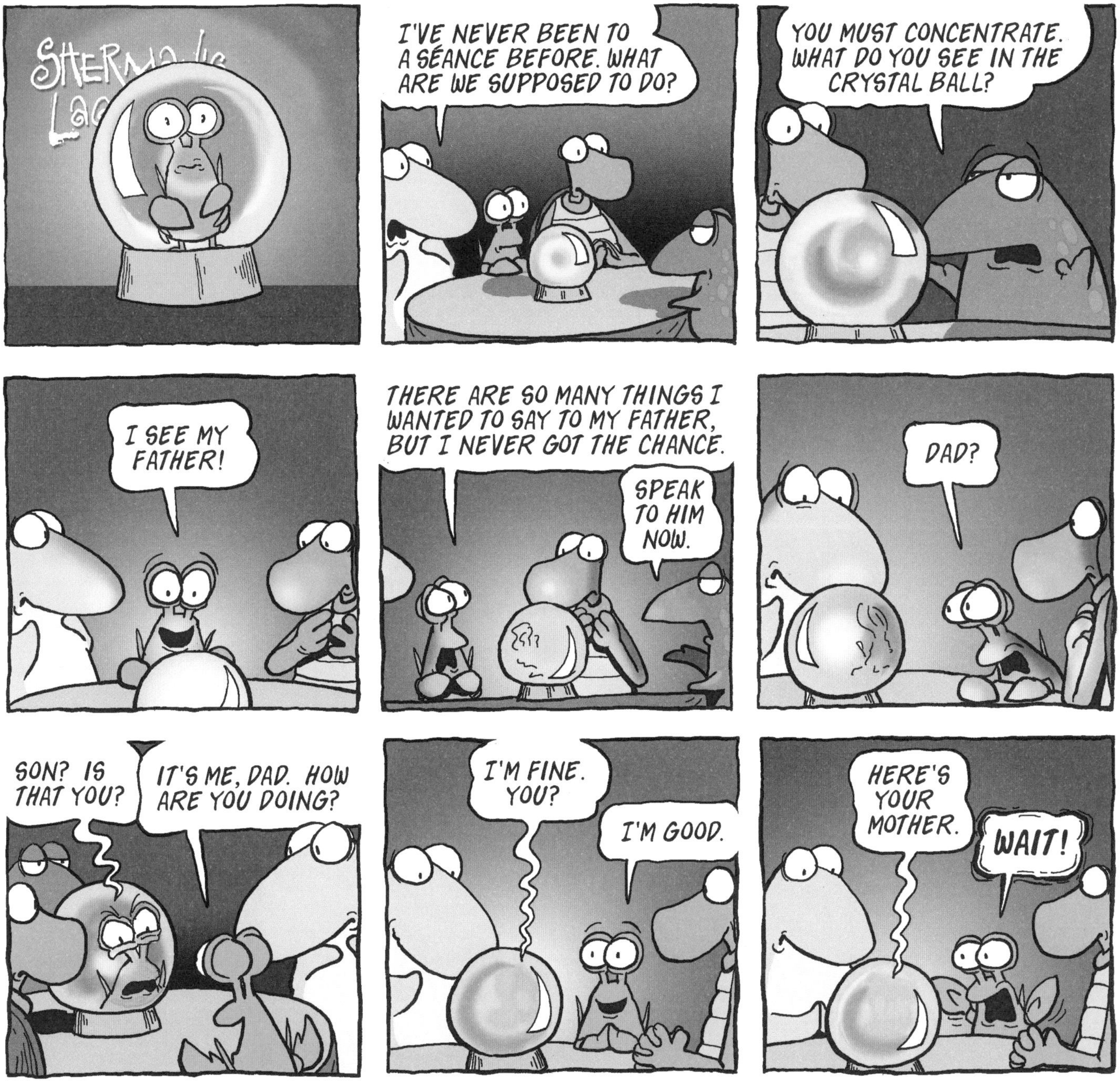
SHERMAN'S LAGOON
I'VE NEVER BEEN TO A SÉANCE BEFORE. WHAT ARE WE SUPPOSED TO DO?
YOU MUST CONCENTRATE. WHAT DO YOU SEE IN THE CRYSTAL BALL?
I SEE MY FATHER!
THERE ARE SO MANY THINGS I WANTED TO SAY TO MY FATHER, BUT I NEVER GOT THE CHANCE.
SPEAK TO HIM NOW.
DAD?
SON? IS THAT YOU?
IT'S ME, DAD. HOW ARE YOU DOING?
I'M FINE. YOU?
I'M GOOD.
HERE'S YOUR MOTHER.
WAIT!

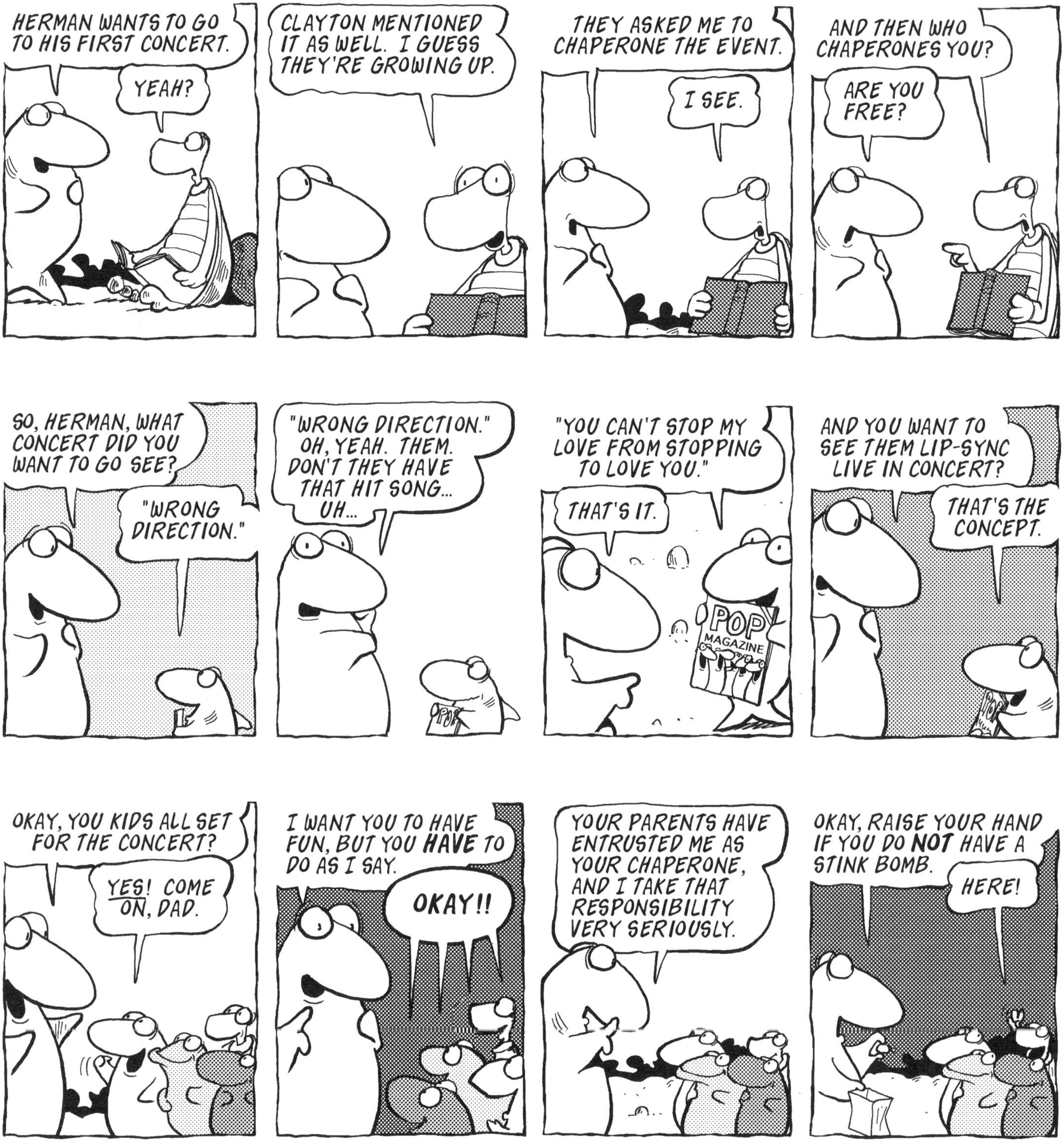
HERMAN WANTS TO GO TO HIS FIRST CONCERT.
YEAH?
CLAYTON MENTIONED IT AS WELL. I GUESS THEY'RE GROWING UP.
THEY ASKED ME TO CHAPERONE THE EVENT.
I SEE.
AND THEN WHO CHAPERONES YOU?
ARE YOU FREE?
SO, HERMAN, WHAT CONCERT DID YOU WANT TO GO SEE?
"WRONG DIRECTION."
"WRONG DIRECTION." OH, YEAH. THEM. DON'T THEY HAVE THAT HIT SONG... UH...
"YOU CAN'T STOP MY LOVE FROM STOPPING TO LOVE YOU."
THAT'S IT.
POP MAGAZINE
AND YOU WANT TO SEE THEM LIP-SYNC LIVE IN CONCERT?
THAT'S THE CONCEPT.
OKAY, YOU KIDS ALL SET FOR THE CONCERT?
YES! COME ON, DAD.
I WANT YOU TO HAVE FUN, BUT YOU **HAVE** TO DO AS I SAY.
OKAY!!
YOUR PARENTS HAVE ENTRUSTED ME AS YOUR CHAPERONE, AND I TAKE THAT RESPONSIBILITY VERY SERIOUSLY.
OKAY, RAISE YOUR HAND IF YOU DO **NOT** HAVE A STINK BOMB.
HERE!

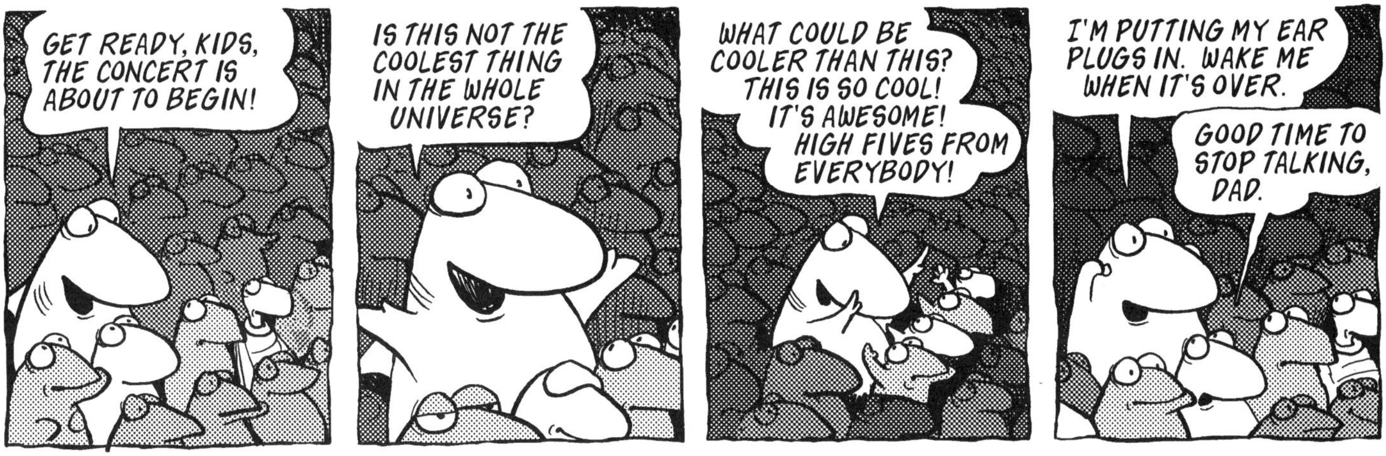
GET READY, KIDS, THE CONCERT IS ABOUT TO BEGIN!
IS THIS NOT THE COOLEST THING IN THE WHOLE UNIVERSE?
WHAT COULD BE COOLER THAN THIS? THIS IS SO COOL! IT'S AWESOME! HIGH FIVES FROM EVERYBODY!
I'M PUTTING MY EAR PLUGS IN. WAKE ME WHEN IT'S OVER.
GOOD TIME TO STOP TALKING, DAD.

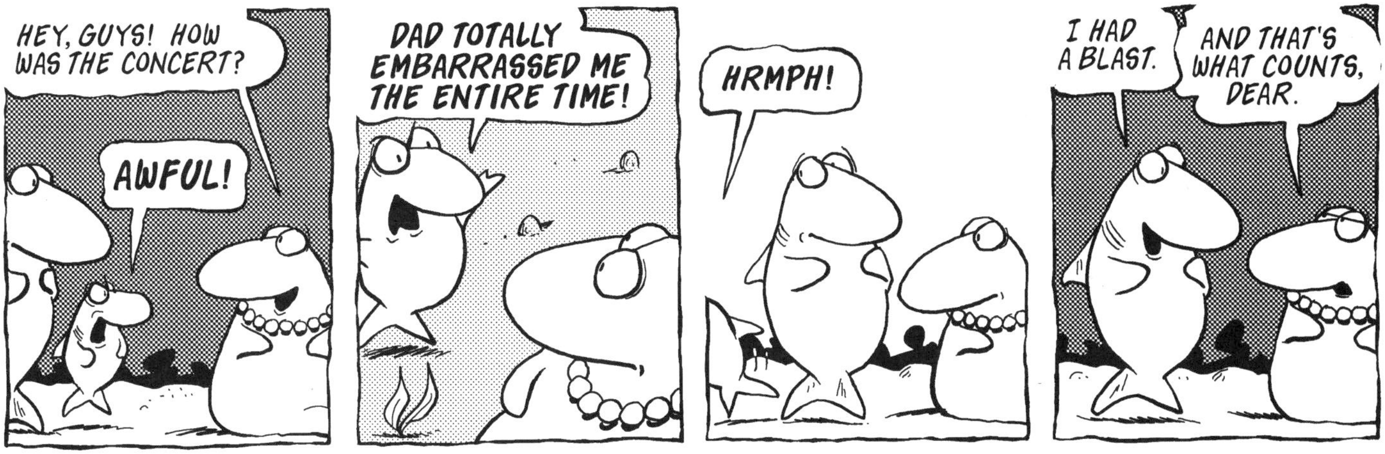
HEY, GUYS! HOW WAS THE CONCERT?
AWFUL!
DAD TOTALLY EMBARRASSED ME THE ENTIRE TIME!
HRMPH!
I HAD A BLAST.
AND THAT'S WHAT COUNTS, DEAR.

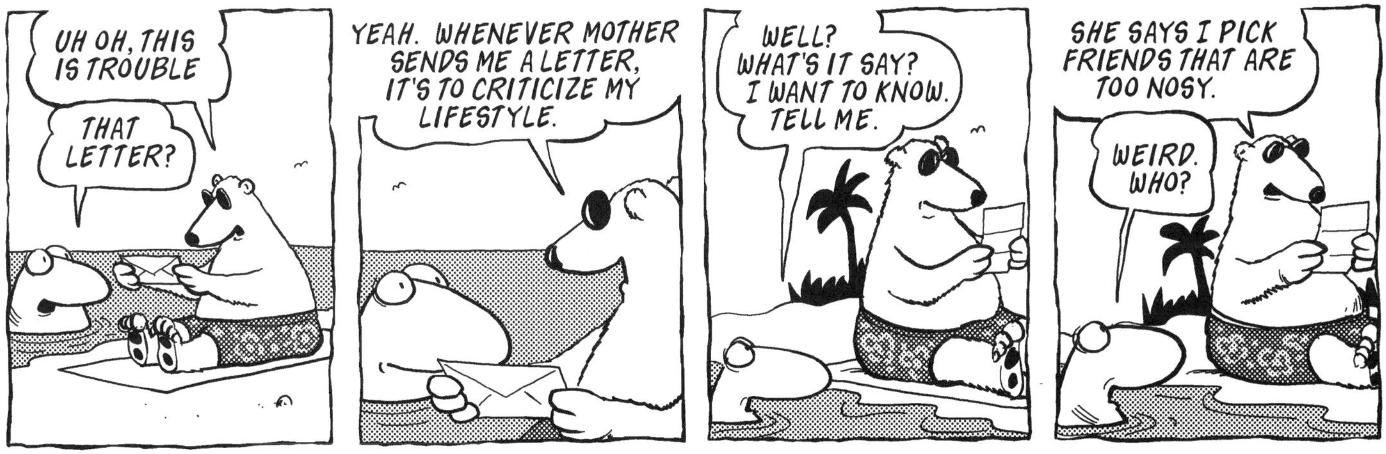
UH OH, THIS IS TROUBLE
THAT LETTER?
YEAH. WHENEVER MOTHER SENDS ME A LETTER, IT'S TO CRITICIZE MY LIFESTYLE.
WELL? WHAT'S IT SAY? I WANT TO KNOW. TELL ME.
SHE SAYS I PICK FRIENDS THAT ARE TOO NOSY.
WEIRD. WHO?

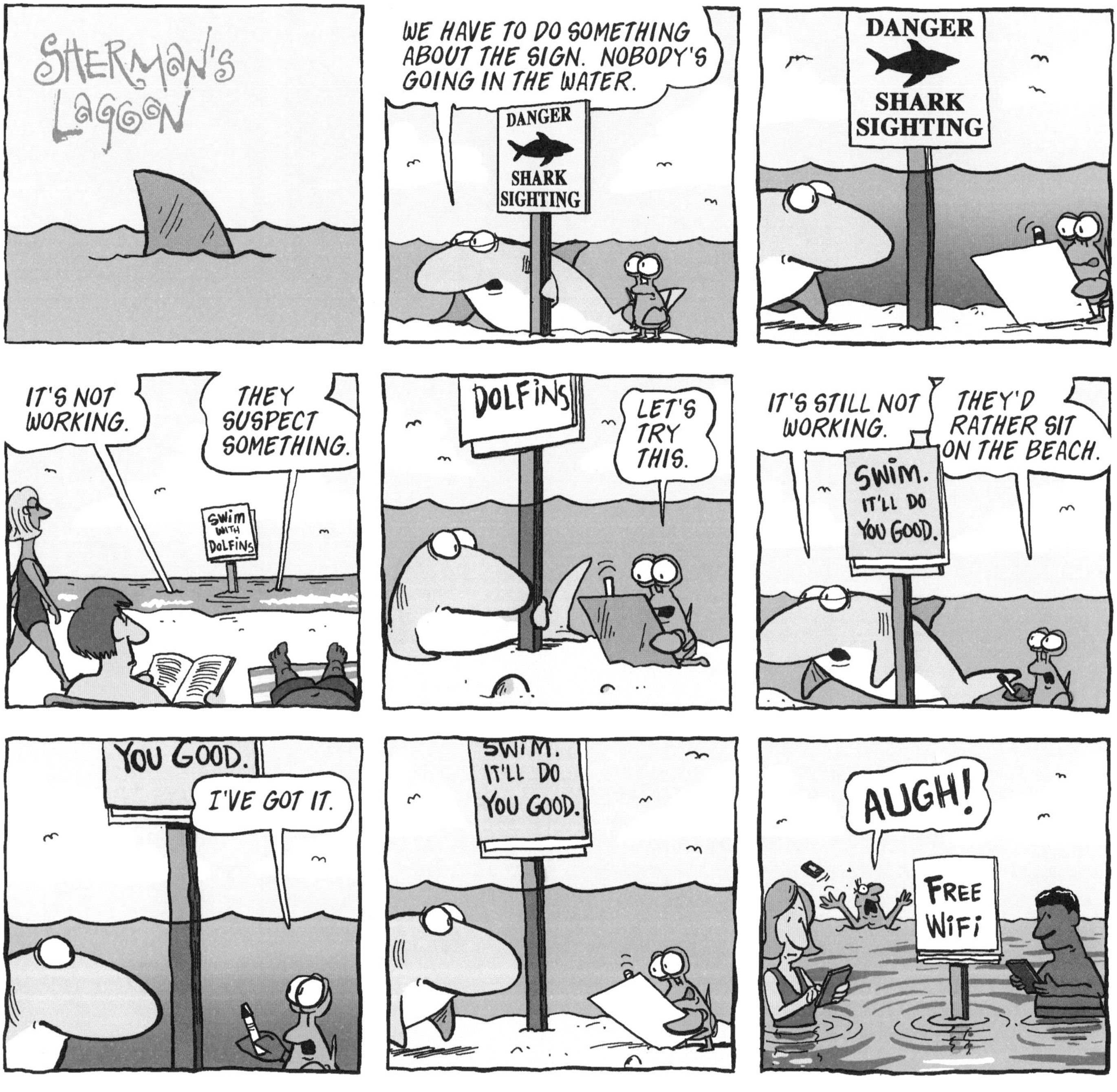
SHERMAN'S LAGOON
WE HAVE TO DO SOMETHING ABOUT THE SIGN. NOBODY'S GOING IN THE WATER.
DANGER SHARK SIGHTING
DANGER SHARK SIGHTING
IT'S NOT WORKING.
THEY SUSPECT SOMETHING.
SWIM WITH DOLFINS
DOLFINS
LET'S TRY THIS.
IT'S STILL NOT WORKING.
THEY'D RATHER SIT ON THE BEACH.
SWIM. IT'LL DO YOU GOOD.
YOU GOOD.
I'VE GOT IT.
SWIM. IT'LL DO YOU GOOD.
AUGH!
FREE WIFI

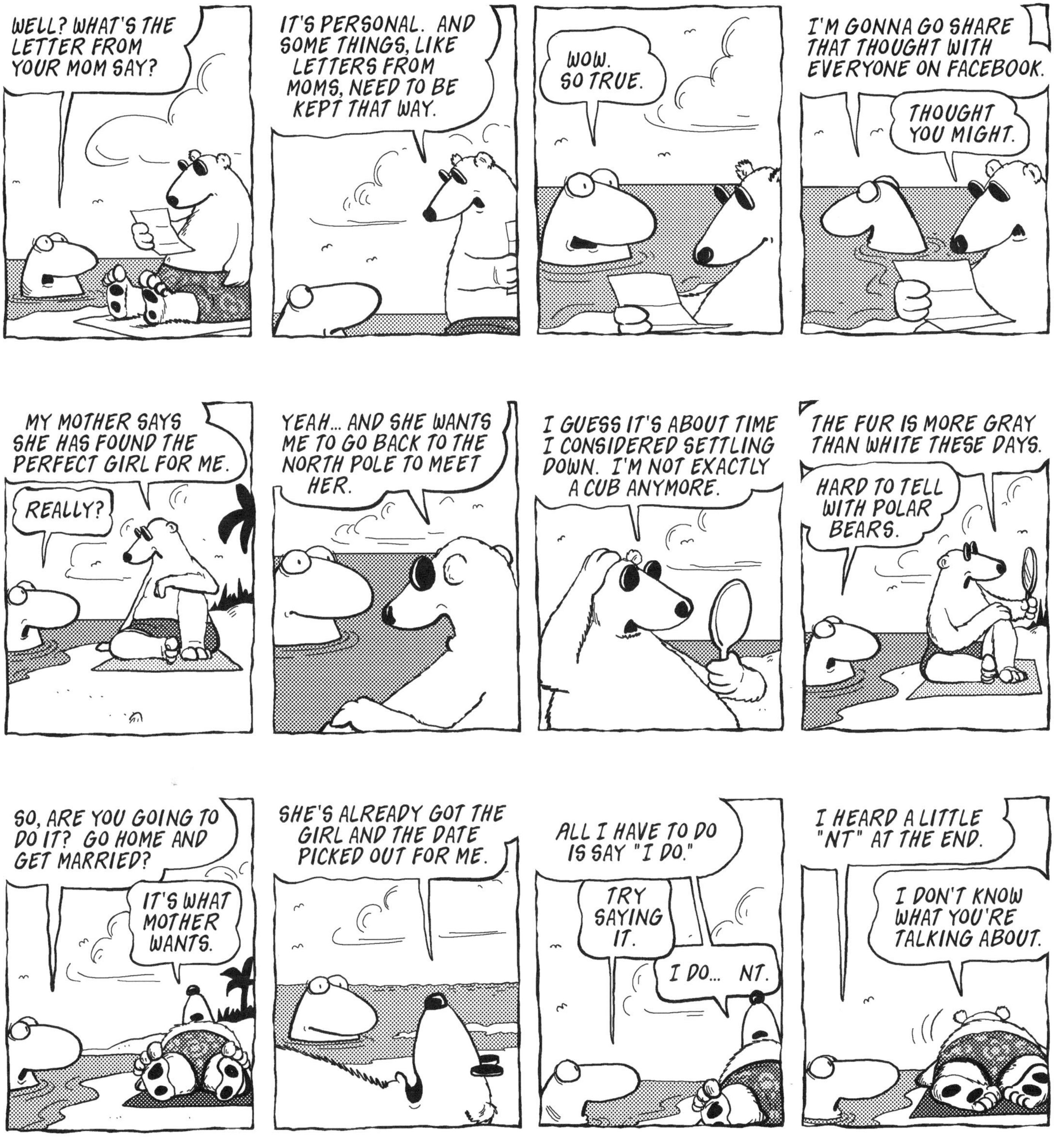
WELL? WHAT'S THE LETTER FROM YOUR MOM SAY?
IT'S PERSONAL. AND SOME THINGS, LIKE LETTERS FROM MOMS, NEED TO BE KEPT THAT WAY.
WOW. SO TRUE.
I'M GONNA GO SHARE THAT THOUGHT WITH EVERYONE ON FACEBOOK.
THOUGHT YOU MIGHT.
MY MOTHER SAYS SHE HAS FOUND THE PERFECT GIRL FOR ME.
REALLY?
YEAH... AND SHE WANTS ME TO GO BACK TO THE NORTH POLE TO MEET HER.
I GUESS IT'S ABOUT TIME I CONSIDERED SETTLING DOWN. I'M NOT EXACTLY A CUB ANYMORE.
THE FUR IS MORE GRAY THAN WHITE THESE DAYS.
HARD TO TELL WITH POLAR BEARS.
SO, ARE YOU GOING TO DO IT? GO HOME AND GET MARRIED?
IT'S WHAT MOTHER WANTS.
SHE'S ALREADY GOT THE GIRL AND THE DATE PICKED OUT FOR ME.
ALL I HAVE TO DO IS SAY "I DO."
TRY SAYING IT.
I DO... NT.
I HEARD A LITTLE "NT" AT THE END.
I DON'T KNOW WHAT YOU'RE TALKING ABOUT.

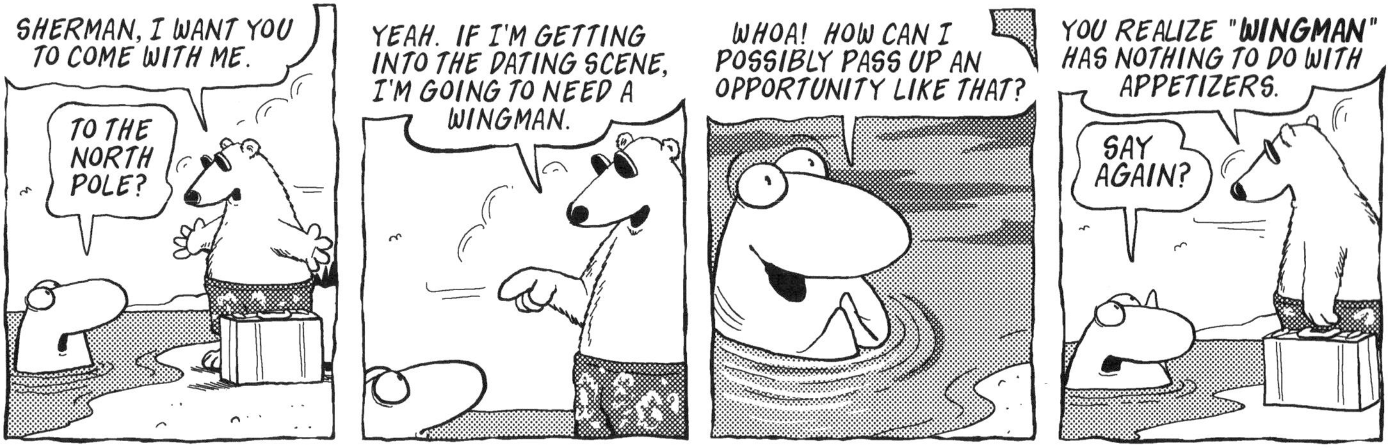
SHERMAN, I WANT YOU TO COME WITH ME.
TO THE NORTH POLE?
YEAH. IF I'M GETTING INTO THE DATING SCENE, I'M GOING TO NEED A WINGMAN.
WHOA! HOW CAN I POSSIBLY PASS UP AN OPPORTUNITY LIKE THAT?
YOU REALIZE "WINGMAN" HAS NOTHING TO DO WITH APPETIZERS.
SAY AGAIN?

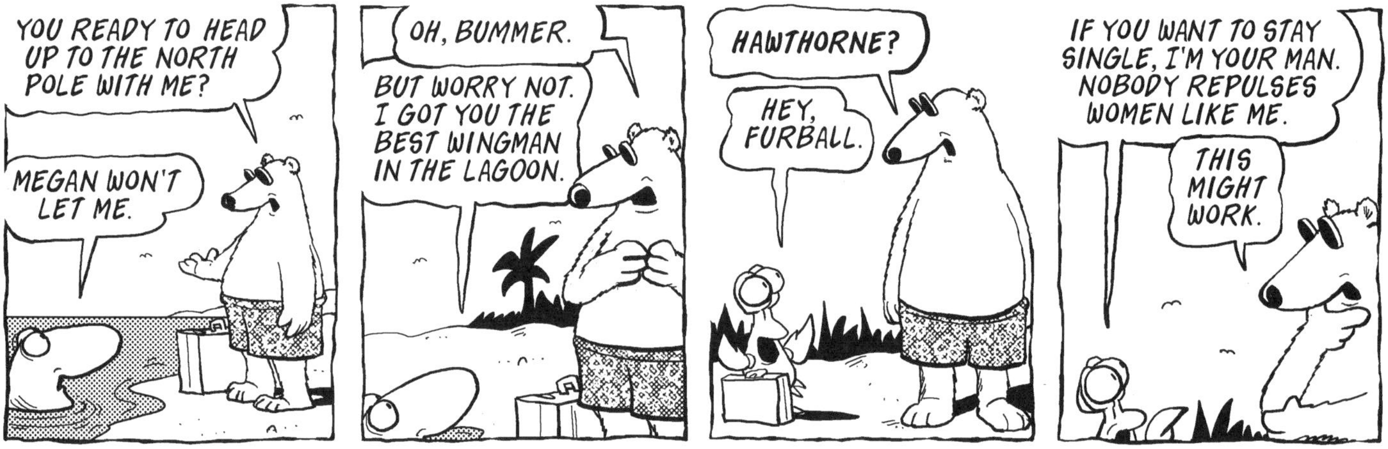
YOU READY TO HEAD UP TO THE NORTH POLE WITH ME?
MEGAN WON'T LET ME.
OH, BUMMER.
BUT WORRY NOT. I GOT YOU THE BEST WINGMAN IN THE LAGOON.
HAWTHORNE?
HEY, FURBALL.
IF YOU WANT TO STAY SINGLE, I'M YOUR MAN. NOBODY REPULSES WOMEN LIKE ME.
THIS MIGHT WORK.

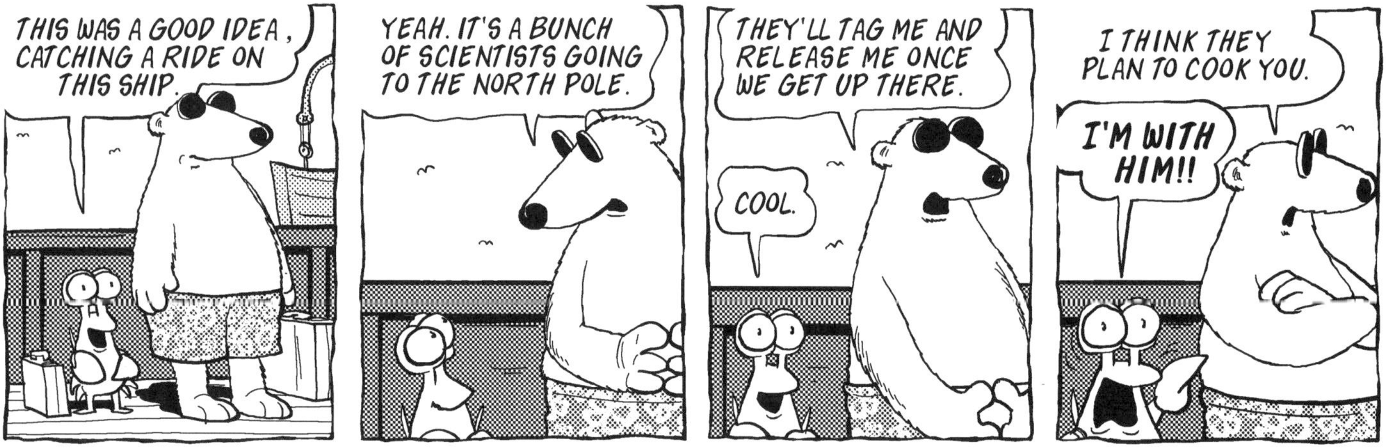
THIS WAS A GOOD IDEA, CATCHING A RIDE ON THIS SHIP.
YEAH. IT'S A BUNCH OF SCIENTISTS GOING TO THE NORTH POLE.
THEY'LL TAG ME AND RELEASE ME ONCE WE GET UP THERE.
COOL.
I THINK THEY PLAN TO COOK YOU.
I'M WITH HIM!!

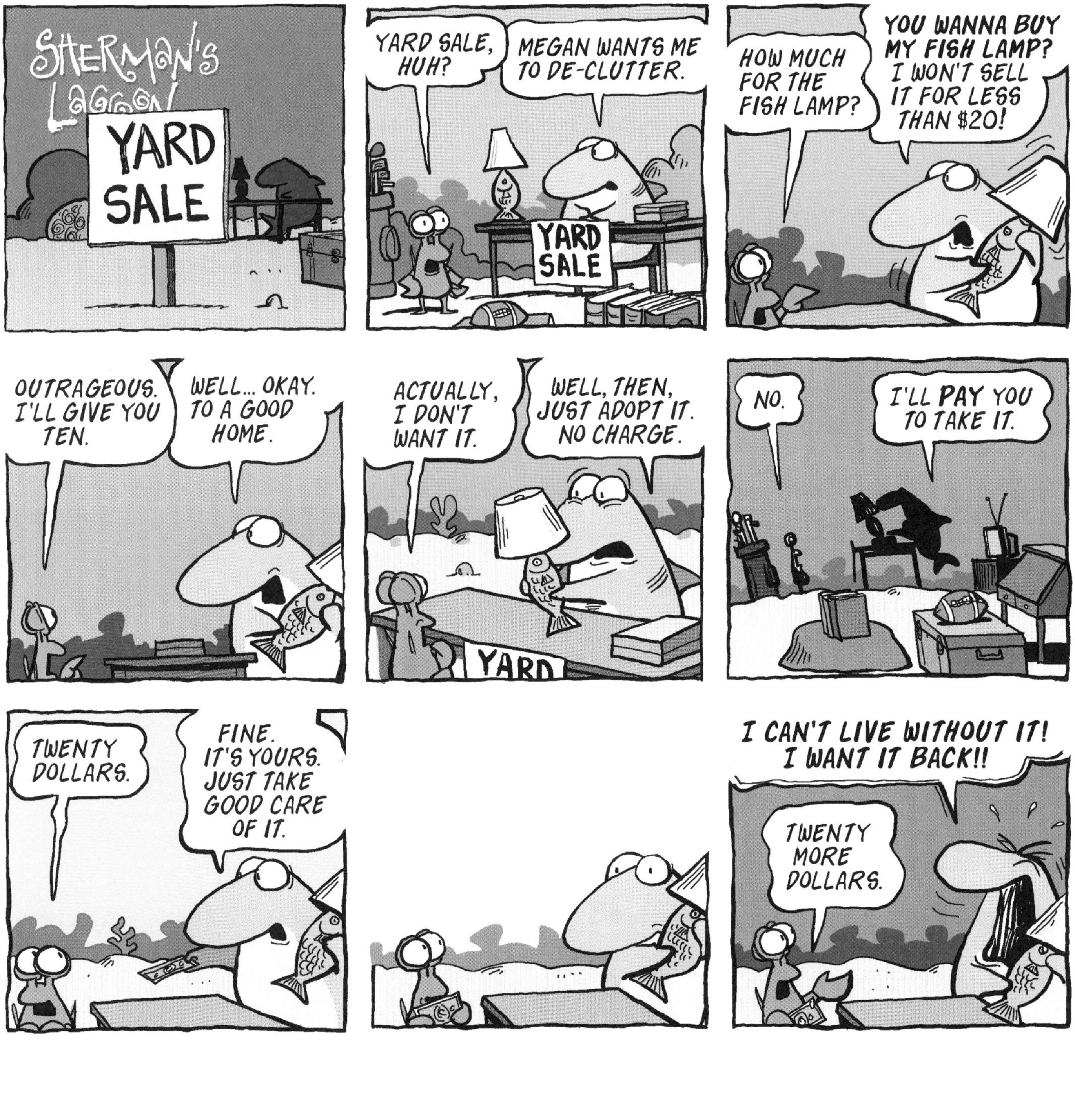

SHERMAN'S LAGOON
YARD SALE
YARD SALE, HUH?
MEGAN WANTS ME TO DE-CLUTTER.
YARD SALE
HOW MUCH FOR THE FISH LAMP?
YOU WANNA BUY MY FISH LAMP? I WON'T SELL IT FOR LESS THAN $20!
OUTRAGEOUS. I'LL GIVE YOU TEN.
WELL... OKAY. TO A GOOD HOME.
ACTUALLY, I DON'T WANT IT.
WELL, THEN, JUST ADOPT IT. NO CHARGE.
YARD
NO.
I'LL PAY YOU TO TAKE IT.
TWENTY DOLLARS.
FINE. IT'S YOURS. JUST TAKE GOOD CARE OF IT.
I CAN'T LIVE WITHOUT IT! I WANT IT BACK!!
TWENTY MORE DOLLARS.

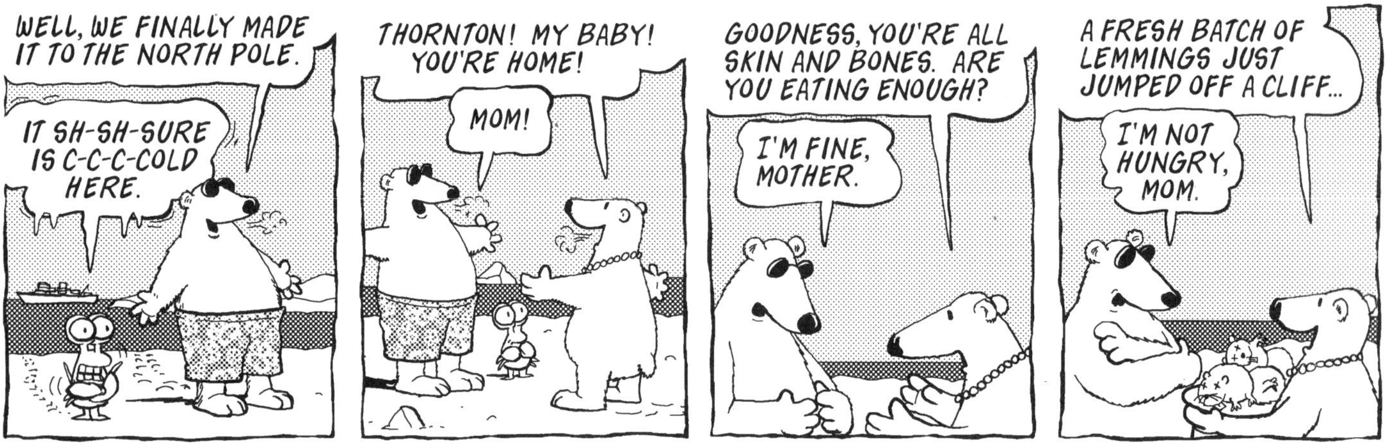
WELL, WE FINALLY MADE IT TO THE NORTH POLE.
IT SH-SH-SURE IS C-C-C-COLD HERE.
THORNTON! MY BABY! YOU'RE HOME!
MOM!
GOODNESS, YOU'RE ALL SKIN AND BONES. ARE YOU EATING ENOUGH?
I'M FINE, MOTHER.
A FRESH BATCH OF LEMMINGS JUST JUMPED OFF A CLIFF...
I'M NOT HUNGRY, MOM.

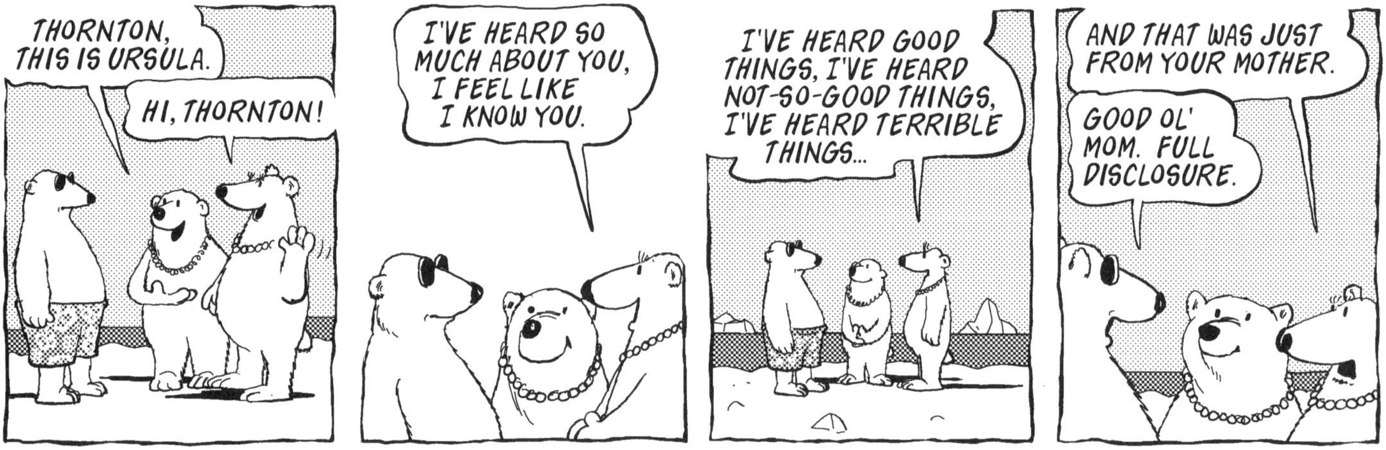
THORNTON, THIS IS URSULA.
HI, THORNTON!
I'VE HEARD SO MUCH ABOUT YOU, I FEEL LIKE I KNOW YOU.
I'VE HEARD GOOD THINGS, I'VE HEARD NOT-SO-GOOD THINGS, I'VE HEARD TERRIBLE THINGS...
AND THAT WAS JUST FROM YOUR MOTHER.
GOOD OL' MOM. FULL DISCLOSURE.

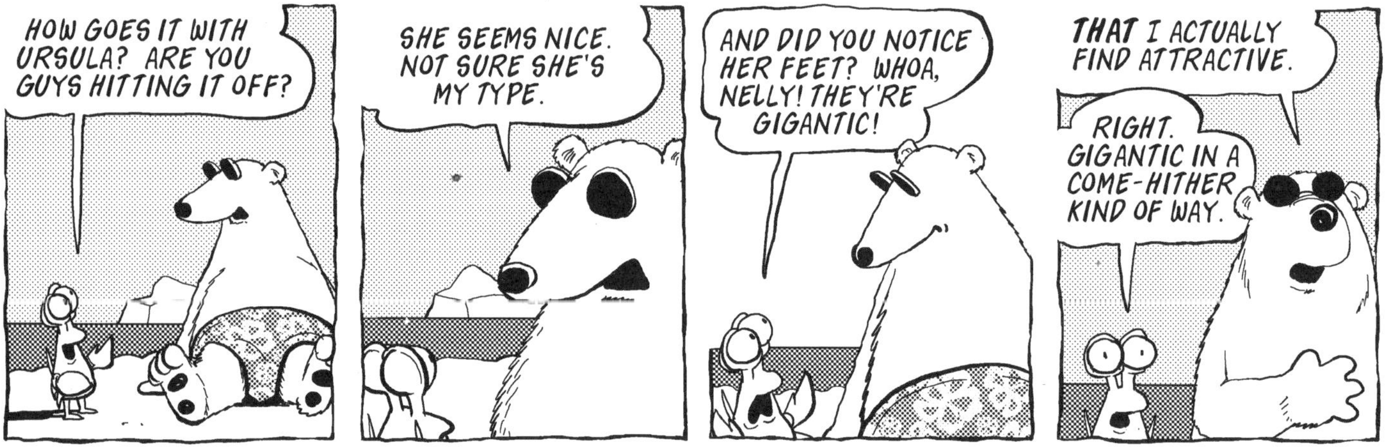
HOW GOES IT WITH URSULA? ARE YOU GUYS HITTING IT OFF?
SHE SEEMS NICE. NOT SURE SHE'S MY TYPE.
AND DID YOU NOTICE HER FEET? WHOA, NELLY! THEY'RE GIGANTIC!
THAT I ACTUALLY FIND ATTRACTIVE.
RIGHT. GIGANTIC IN A COME-HITHER KIND OF WAY.

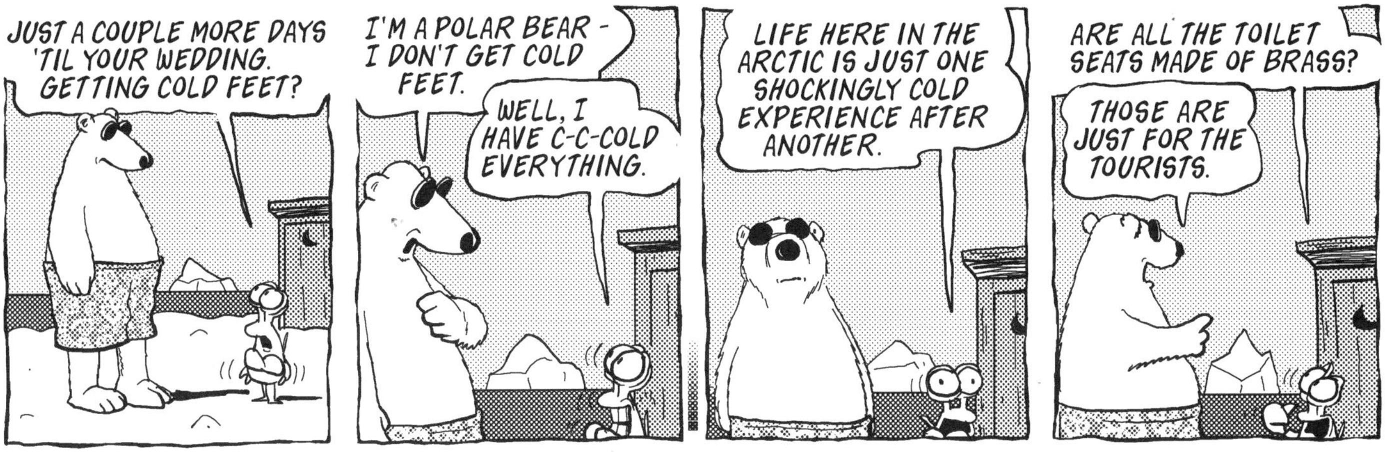
JUST A COUPLE MORE DAYS 'TIL YOUR WEDDING. GETTING COLD FEET?
I'M A POLAR BEAR - I DON'T GET COLD FEET.
WELL, I HAVE C-C-COLD EVERYTHING.
LIFE HERE IN THE ARCTIC IS JUST ONE SHOCKINGLY COLD EXPERIENCE AFTER ANOTHER.
ARE ALL THE TOILET SEATS MADE OF BRASS?
THOSE ARE JUST FOR THE TOURISTS.

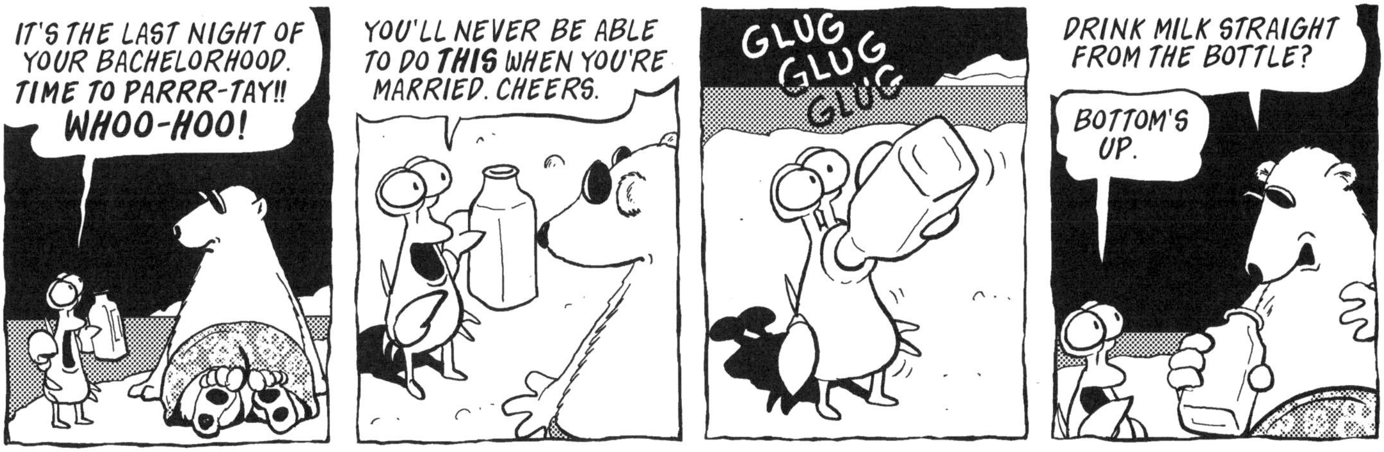
IT'S THE LAST NIGHT OF YOUR BACHELORHOOD. TIME TO PARRR-TAY!! WHOO-HOO!
YOU'LL NEVER BE ABLE TO DO **THIS** WHEN YOU'RE MARRIED. CHEERS.
GLUG GLUG GLUG
DRINK MILK STRAIGHT FROM THE BOTTLE?
BOTTOM'S UP.

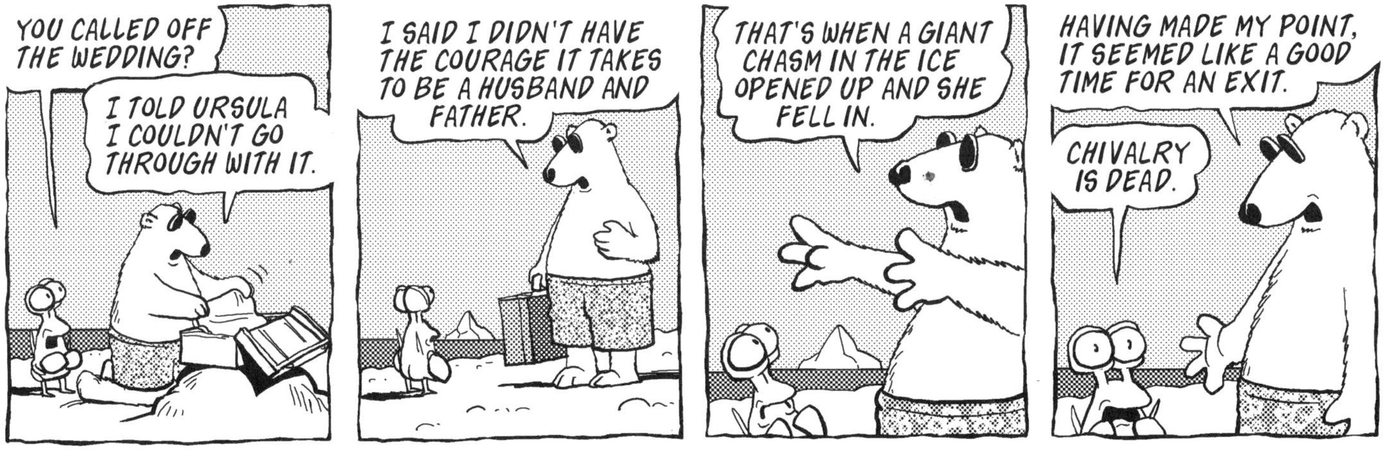
YOU CALLED OFF THE WEDDING?
I TOLD URSULA I COULDN'T GO THROUGH WITH IT.
I SAID I DIDN'T HAVE THE COURAGE IT TAKES TO BE A HUSBAND AND FATHER.
THAT'S WHEN A GIANT CHASM IN THE ICE OPENED UP AND SHE FELL IN.
HAVING MADE MY POINT, IT SEEMED LIKE A GOOD TIME FOR AN EXIT.
CHIVALRY IS DEAD.

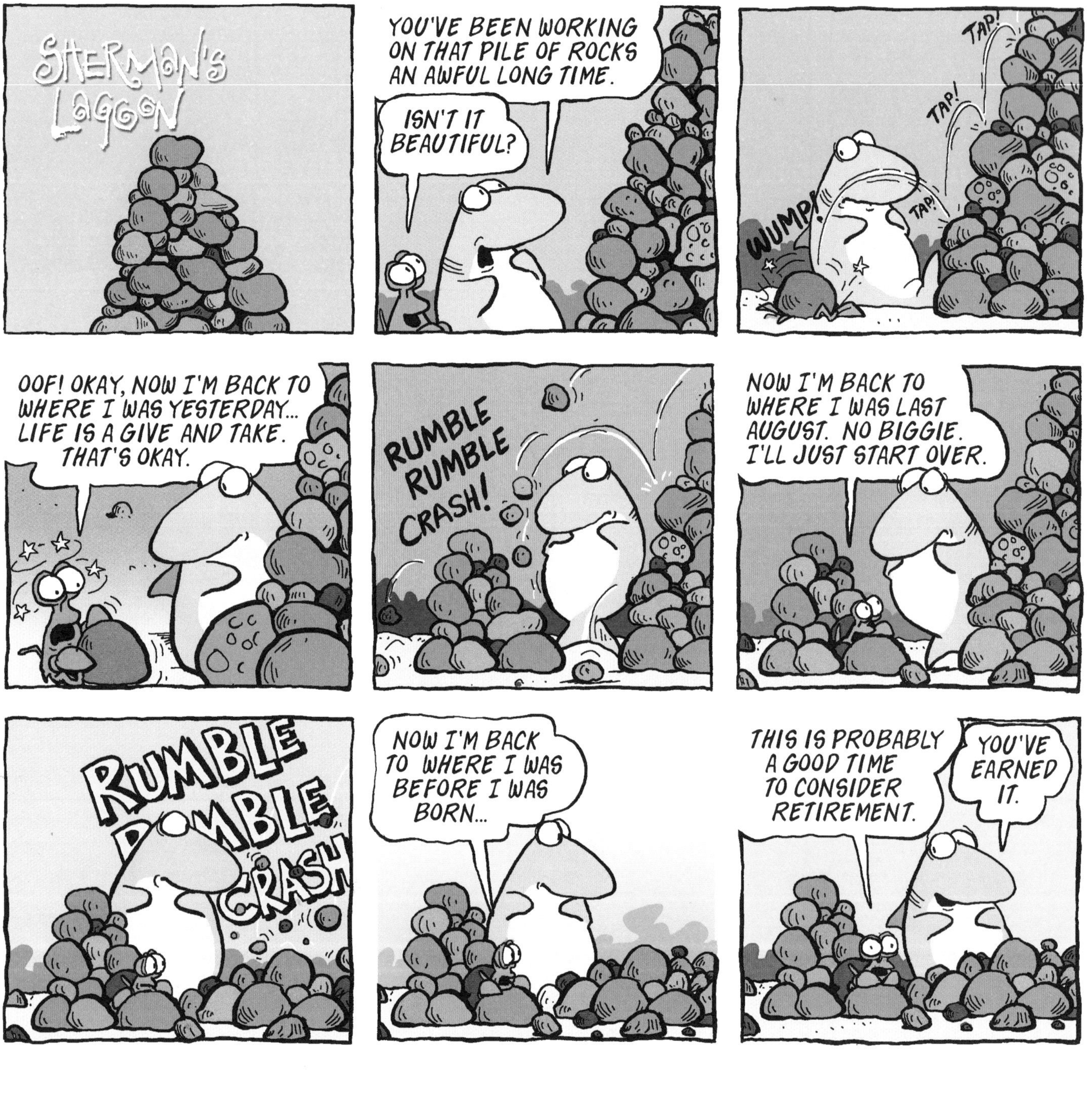
SHERMAN'S LAGOON
YOU'VE BEEN WORKING ON THAT PILE OF ROCKS AN AWFUL LONG TIME.
ISN'T IT BEAUTIFUL?
TAP!
TAP!
TAP!
WUMP!
OOF! OKAY, NOW I'M BACK TO WHERE I WAS YESTERDAY... LIFE IS A GIVE AND TAKE. THAT'S OKAY.
RUMBLE RUMBLE CRASH!
NOW I'M BACK TO WHERE I WAS LAST AUGUST. NO BIGGIE. I'LL JUST START OVER.
CRASH
NOW I'M BACK TO WHERE I WAS BEFORE I WAS BORN...
THIS IS PROBABLY A GOOD TIME TO CONSIDER RETIREMENT.
YOU'VE EARNED IT.

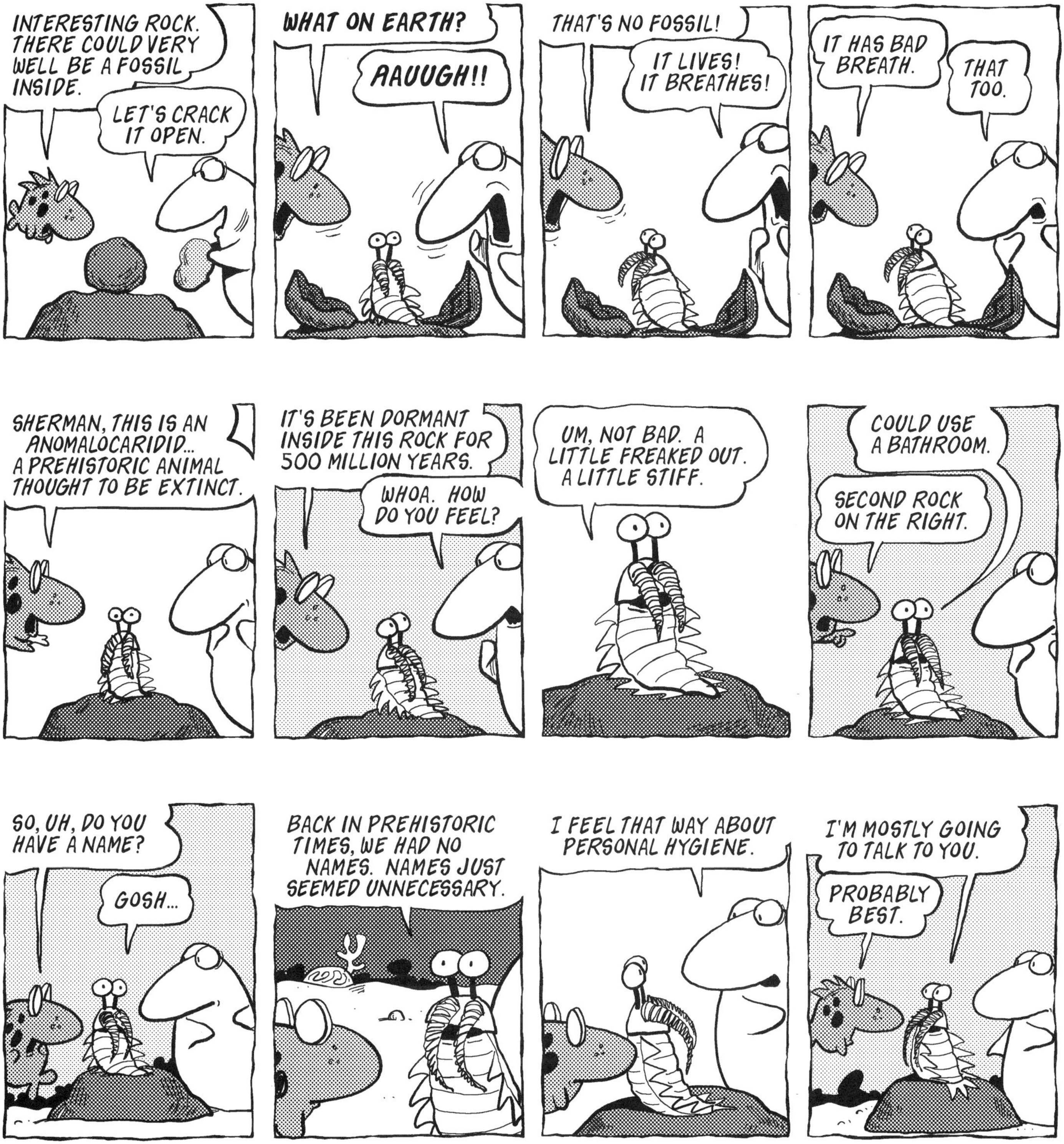

INTERESTING ROCK. THERE COULD VERY WELL BE A FOSSIL INSIDE.
LET'S CRACK IT OPEN.
WHAT ON EARTH?
AAUUGH!!
THAT'S NO FOSSIL!
IT LIVES! IT BREATHES!
IT HAS BAD BREATH.
THAT TOO.
SHERMAN, THIS IS AN ANOMALOCARIDID... A PREHISTORIC ANIMAL THOUGHT TO BE EXTINCT.
IT'S BEEN DORMANT INSIDE THIS ROCK FOR 500 MILLION YEARS.
WHOA. HOW DO YOU FEEL?
UM, NOT BAD. A LITTLE FREAKED OUT. A LITTLE STIFF.
COULD USE A BATHROOM.
SECOND ROCK ON THE RIGHT.
SO, UH, DO YOU HAVE A NAME?
GOSH...
BACK IN PREHISTORIC TIMES, WE HAD NO NAMES. NAMES JUST SEEMED UNNECESSARY.
I FEEL THAT WAY ABOUT PERSONAL HYGIENE.
I'M MOSTLY GOING TO TALK TO YOU.
PROBABLY BEST.

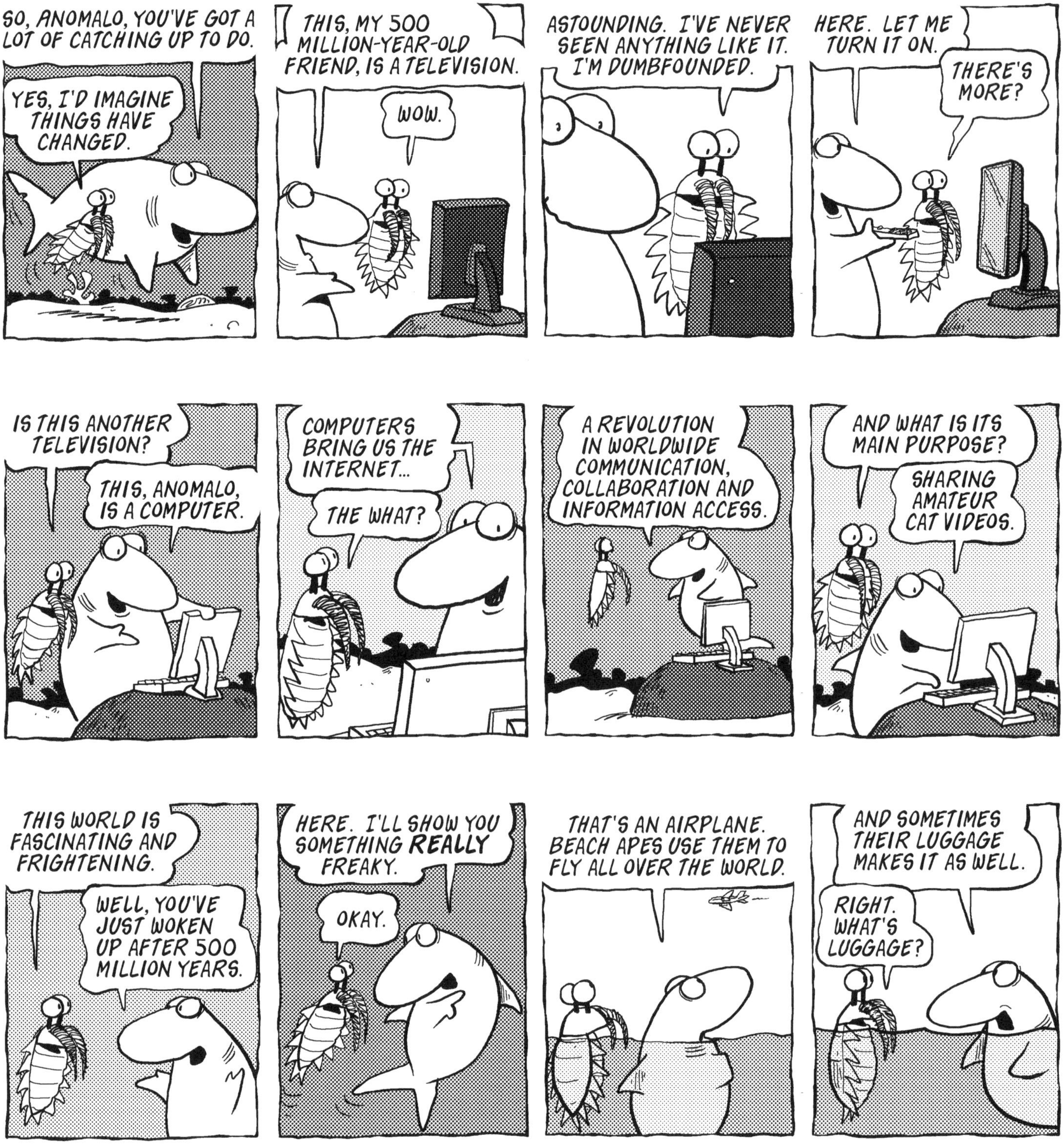
SO, ANOMALO, YOU'VE GOT A LOT OF CATCHING UP TO DO.
YES, I'D IMAGINE THINGS HAVE CHANGED.
THIS, MY 500 MILLION-YEAR-OLD FRIEND, IS A TELEVISION.
WOW.
ASTOUNDING. I'VE NEVER SEEN ANYTHING LIKE IT. I'M DUMBFOUNDED.
HERE. LET ME TURN IT ON.
THERE'S MORE?
IS THIS ANOTHER TELEVISION?
THIS, ANOMALO, IS A COMPUTER.
COMPUTERS BRING US THE INTERNET...
THE WHAT?
A REVOLUTION IN WORLDWIDE COMMUNICATION, COLLABORATION AND INFORMATION ACCESS.
AND WHAT IS ITS MAIN PURPOSE?
SHARING AMATEUR CAT VIDEOS.
THIS WORLD IS FASCINATING AND FRIGHTENING.
WELL, YOU'VE JUST WOKEN UP AFTER 500 MILLION YEARS.
HERE. I'LL SHOW YOU SOMETHING **REALLY** FREAKY.
OKAY.
THAT'S AN AIRPLANE. BEACH APES USE THEM TO FLY ALL OVER THE WORLD.
AND SOMETIMES THEIR LUGGAGE MAKES IT AS WELL.
RIGHT. WHAT'S LUGGAGE?

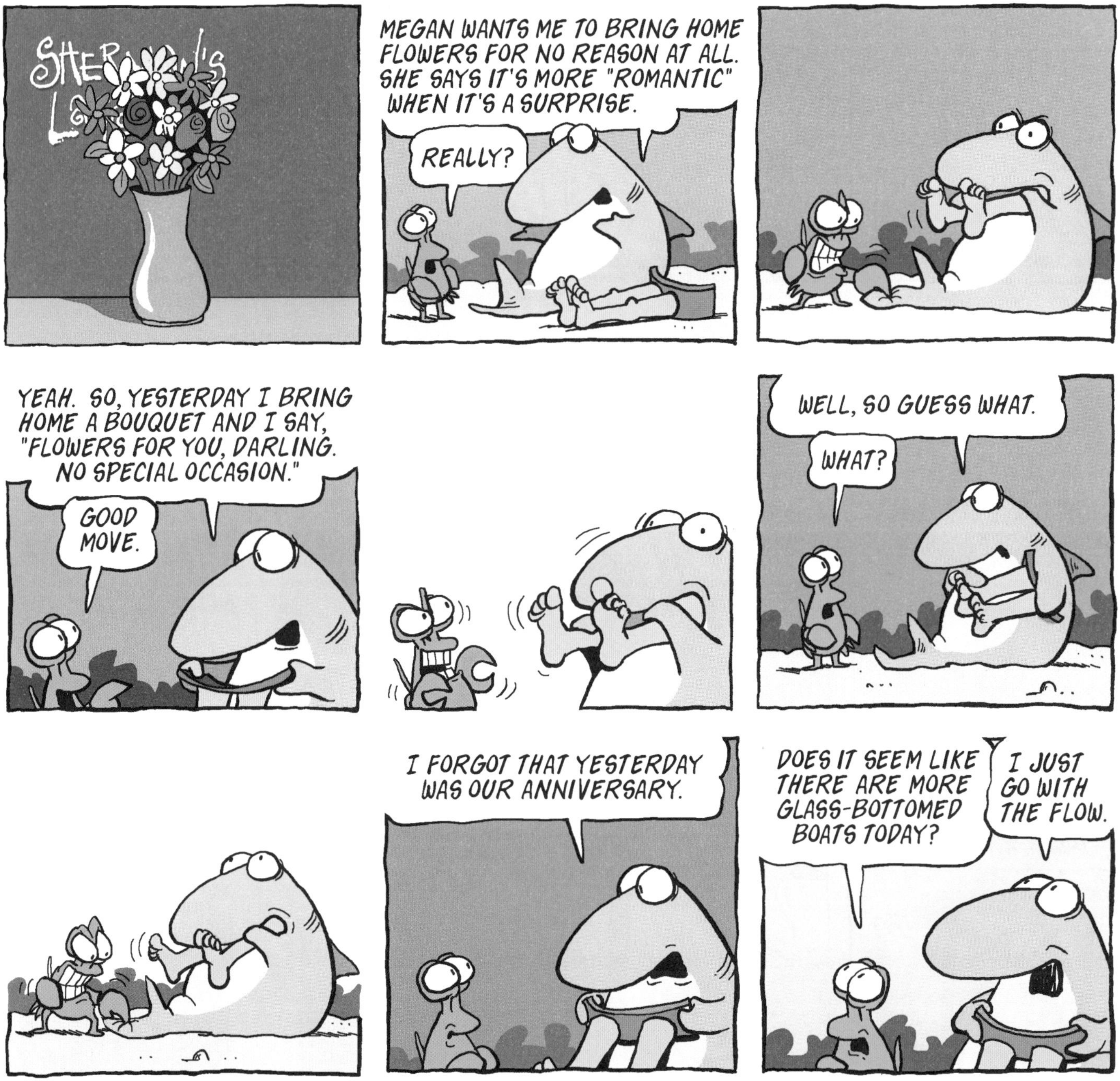
SHERMAN'S LAGOON
MEGAN WANTS ME TO BRING HOME FLOWERS FOR NO REASON AT ALL. SHE SAYS IT'S MORE "ROMANTIC" WHEN IT'S A SURPRISE.
REALLY?
YEAH. SO, YESTERDAY I BRING HOME A BOUQUET AND I SAY, "FLOWERS FOR YOU, DARLING. NO SPECIAL OCCASION."
GOOD MOVE.
WELL, SO GUESS WHAT.
WHAT?
I FORGOT THAT YESTERDAY WAS OUR ANNIVERSARY.
DOES IT SEEM LIKE THERE ARE MORE GLASS-BOTTOMED BOATS TODAY?
I JUST GO WITH THE FLOW.

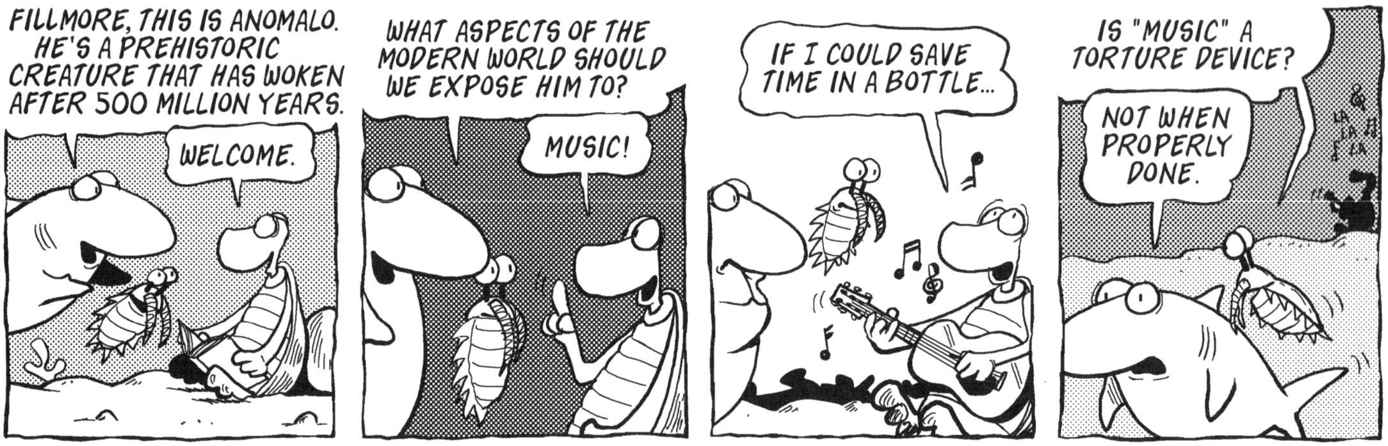
FILLMORE, THIS IS ANOMALO. HE'S A PREHISTORIC CREATURE THAT HAS WOKEN AFTER 500 MILLION YEARS.
WELCOME.
WHAT ASPECTS OF THE MODERN WORLD SHOULD WE EXPOSE HIM TO?
MUSIC!
IF I COULD SAVE TIME IN A BOTTLE...
IS "MUSIC" A TORTURE DEVICE?
NOT WHEN PROPERLY DONE.

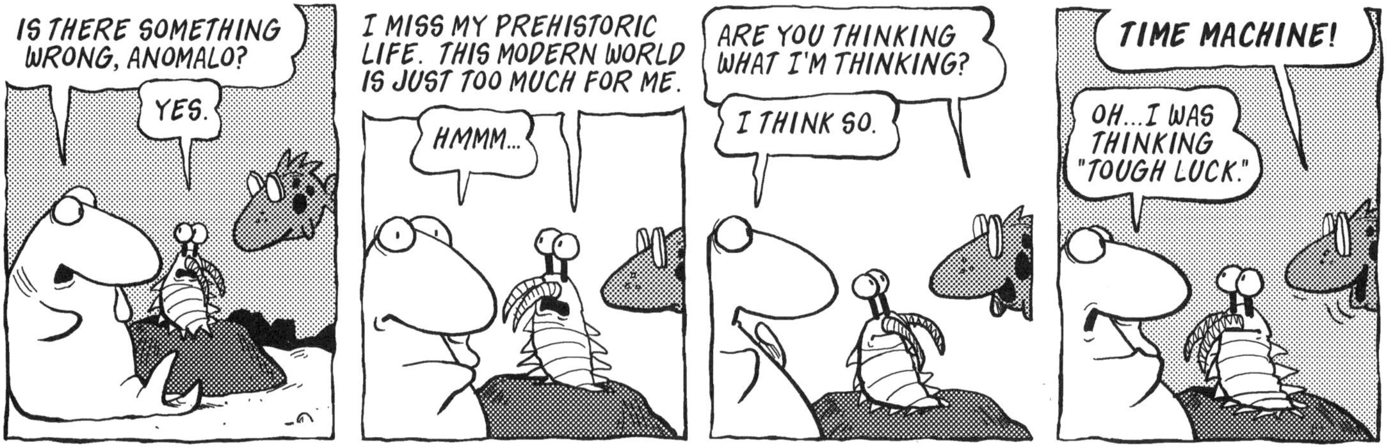
IS THERE SOMETHING WRONG, ANOMALO?
YES.
I MISS MY PREHISTORIC LIFE. THIS MODERN WORLD IS JUST TOO MUCH FOR ME.
HMMM...
ARE YOU THINKING WHAT I'M THINKING?
I THINK SO.
TIME MACHINE!
OH...I WAS THINKING "TOUGH LUCK."

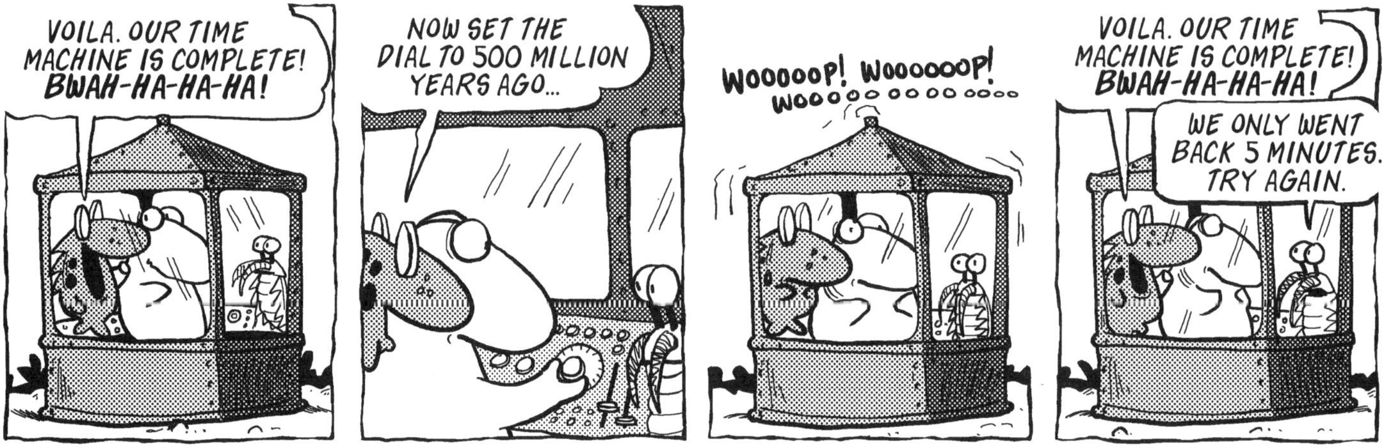
VOILA. OUR TIME MACHINE IS COMPLETE! **BWAH-HA-HA-HA!**
NOW SET THE DIAL TO 500 MILLION YEARS AGO...
WOOOOOP! WOOOOOOP! WOOOOOOOOOOOOO
VOILA. OUR TIME MACHINE IS COMPLETE! **BWAH-HA-HA-HA!**
WE ONLY WENT BACK 5 MINUTES. TRY AGAIN.

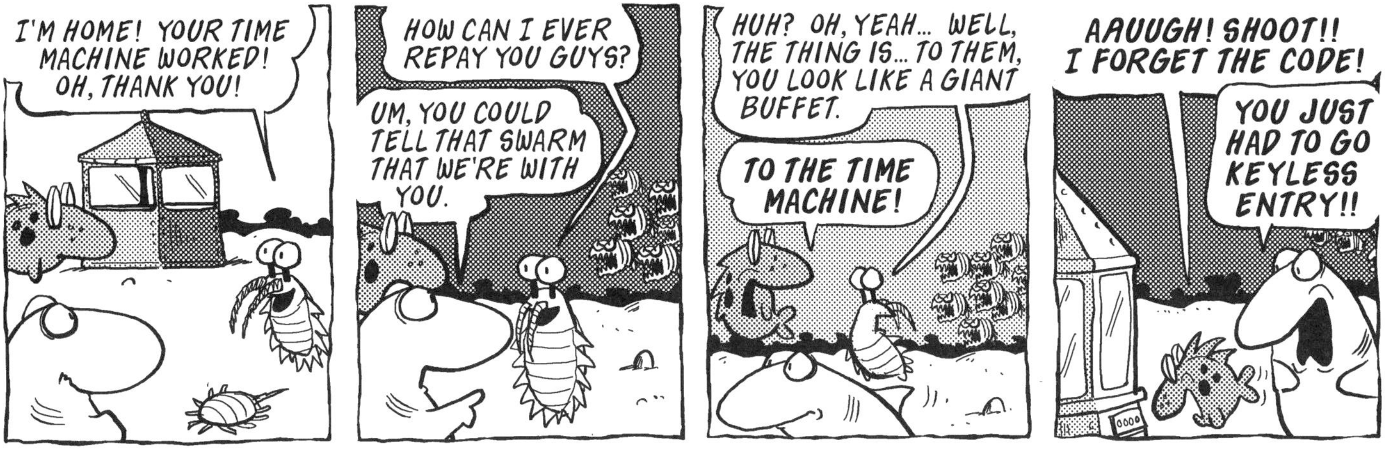
I'M HOME! YOUR TIME MACHINE WORKED! OH, THANK YOU!
HOW CAN I EVER REPAY YOU GUYS?
UM, YOU COULD TELL THAT SWARM THAT WE'RE WITH YOU.
HUH? OH, YEAH... WELL, THE THING IS... TO THEM, YOU LOOK LIKE A GIANT BUFFET.
TO THE TIME MACHINE!
AAUUGH! SHOOT!! I FORGET THE CODE!
YOU JUST HAD TO GO KEYLESS ENTRY!!

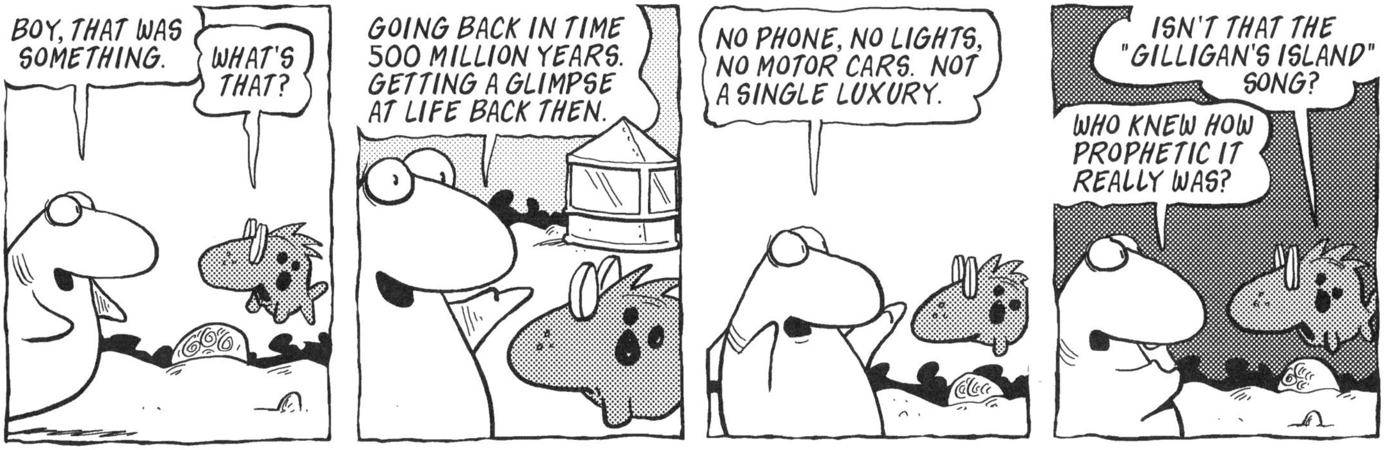
BOY, THAT WAS SOMETHING.
WHAT'S THAT?
GOING BACK IN TIME 500 MILLION YEARS. GETTING A GLIMPSE AT LIFE BACK THEN.
NO PHONE, NO LIGHTS, NO MOTOR CARS. NOT A SINGLE LUXURY.
ISN'T THAT THE "GILLIGAN'S ISLAND" SONG?
WHO KNEW HOW PROPHETIC IT REALLY WAS?

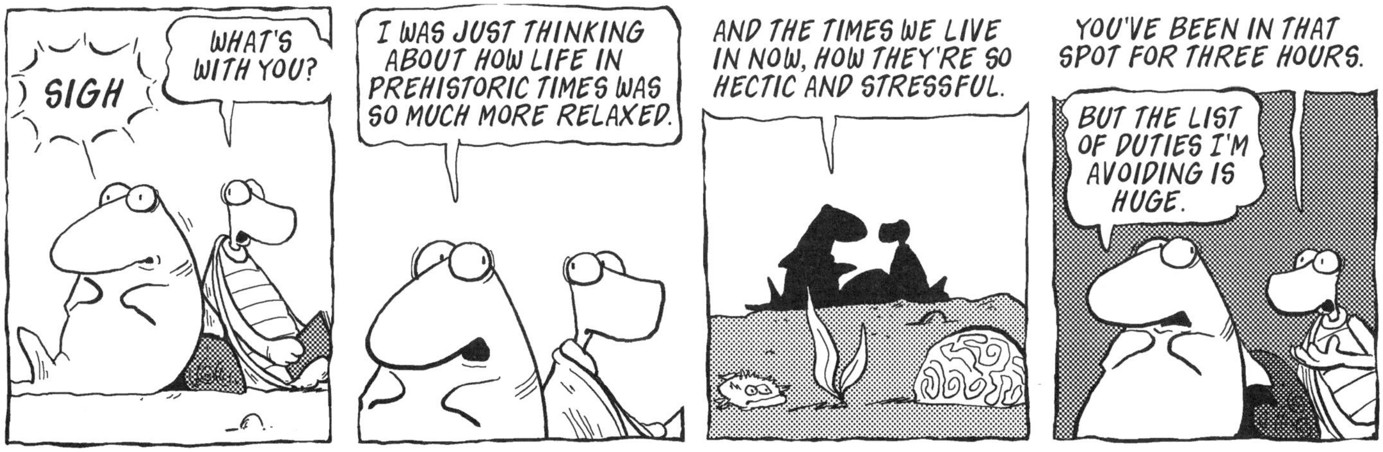
SIGH
WHAT'S WITH YOU?
I WAS JUST THINKING ABOUT HOW LIFE IN PREHISTORIC TIMES WAS SO MUCH MORE RELAXED.
AND THE TIMES WE LIVE IN NOW, HOW THEY'RE SO HECTIC AND STRESSFUL.
YOU'VE BEEN IN THAT SPOT FOR THREE HOURS.
BUT THE LIST OF DUTIES I'M AVOIDING IS HUGE.

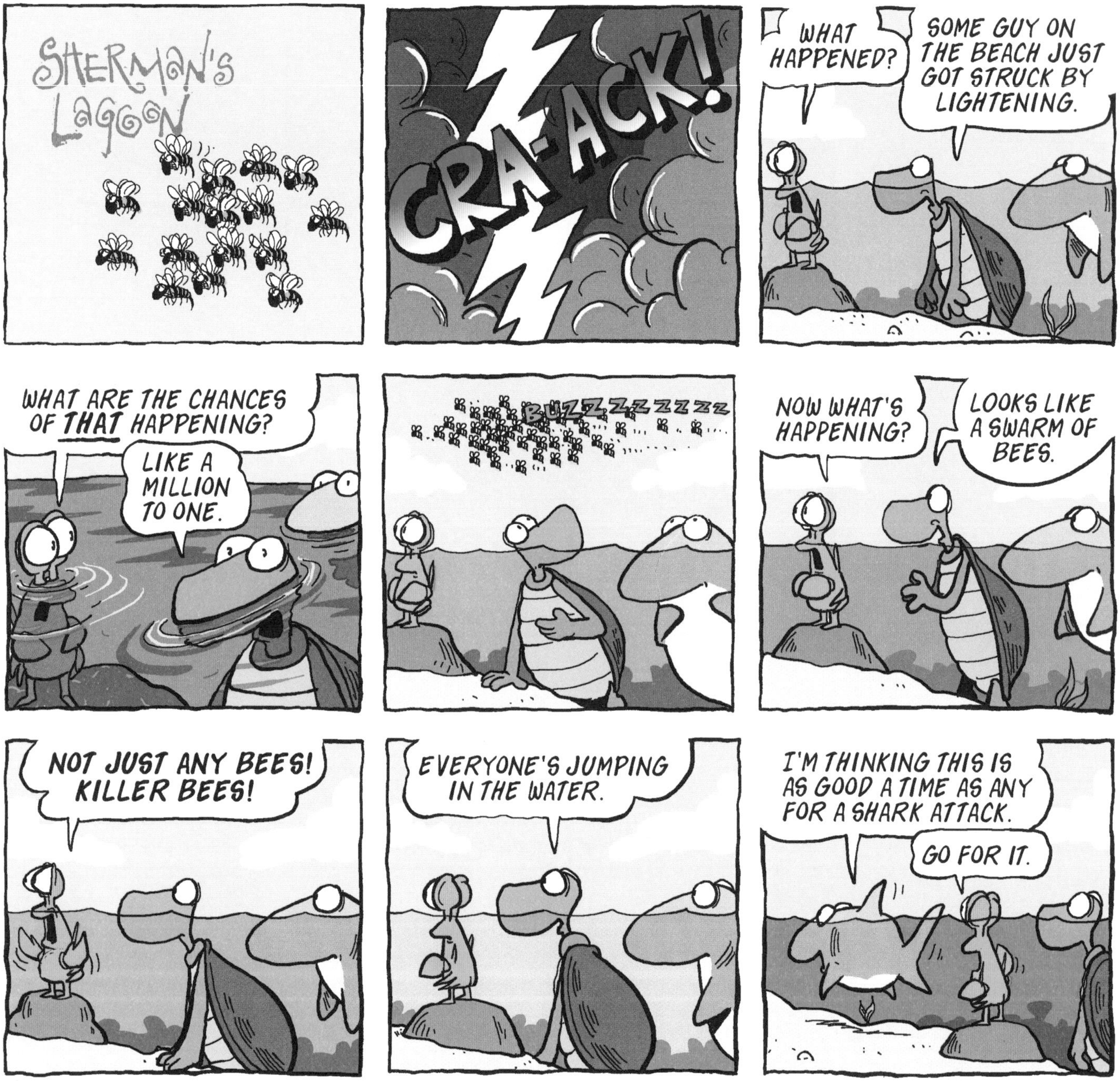
SHERMAN'S LAGOON
CRA-ACK!
WHAT HAPPENED?
SOME GUY ON THE BEACH JUST GOT STRUCK BY LIGHTENING.
WHAT ARE THE CHANCES OF THAT HAPPENING?
LIKE A MILLION TO ONE.
BUZZZZZZZZZ
NOW WHAT'S HAPPENING?
LOOKS LIKE A SWARM OF BEES.
NOT JUST ANY BEES! KILLER BEES!
EVERYONE'S JUMPING IN THE WATER.
I'M THINKING THIS IS AS GOOD A TIME AS ANY FOR A SHARK ATTACK.
GO FOR IT.

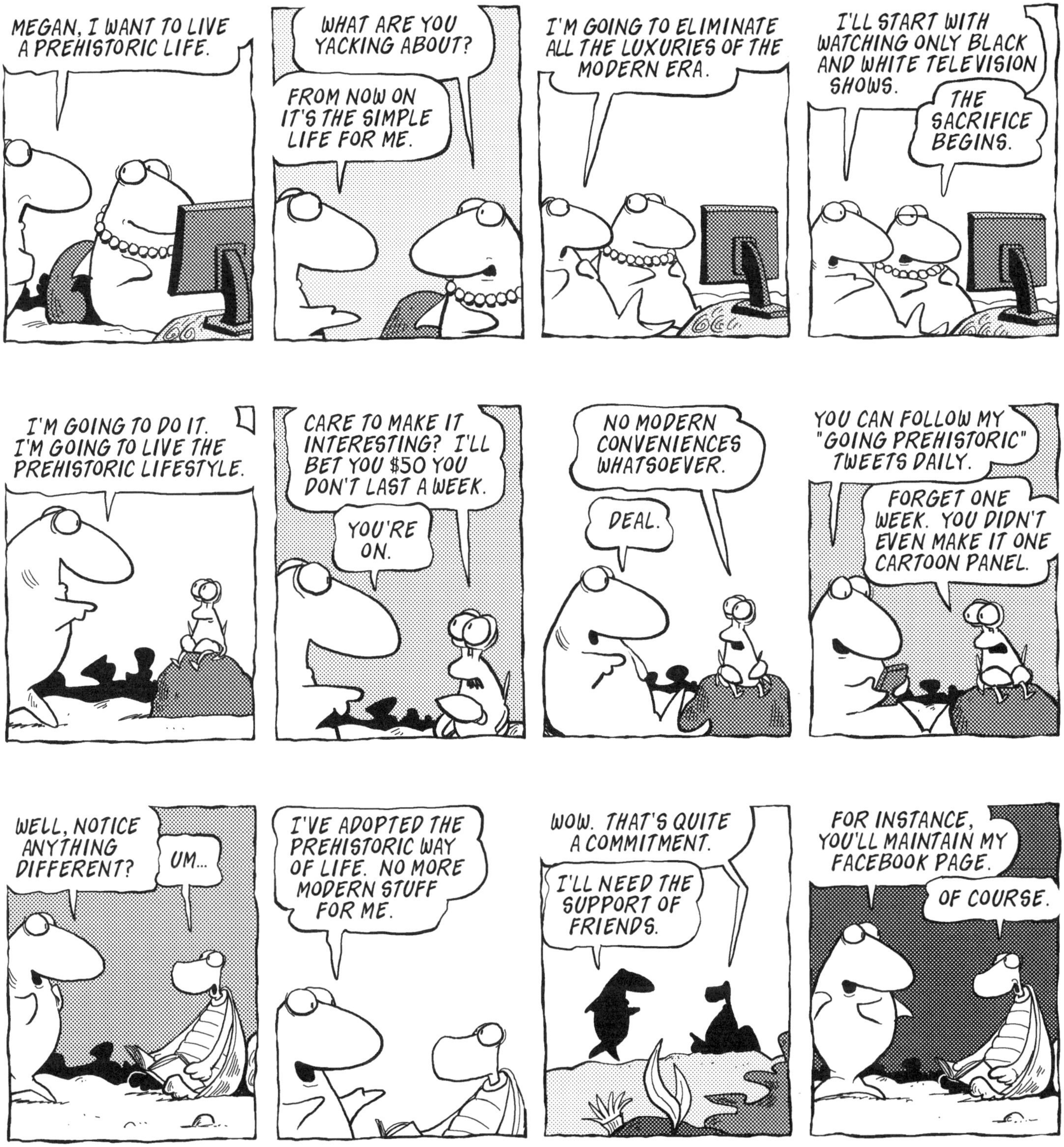
MEGAN, I WANT TO LIVE A PREHISTORIC LIFE.
WHAT ARE YOU YACKING ABOUT?
FROM NOW ON IT'S THE SIMPLE LIFE FOR ME.
I'M GOING TO ELIMINATE ALL THE LUXURIES OF THE MODERN ERA.
I'LL START WITH WATCHING ONLY BLACK AND WHITE TELEVISION SHOWS.
THE SACRIFICE BEGINS.
I'M GOING TO DO IT. I'M GOING TO LIVE THE PREHISTORIC LIFESTYLE.
CARE TO MAKE IT INTERESTING? I'LL BET YOU $50 YOU DON'T LAST A WEEK.
YOU'RE ON.
NO MODERN CONVENIENCES WHATSOEVER.
DEAL.
YOU CAN FOLLOW MY "GOING PREHISTORIC" TWEETS DAILY.
FORGET ONE WEEK. YOU DIDN'T EVEN MAKE IT ONE CARTOON PANEL.
WELL, NOTICE ANYTHING DIFFERENT?
UM...
I'VE ADOPTED THE PREHISTORIC WAY OF LIFE. NO MORE MODERN STUFF FOR ME.
WOW. THAT'S QUITE A COMMITMENT.
I'LL NEED THE SUPPORT OF FRIENDS.
FOR INSTANCE, YOU'LL MAINTAIN MY FACEBOOK PAGE.
OF COURSE.

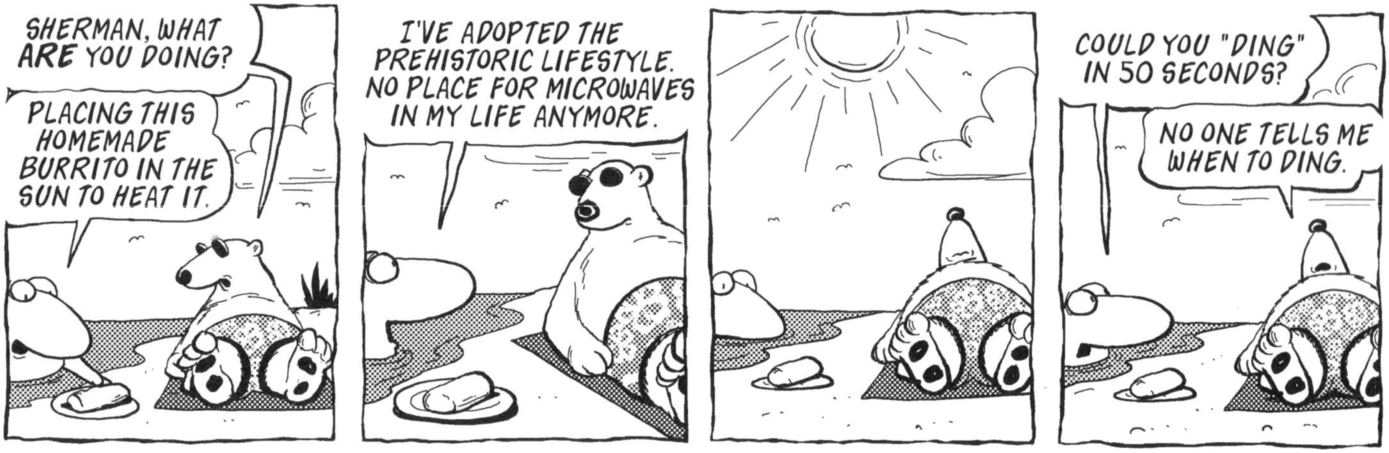
SHERMAN, WHAT **ARE** YOU DOING?
PLACING THIS HOMEMADE BURRITO IN THE SUN TO HEAT IT.
I'VE ADOPTED THE PREHISTORIC LIFESTYLE. NO PLACE FOR MICROWAVES IN MY LIFE ANYMORE.
COULD YOU "DING" IN 50 SECONDS?
NO ONE TELLS ME WHEN TO DING.

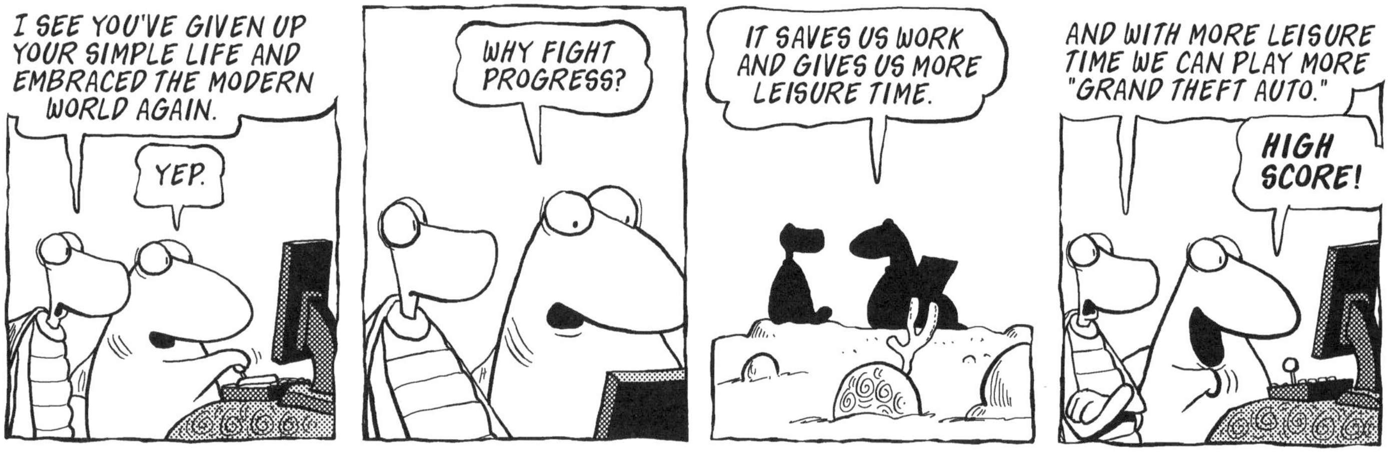
I SEE YOU'VE GIVEN UP YOUR SIMPLE LIFE AND EMBRACED THE MODERN WORLD AGAIN.
YEP.
WHY FIGHT PROGRESS?
IT SAVES US WORK AND GIVES US MORE LEISURE TIME.
AND WITH MORE LEISURE TIME WE CAN PLAY MORE "GRAND THEFT AUTO."
HIGH SCORE!

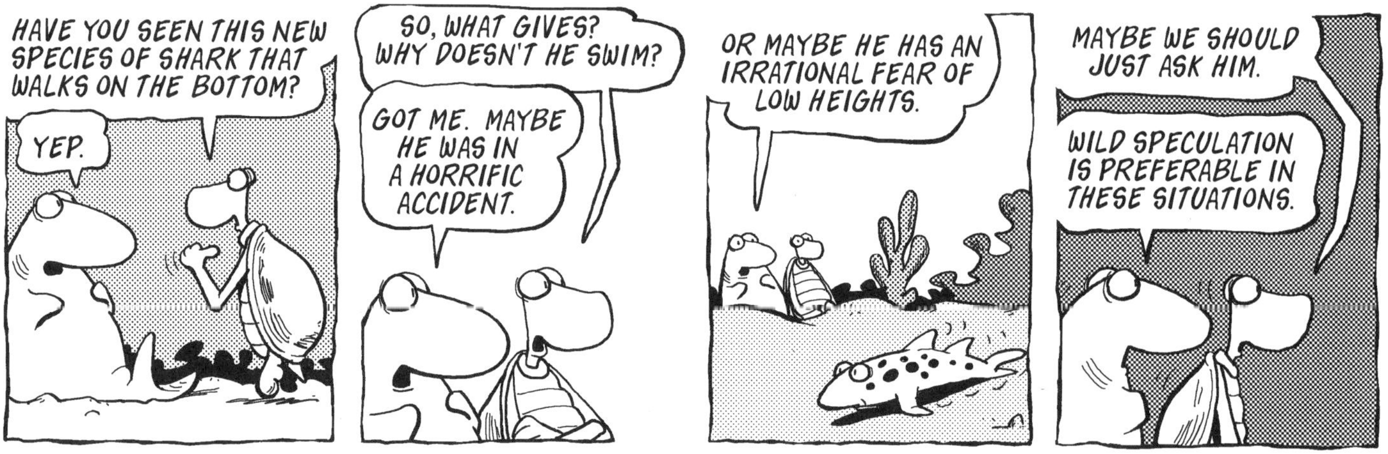
HAVE YOU SEEN THIS NEW SPECIES OF SHARK THAT WALKS ON THE BOTTOM?
YEP.
SO, WHAT GIVES? WHY DOESN'T HE SWIM?
GOT ME. MAYBE HE WAS IN A HORRIFIC ACCIDENT.
OR MAYBE HE HAS AN IRRATIONAL FEAR OF LOW HEIGHTS.
MAYBE WE SHOULD JUST ASK HIM.
WILD SPECULATION IS PREFERABLE IN THESE SITUATIONS.

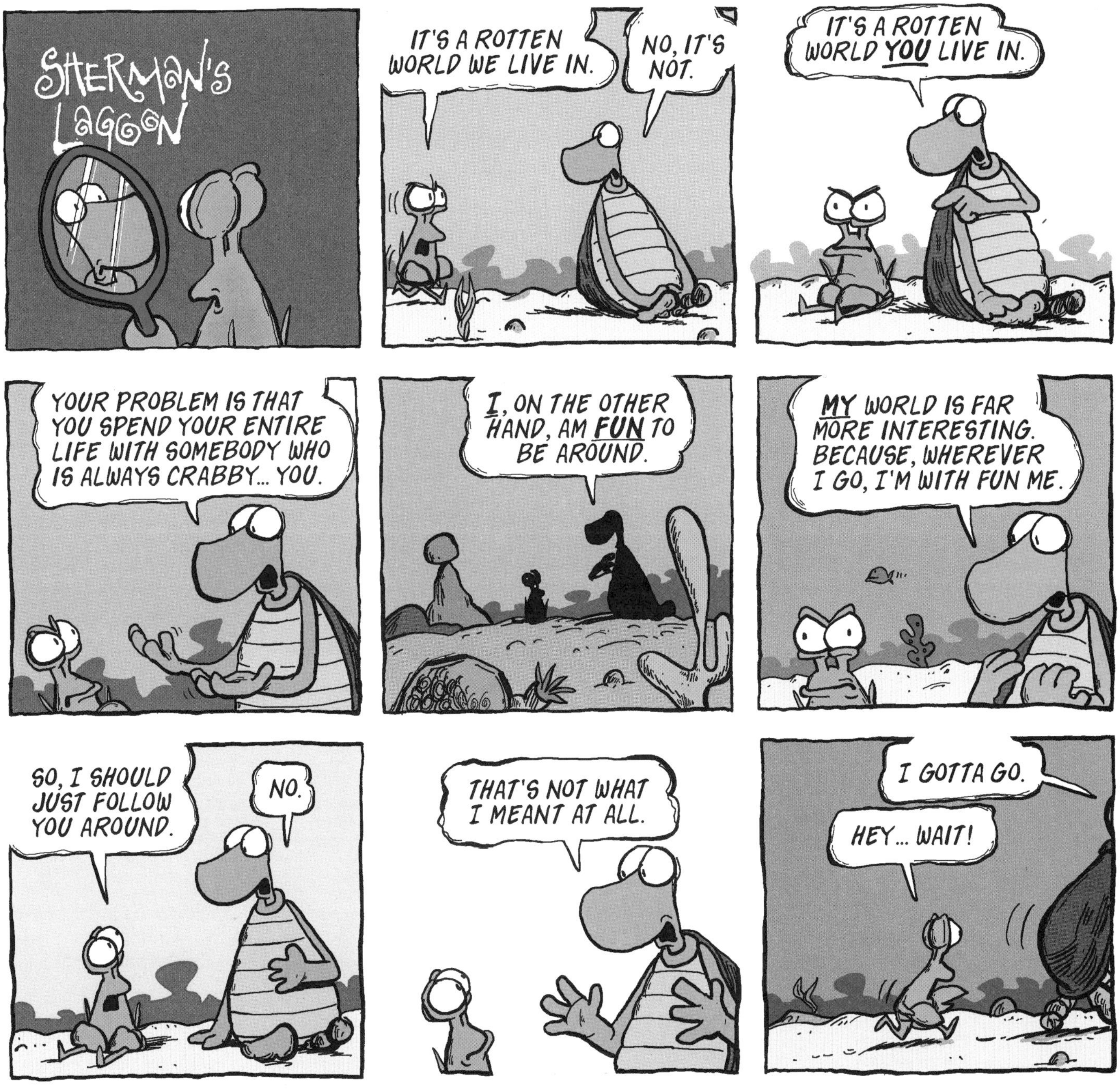
SHERMAN'S LAGOON
IT'S A ROTTEN WORLD WE LIVE IN.
NO, IT'S NOT.
IT'S A ROTTEN WORLD YOU LIVE IN.
YOUR PROBLEM IS THAT YOU SPEND YOUR ENTIRE LIFE WITH SOMEBODY WHO IS ALWAYS CRABBY... YOU.
I, ON THE OTHER HAND, AM FUN TO BE AROUND.
MY WORLD IS FAR MORE INTERESTING. BECAUSE, WHEREVER I GO, I'M WITH FUN ME.
SO, I SHOULD JUST FOLLOW YOU AROUND.
NO.
THAT'S NOT WHAT I MEANT AT ALL.
I GOTTA GO.
HEY... WAIT!

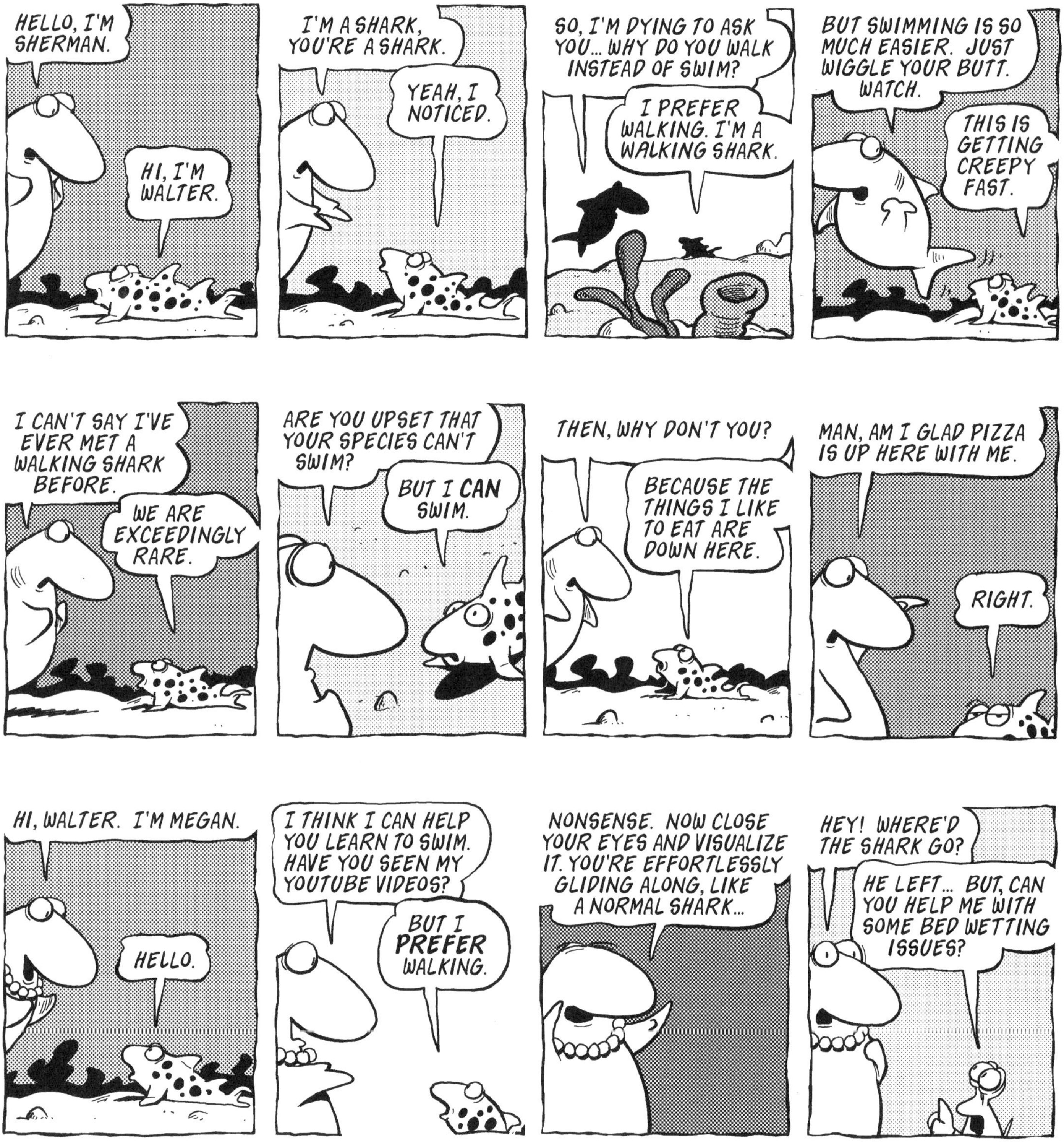
HELLO, I'M SHERMAN.
HI, I'M WALTER.
I'M A SHARK, YOU'RE A SHARK.
YEAH, I NOTICED.
SO, I'M DYING TO ASK YOU... WHY DO YOU WALK INSTEAD OF SWIM?
I PREFER WALKING. I'M A WALKING SHARK.
BUT SWIMMING IS SO MUCH EASIER. JUST WIGGLE YOUR BUTT. WATCH.
THIS IS GETTING CREEPY FAST.
I CAN'T SAY I'VE EVER MET A WALKING SHARK BEFORE.
WE ARE EXCEEDINGLY RARE.
ARE YOU UPSET THAT YOUR SPECIES CAN'T SWIM?
BUT I CAN SWIM.
THEN, WHY DON'T YOU?
BECAUSE THE THINGS I LIKE TO EAT ARE DOWN HERE.
MAN, AM I GLAD PIZZA IS UP HERE WITH ME.
RIGHT.
HI, WALTER. I'M MEGAN.
HELLO.
I THINK I CAN HELP YOU LEARN TO SWIM. HAVE YOU SEEN MY YOUTUBE VIDEOS?
BUT I PREFER WALKING.
NONSENSE. NOW CLOSE YOUR EYES AND VISUALIZE IT. YOU'RE EFFORTLESSLY GLIDING ALONG, LIKE A NORMAL SHARK...
HEY! WHERE'D THE SHARK GO?
HE LEFT... BUT, CAN YOU HELP ME WITH SOME BED WETTING ISSUES?

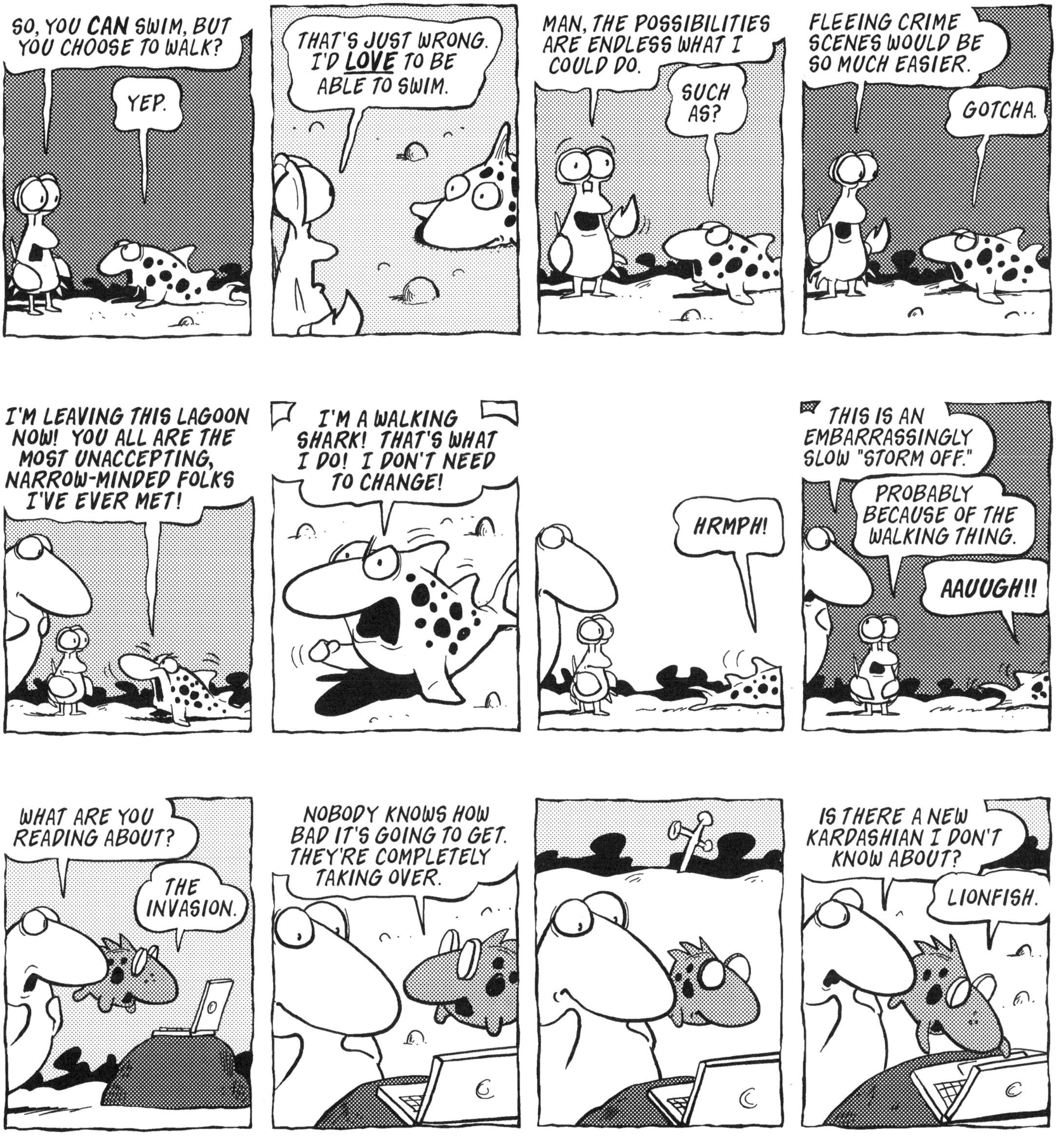
SO, YOU CAN SWIM, BUT YOU CHOOSE TO WALK?
YEP.
THAT'S JUST WRONG. I'D LOVE TO BE ABLE TO SWIM.
MAN, THE POSSIBILITIES ARE ENDLESS WHAT I COULD DO.
SUCH AS?
FLEEING CRIME SCENES WOULD BE SO MUCH EASIER.
GOTCHA.
I'M LEAVING THIS LAGOON NOW! YOU ALL ARE THE MOST UNACCEPTING, NARROW-MINDED FOLKS I'VE EVER MET!
I'M A WALKING SHARK! THAT'S WHAT I DO! I DON'T NEED TO CHANGE!
HRMPH!
THIS IS AN EMBARRASSINGLY SLOW "STORM OFF."
PROBABLY BECAUSE OF THE WALKING THING.
AAUUGH!!
WHAT ARE YOU READING ABOUT?
THE INVASION.
NOBODY KNOWS HOW BAD IT'S GOING TO GET. THEY'RE COMPLETELY TAKING OVER.
IS THERE A NEW KARDASHIAN I DON'T KNOW ABOUT?
LIONFISH.

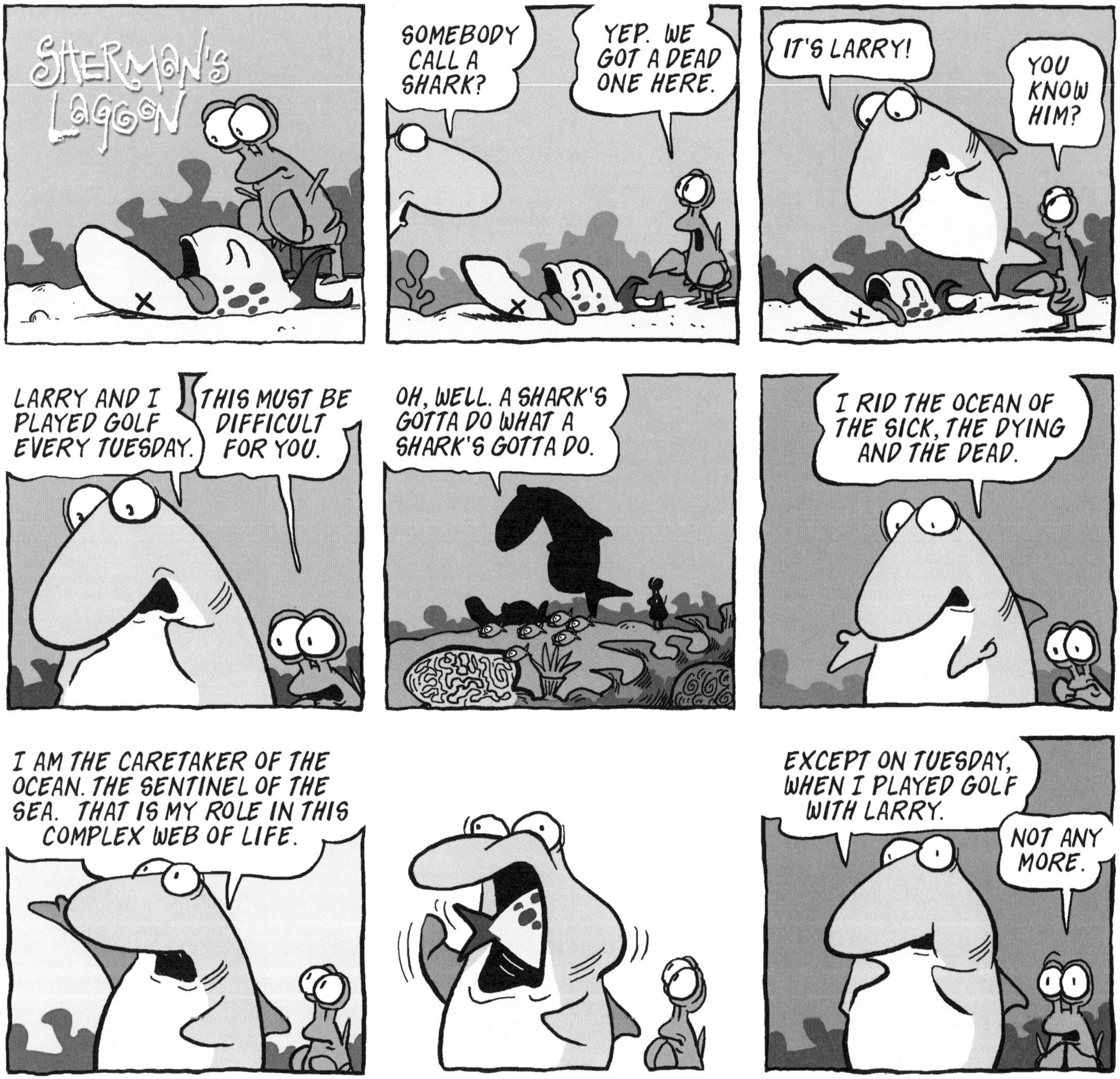
SHERMAN'S LAGOON
SOMEBODY CALL A SHARK?
YEP. WE GOT A DEAD ONE HERE.
IT'S LARRY!
YOU KNOW HIM?
LARRY AND I PLAYED GOLF EVERY TUESDAY.
THIS MUST BE DIFFICULT FOR YOU.
OH, WELL. A SHARK'S GOTTA DO WHAT A SHARK'S GOTTA DO.
I RID THE OCEAN OF THE SICK, THE DYING AND THE DEAD.
I AM THE CARETAKER OF THE OCEAN. THE SENTINEL OF THE SEA. THAT IS MY ROLE IN THIS COMPLEX WEB OF LIFE.
EXCEPT ON TUESDAY, WHEN I PLAYED GOLF WITH LARRY.
NOT ANY MORE.

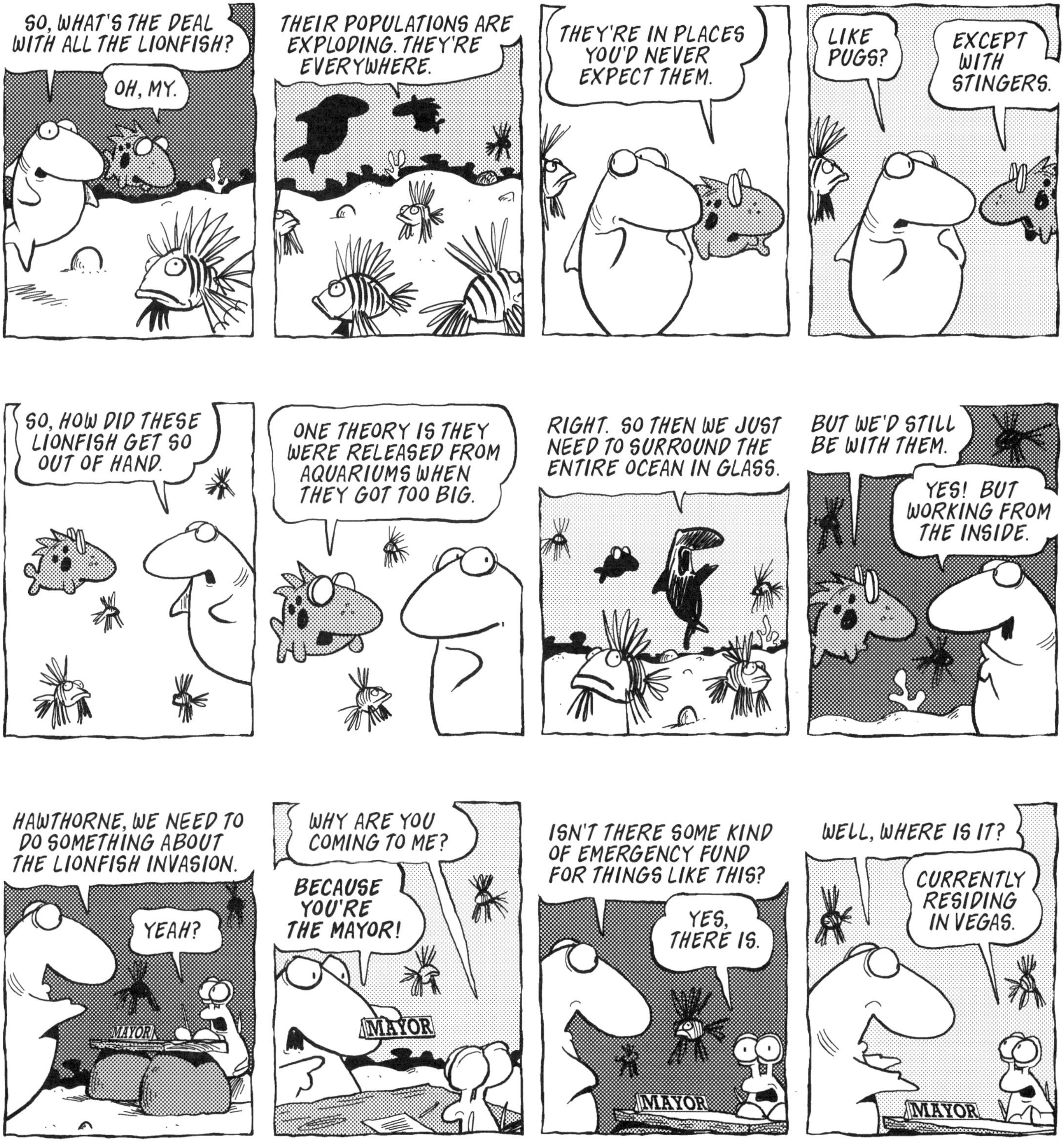
SO, WHAT'S THE DEAL WITH ALL THE LIONFISH?
OH, MY.
THEIR POPULATIONS ARE EXPLODING. THEY'RE EVERYWHERE.
THEY'RE IN PLACES YOU'D NEVER EXPECT THEM.
LIKE PUGS?
EXCEPT WITH STINGERS.
SO, HOW DID THESE LIONFISH GET SO OUT OF HAND.
ONE THEORY IS THEY WERE RELEASED FROM AQUARIUMS WHEN THEY GOT TOO BIG.
RIGHT. SO THEN WE JUST NEED TO SURROUND THE ENTIRE OCEAN IN GLASS.
BUT WE'D STILL BE WITH THEM.
YES! BUT WORKING FROM THE INSIDE.
HAWTHORNE, WE NEED TO DO SOMETHING ABOUT THE LIONFISH INVASION.
YEAH?
MAYOR
WHY ARE YOU COMING TO ME?
BECAUSE YOU'RE THE MAYOR!
MAYOR
ISN'T THERE SOME KIND OF EMERGENCY FUND FOR THINGS LIKE THIS?
YES, THERE IS.
MAYOR
WELL, WHERE IS IT?
CURRENTLY RESIDING IN VEGAS.
MAYOR

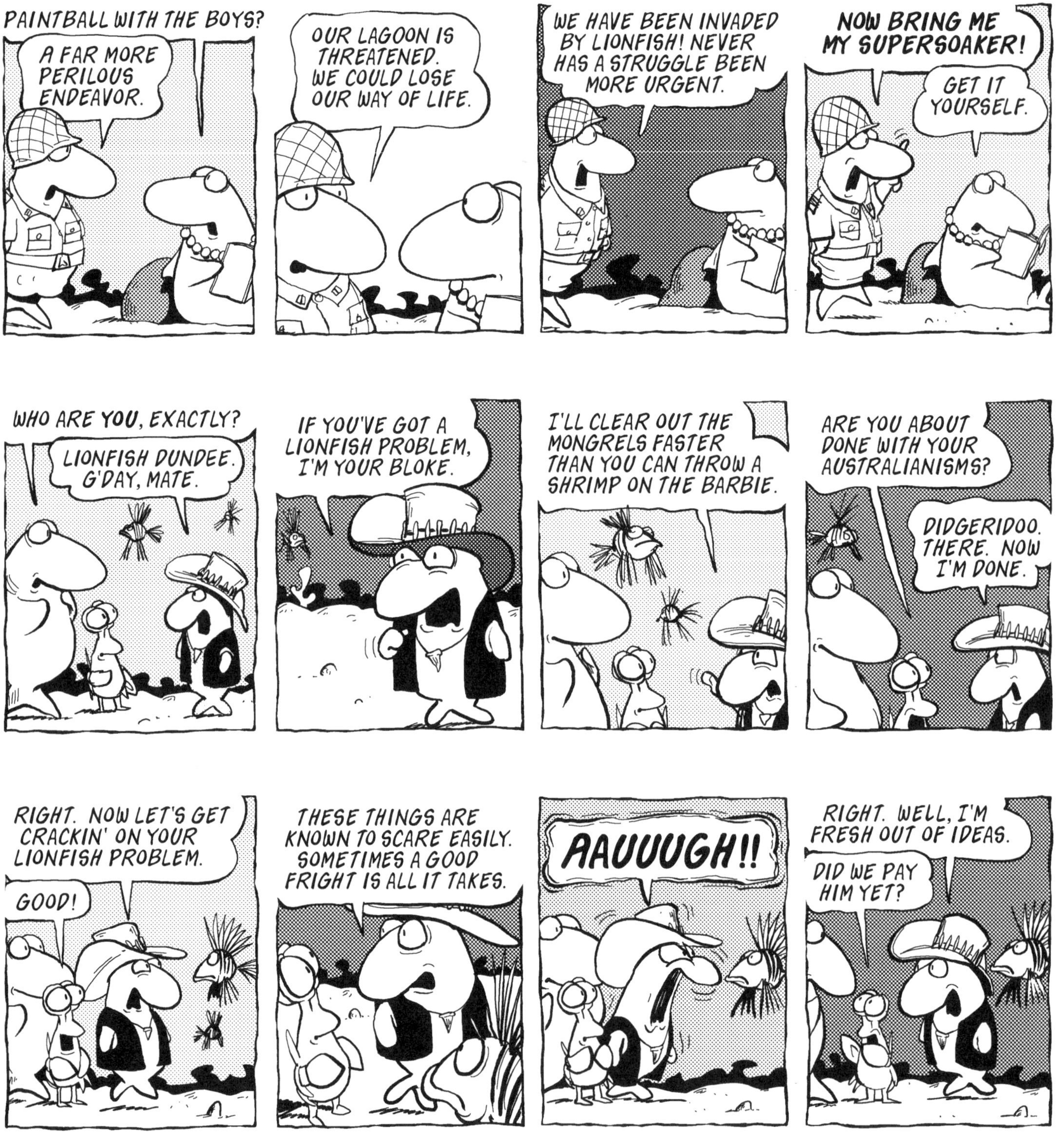
PAINTBALL WITH THE BOYS?
A FAR MORE PERILOUS ENDEAVOR.
OUR LAGOON IS THREATENED. WE COULD LOSE OUR WAY OF LIFE.
WE HAVE BEEN INVADED BY LIONFISH! NEVER HAS A STRUGGLE BEEN MORE URGENT.
NOW BRING ME MY SUPERSOAKER!
GET IT YOURSELF.
WHO ARE YOU, EXACTLY?
LIONFISH DUNDEE. G'DAY, MATE.
IF YOU'VE GOT A LIONFISH PROBLEM, I'M YOUR BLOKE.
I'LL CLEAR OUT THE MONGRELS FASTER THAN YOU CAN THROW A SHRIMP ON THE BARBIE.
ARE YOU ABOUT DONE WITH YOUR AUSTRALIANISMS?
DIDGERIDOO. THERE. NOW I'M DONE.
RIGHT. NOW LET'S GET CRACKIN' ON YOUR LIONFISH PROBLEM.
GOOD!
THESE THINGS ARE KNOWN TO SCARE EASILY. SOMETIMES A GOOD FRIGHT IS ALL IT TAKES.
AAUUUGH!!
RIGHT. WELL, I'M FRESH OUT OF IDEAS.
DID WE PAY HIM YET?

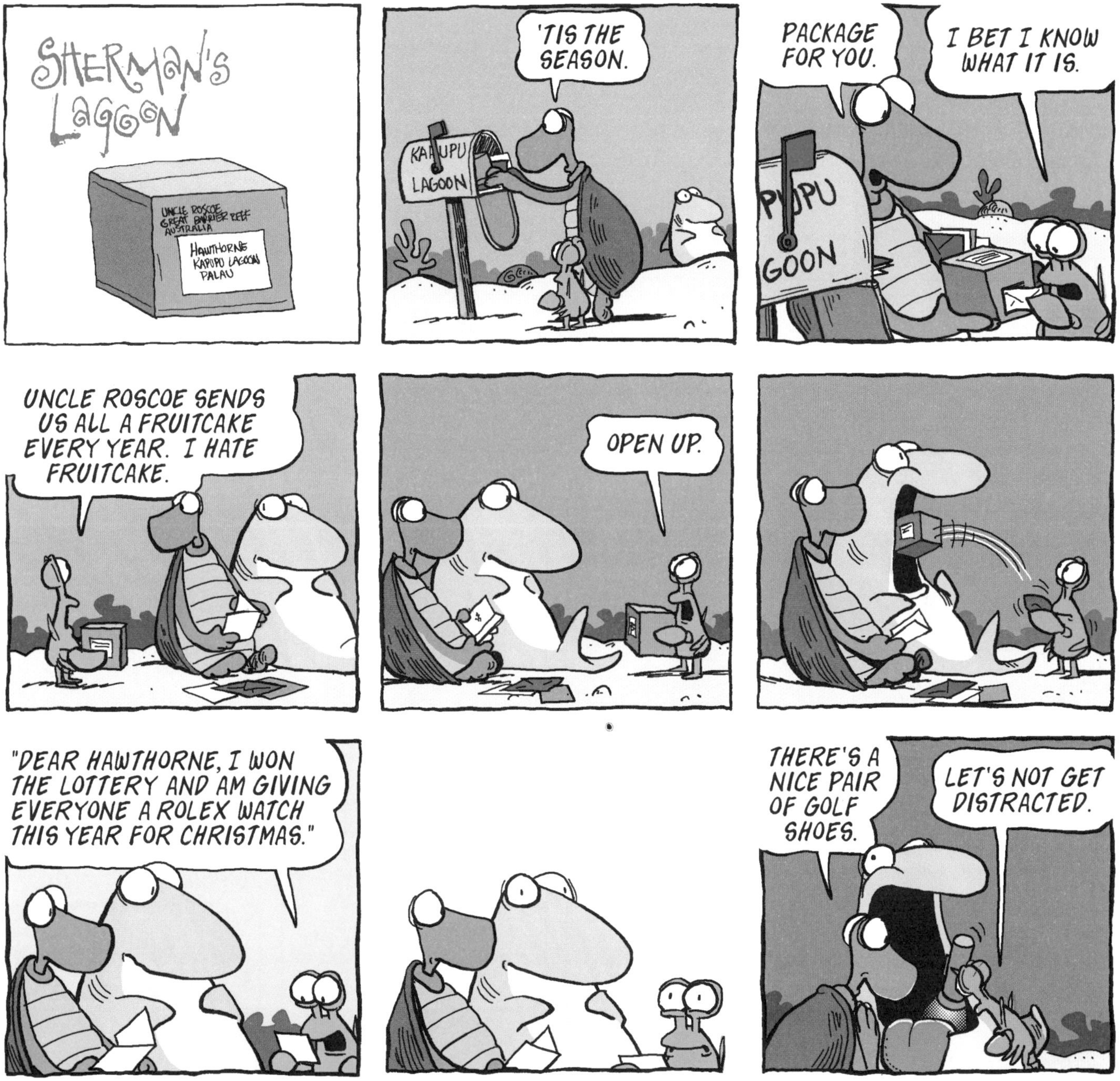
SHERMAN'S LAGOON
UNCLE ROSCOE GREAT BARRIER REEF AUSTRALIA
HAWTHORNE KAPUPU LAGOON PALAU
'TIS THE SEASON.
LAGOON
PACKAGE FOR YOU.
I BET I KNOW WHAT IT IS.
UNCLE ROSCOE SENDS US ALL A FRUITCAKE EVERY YEAR. I HATE FRUITCAKE.
OPEN UP.
"DEAR HAWTHORNE, I WON THE LOTTERY AND AM GIVING EVERYONE A ROLEX WATCH THIS YEAR FOR CHRISTMAS."
THERE'S A NICE PAIR OF GOLF SHOES.
LET'S NOT GET DISTRACTED.

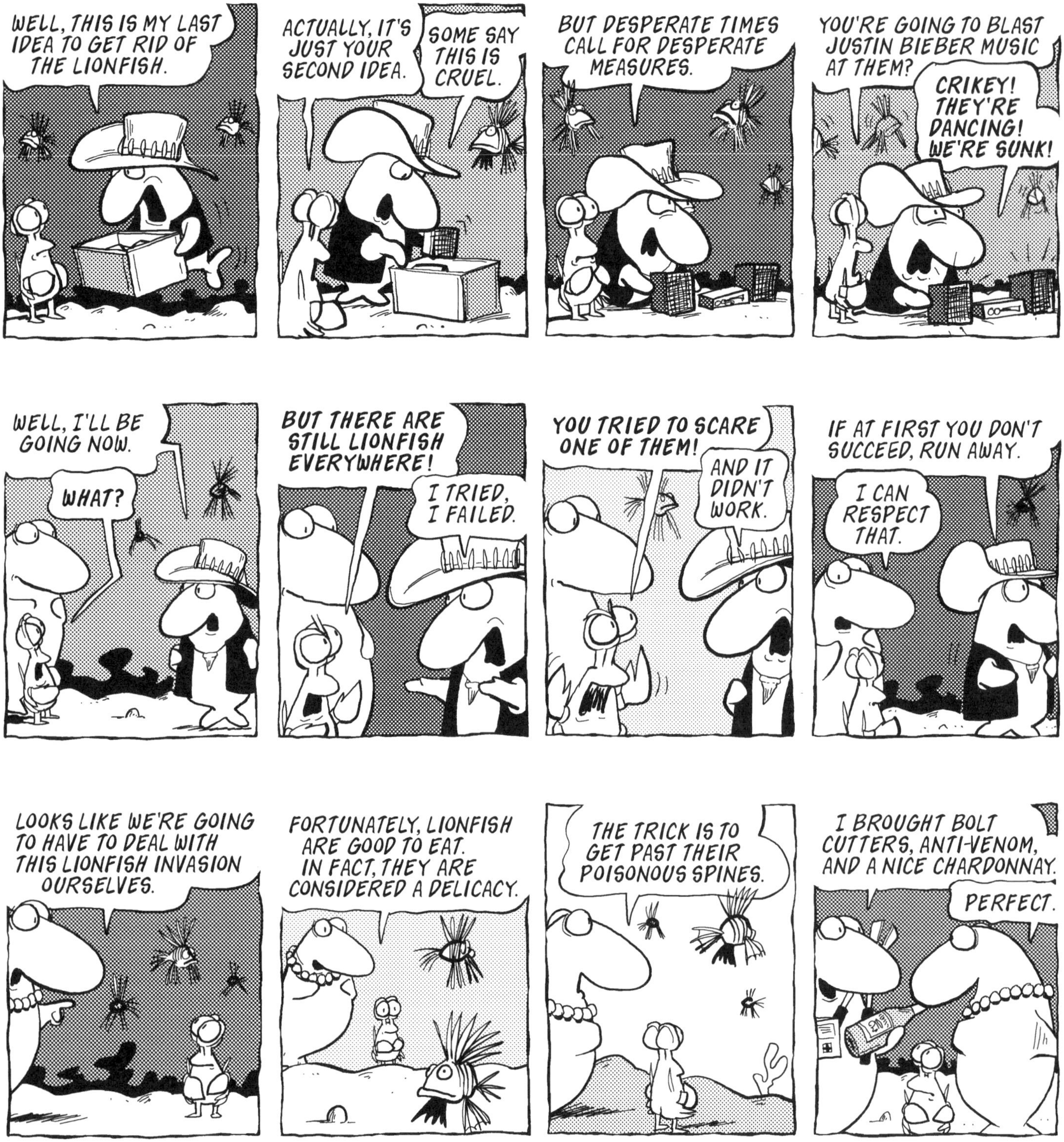
WELL, THIS IS MY LAST IDEA TO GET RID OF THE LIONFISH.
ACTUALLY, IT'S JUST YOUR SECOND IDEA.
SOME SAY THIS IS CRUEL.
BUT DESPERATE TIMES CALL FOR DESPERATE MEASURES.
YOU'RE GOING TO BLAST JUSTIN BIEBER MUSIC AT THEM?
CRIKEY! THEY'RE DANCING! WE'RE SUNK!
WELL, I'LL BE GOING NOW.
WHAT?
BUT THERE ARE STILL LIONFISH EVERYWHERE!
I TRIED, I FAILED.
YOU TRIED TO SCARE ONE OF THEM!
AND IT DIDN'T WORK.
IF AT FIRST YOU DON'T SUCCEED, RUN AWAY.
I CAN RESPECT THAT.
LOOKS LIKE WE'RE GOING TO HAVE TO DEAL WITH THIS LIONFISH INVASION OURSELVES.
FORTUNATELY, LIONFISH ARE GOOD TO EAT. IN FACT, THEY ARE CONSIDERED A DELICACY.
THE TRICK IS TO GET PAST THEIR POISONOUS SPINES.
I BROUGHT BOLT CUTTERS, ANTI-VENOM, AND A NICE CHARDONNAY.
PERFECT.

Sherman's Lagoon is syndicated internationally by King Features Syndicate, Inc. For information, write King Features Syndicate, Inc., 300 West Fifty-Seventh Street, New York, NY 10019.

Andrews McMeel Publishing, LLC
an Andrews McMeel Universal company
1130 Walnut Street, Kansas City, Missouri 64106

www.andrewsmcmeel.com

14 15 16 17 18 SDB 10 9 8 7 6 5 4 3 2 1

ISBN: 978-1-4494-5799-0

Library of Congress Control Number: 2014935609

Sherman's Lagoon may be viewed on the Internet at
www.shermanslagoon.com

ATTENTION: SCHOOLS AND BUSINESSES

Andrews McMeel books are available at quantity discounts with bulk purchase for educational, business, or sales promotional use. For information, please e-mail the Andrews McMeel Publishing Special Sales Department:
specialsales@amuniversal.com